SPACE SHUTTLE

Melvyn Smith FBIS

ISBN 0 85429 480 5

A FOULIS Aviation Book

First published 1985
© Melvyn Smith 1985

Published by:
Haynes Publishing Group
Sparkford, Nr. Yeovil, Somerset
BA22 7JJ, England

Haynes Publications Inc.
861 Lawrence Drive, Newbury Park,
California 91320 USA

British Library Cataloguing in Publication Data

Smith, Melvyn
    An illustrated history of Space shuttle : US
    winged spacecraft, X-15 to Orbiter.
    1. Space shuttles—History
    I. Title
    629.44′1   TL795.5

    ISBN 0-85429-480-5

Library of Congress catalog card number 85-81671

Editor: Mansur Darlington
Page layout: Tim Rose & Barry Griffiths
Printed in England by: J.H.Haynes & Co.Ltd.

Contents

Introduction

During the past quarter of a century so much has been written, documented and filmed about the United States ballistic 'man in space' programmes that it has become commonplace to think only of Mercury, Gemini, Apollo and Skylab as the beginning and end of the US space project. The Space Shuttle is generally regarded as an entirely new concept, initiated only in the post-Apollo era as a result of a cost-conscious Government, commercial pressures, the need to keep a US presence in space and, not least of all, just something for the Space Agency and its facilities to do.

In fact, the Space Shuttle *was* the United States Space programme. The ballistic race into space and to the moon was merely a diversion from the development of the Shuttle as a result of Soviet competition. Indeed, it has been said that *Sputnik 1,* and the flight by Major Yuri Gagarin was, in fact, a clever ruse by the Russians to divert research and development away from what they may have regarded as the greater threat of winged reusable spaceplanes, then in an advanced stage of development in the US. Such a vehicle was far ahead of anything at that time in the USSR.

It is quite conceivable that, had US development continued into this area at the accelerated pace of their new ballistic programme, the X-20, a smaller version of today's *Columbia,* could have orbited the Earth as far back as the late nineteen-sixties. Had that taken place it would have been as

a result of a programme of carefully planned development with rocket-powered aeroplanes that began just after the Second World War. The Americans would then have achieved a level of aircraft and space flight technology that the Soviet Union, even twenty-five years later, has yet to reach.

When *Sputnik 1* was launched in October 1957 there were those who doubted the technical superiority of the US. In fact, all the US lacked was an equivalent ballistic missile capability, having, by political choice, opted for the more sophisticated development of rocket-powered winged aircraft to reach the 'high frontier'. Naturally, such a programme would be immeasurably more complex and time consuming to mature than the 'easy' route taken by the Russians which involved a small, uncontrolled satellite mounted atop a ballistic missile. (In addition, the route to space via aircraft technology had immediate, visible benefits to both civilian and military aviation technology.)

Nevertheless, national pride had been hurt, and the immediate reaction was to speed up US ballistic missile research, firstly to place a satellite in orbit, and secondly a man. The urge to 'be first' finally culminated in the commitment by President Kennedy to 'reach the moon before the decade is out'.

As the mighty missile launches of Gemini, Apollo and Skylab carried through the late sixties and early seventies, manned winged aircraft such as the X-15 and the stubby lifting bodies continued simultaneous development that would ultimately lead to the Space Shuttle.

In addition to the activities of NASA, the USAF were also keen to maintain their own 'key' to space. Although their two projects — the X-20 and Manned Orbital Laboratory — never flew in reality, they nevertheless provided both the technical know-how and the astronauts that would make the Shuttle Orbiter possible. The entire history of winged rocket-powered space plane development has been closely associated with both military and defence applications, and it is therefore no surprise today to find that the Shuttle is heavily committed in this direction.

Even before the end of Apollo the United States and NASA had realised that the future of space research lay not in expensive 'throw away' ballistics but a reusable practical access to earth orbit. By the end of the sixties the US space programme had turned full circle and the Space Shuttle concept as we know it today was reborn.

The story of the Space Shuttle and its pre-

decessors is one of daring, courage, and above all skill. Skill of the pilots and 'forgotten' astronauts of the X-15 programme, skill of the designers and technicians throughout NASA and the US Aerospace industry, and skill of the NASA, the Air Force and Navy Management who, despite rapidly changing political climates, kept the programmes of development going.

The 'other' United States space programme never captured the headlines like Apollo's quest for the moon, yet was every bit as challenging, exciting and revolutionary. Every time a Shuttle Orbiter roars into space and gracefully lands days later back at Kennedy Space Centre it represents, in one sense, the culmination of 35 years of rocket-powered winged aircraft research. A story that began just after the Second World War over the dusty dry lake beds of Muroc Army Air Base, California.

Acknowledgements

In addition to those many people who have freely given their own personal reminiscences over the years, I would also like to thank the following for their assistance in the preparation of this book:-
Mr Walter J. Boyne, Director of the National Air and Space Museum, Smithsonian Institution, Washington DC; Ms Cheryl A.Hartel, Archivist, Office of History, Department of the Air Force, Edwards Air Force Base, California; Mr James D. Grafton, Manager, Public Relations, Boeing Aerospace Seattle; Mrs Francene Crum, Martin Marietta Corporation, Maryland; Mr Charles F. Kreiner, Director, Public Relations, Bell Aerospace Textron, Buffalo, New York; Mr M.V. Brown, Deputy Public Relations Manager, British Aerospace, Hatfield, England; Ms Sue Cometa, Public Relations, Rockwell International, California; Ms Lisa Vazquez, NASA, Houston Texas; Mr Lee Saegesser, NASA Washington DC and Mrs Enid Pond. Also to the staff at NASA's Ames and Dryden Research Centres.

Finally my thanks to my wife Donna, without whose help and support this book would not have been possible.

1 Quest for Mach 1

The Second World War with all its misery and destruction was drawing to a close when, in the United States of America, an organisation set up in 1915 and known as the National Advisory Committee for Aeronautics (or NACA) was meeting representatives of the Navy and the then Army Air Force with a view to developing new high speed and high altitude aircraft. The goal, laid down in March 1944, called provisionally for a 'one-man, rocket-powered aircraft that could exceed the speed of sound in level flight'.

The two services agreed an undertaking with NACA to conduct independent, yet co-operative, programmes to achieve this objective which would clear the path for a new generation of aircraft and a new era in aviation. They began work with the first American military rocket-research aircraft, the Northrop MX-324. This aircraft was originally built as a prototype for the proposed Army Air Force Northrop XP-79 rocket-propelled 'flying wing' interceptor.

The swept wing MX-324 was 14 feet long, and had a wingspan of just over 36 feet. It carried a crew of one and was powered initially by twin Westinghouse turbojets which were later replaced by an Aerojet Inc 2000lb thrust rocket engine.

Although obtaining a maximum speed of 550mph in 1944, and returning valuable information on high-speed rocket aircraft performance, the MX-324 had an inauspicious career and was later superseded by a more advanced version, the MX-653; this, in turn, led directly to the historic 'X' series of rocket aircraft and missiles that were to continue into the nineteen-eighties at the forefront of aviation technology.

It was soon to become apparent, however, to the various US research teams (as, indeed, it had become to others working on the same problem), that the 'Speed of Sound' would not easily be exceeded. The fundamental problem lay in the nature of air itself, and the effect it has on bodies passing through it at increasingly higher speeds. When an object travels through air at relatively low speeds, i.e. below the speed of sound, the air molecules are driven out of the way in a series of pulses, radiating out like ripples in a pond, the air molecules returning to their natural, uncompressed 'static' state as the object passes. As the object nears the speed of sound, the air molecules become progressively less able to be moved aside fast enough. Instead, the air begins to be driven forward at the same speed as the object with the air molecules being compressed more closely together. In an effort to return to their static state the molecules move sideways, transferring their forward energy to adjacent molecules, which, likewise, pass on the energy to their near neighbours. This sets up an expanding pressure pulse which radiates at 90 degrees to the object's direction of motion. The pressure wave continues expanding, though by this time the object has moved on, until the limits of the atmosphere are reached. The moving object continues to generate new expanding waves as it travels on, leaving behind that area of disturbed air, resulting in an ever-expanding cone-shaped pressure area being produced.

Pressure waves moving through air are, of course, perceived as sound. When the boundary of the cone passes over the ear drum the energy involved causes the emission to be heard as a loud crack, the so-called 'Sonic Boom'.

At and beyond the speed of sound, the condition of air 'compressibility' changes the aerodynamic effect that the air has on an object. In an aircraft designed in the knowledge of subsonic flight alone, attempts to attain the speed of sound could — indeed, they did — lead to loss of aerodynamic control and airframe failure. During the war years investigations into transonic and subsonic control problems had shown that the difficulties encountered, though not insurmountable, might make impracticable the operational use and safe attainment of such speeds. In this sense, the speed of sound was considered to be a profound 'barrier'. Not unnaturally, though inaccurately, the term the 'Sound Barrier' was adopted as a popular expression.

The speed of sound is not a constant — it varies with the temperature and, thus, with the height at which an aircraft flies. For instance, at sea level the speed of sound is about 760 mph, whereas at 35,000 ft it is about 660 mph. From the point of view of the aerodynamic effects on the aircraft, however, the critical consideration is the relationship between the aircraft's speed, and the local speed of sound. To simplify such matters, a unit, the Mach (after Ernst Mach, an Austrian scientist) was adopted to relate the aircraft's speed to the speed of sound as a ratio. Therefore, when an aircraft reaches the local speed of sound the ratio is unity or 1, and the aircraft's speed is expressed as Mach 1.

In England in 1946 an experienced test pilot called Geoffrey de Havilland, son of the owner of the famous aircraft company, was to make an attempt on Mach 1 in the firm's own DH-108.

A few days before de Havilland had exceeded

The jet-engined DH 108 is pushed inside its hangar at Hatfield, England after a test flight to determine its high-speed handling characteristics. At the time many were confident that the DH 108 would be the first aircraft to achieve Mach 1. (British Aerospace)

the level speeds of 620 mph, recorded earlier by a rival aircraft, the Gloster Meteor. Now he was set for a final check of the DH-108 at full power before the team attempted an 'official' record across the south coast of England.

It was a pleasant early autumn evening as the tailless DH-108 with its broad swept back wings roared into the sky from Hatfield Aerodrome and disappeared into the slight haze of a cloudless horizon. The weather conditions were ideal. De Havilland had planned a power dive from 10,000 ft at a speed approaching Mach 1 to check the jet engined DH-108's handling and control response. Then he would fly level at full-throttle close to the sea by the Thames Estuary again to check the aircraft handling. After this clearing flight it was hoped that there would be no unpleasant surprises in store on the official record flight some days later.

As dusk began to settle over Hatfield, de Havilland had not returned. The DH-108 had fallen apart in mid-air, spreading wreckage across the countryside north of the little village of Cliffe, near the town of Gravesend. The DH-108's engine,

Geoffrey de Havilland at the controls of the DH 108 flying over Kent. Several days later Geoffrey de Havilland and the DH 108 were lost in the final test flight before the Mach 1 attempt. (British Aerospace)

found almost intact, was faultless. The problem, as anticipated, was in the airframe. The 'sound barrier' was beginning to look as solid as a brick wall.

Back in the United States, Bell Aerospace had, during the final years of the war, developed an aircraft they believed would survive attaining the speed of sound. They called it the XS-1 (later the X-1) and it was to be flown and co-ordinated by the Army Air Force. Conceived in 1943 the first aircraft was delivered in 1946. Shaped like a needle-nosed straight-winged bullet, it was America's first attempt at a supersonic rocket-powered aircraft.

The X-1 was powered by a Reaction Motor Inc XLR-II four-chamber, 6,000 lb thrust liquid-propellant rocket-engine. Since a throttleable rocket engine was well beyond the abilities of early post-war technology, a change in power levels could only be achieved by cutting in or out individual chambers. The pilot could thus adjust the thrust by increments of 1,500 lb. XLR-II would fire (or 'burn') for a maximum of 100 seconds at full power. The fuel, an unpleasant mixture of liquid oxygen and alcohol, was to be carried in the

X-1 fuselage behind the pilot and in front of the rear-mounted engine.

On completion of its tests and proving flights (which would encompass a Mach 1 demonstration), the Army Air Force was to hand the X-1 over to NACA for flight research on aircraft handling at extreme speeds.

The limited engine duration of the X-1 meant that it would have to be air-launched from the only suitable carrier aircraft of the time, a B-29 Superfortress. A huge propeller-driven B-29 was obtained for the project, its bomb bay removed, and the reshaped lower fuselage modified to accept the X-1 and transport it to drop height.

Initially, the X-1 would be winched up into the belly of the B-29 where it would be protected during take-off and climb-out. Shortly before drop its pilot would clamber back down to the converted bomb-bay onto a small ramp alongside the cockpit of the X-1, lower himself and squeeze through a small access hatch in the side of the

canopy and into the cramped cockpit. Once inside, the pilot hooked up his oxygen breathing system, donned his helmet, and connected up his communication links. The B-29 flight engineer would then climb down alongside the cockpit with the hatch door, and locate it in place for the X-1 pilot to lock from the inside of the cockpit. An awkwardly-positioned handle and the cramped dimensions of the cockpit conspired to complicate the latching task which, in any event, needed a fair degree of force. Following release from the mother ship, the X-1 with its pilot would free fall until well clear of the B-29, when the four XLR chambers would be ignited one by one. After its flight, a landing would be made on a standard retractable undercarriage.

Test flights from the Army Air Force base at Pinecastle, Florida were made with the engine switched off, in the summer of 1946, with test pilot

Charles 'Chuck' Yeager alongside the X-1 that finally broke the 'sound barrier' on 14 October 1947. Named *Glamorous Glennis* after Yeager's wife, the X-1 was the first practical step in a series of research aircraft that would ultimately lead to the Space Shuttle. (NASA)

The X-1 was carried aloft beneath the bomb bay of a converted B-29 bomber. The white band around the rocket ship's fuselage is outward evidence of the super-cold liquid oxygen stored inboard just behind the cockpit. (USAF)

Chuck Yeager and the X-1 drop clear of the B-29 and its slipstream. Seconds later he ignited the four-chamber XLR-II engine and accelerated past Mach 1 and into aviation history. (USAF)

Jack Woolams in command. Powered flights commenced in October under Chalmers H. Goodlin and Alvin M. Johnson's control. Finally, in October 1947, after numerous checks and verification flights, both NACA and the new United States Air Force (recently renamed from the United States Army Air Force) felt that they had gathered enough test data and confidence to attempt Mach 1.

This first tentative step to the Space Shuttle was to be taken at what became in 1950 Edwards Air Force Base, then a flight test centre called Muroc Army Air Base, located 2,300 ft above sea level on the high plateau of the Mojave desert in California. This area had been selected for high performance aircraft testing because of its deserted flat landscape with dry salt lake beds. Every spring and early summer the damp salt lake beds dried out under the baking desert sun, leaving a flat, smooth surface for aircraft landings and take-offs. As the year progressed, and the once smooth surface again became rough from constant use, the winter rains covered the area to a depth of several inches, whilst high winds blowing across the surface water once again levelled out the lake bed, and the cycle

began again. Concrete runways maintained year round operations.

World War Two veteran and test pilot Charles 'Chuck' Yeager had flown the X-1 many times under power and, despite the recent death of Geoffrey de Havilland, volunteered to fly the attempt on Mach 1 scheduled for 14 October 1947. The engineers and designers were confident, and so was Yeager who, during his flights over the previous months, had developed a 'feel' for the X-1 whilst putting it through every conceivable type of manoeuvre (both authorized and unauthorized) at speeds up to Mach .9. He later commented, 'Some people figured that the X-1 would break up also, like the DH-108, but I figured that, having a great deal of confidence in it and knowing it as I did, the X-1 wouldn't bite me or swap ends on me without giving me some sort of warning'. Three days before the Mach 1 attempt, Yeager suffered a horse-riding accident which left him with two broken ribs and in constant pain. Reluctant to reveal his injuries, knowing that he would lose the chance to make the first flight, Yeager kept the accident secret. The only aspect of the flight that might prove troublesome to Yeager was the latching of the X-1's hatch. To overcome this, Yeager improvised an additional lever from a sawn-off broomhandle which he smuggled aboard the B-29.

Thus equipped, on 14 October, the B-29 carried Yeager aloft to 37,000 ft and released the sleek X-1 over Rogers Dry Lake in the Mojave Desert in California. Yeager allowed the X-1 to drop clear then ignited the XLR-II chamber by chamber and soared up to Mach .96. ('The machmeter only went up to Mach 1,' Yeager commented, 'I don't think they had a hell of a lot of confidence in us in those days.') At Mach .96 pilot and aircraft were subjected to tremendous buffeting. Then, all at once, the machmeter indicator needle flew past Mach 1 and right off the scale. Almost immediately the buffeting stopped and the X-1 smoothed out as it streaked across the sky above the test range. Yeager then began to shut down the chambers one by one and let the X-1 decelerate back through the buffeting range. On completion of this flight test X-1 came in to land on the same runway that was to take the Space Shuttle *Enterprise* exactly thirty years later on completion of its glide trials.

Such was the state of affairs in the 'cold war' that within two hours of Yeager's X-1 flight the deputy director of NACA classified the programme Top Secret. The X-1 had flown to 43,000 feet and 700 mph, but nobody outside the senior NACA and military would know for several months.

By 1949, the X-1 had pushed the air speed record to nearly 970 mph, and had achieved an altitude of almost 14 miles. In all, three X-1s were constructed, achieving by the end of the programme in 1951 a total of 156 flights.

At the time that the Army Air Force first approached Bell Aerospace for development of the X-1, the Navy Bureau of Aeronautics had contracted with the Douglas Aircraft Company for a turbojet aircraft capable of exploring flight dynamics up to Mach 1, but not exceeding that speed. The D-558-I or Skystreak was merely a step towards a Navy co-ordinated vehicle which would eventually compete with X-1 and the Army Air Force.

The D-558-I Skystreak was to take to the air in March 1947, much later than the X-1, powered by a General Electric TG180 jet engine. In February 1948 a new version was introduced: the D-558-II Skyrocket with swept wings and a Westinghouse J-34 (later a J-40). This was the final interim model before the introduction of the supersonic Skyrocket.

The supersonic D-558-II Skyrocket had, in addition to its existing jet engine, a supplementary rocket motor, enabling it, in theory at least, to achieve Mach 2. Its new Reaction Motors engine, coded the LR8RM6, was designed to give at least 5,950 lb of thrust, and would cut-in after a conventional jet-powered take-off and climb-out, to

accelerate the Skyrocket to even higher altitude and speed. By late 1950 performance was improved further when the jet engine was discontinued altogether, and the Skyrocket joined the X-1 as an air-launched rocket-powered aircraft. The space in the airframe previously occupied by the J-40 jet engine was given over to additional fuel, making for a total engine 'burn' time of 200 seconds or more. Another B-29 was acquired and suitably adapted to support the Skyrocket programme.

The first of the 'all-rocket' Skyrocket planes was delivered to Edwards Air Force Base in January 1951, and was handed over to NACA after a successful series of test flights which began in April of that year, and which culminated in a flight of Mach 1.89.

Already, only six years since the end of the war, such had been the proven and anticipated rate of progress in high speed, high altitude aircraft research, that NACA realized that there would be a future requirement for aircraft that would fly even higher and faster, ultimately reaching beyond the upper atmosphere and into space.

The United States, by design, had started with the rocket engine as a tool that would propel their aircraft higher and faster than any other in the world. The development of turbojet propulsion for such extreme high performance research had been finally abandoned with the Navy's latest Skyrocket configuration. As rocket technology improved they would soon have the power and, with the X-1 and Skyrocket, the foundation of airframe technology, to achieve the 'high frontier' of upper atmosphere flight. In order to achieve flights at extremely high altitude, the rocket engine was, perforce, adopted in favour of the fast-developing jet engine. A rocket engine carries its complete fuel requirements with it, whereas the jet derives the oxygen part of its fuel from the atmosphere. As the oxygen content of the atmosphere diminishes with altitude, the point is soon reached when there is insufficient for efficient combustion to take place. Thus, the rocket is the key to high-altitude flight

NACA knew, of course, that there were two distinct ways of reaching space. The first was by using the ballistic missile, on top of which a small, uncontrolled 'capsule' could be propelled into either an orbital or sub-orbital trajectory. The second was to continue the established line of aeronautical research on its upward trend, eventually achieving, as a matter of course, a manned, practical, winged reusable vehicle that could be used regularly and economically to fly into and out of space.

Politically, the concept of launching a ballistic satellite, manned or otherwise was viewed as of little value. Space, for its own sake, was frowned

Whilst the Air Force was developing its X-1 series, the US Navy was experimenting with aircraft that would lead towards their own supersonic aircraft. The D-558 Skystreak was a subsonic test bed for a supersonic airframe concept. Undoubtedly ugly, but profoundly practical, this aircraft not only established the soundness of the swept wing concept for supersonic flight, but also provided a good deal of feedback for then current jet fighter development. Skystreak contained over 500 lb of instruments to record flight test data. (NASA)

Improvements to the Skystreak cockpit canopy were just some of the many steps on the way to the Skyrocket. Note the similarity of the forward cockpit to that of the later aircraft. (NASA)

upon by post-war American Government as a waste of national effort. NACA knew that, compared to winged aircraft research, ballistic missiles would be the easy option, but there was no hurry, and money would be forthcoming if they pursued aeronautical research with its immediate visible benefits in terms of higher performance military aircraft and safer and cheaper commercial aircraft. In any event, spaceflight was still a long way off and it seemed reasonable to follow an established line of development rather than to branch off into something altogether different. Thus the pattern of progress was becoming clear: spaceflight was to be only the final rung on a ladder of development that was yet only part climbed.

In the meantime, the USAF, ever mindful of its future role in defence, had already made secret moves to retain a leading global position if and when the technology to put men into space became available. Unbeknown to all but the most senior NACA, Government and military staff, the USAF in 1951 were beginning to develop a winged suborbital space shuttle of their own.

The USAF concept of a winged rocket-powered spacecraft originated back in 1933, the year that a pilot named James R. Wedell achieved a new world's air speed record by averaging 305.33 mph in the Phillips Trophy Race, and a Lt Cdr Frank M. Hawks set a west-east USA non-stop record flying from Los Angeles in California to Brooklyn's Floyd Bennett airfield in 13 hours 26 minutes.

As these achievements were headline news across the USA, in Vienna an engineer and physicist named Dr Eugene Sanger completed a book entitled *Raketenflugtechnik* (Rocket Flight Technique), in which he introduced the concept of a rocket aircraft which would fly over fifty times as fast as Wedell's aircraft, and 10,000 miles further than the record achieved by Frank Hawke. The book which laid the conceptual foundations of the Space Shuttle *Columbia* and her sisters achieved barely a mention outside a small technical readership.

In his preface, Sanger wrote: 'This kind of rocket flight is the next fundamental step in the phase of development from the troposphere-flight established during the last 30 years. It is the first stage of space flight, the most colossal technical problem of our time.'

Two years after the publication of his book, Dr Sanger was given notice to quit his position as assistant at the Technical College, Vienna. He had by then completed two years of tests on liquid-fuelled rocket engines. Despite being faced with mounting debts incurred in the publication of his book, Dr Sanger remained convinced of the feasibility of the concept of a winged spacecraft and wrote defiantly in his diary on 28 March 1935, 'Nevertheless, my silver birds will fly'.

Shortly afterwards Dr Sanger was invited to Germany to continue his work under the auspices of the Hermann Goering Institute, the research organisation of the Luftwaffe. He was assigned to a ten year programme to develop his ideas on a long-range rocket aircraft. A research centre at Trauen was specially built as the site for his studies.

During this time Dr Sanger was joined by a young mathematician called Dr Irene Bredt who later became his wife. Slowly, together with a small team of technicians, the various details of rocket aircraft design were painstakingly evolved.

The aircraft itself appeared in their design as a low-wing vehicle with vertical stablilizers at the tips of horizontal tail surfaces. The wing section was that of a thin wedge with sharp leading and trailing edges. A water-cooled rocket engine of 100 tonnes static thrust was mounted in the tail.

Dr Sanger proposed an unique launching procedure. The 100 tonne spacecraft would take off from a railed track two miles long under the boost of a rocket powered sled. The sled would not in itself fly, but bring the vehicle to a ground speed of mach 1.5 before release. At this point the craft would separate from the sled and climb away under its own unpowered momentum at an angle of 30 degrees to around 5,500 ft, before igniting its own rocket engine to take it up to a height of almost 100 miles before falling back to Earth on a planned trajectory.

Instead of re-entering the atmosphere like a 'capsule', however, it would return to Earth along an undulating trajectory skipping along the top of the atmosphere like a flat stone across the still waters of a pond. Using this technique Dr Sanger proposed to achieve ranges of up to 14,600 miles, which would allow use of the craft as an intercontinental bomber.

The idea appealed to the Nazi High Command, but there were major problems which had first to be overcome. The spacecraft's maximum permissible payload allowed for only one crew, even if all the problems of material and propulsion could be solved. (Over a range of 14,600 miles, its payload was only 672 pounds!) Nevertheless, this intercontinental, space bomber which would deliver its cargo of weaponry as far away as the USA and land for reuse, say, in Japanese territory, was just too good a potential weapon to discard.

Although Sanger and Bredt regarded their work as purely a preliminary study, it was continued right up to the summer of 1942 when, according to Dr Sanger, 'The long-term programme came into conflict with the prosecution of

the war'. Hindered by the call-up of key personnel, plus the shortages of such materials as nickel, copper and chrome, the project was faced with increasing handicaps which could no longer be overcome.

Nazi Germany was, meanwhile, losing the war, and its leaders chose instead to gamble their remaining resources on the V1 and V2 rockets. Dr Sanger's 'Silver Birds' were shelved. It is salutory to speculate what would have been the outcome of the Second World War had Germany achieved nuclear weaponry and the space glider. No city would have been safe from complete annihilation!

Fortunately for civilization, such a dual concept was beyond the German resources, but the US Government was, in the post-war years, nevertheless keen to investigate the possibility of building a rocket plane capable of such feats. Moreover, they were concerned as to whether the technology required was within the grasp of the Soviets, into whose hands copies of the captured German plans had also fallen after the war.

So it was that the Bell Aircraft Company, in 1951, came to be working in strictest secrecy with the USAF on a highly classified project codenamed 'Bomi' (Bomber-Missile). At Bell it was no surprise to find the project was being co-ordinated and supervised by Dr Walter Dornberger, former Peenemunde V2 base commandant; Dr Sanger having elected to continue his own research in Europe.

The 'Bomi' concept took shape as two rocket-powered, winged aircraft, one of which, the 'space plane' would ride in piggyback fashion on the larger mother ship. Unlike Dr Sanger's concept, the two would be launched vertically as was then standard ballistic practice.

The mother ship, or first stage with its five rocket engines would, combining with the three engines of the 'space plane', fire for only 130 seconds after lift off before separating and returning to base for a landing. The 'space plane' would continue in the climb using its own internal fuel supply, now no longer supplemented by a flow from the tanks of the mother. The space plane would fly up to a maximum speed of 8,450 mph crossing the US, say, in 70 minutes at an altitude of

At maximum thrust the X-1's XLR-II exhaust creates a pattern of 'shock diamonds' in its wake. The stainless steel, black painted engine, mounted in the tail, was affectionately dubbed the 'Belching Black Bastard' by the Air Force personnel associated with it; although all press releases referred to it, for obvious reasons, as the 'Black Betsy'. (USAF)

Derived from the X-1, the X-1A pushed back even further the frontiers of high-speed high-altitude flight. It was in this aircraft that Chuck Yeager was to make an attempt on raising Scott Crossfield's Mach 2 plus record. (USAF)

40 miles. Because of deep concern over the ability of a human being to function in a zero g (or 'weightless') environment one of the Bomi's three engines would continue to burn at minimum level throughout the flight giving a constant quarter g in the coasting phase.

Calculations disclosed that the 'skipping' procedure advocated by the early studies of Dr Sanger resulted in considerably higher levels of atmospheric heating than a straight, gradually descending glide path. Severe temperatures would result from the 'pull ups' required to generate the increased aerodynamic lift required to 'skip'.

After dropping the bomb, the Bomi space plane would make a 180 degree turn and be boosted back up to the initial velocity and altitude levels for a return flight. This, of course, necessitated yet another rocket engine system for the return boost.

So impressed were the USAF with Dr Dornberger's findings that they provided further funding for development.

It was soon discovered, however, that the Bomi space-plane would burn up in attempting to make the 180 degree turn because of the extreme increase in temperature resulting from this manoeuvre being made in the atmosphere. The additional rocket weight-penalty also required a gigantic first stage mother ship. Before long it was decided a far more efficient and practical method would be to continue the flight path around the Earth after dropping the bomb. In order for any vehicle to achieve and stay in orbit, circling the Earth, it acquires sufficient speed so that the centrifugal force it generates matches the Earth's own gravitational pull. The speed required to do this is about 17,500 mph. If the vehicle exceeds this speed the extra centrifugal force generated will drive it into progressively higher orbits until at 25,000 mph the force of Earth's gravity (which itself diminishes with altitude) will be overcome completely and the vehicle will be able to travel out into the Solar System.

Revolutionary as it was, Bomi remained only a paper study; tantalizingly close, yet just beyond the reach of available technology. For in those days of the early nineteen-fifties, little, if anything, was known about the problems of manned spaceflight and the effects of re-entry loads on a winged vehicle.

It was with this in mind, therefore, that in April 1952 NACA, in line with both current aircraft research and the classified USAF studies, set its laboratories and research centres across the States to work on the analysis of potential problems involved in building manned spacecraft. Later NACA's Langley Aeronautical Laboratory repor-

ted back on two conceptually critical areas. One was the problem of severe aerodynamic heating, and the other, 'the achievement of stability and control at very high altitude and speed'. Of the two, Langley scientists stressed that until aerodynamic heating problems could be resolved it would 'for the foreseeable future prohibit the building of a practical space-plane'.

It was clear to NACA, the Air Force and the Navy that the building of a winged space-plane, secret or otherwise, capable of flights into or out of the upper atmosphere would need continuing data and developmental feedback from an advancing step-by-step rocket aircraft programme.

As a result of the Langley report, on 24 June 1952 NACA's Committee on Aerodynamics set to work on a major programme of, 'research efforts on the problems of manned and unmanned space flight at altitudes of between 12 and 50 miles and at speeds of Mach 4 through 10'. A remarkable task insofar as at that time no aircraft had even exceeded Mach 2.

Back at Edwards Air Force Base, by the end of 1952 the new Bell X-1A was being rolled out in preparation for its first flight scheduled for February 1953. It was designed to go both higher and faster than the X-1 and to facilitate this goal had a 5 ft longer fuselage containing extra fuel. Other changes included a revised cockpit canopy giving greater forward vision. Its flight trials were successful, and it gained such a reputation that by the autumn of 1953 the Air Force decided to celebrate the 50th anniversary of the Wright Brothers' first aeroplane flight at Kittyhawk by flying the X-1A to Mach 2. Naturally Charles Yeager wanted to be the man to do it, but by then he had a rival.

In 1950 Scott Crossfield, a 29-year-old civilian graduate engineer with a masters degree in aeronautics, came to Edwards Air Force Base. Within a year of his arrival he had established himself as a pilot of outstanding ability, gaining a respect amongst his fellow pilots almost equal to that given to Yeager. Up to 1953 Crossfield put in more hours in experimental rocket planes than any other pilot. The Navy wanted to beat the Air Force to Mach 2 but their pilot, a veteran of the D-558-I Skystreak called Marion Carl just could not, despite every effort, achieve that goal (he had nevertheless established a new world altitude record of over 79,000 ft in the process). That was in August 1953. Scott Crossfield, who probably knew more about the handling characteristics of the Skyrocket than any man alive, then saw his opportunity. He proposed to the Navy Liaison Officer at Edwards Air Force Base that he should, in a civilian capacity, be allowed to make a series of last ditch attempts to beat the Air Force, and in particular Yeager with whom he was in healthy professional competition.

After Marion Carl's flights, several engineers doubted whether the Skyrocket, now nearly three years old, could reach Mach 2 at all, but Crossfield was convinced. NACA agreed to release temporarily the Skyrocket from its research programme for this quest, which for them would merely add to their overall fund of knowledge.

Long before dawn on 20 November 1953, Crossfield's ground crew had polished and cleaned every blemish and fly speck from the Skyrocket for this, his seventh and final, attempt. In the cold desert twilight they began loading the super-cold liquid oxygen eight hours early, letting it trickle into the tanks, cold-soaking the entire aircraft. As dawn broke across the flat landscape a cold damp morning was promised at Edwards AFB and Crossfield had the 'flu.

The B-29 rumbled across the runway and climbed slowly up into the crystal blue sky to 72,000 feet where it jettisoned the Skyrocket. Crossfield dropped clear, ignited the engine and nosed down towards the desert below. By the time the engine shut down, 32-year-old Crossfield had become the fastest man alive, at over 1,300 mph, just over Mach 2.

Some years later he recalled, 'It was something I wanted to do,' adding with a grin, 'particularly if I could needle Yeager about it'.

So Mach 2 had been achieved, but lurking beyond it was danger, every bit as deadly as that encountered in the early days at Mach 1.

Three weeks after Crossfield's flight had temporarily put the Air Force's nose out of joint, the honour was to be regained barely days before the Wrights' 50th anniversary by raising Crossfield's Mach 2 record in the X-1A.

On 12 December 1953, Yeager took the X-1A up past Mach 2 into unexplored territory.

Edwards Air Force Base, California, 1952. The Douglas D-558-II Skyrocket poses for photographers. Its sleek lines betray its capabilities. This final, all-rocket-powered Skyrocket was destined to become the world's first aircraft to exceed Mach 2. (NASA/US Navy)

Scott Crossfield and the Skyrocket at the beginning of the record-breaking flight on 20 Novembr 1953. Dropped from the B-29 'mother' ship, the Navy Skyrocket flew on to Mach 2.005. (Smithsonian Institution)

At Mach 2.3, the X-1A began to yaw, then the starboard wing flew up, and nothing Yeager could do would cause the X-1A to respond. Within the space of a few terrifying seconds it had flipped onto its back and pitched up into an end-over-end and inverted spin. Yeager's helmet smashed repeatedly into the canopy, cracking the glass with the force of impact. Down and down they went with Yeager dazed and unable to orientate himself or the aircraft. With no ejection seat he had no means of escape. Yeager blacked out as the X-1A rolled, tumbled and span in one sickening continuous motion, down 51,000 ft in under 50 seconds. When Yeager came round he was bleeding, and dazed. The ground and sky were just a blur outside. The much increased air density at this lower altitude allowed him to convert the end-over-end inverted spin into a normal spin, and then recover from the spin at just 25,000 ft. Below he could see one of the flat lake beds. Thankfully, he glided in and landed in a shower of dust, saving both the X-1A and his own life with seconds to spare.

Yeager and the X-1A had encountered what

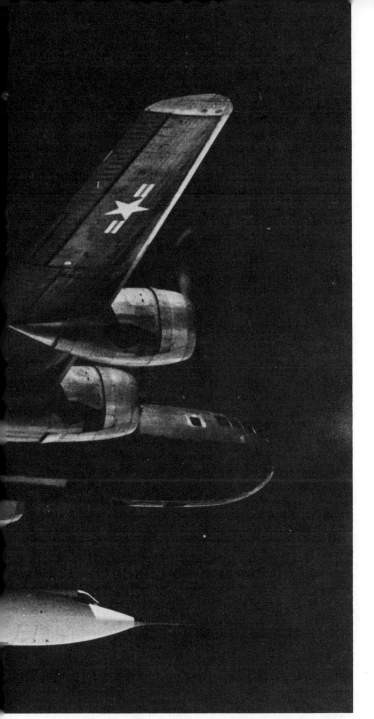

search, when the NACA laboratories and research centres had, as a result of the June 1952 directives issued by NACA management, stepped up their efforts in hypersonic flight and spaceflight research, studying more specific areas such as high-temperatures structure, hypersonic aerodynamics, stability, control and piloting problems. At that time it was decided that a new flight programme should be expedited, with a period of about three years being allowed for the design and construction of a suitable aircraft. This relatively short timescale virtually precluded the development of new materials and construction techniques.

Based on earlier surveys, and the requirements of Dr Dornberger's project, the NACA recommended a manned aircraft capable of a speed of 6,600 feet per second (about six times the speed of sound at altitude) and an altitude of 250,000ft. It was assumed the new aircraft would be air-launched in a similar way to that of the existing research planes it would replace, namely the X-1 series, D-558-11, and the X-2, then under development. This decision limited the vehicle to about 50ft length and a maximum gross weight of 30,000lb.

On 19 July 1954, a joint NACA/USAF/Navy committee met in Washington to consider the need for such a research vehicle, and to discuss other hypersonic aeroplane concepts proposed by the Air Force and Navy. The NASA proposal was finally accepted for further study and NACA was asked to take the initiative in obtaining approval from the Department of Defense.

The first obstacle in the new project was the problem of obtaining a suitable rocket engine. No existing powerplant possessed the reliability and controllability required for a manned aircraft. The committee decided to postpone selection of a propulsion system until these requirements could be more closely defined.

Later in 1954, the National Research Airplane Committee agreed on methods of originating and co-ordinating design requirements for eventual contract competition from industry. A formal memorandum of understanding signed by the Navy, Air Force and the NACA completed initial organization of the project. This memorandum assigned technical direction to NACA, with the advice and assistance of the Research Airplane Committee, comprising representatives of all three agencies.

The Navy and Air Force agreed to finance the programme with the Air Force administering the design and construction phases. Upon acceptance of the aircraft following industry co-ordinated test flights, it would be turned over to the NACA for research.

On 30 December 1954, the Air Force forwar-

the engineers at Langley had predicted exactly eight months before. This was a phenomenon that would become known as 'roll inertia coupling', a condition which occurs in naturally unstable aircraft, when centrifugal and inertial forces multiply in combination to exceed the control capacity, and ultimately the structural strength, of the aircraft. The problem occurs more readily at high altitudes where the air density is low resulting in low aerodynamic damping, and where high angles of attack are needed to maintain lift. Before anyone could even contemplate speeds in excess of Mach 2.5 this aerodynamic problem had to be solved.

In May 1954 the USAF was still committing extra funds to (the still secret) Project Bomi reded 'invitation to bid' letters to 12 prospective contractors. The contractors were briefed on the project requirements on 18 January 1955, which was to carry the designation 'X-15'.

Lack of a suitable engine for the X-15 project was of real concern. Therefore, on 4 February 1955 four prospective engine contractors — Reaction Motors; General Electric; North American and Aerojet — were asked to submit engine proposals as early as possible.

All the time, valuable data relevant to the construction of the X-15 was being gained through continued high speed/high altitude flight research by the X-1A during its 21 flights (including raising the world altitude record to 90,438ft) up to August 1955. But research data from that particular piece of flight hardware was soon to come to an abrupt halt.

On the X-1A's final flight, the pilot was to be Joe Walker, a civilian test pilot with NACA. Born in Washington on 20 February 1921 Joe Walker excelled academically and gained a degree in physics by 1942, subsequently joining the then Army Air Force, flying P38s during the Second World War. At the end of the war he left the Services with many awards, including the DFC and the Air Medal. In line with his desire to remain flying he joined NACA in the spring of 1945, eventually serving as project pilot on the Skyrocket, X-1 and X-1A.

The August X-1A flight was scheduled as a routine investigation of X-1A handling and performance at high altitude. Walker was seated in the cabin of the X-1A at 35,000 ft still inside the protective cocoon of the B-29 Superfortress and over 70 seconds away from the scheduled drop time. As he carried through the final checks, there was an explosion behind the cockpit, and then the X-1A's fuel tanks erupted in flames, fanned out and behind in the B-29's slipstream. Walker wasted no time in unstrapping himself, squeezing out of the cramped cockpit and up into the B-29. Scrambling about — semi conscious in the rarefied air — he grabbed a portable oxygen cylinder from the B-29 and went back down again to the blazing rocket ship in an attempt to jettison the fuel and save both aircraft. As the flames and leaking gases blew all around him, Joe Walker knew that any second another explosion could blast the B-29 out of the sky. His brief attempt at saving the X-1A abandoned, the B-29 jettisoned the X-1A to its fate. As it fell, it pitched up suddenly and climbed almost smashing back into the B-29 before it spiralled down, scorched and smoking to the desert floor below. Soon after, Joe Walker was awarded the Distinguished Service Medal for conduct. As Crossfield would say, 'If you're given to reacting

badly to fear, you've got no business being a test pilot'.

Although the X-1A was now gone, the USAF had had another, better-equipped, version, designated X-1B, in service since October 1954. This aircraft was unique in that it was fitted with a set of small gas thrusters to control its attitude at heights where aerodynamic controls were of diminished effectiveness in the low-density atmosphere. This device, known as a 'reaction control system' or RCS, was a forerunner of similar more advanced equipment to be fitted on the X-15.

By the end of 1955 all the industrial contractors approached by NACA for development of the X-15 rocket aircraft airframe had submitted their proposals and had had them evaluated. Amongst these, North American Aviation (later North American Rockwell) were one of the twelve companies who had submitted airframe proposals. Many more companies had simply rejected NACA's approach, because experimental contracts were, because of high research and development costs coupled with low output, considered to be economically unjustifiable. NAA's subsequent success, though, marked the beginning of major multi-billion dollar space involvement, culminating in their being chosen as prime contractors for the Space Shuttle over twenty years later. Their first contract, however, awarded in November 1955, was for the building and development of three flight-certified X-15s.

Four potential engine contractors were considered during 1955, and when their proposals, too, had been studied, it was to nobody's surprise that Reaction Motors (by then a division of the Thiokol Chemical Corporation) were awarded the contract with their experience gained on the XLR-II and Skyrocket LR8RM6. They agreed to deliver an engine capable of 57,000lb thrust, in-flight variations of between 30 per cent and 100 per cent, and an operating duration of 90 seconds at full thrust.

With the X-15 project well and truly under way the pioneering X-1 series of rocket airplanes was coming to an end. The X1-C was cancelled whilst still in the design stage; the X1-D was destroyed in an in-flight fire under its B-29 'mother', after only one unpowered flight, and was not replaced. This left the X1-B and X1-E as the Air Force's only X-1 series planes performing (relatively) low-speed research up to Mach 2 from December 1955.

Development of the new X-15 was hindered, therefore, by a major shortfall on aircraft handling data at speeds up to Mach 3, in particular the prob-

The family of Air Force/NACA X-1 rocket aircraft continued into the nineteen-fifties with the X-1B and X-1E. Continually expanding the basic aircraft's flight envelope, these aircraft laid the foundations for the next generation of rocket research aircraft. (USAF)

lems associated with Yeager's high-speed instability. To illustrate, no-one had come even close to challenging his Mach 2.45 record in almost two years.

In fact, the only aircraft at that time thought capable of Mach 3 at all was the Bell X-2 and it was, therefore, on that aircraft's performance that future development of the X-15 depended.

The X-2 had been conceived by Bell at roughly the same time as the X-1. The main differences lay in its swept-back wings and a throttle-controlled rocket engine. The latter unit proved difficult, and at times almost impossible, to develop, driving to distraction the USAF who were supervising the

project. Changes of contractors did little to alleviate the problem. Whilst airframe development remained with Bell, engine development responsibility was given to the Curtiss-Wright Corporation. The XLR-25 engine was fuelled by a mixture of alcohol and oxygen. Changes in thrust were to be achieved by varying the fuel feed pressure. Problems arose in the operation of the fuel turbopump unit and associated valves and controls, which prevented a regular, controlled, delivery under different throttle settings. Mainly because of this and other delays and technical problems, the first

The X-2 photographed just days before Frank Everest flew it to Mach 1.4. The X-2 programme had been plagued with problems and catastrophies, but it was on this aircraft that much of the developmental work on the embryonic X-15 project depended. (Smithsonian Institution)

X-2 was not ready for test flights until October 1952, almost eight years since the concept was first laid down. Heavier than the X-1 the X-2 was carried aloft on its first test flight by a converted B-50 bomber with Bell's chief test pilot, Skip Ziegler, at the controls. He conducted that, and one subsequent trial, before the Air Force test pilot Frank Everest conducted the third flight.

On completion of those tentative glide flights it appeared that, at last, the long delayed X-2 programme was beginning to gain momentum. The X-2 was then ferried back to the Bell factory for the installation of its XLR-25 rocket engine. This latest engine, the most advanced of its type, had a thrust output of between 5,000 and 15,000 lb, giving the X-2 the capacity of Mach 3.

By 1953 the X-2 was prepared for its first powered flight, this time away from Edwards Air Force base, with, once again, Skip Ziegler at the controls. High in the sky, fully-fuelled and slung under the B-50 the X-2 blew itself apart. Skip Ziegler and an engineer from Bell were killed. Somehow though, the B-50 remained airborne, limping back to base and crash landing; fortunately the rest of the crew, unlike the B-50, survived.

Skip Ziegler's death and the X-2's destruction had a material effect on the development of high-speed aircraft. The engine which had instilled so much confidence was now suspect, and it was to be a full year before a new X-2 and B-50 were to take to the air again to resume the whole glide test programme. Even then, it seemed, that fate conspired against the project. On the first glide test landing of the second X-2 on 5 August 1954, the landing gear broke, and by the third, so many problems were uncovered that the X-2 was wrapped up and sent back to Bell for repair and complete reassessment.

With their patience exhausted, the USAF gave Bell until the end of 1955 to get the X-2 into the air and flying under its own power. If not, the project would be cancelled and the X-15 would have to proceed on the basis of flight data already obtained.

The X-2 returned to Edwards in October and Frank Everest was to fly it. As he dropped away from the B-50 he went to ignite the engine and —

nothing! A small fault had prevented ignition and yet another unplanned glide flight ensued.

Next month, on 18 November, Frank Everest tried again. As he hit the engine ignition the engine caught fire, then coughed, spluttered and wheezed its way to an embarrassing Mach .95. The Air Force were not very pleased, but NACA was becoming increasingly desperate for high-speed flight data past Mach 2.5, and at that time the X-2 was the only aircraft in the world capable of meeting that requirement. Without the X-2 the entire X-15 programme would hang in the balance.

Slung under the converted bomb bay of a Boeing B-50, the X-2 was air launched in much the same way as the X-1 series and Skyrocket rocket aircraft. In this photograph, Melburn Apt was preparing to make an attempt on Mach 3, a flight that was to prove fatal.

With NACA pressure, the Air Force granted a stay of execution on the X-2 (now just about 10 years late) until early in the spring of 1956. It was a time of crisis for the rocket planes: the X1-A had almost killed Joe Walker and an entire B-29 crew, Skip Ziegler had died along with a Bell engineer in similar circumstances, and the third basic X-1 had likewise perished in flames whilst in mid-air. It was time for what engineers called an 'agonizing reappraisal'.

Finally, on 26 March 1956 the X-2 broke back into the skies reaching Mach .91 then later Mach 1.4, 1.5, 1.8, and then, almost two and a half years after Yeager's record, Frank Everest pushed X-2 past Mach 2.5. At last it seemed that the old X-2 had 'made good'. The Air Force selected the date of 1 November 1956 to hand over formally the X-2 to NACA.

All that remained for them to do was to fulfil the X-2's design criteria.

Frank Everest was due to leave the X-2 programme in the summer of 1956, whereupon he would be succeeded by Ivan Kincheloe and Melburn Apt, who were to take the X-2 to its design limits in both speed and altitude.

Kincheloe made his first flight in X-2 on 25 May with Frank Everest flying in the chase plane, monitoring progress and assisting in final approach. Frank Everest was, however, not going to leave Edwards without leaving his mark. He set out to exceed his own speed record on 12 July 1956 but, reminiscent of its earlier form, the XLR-25 cut out prematurely at Mach 1.5. Determined not to be

beaten by this temperamental machine Frank Everest tried again on the 23rd, this time punching through to Mach 2.93. With that he left the programme.

Contrasting the speed record, Kincheloe aimed for a similar record in altitude, finally achieving over 126,200 ft on the 7 September.

The November hand-over to NACA was approaching and only one test remained. An all out flight at maximum power to attain the X-2's maximum possible speed. The heating problems caused by aerodynamic friction at these high speeds had been overcome by using an airframe of stainless steel and of copper and nickel alloy.

Captain Melburn Apt was to make the attempt on his first flight in the X-2 on the 27 September 1956. Away from the B-50 he hit the throttle and soared the sleek X-2 to Mach 3.2, thus becoming the fastest man alive. But the X-2 had one final, wicked trick to play. As Captain Apt shut down the XLR-25, X-2 began to yaw uncontrollably; within seconds it pitched down and was totally beyond recovery. Instinctively, Captain Apt tried to activate the emergency escape mechanism, but it was too late. The X-2 ploughed into the desert scrub, deep gouges in the soil were interspersed with tailplane, forward fuselage and pieces of wing. The old instability problem had occurred again. Work on the X-15 was halted.

The wreckage of X-2 was taken back to Edwards Air Force Base whilst engineers tried to find out just what had gone wrong. At NAA the news of the X-2's fatal crash stunned engineers who were convinced they had overcome the high-speed handling and control problems. From then on they knew that only the pieces of X-2 and its last flight data could prevent the same thing happening to the X-15. After many weeks of painful reassessment the message became clear: an increased tailplane area was needed to overcome the problems of flight control in the tenuous upper atmosphere. The X-15 was accordingly modified.

Whilst confidence in the X-15's design steadily increased so did the headaches concerning the aircraft's heat-resisting outer skin. As Langley Laboratory had predicted in 1952 the new thermal protection system was causing problems — in addition X-15 was becoming overweight.

The new Inconel 'X' heat resistant X-15 skin was a product of the International Nickel Company, and was widely used in heat-stressed industrial processes. In its application to the X-15 it would need to provide protection from 820 °C on the wing and tailplane leading edges, and 730 °C on the surface panels. NAA metallurgists had tested the alloy to over 870 °C for what would provide an adequate safety margin, necessary if the X-15

was to explore hitherto unknown areas of flight. Finally, the Inconel 'X' skin was to be assembled over a titanium and stainless steel structure.

In September 1957, construction began on the X-15 airframe at NAA's plant on the outskirts of Los Angeles, California. No sooner had the jigs and frames been assembled and positioned, than an event occurred that shocked the world. To many at NACA it seemed more than just a coincidence.

On 4 October 1957, at Baikonur in the Soviet Union, a ballistic R7 missile roared into space taking *Sputnik 1* into orbit. The little sphere's constant bleeping signal seemed to demonstrate Soviet superiority in space. A further blow came on 3 November when *Sputnik 2,* with the dog Laika, was sent into orbit only to burn up in a planned re-entry some weeks later with Laika already dead.

Ken Leonarde, at that time a consultant engineer at NAA, recalled the general mood: 'I suppose no-one sort of liked the idea of the Soviets in space before us, but again, many of us realized that given a little time almost anybody could place an object in orbit by a rocket just so as it stays up a couple of days before burning up. All of a sudden because we hadn't done this thing first, because we reckoned that was not the best way, we were suddenly told we were technically inferior to the Soviets. Let me tell you, when I looked at the X-15 and what it could do, I just know that wasn't the case at all; no, we were far and away ahead in aircraft sophistication at that time, and the Soviets knew it.'

NAA assured NACA that they believed that the stability problems had been finally solved once and for all. But it had taken the X-2 and three lives to provide the answer. If anything were to go wrong with the X-15, designed to go twice as fast and almost three times as high as the X-2, it would not be the first time that theory proved wrong in practice.

With the X-15 airframe configuration formalized, in the autumn of 1956 the project's first industry-wide conference was held at the NACA Langley Aeronautical Laboratory, Langley Field, Virginia. Technical papers were presented by engineers and scientists from NACA, North American and Reaction Motors. The conference was primarily concerned with design and construction problems, and areas to be investigated once the flight programme was underway.

During this period it was determined that the X-15 would be equipped with a cockpit-side located aerodynamic flight surface controller (or side-stick), designed for use during periods of high acceleration forces. Also, it was agreed, a series of tracking stations were to be constructed to assist the pilot with information and guidance. This complex of stations, later known as the X-15 High Range, stretched from Wendover, Utah, to Edwards Air Force Base, California. It comprised radar stations at Ely and Beatty, Nevada, and a master station at Edwards. The range was also designed to aid in locating both X-15 and pilot in the event of an emergency landing.

Other systems considered at the time included an inertial guidance system to provide data on the X-15's velocity, altitude and pitch, roll and yaw; an attitudes ejection seat escape system for the pilot — later successfully tested at Edwards Air Force Base to speeds of Mach 4, and an altitude of 120,000ft — and a cockpit pressurization system, supplied by gaseous nitrogen and capable of pressurizing the X-15 cabin to an ambient 35,000ft level.

As work continued on the X-15 airframe and its rocket engine, several NACA, Air Force and NAA research pilots completed a programme on the human centrifuge at the Naval Air Development Center, Johnsville, Pennsylvania. Participants in the dynamic simulation included Captain Iven Kincheloe and Captain Robert M. White (USAF); Joseph Walker, Neil Armstrong and John B. McKay (NACA); and Scott Crossfield and Alvin S. White of NAA. (Scott Crossfield had left NACA to enter industry shortly before.) The centrifuge programme was devised to assess the pilot's ability to make an emergency re-entry into the Earth's atmosphere following control damper failures, and to determine piloting limitations in accomplishing a safe recovery from extremely high

altitudes and under varying g-loadings. The studies revealed no major difficulties in either case.

Whatever the X-15 team thought, the American public wanted a tit-for-tat effort to repair what the media deemed 'dented national pride'. President Eisenhower ordered an immediate acceleration of the long underfunded and relatively undeveloped US ballistic missile programme. On 7 December, a Vanguard rocket with a small US satellite on top was rushed into readiness and launched; it blew up on national live TV. The Soviets had a field day. Khruschev made the most of it as usual, and the American public wanted results — fast. The quickest way to space was via ballistic rockets, and so for the first time, emphasis

A line-up of X-series rocket- and jet-propelled aircraft that contributed to X-15 development. Surrounding the Douglas X-3 Stiletto clockwise is the Bell X-1A, Douglas Skystreak, Convair XF-92A, Bell X-5, Douglas D-558-II Skyrocket and Northrop X-4. (NASA)

began to shift away from winged rocket-powered aircraft. If the Soviets had indeed intended this to happen, their plan was succeeding.

During a series of meetings over Christmas 1957 and the New Year NACA's director, Dr Hugh L. Dryden, had, in conjunction with his staff, reappraised the administration's attitude to space-flight. A National Research Programme for Space Technology was prepared. Effectively, this did nothing to alter NACA's then current commitments, but it did establish a base for ballistic and space research that would culminate in the manned Project Mercury.

Ken Leonarde and the NAA team would have been even more suspicious of the Soviet's motives in launching *Sputnik* if they had known of the top secret meetings being held between senior Government, USAF and NACA staff over the past months. The USAF had proposed a project for a winged, orbital space plane to supplement and then replace X-15. Fired with enthusiasm for the Bomi project studies, and concerned about possible Soviet developments in that field, the USAF were set to climb the last step to the 'high frontier' with a winged reusable space plane.

Classified studies in the United States relating to a winged space plane had, since Bomi, progressed through many phases involving different proposals but still based on this same concept. By 1954, the Government began to consider the project more seriously. A series of studies by the USAF, NACA and industry followed. Included were 'Hywards', a winged hypersonic research and development system; 'Brass Bell' for various military reconnaissance applications; and 'ROBO' a rocket bomber system.

As for NACA, their interest lay in the research data that would inevitably result from such a programme, with a vehicle capable of over Mach 7 and prolonged spaceflight. In addition the Sputnik shock had not yet changed the minds of top NACA management that a winged rocket-powered Shuttle would be the best way to make routine flights into and out of space. A meeting on 14 October 1957 between NACA and the USAF was the genesis of the next step, the X-20.

By November 1957, the USAF had an approved plan for development of this X-15 follow-on. The X-20 space plane would be boosted into orbit via a converted ballistic missile, then glide back to Earth to land on a conventional runway under total control of the pilot. This concept of 'boost-glide' led to the project's better known title 'Dyna-Soar', an abbreviation of dynamic-soaring. It meant, in essence, that the X-20 would utilize in its flight profile both centrifugal force and aerodynamic lift. Centrifugal force would

keep the X-20 in space once it achieved orbital speed of around 17,500 mph. At this speed it would be flying just fast enough to offset the opposite pull of the Earth's gravity. The X-20 would remain in orbit like a conventional satellite until the pilot or ground control decided to return. The firing of small gas thrusters similar to those employed by the X-15 would control the X-20's attitude in space and align it finally for re-entry into the atmosphere.

The X-20 would return to Earth in a single long glide; its wings giving it aerodynamic lift and manoeuvrability as it descended through the atmosphere. This combination of high speed, extreme altitude and manoeuvrability would permit the pilot to shorten or lengthen the landing point range by thousands of miles and to manoeuvre far to the left or right of his flight path centre line. Landing was expected to be no more complicated than landing an X-15 or modern jet fighter.

The X-15 would take men briefly into the edges of space, whilst the accelerating ballistic programme and Mercury would launch men in capsules atop converted missiles into orbit. In the case of the latter, the crew would have to rely on parachutes to land gently and massive recovery fleets to get them home again. Nevertheless, even though the X-15 pilots would fly back to conventional landings on Earth, the speed and altitude they would attain would not be nearly as impressive as the capsules. The X-20 would attempt to combine the best features of these two approaches — high speed flight into space and return with aeroplane-like control.

On 1 January 1958, the USAF cast their net among the US aviation industry for design proposals. By March 1958 eight companies had submitted concepts. In June of that year the USAF selected two major teams to prepare competitive studies of the X-20. Boeing headed one team and the Bell Aircraft Company in association with Martin, the other. (One of the X-20 teams rejected, that of the McDonnell Corporation, subsequently went on to build the Mercury capsule.)

The unknowns which faced Boeing Aerospace division in Seattle in 1958 were daunting, and typical of these confronting other members of the two teams. The X-20 Dyna-Soar would fly at high Mach numbers and there were few men in the country who had much knowledge of hypersonics. Boeing was known for its experience in supersonics, engine inlets, and other related fields, but this was altogether different.

As the X-20 would have to withstand blast-off, spaceflight and re-entry into the atmosphere an entirely new approach to materials and structures was demanded. One of the first steps towards a solution of the problems was to select preliminary design experts whose work in other areas of research fitted the needs of the X-20 programme. Advance structures engineers who had conducted research into 'hot' aircraft frames were added to the growing team. Also brought into the project were engineers who had worked on the ROBO and Bomi programmes.

Aerodynamicists began wind tunnel testing hundreds of models to gain predictive data on hypersonic flight. Starting with simple, fundamental shapes, they progressed through to the vehicle configuration Boeing were to propose to the USAF in 1959.

One of the most significant combinations made to the X-20 project at this stage was that of Del Nagel, a young Boeing engineer who had recently graduated from the University of Washington.

Del Nagel's discovery of the 'outflow' phenomenon (a method of predicting flow and heat transfer characteristics) permitted Boeing to understand aerodynamically what heating problems they would face, and, most importantly gave them a 'feel' for predicting and correlating test model results to the full scale vehicle.

As new heat resistant materials were developed, they were tested at the company-owned 5,750 kVA radiant heat facility. Built specifically by Boeing to conduct heating tests on supersonic space vehicles, it would simultaneously subject the airframe to high mechanical loads, reproducing in effect the same stresses that would be encountered in re-entry. The heat from each test was so intense that, on one occasion, insulation on wires carrying electric current into the test chamber burst into flames!

Finally, engineers realized that they had almost beaten the 'heat barrier', and the X-20 began to look a workable proposition.

At NAA, work continued on the X-15, final assembly being made to the almost complete airframe of the first vehicle. Continued Soviet space successes added a spur to the X-15 work. At that time it was the nation's only potential 'spacecraft', and public, media and politicians alike were taking an increasing interest in the X-15's fortunes. Project Mercury was still some time away. Indeed, NAA had come up with several proposals during 1958 to orbit an X-15. One of the most practical of these proposals envisaged an X-15 launched by a conventional three-stage rocket booster on a single orbit flight around the Earth, followed by a re-entry, and immediate ejection of the astronaut because such a modified X-15 would not be capable of landing. Thankfully, this proposal by NAA was turned down by the Space Agency when the McDonnell Corporation's Mercury capsule concept was accepted on 6 February 1958.

The X-15 was to emerge as being just over 49½ ft long, with a roughly oval cross-section fuselage, from which short, thin wings were mounted on two large fairings both port and starboard, giving a wing tip to wing tip width of 22½ ft. The sleek jet-black fuselage ended in a stubby tail with a dorsal and ventral fin forming the upper and lower vertical members, whilst two horizontal

elevons with a downward sweep were mounted either side of the cavernous thrust chambers of the engine exhaust. Its total height was around 13 ft and it was to weigh 33,800 lb fully-fuelled, ready for launch and 15,000 lb on landing.

The engine for the X-15, designated the XLR-99, was built by the Reaction Motors Division of the Thiokol Chemical Corporation. In effect, the XLR-99 was a heavily-adapted version of the rocket motor used on the Viking ballistic missile. Fuelled by 8,400 lb of anhydrous ammonia and 10,400 lb of liquid oxygen, it consumed on average 12,000 lb of fuel a minute. A unique feature of this engine was that it could be throttled from 25,000 lb minimum thrust right up to a maximum of 60,000 lb and was also capable of being stopped and re-started in flight.

The X-15's propellant was stored in cylindrical tanks mounted inside the fuselage between an equipment bay just aft of the cockpit, and the rocket engine itself at the rear of the plane. The tanks were pressurised with helium gas. An on-board supply of hydrogen peroxide served as fuel for the X-15's auxiliary propulsion units (or APUs) that provided both electrical and hydraulic power. The APU system consisted of two 40 horsepower units which operated independently from the XLR-99 rocket engine. The hydrogen peroxide fuel, once burnt, decomposed harmlessly into steam and oxygen, which was vented outboard. The electrical power thus generated energized the X-15's instrumentation, heating elements in the pilot's pressure suit and throughout the aeroplane, the inertial guidance system, and communication, telemetering and recording equipment. The hydraulic power operated the X-15's air brakes, landing flaps and control surfaces.

The XLR-99 engine had to be exceptionally accurate and reliable, the fuel controls being able to supply the engine with adequate volume and the most efficient mixture. The XLR-99 received ammonia and gaseous liquid oxygen through a main propellant valve and two 'igniter' stages. A hydraulic cylinder actuated the mechanical linkage that sequenced two joint stage valves connected in parallel. With the cylinder extended, it first opened the gaseous oxygen valve, then the ammonia valve. The timing had to be exact. The cylinder was spring-loaded so that it would 'fail safe', retract and shut the valves if hydraulic pressure failed. A toggle linkage provided a secure 'lock' to the valves when in the fully closed position. This was a safety feature so that neither vibration nor dynamic forces on the valves could open them.

After the XLR-99 fuel pump was primed with oxygen and ammonia fuel fed through the two ½ inch diameter two-way first stage valves (each valve had a safety vent to release fuel in case of leakage), a pressure switch sensed satisfactory operation of the first stage and sequenced the control system to operate the second stage igniter. Liquid oxygen and ammonia for the second stage igniter were supplied directly from the X-15's turbopumps.

Two one inch diameter valves were linked to a single stage actuator. As with the first stage igniter controls, they also had a venting arrangement in case of leakage. The second stage igniter valves were 'three-way', being used for the priming operation and to cool the system to required temperatures before ignition. Activation of these valves, again like the first stage igniter, was sensed by a pressure switch which regulated the opening and closing of the main turbopump-fed propellant valves and subsequent ignition in the thrust chamber.

The main propellant valves mixed liquid ammonia and oxygen at a pressure of 1,200 psi. A pressure switch triggered the three-way, two-position spring return ball-valves which opened when energized. It took only a quarter of a second to shift the valves from the fully-open 100 per cent power level to fully-closed shutdown.

The X-15 cockpit was similar to that of a contemporary high-speed jet fighter. The instrument panel gave the pilot readings for speed, altitude, rate of ascent and descent, attitude and APU and propulsion system performance.

The pilot could control the X-15's attitude at extreme altitude by firing any combination of eight small hydrogen peroxide gas jet thrusters via a three-axis control column in his left hand. Pitch and yaw control was made possible through four thrusters in the X-15's nose, whilst a roll could be executed by firing two similar thrusters in each wing tip. Based on the valuable research carried out by the X-1B these thrusters (developed by Bell Aircraft Co) could be fired in short bursts of between 40 and 100 lb of thrust each. Also located on the left-hand control column was the XLR-99 engine throttle.

To aid the pilot when encountering high g forces during acceleration and deceleration, an aerodynamic control stick which could be operated by wrist movement was located on the right of the cockpit. This was integrated with the conventional centre stick. The ejection seat featured a ballistic

Close-up of the X-2 cockpit and nose. In an emergency this entire section could be jettisoned from the main body of the fuselage, whereupon the pilot would, it was planned, climb out and parachute to the ground. (Smithsonian Institution)

rocket which could, in an emergency, propel the pilot out of the cockpit. The seat had been successfully tested on high-speed rocket sleds at Edwards Air Force Base prior to being installed in the X-15.

During flight the pilot would be protected inside the nitrogen-pressurized cockpit by a new type of lightweight slip-knit nylon fabric pressure suit which replaced earlier pressure garments with their awkward rigid sections and bulky arm and leg joints. (In fact, the X-15 pilot's garment was a direct ancestor of the type later used by Mercury and Gemini astronauts.) This pressure suit, worn by all X-15 pilots during missions in the research plane, was manufactured by the David Clark Co. Apart from allowing complete freedom of movement it was also designed to provide physiological readings of the pilot during flight. It was pressurized by gaseous nitrogen. A neck dam around the suit's collar prevented seepage of nitrogen into the oxygen-filled helmet. The full pressure suit also provided the pilot protection from aerodynamic heating, loss of cabin pressure and wind blast and acceleration in the event of an ejection.

An internal guidance system, similar to that used on contemporary ballistic missiles, was developed for the X-15 by the Sperry Gyroscope Co. The system provided information to the pilot for precise control of the X-15, including critical attitude, velocity, distance and altitude sensing. A small computer digested and interpreted the information before presenting it to the pilot via the instrument panel.

During re-entry a liquid nitrogen system, designed by the Garrett Corporation Air-research Division, provided a cool environment inside the cockpit and instrumentation compartment.

For its launch at around 45,000 ft and 500 mph, the X-15 would, because of its limited fuel endurance, need to be carried aloft under the wing of another larger aircraft. Two modified B-52 jets, built by Boeing, served as carrier planes for the X-15. The B-52 was an eight-jet, swept-wing aeroplane capable of very long-range flights. X-15 would be carried underneath a B-52's starboard wing on a specially constructed pylon inboard of the converted bomber's starboard inner engines.

For the X-15 programme, the B-52's crew would consist of a pilot, co-pilot, launch panel operator (who monitored the liquid oxygen and the inertial guidance platform for the X-15) and a flight engineer. A closed-circuit television system gave the launch panel operator a view of the X-15 prior to launch. In addition, a 1,500 gallon liquid oxygen (LOX) tank was installed on the B-52's bomb bay. This provided an adequate top-up for the X-15 in flight and prior to launch. The B-52 pilot could, in theory, perform the launch, but it was expected that the X-15 pilot would initiate the mid-air separation. Each B-52 used in the programme was 157 ft long, 40 ft high and had a wing span of 185 ft. Gross weight (with X-15) was 300,000 lb.

1 Quest for Mach 1

On completion of each free flight, the X-15 would land at over 200 mph back at Edwards Air Force Base using 'conventional' aerodynamic controls (ie ailerons, rudders and elevons) and on its own retractable undercarriage. This consisted of two extendable steel skids mounted on the rear of the fuselage, whilst a nose-mounted retractable two-wheel leg provided support for the front end. The undercarriage would be deployed just before touchdown, the pilot landing the X-15 in a nose-high attitude, touching down the tail skids first. The lower ventral fin, because of its size, would be jettisoned as the X-15 approached the landing site and be recovered as its parachute deployed thereby giving the rear of the X-15 fuselage adequate clearance above the tail skids.

On 1 October 1958 the National Aeronautics and Space Administration (NASA) came into being as a result of the Space Act passed by the US Congress in the summer of 1958.

NASA inherited all the old facilities and personnel of the now defunct NACA which was set up in 1915. This comprised chiefly a Washington headquarters; the Langley Aeronautical Laboratory and its neighbouring Pilotless Aircraft Research Station; the Ames Aeronautical Laboratory; and later, the High Speed Flight Station at Edwards Air Force Base. NASA also took over a total of 7,900 staff. NASA's prime objective was to put the first man into space. No one would have guessed that the Soviets were about to do just that. The USAF's ambitions now centred around the X-20 as every other manned space related study had been handed over to NASA in a single-minded effort to achieve a 'man in space soonest' goal.

Only 24 hours after the official 'birth' of the National Aeronautics and Space Administration, its new administrator, Dr Keith Glennan, deputy administrator Hugh L. Dryden and retired Admiral Paul Smith (consultant to the Air Force's Roy Johnson Aerospace Research Pilot School) visited North American Aviation for a first hand report on the X-15's progress.

The new NASA officials met division assistant general manager, Ralph Ruud and chief engineer Harrison Storms. Project engineers Charles Feltz and Bud Benner and X-15 pilot Scott Crossfield also briefed the group.

Roll out of X-15-1 (serial number 56-6670) on 15 October 1958 was just over 11 months after construction began. However, it was not as everybody wanted. Contrasting the development of the airframe, the new XLR-99 engine was, even in February 1958, exactly one full year behind schedule. The XLR-99 was undoubtedly underfunded, and the engineering under-estimated. To create a reliable and throttleable engine of the type and power required for X-15 pushed at the very forefront of known technology. It was against objection from Scott Crossfield (who had left NASA to work on X-15 with NAA) that the Air Force accepted the installation of two X-1 XLR-II engines which, nevertheless, could take X-15 to 2,300 mph and 25 miles high as a makeshift substitute until the XLR-99 was ready. It was in this configuration that the first X-15 saw the light of day at the NAA plant roll-out ceremony.

Vice President Nixon in his address to assembled employees, guests, media and VIPs proclaimed the X-15 as the vehicle that 'regained America's lead in space'. Only those familiar with flight testing realized that the X-15 was still unproven; memories of X-2 were still fresh.

Moments after Vice President Nixon's speech came the first public viewing of the aircraft that would take an American to the fringes of space. Military dignitaries, scientists, engineers, government officials and newsmen all broke into spontaneous applause as the sleek, needle-nosed, black-painted X-15-1 was towed out of its hangar and before the speaker's stand in a standing-room-only crowd of shirt-sleeved spectators, at NAA's Downey plant outside Los Angeles.

For the 700 guests sweltering in the mid-October sun it was a moment of high drama. Here at last was an aircraft that would be piloted to an altitude where over 99.9 per cent of the atmosphere would be below it — and it would travel at speeds in excess of 3,600 mph.

The post-*Sputnik* atmosphere in the US was well illustrated by Vice President Nixon's next speech extolling both America's tradition and heritage in exploring the unknown 'because it is the unknown'. He continued: 'We seek knowledge for the sake of seeking knowledge. We should not take a superior attitude [because of the development of the X-15] but we should be proud of America's workmen, its scientists, engineers, businessmen and industries — and I am proud of its system of government and its heritage'. Then, in an obvious reference to the Soviet's achievement he said, 'Free men always out-produce the slaves of government and providing that free men work, there is nothing that we cannot do'.

Across the nation the media was gripped with X-15 fever. CBS television devoted major programming slots to cover the project's aims and objectives. Walter Cronkite, part of the coast to coast CBS channel's 'X-15 special' noted that as NAA were building three X-15s, 'They might be appropriately called the *Nina,* the *Pinta* and the *Santa Maria'*.

Congressman Yates, a member of the House of Representatives Committee on Appropriations followed an off-the-record briefing on the X-15 project by calling its capabilities 'stranger than fiction'. To most Americans the X-15 concept was nothing short of miraculous. Vice President Nixon summed up the general mood of euphoria in his opening remarks at the roll-out ceremony. He mentioned that he had appeared at many events, before emperors and kings, 'but there will be no day more exciting than this'. (He was not to know then that a decade later he would be at sea on the USS *Hornet* welcoming back to Earth the first men to set foot on the moon.)

2 Wings into Space

With the pressure on, and in order to minimize delay, X-15-2 (serial number 56-6671) was, like X-15-1, also fitted with two XLR-II engines. The third production aircraft, X-15-3 (serial number 56-6672) would remain engineless until the XLR-99 was ready.

Scott Crossfield was to fly the initial flight tests for NAA and was confident he would be able to stay with the programme right through, particularly if NAA were to co-ordinate the entire project. Even before the X-15 had been rolled out, however, provisional Government X-15 pilots had been selected to take over when X-15 became Government property. The Air Force pilot was Captain Ivan Kinchloe, former X-2 pilot and holder of the altitude record of 126,200 ft. Lt Commander Forrest Petersen was the Navy man, and Joe Walker was the NASA pilot. Of the four, Scott Crossfield would be the sole pilot for the first series of NAA demonstrations and test flights.

Within weeks of the crew selection announcement Captain Kinchloe was killed when his F-104 fighter flamed-out after take-off. He managed to eject but, tragically, was too low. (In his memory the Society of Experimental Test Pilots' award was established.) It was thus, under the worst possible circumstances, that his back-up, Robert White, became prime Air Force X-15 pilot.

Robert White was born in New York City on 6 July 1924. He gained degrees in both electrical engineering and business administration. During the Second World War he flew P-51s over Europe before being shot down on his 52nd mission and captured by the German army, only to be released at the end of hostilities. After a brief period he returned to the Air Force and by 1954 he had graduated from the famous Experimental Test Pilot School at Edwards Air Force Base. He was selected as the Air Force X-15 back-up pilot in 1957. Commander Forrest Silas Petersen was born in Nebraska on 16 May 1922. He had served with the US Navy since June 1944, when, as an ensign, he completed a period of duty on board destroyers in the Pacific during the Second World War. At the end of the war he was assigned to the Naval Air Station, Pensacola, Florida, gaining his wings on 14 June 1947. Before being assigned to the X-15 project, Forrest Petersen obtained two Bachelor of Science degrees and a Master of Science degree in engineering.

By the time X-15-1 was on its way, wrapped up, by road to Edwards on 16 October 1958, Yeager had left and Scott Crossfield, at 38, was the pilot everyone looked up to, whilst those concerned with the project knew that at that time the whole of the USA was looking to the X-15 to restore self-confidence.

Flight tests began on 19 March 1959, and initially things did not go well. Time after time the X-15 would take off only to return again later, still under the B-52 wing, because some or other minor fault prevented a free flight. Despite media and other pressures, the X-15 team was not going to be rushed into another 'Vanguard' disaster. They knew that the nation was watching and that made them even more determined not to make any mistakes.

Repeated problems, however, did start to take a toll on the project team and particularly the ground crew who would often work all night on the cold desert airstrip to get the X-15 ready, only to have the flight cancelled at the last minute. As Crossfield put it, 'As soon as we encountered any difficulty, if just one person gave up, everyone would give up'. As things began to slide, Crossfield used a ploy that only he could carry off. Every morning before a flight was scheduled he would be up and ready several hours early, go out across the airstrip and get into the X-15 cockpit as the ground crew continued to prepare the aircraft. He knew that as long as he sat there (up to eight hours on one occasion) the crew would do their best not to let him down, and get the X-15 ready.

On 8 June 1959, technicians closed the X-15's hatch as Scott Crossfield adjusted his helmet. Around him the X-15 cockpit hummed into life as assembled fuel and service trucks began to leave.

Over his headphones control radioed: 'OK — here we go'. Crossfield called back, 'Good morning Al — how are you this morning?' 'Fine Scott,' came the reply, 'how are you?' 'All I need now is a pilot's licence.' Crossfield quipped.

The B-52 with X-15-1 and Crossfield taxied across the runway followed by the smaller F-104 chase planes, then up into the air. Everything was working to plan. This was to be the one — the first free flight of the X-15. Chase planes flying alongside could see clearly Crossfield's white helmet moving inside the X-15 through its small cockpit windows as he went through the final checks. The B-52 captain then radioed the 'drop minus one minute' warning. Crossfield came back with, 'One minute — roger — data on — emergency battery

The completed X-15-1 looks profoundly sinister, shrouded up before the roll-out ceremony and screened off from the rest of the NAA plant in Downy, Los Angeles. Alongside, Scott Crossfield (left) and NAA assistant project engineer Roland 'Bud' Benner (right) pose for the camera. (Rockwell International)

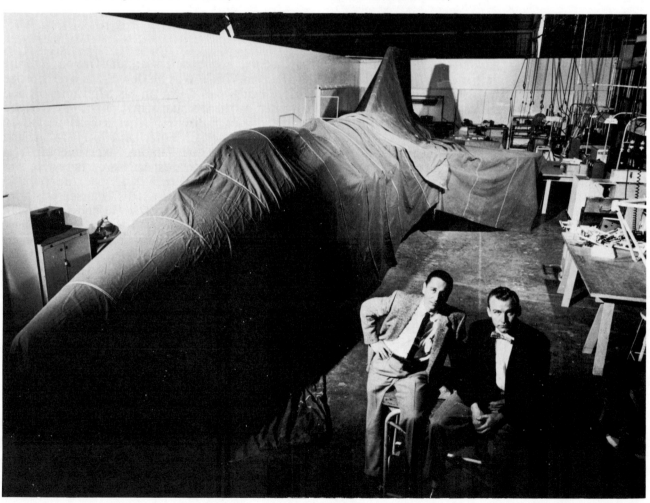

The day of the X-15 roll-out. Left to right, Howard Evans, who headed NAA's preliminary design engineering function (research); Rawn Robinson, assistant project engineer; Charles Feltz, project engineer; and Bud Benner. The X-15-1 fuselage has US Air Force markings, and on the nose is stencilled North American Aviation Inc. (Rockwell International)

This photograph of the roll-out shows a group of engineers and pilots assigned to the X-15 programme from NAA, NASA, USAF and US Navy. Kneeling from left, the second person is Scott Crossfield and the fourth is Joe Walker. Sixth is Walt Williams of NASA Edwards, and seventh from left is Charles Feltz. (Rockwell International)

on — ventral is armed — I'm ready when you are buddy. Master arm is on, system arm light is on.' The B-52 called out the 15 second mark to separation; the chase planes — Crossfield's guides on this mission — closed in around their charge. 'Chase on target, Scott.' 'Ten seconds,' Crossfield started counting down, '3 — 2 — 1 — Release!' The X-15 snapped away from the B-52's wing pylon. 'It's a clean break,' radioed the chase planes. Crossfield was in control as X-15 streaked like a black-winged needle through the sky above the desert, a thin wispy vapour trail in its wake. 'Looks pretty good here at 36,000 ft — Yeah, the APUs are looking real good — I wish I could get enough to do a barrel roll here — I feel as if I'm back in the saddle again buddy.'

Within seconds Crossfield was preparing for

landing. Nearer the ground, the chase planes called, reminding Crossfield to jettison the X-15's ventral fin ready for touchdown. 'OK, wait till I clear the edge of the lake here — ventral coming off now.' The stubby tail plane fell away. 'Clean separation,' radioed the chase plane. 'Good deal buddy,' said Crossfield. At 260 mph and 5,000 ft Crossfield called, 'All right — she handles nice, right along here.' But suddenly something was badly wrong. X-15-1 was developing a severe pitching motion as the airspeed fell away. His vision was restricted so that he had to rely on both instruments and the chase pilot's instructions to land. The controls in the cockpit that powered the X-15's ailerons, elevons and rudder had been set at too sensitive a level; the more Crossfield attempted to

The first three pilots to fly the X-15. Left to right are Joe Walker (NASA), Scott Crossfield (NAA), and Captain Bob White (US Air Force). Note the attitude thruster orifices on the nose and the warning 'Beware of Blast'. (Rockwell International)

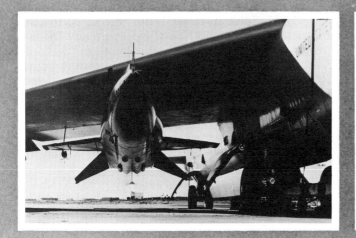

A pylon under the wing of the B-52 mother ship holds the NAA X-15-1 in the position occupied for its flight to drop altitude. Three main fittings secure the X-15, and additional quick-disconnect lines allow a launch panel operator in the B-52 to feed nitrogen and liquid oxygen to the rocket ship. The blisters on the B-52's fore and aft fuselage exterior housed two closed-circuit TV cameras for observations of the X-15 pilot, and the XLR-11 chambers and fuel venting tubes at the X-15's rear. (Rockwell International)

Close-up of the twin, four-chamber XLR-11 rocket engine exhausts. In this photograph the lower ventral fin, jettisoned for landing to provide clearance for the tail skids, has been removed. (Rockwell International)

X-15-1 takes off for what was to be its first, unpowered glide flight after months of delay on 8 June 1959. (Rockwell International) correct the pitching the worse it got. As he made his final approach he was in deep trouble. Over the radio he could be heard breathing heavily into the microphone as the X-15 raced in at over 200 mph. 'Rear flaps — they're down.' The chase planes closed in and radioed, 'Scott you're now 230, take it easy — the gear is down — OK 30 ft — 20 ft — Right, just hold her steady and you'll set her right there.' X-15-1 hit the desert airstrip like a brick,

By 17 September 1959 the second X-15 had been checked out and Crossfield was ready for the programme's first powered flight in X-15-2. Throughout the cold, damp, early morning hours technicians had loaded the liquid oxygen and alcohol fuel into the X-15 as it hung under the B-52's wing. Not far away Joe Walker of NASA and Major Robert White of the Air Force climbed aboard their respective jet chase planes to begin their own pre-flight checks. They were visibly in

This sequence of photographs follows X-15-1's approach and landing after its successful first glide flight. (NASA)

showering dust in a long billowing plume fanning out behind, marking its progress across the dry lake bed. But both Crossfield and X-15-1 were in one piece.

Meanwhile, X-15-2 was undergoing ground runs at Edwards in May and June. During July and August, several attempts at a powered free flight were cancelled because of leaks in the auxiliary power units and malfunctions caused by propellant tank pressure regulators.

the background, anxiously awaiting their turn to fly Crossfield's X-15-2 when NAA turned it over to the Government.

In common with the usual constraints when flying a new vehicle, plans called for a 'safe' flight of under Mach 2 and a maximum height of 60,000 ft. As the B-52/X-15-2 and chase planes took off in formation, Crossfield was aware that he was sitting in a vehicle with the explosive equivalent of a 17,000 lb bomb. Recalling events with the X-2, in case of emergency Crossfield made the B-52 commander agree to drop the X-15 to its fate, saving the lives of his own crew.

Twenty seconds from the planned drop time the launch light flashed on the X-15's instrument panel to show all was well. The B-52 pilot marked off the final seconds over the radio, '... 10 seconds — 5 — counting down Scott — 4 — 3 — 2 — 1, sep.' X-15-2 made a perfect break from the B-52 and within seconds Crossfield had stabilized ready for ignition.

Above and behind, Walker and White watched Crossfield ignite the first XLR-II engine and gracefully pull upwards and away. Such was the power of the X-15 that with both engines running Crossfield could not keep the space plane below Mach 2.1 even with the air-brakes fully extended. At the end of the brief powered portion of the flight, Crossfield showed his delight by performing a long, lazy barrel roll in the new rocket aircraft, for the benefit of Walker and White who had by then managed to catch up. Turning and gliding into a perfect landing Crossfield completed the first powered flight of the X-15 programme.

X-15 First Powered Flight Countdown Procedure

Prior to Flight Day
1. Flight briefing
2. Pre-mating inspection, including systems checkout
3. Mate B-52/X-15

Flight Day
1. Service; X-15 pilot's suit vent nitrogen
2. Service; X-15 pilot's oxygen
3. Service; B-52 pneumatic system servicing
4. Service; B-52 nitrogen top-off
5. Service; X-15 APU (hydrogen peroxide and helium)
6. Service; X-15 liquid nitrogen
7. Service; X-15 helium
8. Service; X-15 water alcohol and nitrogen
9. Final briefing of X-15 pilot and B-52 crew
10. Tow B-52/X-15 to engine start area
11. B-52 crew board aircraft
12. X-15 pilot boards aircraft
13. Close and lock canopy
14. Chase pilots man aircraft
15. Start B-52 engines
16. B-52 cockpit check
17. B-52 taxis to runway for take-off
18. Chase aircraft take off
19. B-52/X-15 takes off
20. Climb to 38,000 feet
21. *12-minute warning*
    X-15 pilot checks:
    Gauge readings
    Ram air closed

Pressurization cooling ON
Blowers ON
22. *8-minute warning*
    Chamber pressurization check
23. *7-minute warning*
    Data ON
    APUs ON
    Reset generator
    Reset stability augmentation
    Hydraulic pressure check
    Electrical pressure check
    Control motion check
    Rudder check
    Lateral control check
    Stability augmentation check
    Launch light ON
24. *1-minute warning*
    Emergency battery ON
    Fast slave Gyro ON
    Arm ventral jet
    Final OK
25. B-52 pilot; move master arming switch ON
    radio countdown:5-4-3-2-1, drop
    At drop turn launch switch ON
26. X-15; Recovery from drop:
    Emergency battery OFF
    Start engines

X-15-2 made another successful powered flight exactly a month later, that time reaching Mach 2.15 at a maximum altitude of 61,781 ft. On 5 November 1959 Crossfield was to undertake the third powered flight of X-15-2. As he dropped cleanly away from the B-52, chase planes watched the vapour trail thicken into exhaust plume from the two XLR-II engines. Crossfield began to accelerate away when one of the closest chase pilots saw, instead of the smooth controlled rocket plume, tongues of flames rushing from one of the chambers. 'There's something there... Hey!... You're on fire Scott.' 'Right,' snapped Crossfield, 'shut down — how much fire have I got?' 'Right by the rear of the engine,' came the reply.

Crossfield remained calm and professional; he knew that he had to jettison fuel quickly. 'Right [engine] arm is off — going to jettison — am I jettisoning?' The chase pilots confirmed, seeing a long white stream of billowing fuel flow from the crippled X-15 as it nosed downwards. Crossfield judged that he could just about make the safety of Rosemund Dry Lake, near the NASA flight research station at Edwards, and advised the chase pilots accordingly: 'Landing at Rosemund. Still have a fire warning light on.' The jet aircraft closed in protectively and confirmed, 'Jettison is still full blast'. Every second in the air lowered the level of explosive fuel aboard. Crossfield knew, however, that in his steep 'dive' attitude with the nose down the speed of the gravity-assisted fuel jettison system would be less than in level flight and that because of remaining fuel on landing he would be nose-heavy. He called up the chase planes once more. 'When over the centre of Rosemund I'm going to make roughly a 360.' As the mid-air crisis developed Control on the ground were mustering fire-tenders and crash equipment to Rosemund Dry Lake — above Crossfield prepared for his turn. 'OK — I think you can turn now, Scott,' called the chase pilot. 'Roger.' 'OK, don't forget to arm your ventral.' 'Ventral coming off now,' responded Crossfield as the black stubby lower tailplane tumbled away to make clearance for the rear tailskids. 'Roger; here come the flaps.' Crossfield

could feel the X-15 respond sluggishly, still nose-heavy, as the dry lake rushed up to meet him. For a few brief seconds X-15-2 soared just feet above the shimmering reflected heat of the lake bed, then at 200 mph the tailskids ploughed into the ground, followed almost immediately by the nose wheel, which, with all the extra weight forward, slammed down hard. It was too hard; almost a full second after X-15-2 had landed Crossfield heard the buckling twisting sound of the fuselage breaking up. Observers saw the main body of the rocket plane buckle just behind the cockpit as the X-15 slowed to a dusty halt.

For a few agonizing moments the emergency services watched, knowing that, if the fuel tanks had ruptured, Scott Crossfield would be incinerated in a ball of flame. Control radioed concern, 'What's happening out there? Does anyone read

X-15-1 with Scott Crossfield at the moment of ignition on its first powered flight, 23 January 1960. (NASA)

Scott at all?' Crossfield was unhurt and, by a miracle, the fuselage had buckled just aft of the cockpit and only inches in front of the fuel tanks. Within minutes of the landing Crossfield was out of the cockpit wryly examining the damage as firemen made safe the remaining fuel. It had been a close thing, and it would be almost a year before X-15-2 would fly again.

Crossfield dismissed the landing accident as one resulting from a design oversight in the nose gear, causing excessive stresses in the structure of the fuselage. In fact, he later commented, 'It probably should have broken on any previous landings that I made, because the deficiency was there all the time.' Crossfield's 'all-in-a-day's-work' attitude typified the testing of the X-15 in its early days.

On 9 December 1959, just over a month since Crossfield's most recent (and nearly fatal) flight, the USAF, having looked at both Boeing's and Bell/Martin's X-20 proposals, decided that the latter's design relied too heavily on unproven technology and should therefore be rejected in favour of a much less complex configuration proposed by Boeing. The company was therefore awarded the X-20 'Dyna-Soar' contract. (The Martin Company was named 'Associate Booster Contractor'.)

Development work on the programme, however, did not begin immediately. Because of the high costs involved, as well as serious doubts among many of NASA's top scientists and engineers that the programme would be successful,

the USAF was ordered to perform a configuration verification study. Code named 'Phase Alpha' this study began in mid-December 1959 and was to last until April 1960. In that time suggestions and comments on the Boeing concept were sought from other companies in the US Aerospace Industry. All of the technical data generated to support the programme was collected and catalogued, and all the possible re-entry vehicle designs were reconsidered.

Meanwhile, as X-15-2 was undergoing major repairs, X-15-1 flew just one more flight, with Crossfield at the controls on 23 January 1960, after which it was turned over to NASA. Their chief X-15 pilot, Joe Walker, flew the first Government mission on 25 March 1960, flying the X-15-1 to both 248,630 ft and Mach 2.

When the X-20 'Phase Alpha' was completed, on 25 April 1960, the original Boeing design re-emerged unaltered. If anything, the review had strengthened confidence in the concept and served to illustrate the feasibility of the programme.

The pilots of X-15. Left to right are Robert Rushworth, Jack McKay, Forrest Petersen, Joe Walker, Neil Armstrong and Robert White. (Smithsonian Institution)

The cockpit of X-15-1 taken midway through the flight programme shows general wear sustained during repeated high-speed flights into the upper atmosphere and space. (Rockwell International)

The X-15-1 cockpit, and the ejection seat. This photograph, again taken in the mid-sixties during overhaul, shows the open hatch and its nitrogen-inflated rubber pressure seals. (Rockwell International)

The X-20 Dyna-Soar prototype mounted on its ground-handling trolley at the Boeing factory. The cockpit windows were to be shielded during launch by a detachable metal plate, shown here in position. (Boeing)

Another close-up of the X-20, this time with the six prime crewmembers. Nearest the camera is Major William 'Pete' Knight, with Major Henry Gordon, Milton C. Thompson (civilian), Major James Wood, Major Russell Rogers, and Captain Albert Crews Jnr. (Boeing)

The Boeing/USAF X-20 emerged as a delta-winged space glider. It was to look and behave more like an aeroplane than any spacecraft either planned or in existence. Lt General Roscoe C. Wilson, former Air Force Deputy Chief of Staff for Development, called the X-20, 'the most important research and development project the Air Force has'.

The X-20 programme was to be conducted in three distinct stages. First, a series of developmental test flights was to be made. In June 1962 seven scale models of the X-20 were to be launched on top of a Scout rocket into a sub-orbital trajectory to test the high-speed flight characteristics of the vehicle. These models would also test the various types of thermal protection then under development for the full-scale series.

Space Shuttle

In 1963 a series of manned air drop-tests of unpowered X-20 gliders would be made from a B-52 mother ship at Edwards Air Force Base to check the craft's stability and control at low speeds and to give the pilots opportunities to perfect landing techniques. Later, X-20 gliders would be equipped with rocket engines and flown faster than sound to see how they handled at supersonic speeds. These tests would be followed in early 1964 by the launching into a sub-orbital trajectory down the Atlantic Missile Range, of an unmanned X-20 on top of an Air Force Titan II rocket. 1965 would see the first manned sub-orbital flight of the X-20 in this, its first stage, of development. Construction of eleven full scale X-20s was envisaged; three of these were to be used as flightless ground based 'test beds', four would be equipped for remotely-controlled unmanned flights, and four for manned flights into space.

The second stage of the X-20 project would be to orbit. This would necessitate the use of an improved booster capability (then under development by Martin) because at that time, in the early sixties, no rockets were available capable of placing the X-20 into such a trajectory. Stage three would coincide with the first Saturn launch vehicle rockets, and would give the USAF a fleet of X-20s with full range of orbital weapons systems.

Whilst the USAF, Boeing and the Government were drawing up their X-20 plans, on 12 May 1960 Joe Walker flew X-15-1 up to Mach 3.19 to equal Mel Apt's record set on his tragic X-2 flight almost four years before. The X-15 had behaved flawlessly and was returning valuable research data to both NASA and the X-20 teams.

A month earlier, in April, just 18 months after X-15-1's roll out, the XLR-99 engine was ready at last and two units were delivered. One was retrofitted to X-15-2 after its flight with Crossfield at the controls on 26 June, having made five successful flights previously since the accident. The other XLR-99 was fitted to the engineless airframe of X-15-3 for static ground tests during the summer of 1960, a prerequisite before X-15-2 could commence flight tests.

On the afternoon of 8 June 1960, X-15-3 stood rigged and ready at Edwards for the first static ground test of an installed XLR-99.

Bob Thompson, then a civilian engineer with NAA was assigned to the test as observer.

'When they completed fuelling of X-15-3's XLR-99 I was in the low concrete reinforced blockhouse on site. This building we called the pill box housed both the ground test monitoring staff and a bunch of equipment to record the engine test data. The pill box was blast and flame proof because we knew we had quite an explosive potential out in the

X-15. As usual in tests like that you aim to risk as few people as possible. Test auxiliary staff were filling the LR-99's flame trench with water right up to the siren call. When they were clear, we closed the double blast-door at the pill box and gave a final blast on the siren to make sure everyone knew we were going for ignition. The only person outside at that time was Scott Crossfield who, of course was sat in the X-15's cockpit. Anyway, we checked out the systems, found them OK and gave Scott the 'Go'. Now he ran the LR-99 up to around 30 per cent for ten seconds while we checked the performance data. We figured everything was OK so we shut down and opened her up for a burn of 50 per cent power for 15 seconds. Well, Scott sure seemed calm enough. Then he called in that the malfunction light was on and that he had the throttle off. The engine stopped and the malfunction light went out. So I guess he figured that whatever the problem was had cleared itself. I heard him say he was going to reset; the engine fired and the roof nearly fell in! I tell you, I never heard such a noise as loud as that explosion. The whole building shook and plaster fell in on us together with a piercing white light. Outside I could hear a sound like a high pitched scream; it was really frightening. My first thought was that we had lost Scotty.'

On the test stand, where only seconds before the sleek X-15-3 had been anchored, there was nothing but flames and debris. Rescue and emergency staff rushed out oblivious of their own safety, to find the only piece of recognizable airframe, the cockpit, over 40ft forward of its original position but intact. In specially-made flame resistant suits, the rescuers concentrated on reaching the cabin section which remained upright. Crossfield himself recalled: 'It was the biggest bang I ever heard, it was like being in the centre of the sun and the cockpit and instrument bay was blown about 30-40 feet from its original position and the fire was burning all around me.'

Crossfield's life had certainly been saved by the construction of the cockpit he himself had helped design to withstand both heat and stress, though under somewhat different circumstances.

Bob Thompson recounts: 'As things turned out, the engine was just fine; what we had was a faulty fuel tank pressure-relief valve which caused the Lox tank to over-pressurize and explode. The valve was comparatively a 10 cent piece of equipment, but the media really overplayed the significance of the incident. That kinda bugged us at the time, but that's what you have to expect when you carry out a test programme in the public eye.'

Scott Crossfield had his own version of media harrassment. 'The newspapers started calling me, so I made an attempt to calm them down and get them to relax — I told them that the only damage I had was the press in my pants. Sure enough, the next day an East Coast newspaper carried a headline, 'X-15 BLOWS UP — PILOT WETS PANTS'.

46

What was left of X-15-3 was picked up and the remains shipped back to NAA's plant at Los Angeles for a complete rebuild.

As part of X-15-3's refurbishment, engineers installed a Honeywell MH96 'adaptive flight control system' (AFCS). NASA had decided to make the third X-15 uniquely capable of high altitude flight, and the AFCS would overcome the major problem of adjusting the response of the aerodynamic control surfaces to meet the differing requirements of varying atmospheric density. Using the AFCS, X-15-3 would in theory have the same handling characteristics under all atmospheric flight conditions.

The X-15-3 aircraft was equipped with three control surfaces for aerodynamic control. The top of the vertical fin moved as a unit for rudder control, and two horizontal tail planes provided control in both pitch and roll. The planes moved differentially for roll control and together for pitch control. All three surfaces were fully boosted by means of hydraulic servo-mechanics. The servo-mechanisms were normally controlled electrically through the MH96 adaptive control system, but in the event of a failure of the MH96 system there were mechanical links from the pitch control stick and rudder pedals.

X-15-3 also had a dual set of rockets for attitude control about all three axis when at altitudes too high for aerodynamic control. One set of rockets operated automatically through the MH96 adaptive control system and was the normal mode of control. There was also a mechanical system, completely independent of the MH96, that allowed the pilot to fire both reaction control systems by moving a separate, left-hand, three-axis mechanical controller. No feedback was provided in the system, and the pilot had to provide damping inputs manually.

X-15-3 was the only X-15 equipped with the MH96 adaptive control system. This system was a rate-commanded type with automatic damping and variable gain features. Furthermore, the variable gain was self-adaptive and adjusted itself to the requirements of the various flight conditions encountered. The gains remained low, that is, there was less control surface movement for a given pilot input, when the aerodynamic control effectiveness was high (lower altitudes). The gains increased automatically as the aerodynamic control effectiveness decreased (high altitudes). When the average gain for all three axis reached a level of 90 per cent of the maximum, one set of the reaction control rockets was engaged automatically so that the pilot could continue to control the X-15 with the centre or right-hand controller and the foot pedals when in the ballistic portion of the trajectory. To conserve RCS fuel, the system was preset to disengage the rockets whenever the average gain for the three axis decreased to 60 per cent of the maximum.

The control system, being a rate command type, received the command signal from the pilot,

matched with a rate input from the angular rate gyros, and actuated the appropriate control surface and rockets to balance the two inputs.

The pilot's display panel in the X-15-3 differed significantly from those in the other two X-15s. The primary flight control instruments and their arrangement on the X-15-3 panel were experimental, using concepts developed by the Air Force Flight Dynamics Laboratory.

On completion of its rebuild and modification, X-15-3 was to be handed directly over from North America to NASA and the government. The extent of the repairs needed, however, meant that it would not be making its first flight until 20 December 1961.

On 4 August 1960, NASA pilot Joe Walker in X-15-1 had broken through to Mach 3.31. On November 15 1960, Scott Crossfield flew X-15-2 complete with the XLR-99 engine. For the first time, an X-15-2 was in the air as the designers had intended it, the culmination of many years work that began in 1954. Even at the lowest throttle opening, and with the air-brakes fully deployed X-15-2 reached Mach 2.97. Shortly after the flight, Scott Crossfield proposed that NASA allow him to fly most of the 'follow-on' X-15 missions for the Government. However, Scott Crossfield's earlier decision to leave NASA (then NACA) and join NAA had worked against him. He had hoped that NAA would be allowed to carry out the entire programme, but his gamble had not paid off; he was refused. The official reason for turning him down was that it would not have been good policy to have one pilot do most of the flying. Crossfield dearly wanted to stay with the programme and fly into space, but so did many other younger ambitious NASA, Navy and Air Force pilots who felt that perhaps Crossfield had had his fair share. Without a doubt, had Crossfield stayed with NASA he would almost certainly have made the trip into space; that is assuming, of course, that without Scott Crossfield's assistance in the design, development and flight testing of X-15 it would ever have succeeded at all!

Crossfield was, of course, terribly disappointed not to have been able to take X-15 to its design limits but said later: 'I got just about all out of it [the X-15] any man could get out of a single programme — and I can't ask for it all you know — I got all eight yards, didn't get to nine yards that's all.'

After two more flights, on 22 November and 6 December 1960 Crossfield's last X-15, number 2, was handed over from NAA to the Government.

Scott Crossfield left the flight programme but continued to work for NAA, as Director of Test and Quality Assurance, up until 1967 when as a result of reorganizations he left that position, to direct research and development programmes for Eastern Airlines, and conduct his own consultancy in Washington DC.

As Scott Crossfield bowed out of the X-15 programme, on 7 February 1961, Bob White (who flew his first X-15 mission the previous April) pushed the X-15-1 to Mach 3.5, and then, one month later, exceeded that record by almost a whole Mach number in X-15-2 establishing a new world speed record of Mach 4.43.

At the same time that speed records began falling, the X-20 was literally given an extra boost. Instead of the planned Titan I rocket launch, on 13 January 1961, the USAF decided that the X-20 would now ride instead the more powerful Titan II, giving both a test of higher re-entry speeds at just under orbital velocity. Meanwhile more and more pilots at Edwards were looking to the X-15 as a career stepping-stone to X-20 and space.

On 12 April 1961 something happened that would affect the whole future of high-altitude winged vehicle research and space exploration. The Soviet Union launched Major Yuri Gagarin into orbit. Unfortunately, the X-15 unlike the simpler Mercury or Vostok capsules, could not orbit. So, as the US emphasis on manned spaceflight grew along the lines of ballistic research, simultaneously Government and public interests in the X-15 and high altitude winged research began perceptibly to wane. Ken Leonarde of NAA commented: 'I guess at the time we thought that the Soviets were trying to pull us down a track we didn't want to go along. We figured the Soviets had a pretty good idea how far we had got with Dyna-Soar [X-20]and that they knew how advanced our high-altitude planes were getting. Making us compete with ballistics would throw us off course and slow us down, which of course in the end they did, with more and more dollars going into Mercury, Gemini and Apollo.'

On 25 May 1961, the same day that Joe Walker broke all previous air speed records in X-15-2 at Mach 4.95, President J.F. Kennedy at a joint session of Congress declared: 'I believe that this nation should commit itself to achieving the goal, before this decade is out, of landing a man on the moon and returning him safely to the Earth.' It is an interesting speculation whether the Soviets were concerned or relieved.

By the late spring of 1961 most of the X-20's major structural and aerodynamic configuration had been set. Boeing's 1,600 strong team was building and integrating new sub-systems, electronic controls and other pieces of hardware.

In May 1961 the Appropriations Committee of the US House of Representatives announced: 'The Committee foresee the need for an opera-

tional, manned military space vehicle over which the pilot has the greatest possible control and believes that the Dyna-Soar concept provides the quickest and best means of attaining this objective.'

On this and further recommendations of the Appropriations Committee, Congress appropriated an additional $85.8 million over and above the initial $100 million allocated for Fiscal Year 1962 to the X-20 project (at that level alone still $30 million more than that proposed under the Eisenhower Administration), and urged that the X-20 programme be speeded up in Fiscal Year 1962. At the same time, however, in Washington, the controlling voices were beginning to get cold feet in the light of the moon commitment. Chief of the high level 'doubters' was then Defence Secretary Robert S. McNamara who in mid-1961 cancelled the additional $85.5 million voted to the project by the Senate, and demanded that the USAF should justify the X-20 to him solely on the grounds of a projected military capability. Naturally the Air Force, being the military, could only put forward their case on purely military grounds, and not include the many civilian benefits to be derived from X-20. NASA on the other hand would have been ideally placed to take over such a project had the Air Force been willing and had NASA not now become so preoccupied with 'men on the moon'.

Both the USAF and NASA (participants in the programme's technical development) expected to gain valuable data from early tests of the X-20. The project would help determine what future military uses of space were feasible and aid NASA in space research.

As a test bed the X-20 spacecraft would provide an opportunity for the USAF to test military systems under actual space conditions, whilst at the same time demonstrating the capability of a man to operate them.

Early planned X-20 flights would achieve more than twenty times the speed of sound and last for more than an hour. They would provide a means of conducting research and development tests in a true spaceflight environment. Compared with the sparse data then available from brief free-flight tests of scale models or components mounted

Following assembly and check-out, diesel locomotives pushed the assembled Titan IIIC, complete with Solid Rocket Motors, to the launch pad. There, following flight tests, the X-20 would be hoisted into position, on top of the core vehicle. In this photograph, depicting preparation of a test launch of the Titan IIIC vehicle, the X-20 is replaced by an inert streamlined cone. (USAF)

In much the same way that the Shuttle would fly into space, the X-20 was to ride atop a main liquid-fuelled stage, supplemented with two solid rocket motors. This sequence of photographs shows the point of booster separation. (USAF)

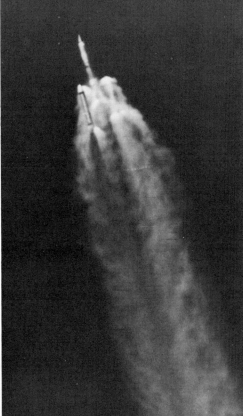

Arching eastward from Cape Kennedy on 2.4 million pounds of thrust, a Titan IIIC carves a brilliant trail across the pre-dawn sky. Following cancellation of X-20 the Titan continued in service to launch a variety of civilian and military payloads including the Viking Marslanders of the mid-seventies. (Martin)

The core vehicle of the Air Force X-20's launch vehicle Titan IIIC is pushed into the Solid Motor Assembly Building (SMAB) at Cape Kennedy's integrated-transfer launch area where twin 85 ft solid-propellant rocket-motors were attached. The three-stage liquid-propellant core vehicle seen here was assembled and checked-out by crews from the Martin Company. (USAF)

on rocket nose-cones, the X-20 flights would be a long, detailed investigation of the systems of winged vehicle spaceflight.

It was not possible in the early sixties to simulate accurately all the environmental conditions of hypersonic and space flight by utilizing ground test facilities. Communications experiments with the X-20 in actual hypersonic flight — just one of the many tests planned — would contribute understanding of the problem of sending and receiving radio signals during atmosphere re-entry.

Within weeks of McNamara's orders, the Air Force came back to him with a set of proposals for manned reconnaissance missions, satellite repair and retrieval, a bomber, or a transporter of four men in the pressurized equipment bay. (X-20 could carry up to half a ton in cargo.) McNamara was not impressed. Such missions could, he believed, be carried out quicker and just as effectively with the manned Gemini capsule launched atop a Titan II rocket. There was, in his view, no use for a manned sub-orbital shuttle that justified its cost.

Boeing countered this argument with a strong counter-measure. They had reviewed all available and potential launch vehicles in the light of rapid developments in that field, and come up with their 'Project Streamline'. Streamline would by-pass all the sub-orbital X-20 flights and put first the unmanned, then manned, X-20s straight into orbit on board one of the new powerful Saturn I launch vehicles. Orbital flights commencing at Cape Canaveral, Florida, would increase X-20's value immediately, not only supporting current NASA space programmes but also by providing a relatively cheap, reusable cargo-carrying space plane and transportation system that could land on conventional runways anywhere in the world much like an ordinary aircraft.

These orbital flights would test and check every phase of the X-20's operation, including stability and control performance and the effects of aerodynamic heating on the craft during re-entry. Military flights would originate from the West Coast Air Force base at Vandenburg, landing at Edwards. All at once the USAF were presented with the concept of a mini shuttle orbiter, capable of a variety of flight profiles including 'in orbit' rendezvous as early as 1961.

Of course, such increases in performance meant a certain re-think in terms of X-20 design, and in particular protection from the frictional heat generated by atmospheric re-entry loads. Leading edges of the wings, nose, and underside were to be covered with a ceramic zirconium graphite material, the rest of the skin to be either columbium alloy or coated molybdenum. Corrugated skin patterns would permit airframe expansion under heat. In addition, expansion joints would be incorporated between these skin panels.

Unlike manned ballistic capsules such as Mercury, which had their blunt ends covered with an ablative material which could 'boil away' heat, the X-20 would radiate heat from its surface area back into the atmosphere.

As the Mercury capsule plunged back into the atmosphere in a matter of seconds it had to endure severe temperatures for a relatively short time. The X-20 would, on the other hand, come back in a more leisurely manner and would take a longer time (upwards of 30 minutes) to dissipate the lesser heat of a shallower re-entry.

Much had been written and discussed among the US media about the high g-loads which the Mercury astronauts encountered when they returned through the atmosphere to Earth. Their capsules' deep, ballistic re-entry (with up to 10 or 11 times the normal pull of gravity) would be in contrast to the shallower glide re-entry of the X-20, where its astronaut pilot would encounter barely more severe g-forces than a commercial jet airline pilot.

Even this type of re-entry, however, would scorch and burn the surface of X-20 until it looked like an old fashioned wood stove! Nevertheless, engineers predicted that it would be a simple task to pepare it for relaunching.

The soaring temperatures encountered by the X-20 when it re-entered the Earth's atmosphere ruled out the use of a conventional undercarriage with rubber tyres and lubricated bearings.

Thus, the landing gear of the X-20 would be different from any then in production. The Goodyear Tyre and Rubber Company had developed a retractable main landing gear for the X-20 which to all intents and purposes consisted of wire brushes mounted on skids. The X-20 would not be equipped with brakes; the wire brushes and the friction they would create upon landing would bring the vehicle to a stop. Work on the unusual undercarriage was performed at Goodyear's, Akron, Ohio plant under a $45,000 sub-contract to Boeing.

Concurrently, Bendix Corporation's Bendix Productions Division of South Bend, Indiana, was developing a retractable nose-gear for the X-20 fitted with a circular steel skid resembling a shallow kitchen dishpan. In the early nineteen-sixties no tyre technology available could meet the environmental and mechanical stress levels inherent in a vehicle such as the X-20. The convex nose skid was designed for repeated landings on the Edwards lake beds, and not for conventional 'hard' concrete or tarmac runways. Work was being performed under

another $75,000 sub-contract to Boeing.

As the X-20 returned from space, parts of its airframe surface skin would be heated to between 2,000 and 4,000 °F. Its pilot, however, would remain in a cockpit maintained at room temperature.

Outside, the air in front of the aircraft would heat up to 20,000 degrees or more, to the so-called stagnation temperature. This super-hot air, or plasma, was expected to behave completely differently from air in its everyday form. Plasma (sometimes referred to as the fourth state of matter) is an excellent conductor of electricity and its flow can be affected by a magnetic field. Air in its natural state has neither of these properties. Preliminary studies into both X-20 and Mercury programmes indicated that it would be very difficult to communicate with the returning space plane whilst enveloped in this plasma which acted like a shield to radio waves.

Boeing scientists and others were experimenting with various techniques in an effort to solve this problem before the first X-20 was launched into space. A report by Dr James E. Drummond of the Boeing Scientific Research Laboratories early in 1961 indicated that low-frequency waves of electrically charged particles calles ions could be used to 'bore' holes in the plasma through which radio waves could travel. Other studies offered hopes that certain very-high-frequency (VHF) radio waves might hold an answer to the re-entry black out. Whilst the plasma sheath created problems for engineers, for observers of the space plane's return to Earth the plasma would afford a spectacular sight, the X-20 looking just like a shooting star as it blazed its way across the sky.

The most exhaustive series of wind tunnel tests in the history of flight were conducted by Boeing on the X-20 spacecraft. By the time it was completed it had tripled the total time spent in similar developmental data-gathering tests on the X-15. Even the eight-engined Boeing B-52 global bomber, under whose fuselage the X-20 would be carried into the air in early flight tests, required only half as much wind tunnel time.

The X-20 would need to gather as much information as possible, if it were to fly within the wide speed range from subsonic landing speeds to those of orbital velocity. In addition, the fact the X-20 would be lifted into space by a multi-stage rocket emphasized the need for tests of every conceivable combination of the X-20 and its booster. Tests of the X-20 atop the complete launch booster, the X-20 and the booster minus its first stage, the X-20 in flight without the booster and so on made an extensive wind tunnel programme necessary.

Wind tunnels used on the X-20 included subsonic and transonic tunnels, from low speeds up to Mach 1.4, supersonic tunnels (from Mach 1.5 to Mach 5.5) low hypersonic tunnels (from Mach 6 to Mach 10) and high hypersonic tunnels (from Mach 12 to Mach 25).

Even the effects of gentle breezes which would simulate off-shore winds at Cape Canaveral were directed at models of the X-20 booster combination, to determine how it would react whilst standing on a launch pad.

Of particular importance to the X-20 project was the so-called 'hot shot' and 'shock tube' tunnels which simulated speeds up to Mach 20 and beyond. Although ballistic rocket nose-cones and other ballistic shapes had generated considerable information in this speed range, X-20 was the first attempt to build a manned winged vehicle which would survive intact the blistering hypersonic speeds.

Started in earnest in early 1958, wind tunnel tests of X-20 models had been gathering data to answer questions on performance stability and control, plus aerodynamic and structural heating loads.

Virtually every major wind tunnel facility in the US had contributed to the development of X-20. Included in the wind tunnel programme were facilities at Boeing, AVCO Connell Aeronautical Laboratory, General Electric, Martin Marietta, the University of Washington, Ohio State University and the University of Southern California. Also included were the USAF's Arnold Engineering Development Centre and NASA's own Ames Research Centre, Langley Research Centre and Jet Propulsion Laboratory at Pasadena.

The Air Force never said publicly how much time would be saved in X-20's development by the decisions to give it an orbital booster. The initial announcement only said that, 'The new booster would assume early attainment of manned orbital flight'. It did not disclose when the first flight would take place. No official schedule for the X-20 development from this point was ever announced.

The main purpose of the abandoned sub-orbital flights was to gain data on hypersonic flight at speeds beyond Mach 6, never before sampled by manned winged vehicles. The rearranged X-20 programme would, however, explore this area as well as accomplishing orbital flight.

Orbital flight was expected to pose fewer problems for the pilot than the sub-orbital hops. The extra hour in space as a result of an 'around the world flight' would give the astronaut pilot more time to adjust to his environment, set up for re-entry and make the necessary preparations before beginning his descent through the atmosphere.

Whilst X-20 continued its complex series of design tests the X-15 flights soared higher and faster, and records continued to fall.

When Crossfield flew the X-15 in its first flight on 8 June 1959, the altitude record stood at just 79,000 ft, set up by Ivan Kinchloe in the X-2 during his attempt at Mach 2 in September 1956. This was exceeded on 12 August 1960 with X-15-1 in a flight to 136,500 ft at the hands of Bob White, and was exceeded again on 30 March 1961 when

Joe Walker reached 169,600 ft. At the same time, the speed records were being broken at an outstanding rate. On 23 June 1961 Bob White reached Mach 5.27. Petersen and Walker followed up in September and October with flights to Mach 5.3 and 5.74 respectively, closing inexorably on the design speed of Mach 6.

Finally, on 9 November 1961, Bob White climbed aboard X-15-2 for the series' 45th flight. The objective was to achieve the X-15 design speed of around 4,093 mph (or Mach 6.04, at 95,800 ft). Following release from the B-52, Bob White ignited the powerful XLR-99 rocket engine, and climbed to an altitude of 101,600 ft. With the throttle fully open Bob White nosed X-15-2 down and watched the machmeter rise to 6.04, when the engine, its fuel exhausted, shut down after a burn of 87 seconds. As he pulled out a loud crack shook the cabin — the right window glass had split as a result of unequal frame thermal stresses encountered during the flight. (A similar occurrence happened during his flight on 11 October 1961 when in X-15-2 again the window cracked for the same reason.) The problem was considered minor and (on both occasions) the flight pronounced a success.

On 20 December 1961, flight 46 in the X-15 programme saw the first flight of X-15-3 with the XLR-99 engine. This was eighteen months after it had blown apart on the engine testing rig with Scott Crossfield at the controls.

The first flight of this new X-15 was assigned to Joe Walker's back up, a 31-year-old civilian NASA test pilot named Neil Armstrong. Armstrong was born in the town of Wapakoneta, Ohio, on 5 August 1930. As a Navy pilot between 1949 and 1952 he flew 72 combat missions in the Korean war. On one sortie he was shot down and parachuted safely into friendly territory. Back as a civilian, Armstrong went to Purdue University where he graduated in 1955 with a degree in aeronautical engineering. He then joined NACA, stationed at Edwards Air Force Base, and was selected for the X-15 programme in 1960.

Armstrong was one of the pilots who saw the X-15 as a career route to the X-20 and space. His first X-15 flight had been on 13 November 1960 in X-15-1, and his second in the same rocket plane came on 9 December 1960. It was to be over a year before he was to make his third flight and the first of X-15-3 on 20 December 1961. The new rocket plane had to be well-tested before its high altitude research programme could begin. Armstrong took X-15-3, on its first flight, to 81,000 ft and 2,502 mph (Mach 3.76).

On 10 January 1962, while attempting his last flight in the project, the Navy X-15 pilot, Cdr

Forrest S. Petersen, safely completed an emergency landing in the X-15-1 at Mud Lake Nevada, about 200 miles northeast of Edwards AFB. After two unsuccessful attempts to start the engine Cdr Petersen jettisoned his fuel and landed X-15-1 without incident, the first such 'remote' landing since the project began. The engine failure was caused by a faulty pressure switch.

In the meantime things were beginning to look bad for the beleaguered X-20 project. Following a review of a full-scale mock-up of the X-20 glider and its related systems by a Government inspection team in September 1961 (as a result of which no further major changes in design were ordered), Secretary McNamara, in October 1961, wrote to President Kennedy with the suggestion that all military aspects of X-20 should be dropped to speed up development, 'against the day when such a system might be required. The best way to do this is to reorientate the programme to solve the difficult technical problems involved in boosting a body of high lift into orbit, sustaining man in it, and recovering the vehicle at a designated place rather than to press on with a full [weapons] system development programme'.

For several weeks the whole X-20 project hung in the balance. That was not all; performance data on the new Saturn I launch vehicle, then provisionally scheduled as the X-20's booster, showed it to be much too powerful, placing impossible aerodynamic launch loads on the space plane.

Finally, the President agreed to McNamara's proposal and the Air Force, keen to maintain their own access to space, accepted the Boeing 'Project Streamline'. Without a doubt, Project Streamline saved the X-20, for without it Boeing would not have been able to justify continued development in the light of changed circumstances. By the end of 1961 X-20 was once again back on the rails. Flight vehicles were to be assembled in Seattle at Boeing's Missile Production Centre. In his budget message to Congress in January 1962, President Kennedy asked for $115 million to be spent on the X-20 during Fiscal Year 1963. This represented an increase of $15 million over the amount designated by the Kennedy Administration for the programme during Fiscal Year 1962.

Further good news came in February 1962 when Martin, the builders of the Titan II liquid-fuelled booster rocket proposed a modification of the existing launch vehicle by the addition of two solid propellant 'strap on boosters' as a tailor-made launcher for X-20. It appeared at last that the X-20 would make it to orbit at least by 1965, powered by this new 'Titan IIIC'.

As part of their preparations for manned spaceflight the USAF organised three concurrent eight month training courses commencing between March and October 1962 at their Air Force Aerospace Pilots Training School at Edwards Air Force Base.

The first group of potential USAF astronauts designated 'Pilot Engineer Consultants' were selected in support of the X-20 project on 15 March 1962. They were: Neil A. Armstrong (NASA), M.L. Thompson (NASA), Captain H.C. Gordon (USAF), Major J.W. Wood (USAF), Captain R.L. Rogers (USAF) and Captain W.J. Knight (USAF).

The second group selected on 20 April comprised Captain R.H. McIntosh (USAF), Captain C.C. Book (USAF), Captain A.H. Crews (USAF), Major D.L. Sorlie (USAF), Major B.F. Knolle (USAF), Captain T.W. Tivinting (USAF), Captain R.W. Smith (USAF) and Lt Commander L.N. Hoover (USN).

Out of these fourteen men, six were to be selected in the autumn as prime pilot/astronauts of the X-20.

Then, out of the blue, Robert McNamara played yet another delaying tactic. Testifying before a House sub-committee of the Appropriations Committee in the spring of 1962, Secretary McNamara said: 'I have personally reviewed the project and concluded that, while we cannot say, categorically, it will yield an important military weapon, we do believe that its potential is sufficiently great to warrant what we have proposed [a $100 million budget].

'The military applications of manned orbital flights of the type towards which Dyna-Soar is directed are likely to be great. We can conceive of a number of such applications, although we have not developed them specifically, because we are trying to achieve the objective of the Dyna-Soar programme.'

He ordered a second 'Phase Alpha', freezing development whilst programme definition studies, reviews and analysis were undertaken, particular attention being paid to Martin's new, more powerful launch vehicle, the Titan IIIC. Effectively, all work was held up until August 1962 when McNamara finally signed the go-ahead order.

The first B-52 glide tests were to proceed as planned in early 1964, followed by a single unmanned flight to orbit, landing at Edwards Air Force Base. The first manned flight would probably take place in 1965. All the time its front-runner, the X-15, continued to climb higher and faster. By 11 October 1961 when the future of X-20 seemed so uncertain White flew the X-15-2 to 217,000 ft, followed on 30 April 1962 with the fulfilment of the design altitude goal, as Joe Walker in X-15-3 reached a height of 246,700 ft (over 46 miles). The X-15 had achieved both design speed and design altitude in just thirty-six build-up flights (excluding Crossfield's 14 NAA flights and White's Mach 6.04 flight in November 1961), almost exactly the number expected.

On 13 April 1962, NASA announced that the

X-15 would carry out new experiments in aeronautical and space sciences, in a programme planned to make use of its capabilities for hypersonic speeds, i.e. over Mach 5, and altitudes beyond the earth's atmosphere. The new programme would add at least 35 flights and two years to the schedule set originally for X-15 research objectives.

The National Research Airplane Committee, representing NASA, Air Force and Navy sponsors of the X-15 project, had approved a group of experiments to be carried out as soon as equipment and modifications could be completed. Some of the new studies would be conducted on research flights scheduled for the X-15's basic studies of aerodynamic heating, operational and control problems, biomedical data on pilots, hypersonic aerodynamics and structures, and problems of exit and re-entry into the earth's atmosphere.

Dr Hugh L. Dryden, Deputy Administrator of NASA, said the decision to utilize the X-15 in additional research effort was logical in view of its capabilities demonstrated since its first flight in 1959. Designed for speeds over 4,000 mph and altitudes above 250,000 feet, it had already flown to 217,000 feet. Much higher altitudes were anticipated.

'The X-15 is the most successful research airplane ever built,' Dr Dryden said, 'It has made repeated flights above 125,000 feet and flown faster than 2,000 mph. As a test bed and platform for carrying out new studies in aeronautics and space, it is unique. I believe the X-15 programe since its inception in 1954 has been a prime example of orderly step-by-step progress in research, and the new program should be very productive.'

Dr Dryden had been chairman of the Research Airplane Committee since it was first formed. Other members were Major General Marvin C. Demler for the Air Force, and Vice Admiral W.F. Raborn for the Navy. The NASA office of Aeronautical Research conducted the overall X-15 research programme, whilst the flight programme continued to be managed by NASA's Flight Research Centre at Edwards Air Force Base, California, in co-operation with the Air Force.

All of the follow-on experiments approved were sponsored by NASA and the Air Force, and were funded by the two agencies. Some of the more complex equipment would not be ready for several months, but necessary modifications were to begin soon on X-15-1 and X-15-2.

Work had started in early April 1962 on one of the primary projects: an experiment in ultraviolet stellar photography. The University of Wisconsin, under a contract awarded by NASA's Office of Astronomy and Solar Physics, devised and conducted a study of photographing the stars from altitude above 40 miles.

Doctors A.D. Code and T.E.Houck of the University's Space Astronomy Laboratory hoped to test their current theories pertaining to the origin

and make-up of stars by using this method.

On the ground, and at moderate altitudes, ultraviolet emissions from the stars are obscured by ozone in the earth's atmosphere. The main advantage sought was the X-15 pilot's ability to orientate the aircraft to face the stars above the ozone layer, plus the aircraft's capability to return and repeat the experiment.

The instrumentation for the 'star tracker' consisted of a gimballed platform containing four cameras, mounted in the X-15 instrumentation bay behind the cockpit. Clamshell doors atop the aircraft opened as the X-15 arched over into its long ballistic trajectory and was manoeuvred under the pilot's control to give the cameras a clear view of distant stars, thus making possible a continuous, simultaneous series of photographs in different, ultraviolet wavelengths.

Sounding rockets had been used for this purpose but their spinning action, required for gyroscopic stabilization, generally did not permit precise orientation for selected targets. Occasionally, too, the photo information was lost when the payload failed to be recovered.

By a similar method, a horizon scanner was to be used for the study of light across the spectrum. The objective, to obtain information on means for accurate attitude and guidance references for earth orbiting spacecraft.

An 'alphatron ionization' gauge was scheduled to be mounted in a small wing-tip pod for density measurements of the atmosphere above 100,000 feet, and a similar pod would house equipment for the measurement of micrometeorites. Several other Air Force experiments would investigate infra-red and ultraviolet data at the extremes of the X-15's higher altitude capabilities.

Besides these studies, the X-15 programme involved evaluation of advanced vehicle systems and structural materials. The Air Force tested an electric 'joystick' controller for possible application in manned spacecraft, and an airborne letdown computer to enable the pilot to plan his landing approach from re-entry to touchdown on the ground.

According to Paul Bickle, Director of NASA's Flight Research Centre, about half of the original research mission had been completed with the X-15-3 which, by mid-April 1962, had been rebuilt after its ground explosion incident. X-15-1 and X-15-2 had undergone extensive modifications in preparation for advanced flight work. The most important change was the installation of a back-up stability augmentation system (SAS) for complete pilot control in case the primary system failed during a high altitude flight. The back-up was an independent unit which could be energized manually or automatically by the pilot in the event of a primary SAS failure. The X-15's SAS provided servo-actuation for the pitch and roll controls, and was powered by one of two 3,000 psi hydraulic systems. Normally, system number 2 pressurized the pitch and roll servo-actuators directly, yaw being controlled by system 1. In the event of a system 2 failure, a spring-loaded selector valve shifted when the pressure dropped below a predetermined value. Fluid from system 1 was then directed to the emergency motor pump auxiliary power unit (APU) to maintain SAS hydraulic power. The reason for using the motor pump APU rather than using the system 1 flow directly, was to have an isolated closed-loop pumping circuit. This avoided loss of system 1 fluid should there be a leak in the SAS. In addition, the motor pump APU provided constant pumping pressure irrespective of variations in system pressure. To summarize, the emergency SAS would operate when pressure in system 2 dropped excessively. Use of the motor pump APU avoided the mixing of systems 1 and 2 fluids. Thus, system 1, being independent, was maintained for normal hydraulic operation of the plane and was not affected by system 2 or SAS failure.

X-15-1 was being prepared for a flight to a new official world altitude record of 250,000 feet. NASA research pilot, Joseph A. Walker, was scheduled to make the flight. In the meantime, Neil Armstrong of NASA Flight Research Centre had completed the third checkout flight in X-15-3.

To NASA, the X-15 presented new possibilities. Walker's record altitude flight had convinced them that X-15-3 was capable of going even higher, even into space. Bob White was assigned to X-15-3 and after a series of build-up flights was to take the rocket plane as high as it would go. As usual in test flying the step-by-step approach was to be adopted. X-15-3 went to 184,000 ft with White on 12 June 1962, then to 246,700 ft on 21 June equalling Walker's record. By 17 July both White and X-15-3 were ready to put the first wings into space.

Out on the cold flat airstrip of Edwards, X-15-3 was receiving last minute attentions from engineers and technicians. Before long the loading of liquid oxygen and anhydrous ammonia fuel was complete, and the X-15 hung ready beneath its pylon on the B-52's wing.

Inside the B-52's cockpit, Project Pilot Major John Allavie and Air Force Group Captain Harry Archer were going through their final pre-flight checks as Bob White, in his silver pressure suit and white helmet, was being strapped into the cockpit of X-15-3, to join the B-52 pilots in their final countdown to take-off. Out of the small X-15 cabin windows Bob White could see the ground crew and tenders disperse. As the sun rose above

the desert horizon the B-52 and X-15 stood ready.

The giant B-52 bomber started its engines and began to trundle across to the take-off position. Bob White, alone under the flexing wing of the B-52, was cocooned inside the pressurized X-15 cockpit, insulated from the noise of the B-52's engine just feet away by its thick protective shell. Down the flat lake bed runway, building up speed, the B-52/X-15 combination roared into the sky, as on the ground everyone concerned with the flight watched the disappearing vapour trails, aware that this was, in one sense, the culmination of all the effort and sacrifice spent on high-speed high-altitude research since the X-1 and Charles Yeager first passed through the sound barrier.

Soon the chase planes joined the B-52 having taken off from separate runways. Inside their cockpits were pilots who had already flown the X-15 and who, therefore, knew exactly what to look for, and the best advice to give if needed.

Bob White, in the meantime, awaited his time whilst buffeted by the B-52's turbulence. He was powerless to control anything until the moment of drop. He monitored his instruments as the altimeter climbed steadily towards 45,000 ft. 450 miles out from Edwards over a map reference known as 'Smith Ranch' in Nevada, Allavie and Archer banked the B-52 out west to the town of Delamar. The time had come for the parting of the ways. At 500 mph White armed the jettison control and joined the B-52 pilots in a countdown to separation. The chase pilots closed in around the two aircraft, eyes alert, ready to guide and otherwise assist White back to a safe landing should anything go wrong.

The X-15 snapped away from its pylon, rolling slightly as it fell. Bob White was in full control. He stabilized the X-15's flight attitude, then ignited the XLR-99 as the black rocket plane surged forwards and upwards, a plume of white exhaust in its wake. Chase planes were left behind as X-15-3 established a 41 degree climb angle towards space.

Moving the XLR-99 throttle to maximum thrust, White was forced back into his seat by a force of 4.5g. Already, ahead and all around him, the sky had turned from pearl blue to a dark blue. He knew that, at 250,000 ft, he had gone higher than any pilot had flown before. X-15-3 continued to rise. The objective of the flight was to reach 280,000 ft, but already he was at 300,000 ft with plenty of fuel remaining. Bob White was in space, the sky outside the tiny cabin was a deep blue-black. He shut down the XLR-99 engine just one second later than planned and 284 miles per hour faster than expected. Carried forward under its own momentum at 3,832 mph, the X-15 climbed an arc that peaked at 314,750 ft (59.61 miles). Below him White could see the Western seaboard of the USA all the way from San Francisco to Mexico; ahead the curvature of the Earth's horizon was clearly visible, as was the clear band of denser atmosphere that surrounded it. Firing the RCS thrusters to align the X-15 White saw something out of his left cabin window that caught him off guard. He later explained: 'First, three or four particles went by. At first I thought they were flakes or bits of ice from the hydrogen peroxide reaction control system. Then, through my left windshield I saw something that looked like a piece of paper the size of my hand, tumbling slowly outside the plane. It was greyish in colour, about 30 to 40 feet away. I paid attention to it for about five seconds. It gradually moved away towards the rear of the plane. He recalled John Glenn's orbital Mercury flight and his sightings of 'fireflies' that later turned out to be particles of ice from the control thrusters. Satisfied that the X-15 was in good shape and after three full minutes of weightlessness White fired the RCS once more to position the X-15 for re-entry. No one knew for sure how the X-15 would react or what would happen during the next few critical minutes. The effects of re-entry had been calculated and theorized but never proven in practice. The transition from reaction to aerodynamic controls, and the steep re-entry path of up to −38 degrees coupled with high angles of aerodynamic attack at speeds approaching Mach 6, faced White with piloting difficulties never before experienced (though he did have the assistance of the new adaptive flight control system).

Bob White was entirely alone, whilst the next few minutes would call on all his piloting skill and judgement. Since there were none of the usual acceleration forces acting on the pilot and since, because of the extreme altitude, the visual referen-

ces were difficult to interpret correctly, X-15 missions were primarily flown using the flight instruments alone. Like all pilots when operating in 'non-visual' conditions, Bob White was trained to rely solely on instruments in order to fly a precise flight profile and maintain orientation. Looking outside was discouraged except in the unlikely event that instrument failure was suspected. Gradually the black nose of the X-15 began to glow in the friction of the upper atmosphere, the impression of speed, lost in the airless, weightless environment of space returned with a negative force of 5g as X-15 decelerated. The leading edges of the wings glowed a dark, threatening red as White held a 20 degree nose upward angle of attack and opened the air-brakes. Sensors attached to his skin measured his heart's response to repeated changes in g force, whilst nearly 600 instruments clinically recorded the stresses on the X-15.

Edwards rushed towards them as at 18,000 ft White pulled in the air-brakes and used the X-15's aerodynamic controls to initiate a corkscrew dive to lose excess speed. By flying a descending spiral the X-15 was able to dissipate the maximum pos-

The effects of re-entry. The skin of X-15-3 after landing is scorched and discoloured after the record flight. (Smithsonian Institution)

sible amount of energy. At 1,000 ft above the dry lake bed White pulled the X-15 out of its dive and with the slipstream roaring past he jettisoned the ventral fin. Ahead the runway at Rogers Lake stretched out before him. White extended the X-15's landing flaps, at the same time bringing up the X-15's blunt nose, scorched and blistered from the heat of re-entry. Just feet above the runway at 200 mph, the landing gear dropped into place and locked with a satisfying 'thunk'. Alongside chase planes flew parallel watching every move.

Then White and X-15-3 were down, the rear skids sending a cloud of dust into the now hot desert air, the nose wheel held aloft for a few brief seconds thudding down to add to the plume of dust. A mile from touchdown, the X-15 came to a halt, whilst in the distance the X-15's ventral fin dropped gently to the ground under its billowing parachute, and the chase planes roared overhead in salute.

Ballistic missiles had reached space first, and by the time of White's flight four Americans — Shepherd, Grissom, Glenn and Carpenter — and with two Russians — Gagarin and Titov — had all exceeded 264,000 ft. Bob White, however, was the first to pilot a winged aircraft into space and return it safely to the Earth.

The following day, 18 June 1962, Air Force Major Bob White travelled to Washington to receive American aviation's highest honour, the Robert J. Collier Trophy, from President Kennedy in a White House ceremony. Joining Bob White in receiving the award were fellow X-15 pilots Scott Crossfield, Joseph Walker and Navy Commander Forrest Petersen. President Kennedy announced on the White House south lawn that the four men, 'represent the kind of Americans we are most appreciative of, and want the United States to be identified with'.

The President then examined the seven feet tall 500lb Robert Collier Trophy and said in an aside to Bob White, 'I don't know what you're going to do with it,' a remark missed by many of the media representatives in attendance. Bob White stepped up to the microphone as spokesman for the quartet and accepted the trophy 'on behalf of all the X-15 pilots'.

Following the presentation in the evening, the four X-15 pilots attended a dinner held in their honour by NASA, and were presented with the Space Agencies Distinguished Service Medals from Vice President Johnson. In a speech the then NASA administrator, James E. Webb, pronounced the X-15 as a 'classic example of a most effective way to conduct research'. The following day Bob White attended a Pentagon ceremony where he was awarded his 'astronaut wings'. He was the first

aviator in history to pilot an aeroplane to over 59 miles altitude. The USAF had ruled that any military pilot exceeding a height of 50 miles altitude would be awarded the status of 'astronaut wings'. By this definition Major Bob White became the first of eight X-15 astronauts. (In France, on the other hand, the Federation Aeronautique Internationale (FAI) regarded the boundary of space as 62 miles (100 km) altitude. They nevertheless had to acknowledge White's flight as a new aircraft altitude record, even though at 59 miles it was just three short of their 'definition' of space.) Military regulations prohibited the garish publicity and life story contracts of say, the Mercury astronauts, so for Major White, once the ceremony was over, it was back to work as usual.

Around the time of White's flight the X-20 was first put on full public view, at the Air Force Association's 1962 convention in Las Vegas. The six men finally chosen to fly it were also present, having been selected individually on 30 September from the first two groups of fourteen 'Pilot Engineer Consultants'. They were Captain Albert Crews Jnr, Major Henry Gordon, Major James Wood, Major Russell Rogers, Captain William 'Pete' Knight and NASA test pilot Milton O. Thompson.

Neil Armstrong would have been among the 'six' had he not been already selected for the NASA astronaut corps as their first civilian recruit on 17 September of that year. His X-20 place was taken by Captain Albert Crews Jnr.

On 26 July 1962, Neil Armstrong made his final X-15 flight, in X-15-1. That flight, to 98,000 feet at a speed of 3,989 mph was his seventh in the project. Immediately afterwards he turned all his attention to the X-20 whilst awaiting assignment to NASA.

A final X-20 group of 'Pilot Engineer Consultants' were recruited on 22 October 1962. They were: Captain J.M. Engle (USAF), Captain C.A. Bassett (USAF), Captain M. Collins (USAF), Captain J.A. Roman (USAF), Captain F.G. Newbeck (USAF), Captain N.R. Garland (USAF), Captain E.G. Givers (USAF), Captain A.H. Uhalt (USAF), Captain A.L. Atwell (USAF), and Major T.D. Benefield (USAF).

The next significant X-15 flight was to be made by another NASA pilot, John B. McKay. Jack McKay, as he was known, was born in Portsmouth, Virginia, on 8 December 1922, and flew for the US Navy during the Second World War, earning both the Presidential Unit Citation and the Air Medal with seven clusters. In 1950, he obtained a science degree before joining NACA in 1951 to fly both the X-1 and the Skyrocket before becoming the third civilian X-15 pilot on 28 October 1960.

On 9 November 1962, Jack McKay was strapped into X-15-2 for what was to be his seventh X-15 flight. Only six weeks earlier McKay had flown X-15-2 on a low-altitude low-speed flight gathering important data on X-15 flight characteristics with the detachable lower ventral fin removed. Various concepts concerning the dissipation of and the effects of extreme temperatures would later be studied using the space provided by removing the lower ventral fin. His flight on 9 November, the programme's 74th, was to be a continuation of this research.

As the B-52 reached separation altitude and speed, McKay flipped the jettison drop switch and fell away cleanly before igniting the engine. No sooner had the XLR-99 roared into life than McKay realized that there was something seriously wrong. The XLR-99's power output was stuck at 30 per cent and no amount of effort would push it past that mark. At over 1,000 mph and at an altitude of 53,950 feet, McKay's only available action was to abort. Shutting down the engine and jettisoning the remaining fuel, he turned the rocket plane around for an emergency landing. Soon the F-104 chase planes caught up and formated above, behind and on each side of him. The nearest suitable landing strip was at a site known appropriately as 'Mud Lake'. All went well until McKay was making his final approach. He attempted to deploy the landing flaps, but there was no response to the controls. The flat expanse of Mud Lake hurtled towards McKay and the crippled X-15 at over 290 mph. Holding off contact until the last possible moment McKay dropped the landing gear seconds before the tail skids hit the ground. Then, almost simultaneously, the nose wheels slammed down with all the force of a blacksmith's hammer on an

anvil. The front landing gear rebounded and fractured as X-15-2 with McKay inside gouged nose first into the ground. McKay knew he had lost the X-15-2 and that all he could do was attempt to stay alive over the next few seconds. Suddenly, the left tail skid gave way under the strain and the aircraft slewed sideways and rolled over the ground. Pilots in the chase planes watched in horror, helpless as the X-15-2 tore itself into pieces on the desert floor. Rolling over and over X-15-2 ended upside down in a cloud of dust and debris. McKay, still strapped in his seat was trapped and badly injured. Around him residual fuel leaked, and torn electrical circuitry crackled amidst the confusion. The rescue teams raced to the crash site as chase planes landed and pilots rushed to the scene. For McKay, it was to be over four hours until he was finally freed from the charred, smouldering wreck of X-15-2.

John McKay never fully recovered from the crash which left him with three crushed vertebrae in his spine and in constant pain. Nevertheless, he lived to fly the X-15 again 22 times. He had survived, like Scott Crossfield, because of the inherent strength of the X-15's cockpit structure.

A diagram of Bob White's X-15 flight profile.

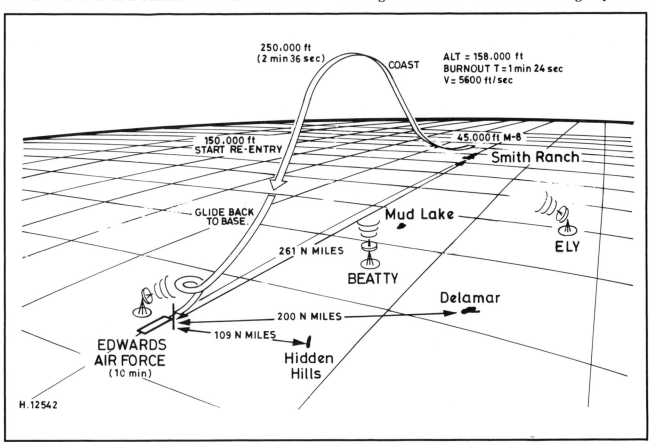

X-15-2 was pieced together and returned to NAA for a rebuild. It was, however, to return to flight status in an altogether different form some time later, adding another chapter to the X-15 story.

On 14 December 1962, Bob White made his final X-15 flight in X-15-2; a routine mission to 141,400 feet at a relatively low speed of 3,472 mph. He then departed the X-15 programme and Edwards to continue flying duties with the USAF in Germany. He is currently Chief of Staff, 4th Allied Tactical Air Force, Ramstein Air Base, West Germany. His position as prime Air Force X-15 pilot was taken by his back-up, Major Robert Rushworth.

Born in Madison, Maine, on 9 October 1924, Major Rushworth flew transport missions over China during the Second World War and, later, combat missions in Korea. After the Korean War ended Major Rushworth graduated in 1954 with a Bachelor of Science degree in aeronautical engineering from the USAF Institute of Technology and in 1958 was selected as an X-15 pilot, flying the first of his thirty-four X-15 missions on 4 November 1960, in X-15-1.

On 17 January 1963, Joe Walker, who by then had become something of a legend, flew his X-15 mission, the fourteenth by X-15-3, and the entire programme's 77th. His brief was to study the handling of the aircraft without the ventral fin at extreme altitude, and to conduct an infra-red astronomical star observation experiment.

The B-52 took X-15-3 with Joe Walker up over Delamar Lake, Nevada; when Walker dropped clear, he ignited the XLR-99 and accelerated to 3,677 mph (Mach 5.47) at 146,000 ft. As the engine cut off on schedule after a burn time of 81 seconds Walker continued on up to a maximum altitude of 272,700 ft (51 miles). Had he been a USAF pilot Walker would, of course, have qualified for his 'astronaut wings'. But NASA was and is a civilian organization and so Walker had to be content with being an 'unofficial' astronaut. He was only the 11th man in the world to exceed 50 miles high. The X-15 had now made two 'USAF defined' spaceflights. Data from Joe Walker's flight revealed that the lower ventral fin could safely be detached for future flights. This would lead to the X-15 being available as a hyper-sonic test-bed, with an assortment of flight test articles being mounted on the truncated fin stub.

On 11 April 1963, USAF prime pilot Major Rushworth took the X-15-1 to 74,000 ft at a maximum speed of 2,864 mph, the first of a series of extended test flights with a camera mounted in the aircraft nose to monitor photographically airframe distortion during high-speed flights.

Soon after the X-15 project management decided that an attempt would be made to break the world altitude record yet again. An objective of at least 350,000 ft was announced, 35,000 ft higher than the current record set by Bob White in July 1962. Careful planning was again required in the usual conservative 'stair-step' testing programme. As usual, as few unknowns as possible were to be tackled on each flight. Prime pilot for this attempt would be Joe Walker.

With the altitude commitment already made, on 13 May 1963 NASA and the Air Force sanctioned NAA to rebuild and modify the X-15-2, still in pieces following its 9 November 1962 crash. Since Air Force headquarters in Washington did not feel that merely rebuilding X-15-2 was of sufficient worth so long as X-15-1 and X-15-3 were still doing excellent work, NAA's Aerospace Systems Division personnel submitted a proposal for an advanced X-15 version. The project to upgrade aircraft number two started in May 1963 on an 'incentive contract' basis. Larry P. Greene, NAA's Vice President for research and development, conceived the improvement approach and the project was to be directed by Howard Evans, programme manager, with W.E. (Bill) Johnston, assistant.

The complete modifications, which would enable the then designated X-15-A2 ('A' for advanced) to reach speeds of Mach 8 at 100,000 feet were to take quite some time, so the X-15-A2 was to be returned to service as soon as it was flight worthy and extra components added and flight-tested piece by piece over successive months.

June 27, 1963 was the date for the 37th mission in the X-15 programme, the 20th flight of X-15-3, the 14th X-15 flight by Major Robert Rushworth, and the third X-15 space flight. It made Major Rushworth the 15th man above 50 miles and earned him his USAF 'astronaut wings', as he gained valuable experience in high altitude X-15 handling.

X-15-3 was released over Delamar, Nevada, with the engine burning at 100 per cent for 80 seconds, taking the rocket plane to a top speed of 3,425.00 mph (Mach 4.89) and an altitude of 285,000 ft (almost 55 miles). Mission duration was 10.46 minutes.

On 19 July, Joe Walker made history by becoming (unofficially) the first man to make two spaceflights. Walker made this, his 24th X-15 flight and the programme's 90th, in X-15-3. The aircraft was to be flown to high altitudes to allow studies to be made of the airframe's expansion during re-entry and flight behaviour of the X-15 with the lower ventral fin again removed. It was to be the first flight before the planned 'all out' altitude attempt. Walker was also to deploy a small nitrogen-filled balloon from the X-15 and tow it along to enable atmospheric density checks to be made. In addition, other tasks included the testing of a horizon scanning photometer, and infra-red/ultraviolet observations of stars.

Walker was launched over Smith Ranch, Nevada and the engine fired at full thrust for 85 seconds, two seconds longer than had been planned, taking the X-15-3 up to a height of 347,000 ft or 65.3 miles (higher than the planned 315,000 ft). Walker had officially become an astronaut. 'I thought that my altimeter had gone wacky,' he said on completion of the flight that lasted just 11.4 minutes and which attained a maximum speed of 3,710 mph (or Mach 5.5). Only one failure occurred on the flight, the nitrogen-filled balloon failed to deploy. The philosophy associated with X-15 research flights was to discontinue the research objectives when aircraft malfunctions impaired safe recovery of the aircraft, or when the pilot became so overloaded with aircraft malfunctions or experimental tasks that he was unable to attend to either! The experiments on board the X-15 were designed so that they did not have to be retracted before re-entry, though if left deployed they could be damaged by high aerodynamic pressure and heat from re-entry. In any event, they would not compromise the safety of the X-15.

On 22 August 1963, Joe Walker made his last X-15 flight. This was to be the attempt at the world aircraft altitude record, and if successful would not only make Walker the first man ever to enter space three times, but also provide invaluable data on aircraft control and stability during re-entry.

X-15-3 was launched on its 22nd flight over Smith Ranch, Nevada. It was the programme's 91st mission. Walker kicked in the XLR-99 engine and adopted the 41 degree climb angle for maximum altitude. Shut-down occurred after a burn time of 85 seconds and X-15-3 continued to rise. Walker monitored the newly-installed altimeter, that measured both the X-15's climb angle and energy to calculate a predicted maximum altitude, whilst ground radar tracked him up to 354,200 ft or 67.08 miles. Walker was weightless for over three minutes as X-15-3 spanned an airless arc over the Western coasts of the USA. Re-entry, accompanied by intense heat and atmospheric friction, preceded a perfect landing after a flight of 11 minutes that reached a maximum speed of Mach 5.58.

No other X-15 was ever to achieve the heights reached by Walker on these his two last flights. Shortly afterwards, Walker left the programme, joining among others, Neil Armstrong, testing the NASA Apollo lunar landing research vehicle, a curious 'flying bedstead' device that simulated the controls and handling of the lunar module, with vertical jet engines.

Soon after Walker achieved his third space-flight the X-20 flight programme was further defined. Following the B-52 glide trials in 1964, there were to be two X-20 unmanned orbital flights to test both the heat protection airframe coatings and the separation of the X-20 from the Titan IIIC. Both unmanned flights would be controlled from re-entry to landing via a Sperry Drone control sys-

tem. Recovery would be at Edwards. The first space flight was scheduled for later summer/early autumn 1965.

The first manned flight of the X-20 was to take place in the spring of 1966. Like the unmanned flights, they were initially to be single-orbit missions of around 90 minutes' duration at a maximum altitude of 50 miles which was relatively low for a 'spacecraft'. The subsequent flights in the development programme were to be at three-monthly intervals. Funding of approximately $1,000 billion would allow for 12 such flights.

Once the initial orbital flight trials were completed, extended missions could be considered using a special service module attached to the X-20 providing additional consumable items like propellant, oxygen and electrical power enabling flights of several days and at much higher altitudes.

Most of the equipment to be installed in the first X-20 was as far as possible tried and tested hardware from other spacecraft and launch vehicles. (The X-20's inertial platform was a direct derivation of that used in the Atlas Centaur missile, of which vital components, the gyroscopes, had been in production for several years.) Other pieces had to be developed specially, such as automatic flight control systems and a guidance computer.

A further device, designed to assist the pilot in the final stages of re-entry and landing, was being perfected. Energy management during the glide portion of atmospheric flight needed a very quick and accurate measurement of the potential energy to be dissipated during the atmospheric drag-breaking manoeuvres following re-entry. Constant comparison of the energy to be dissipated and the energy being lost due to aerodynamic heating and drag allowed the pilot maximum manoeuvrability during decent and landing. The energy management displays were in the form of two television screens mounted in the instrument console facing the pilot. Each screen had an overlay of several possible flight paths giving the pilot a choice of routes to follow. Not only could this system be used on a normal flight, but it could also assist in the event of an early aborted mission.

By maximizing the glide potential of the X-20 in this way the space plane could, in effect, have a landing 'footprint' several thousand miles wide on either side of its flight path, reaching any airport along the entire western side of the USA.

Everything technical pointed towards success, but the cost was frightening. Already X-20 had run up as much expenditure as the entire Mercury programme, due partly to the delays and reappraisal instigated by management and the Department of Defense. The Air Force was also contacting NASA with a view to adapting the Gemini spacecraft to meet their military ambitions. X-20 was becoming an expensive anachronism. The two-man Gemini could perform all the current and anticipated roles of the X-20 more cheaply and more quickly. NASA were to use Gemini as an interim programme to link Mercury to Apollo, testing orbital rendezvous techniques and conducting Earth observations. The military uses were obvious to the Air Force, as was the chance of acquiring some 'off the shelf' hardware.

Continued Air Force interest generated initially by McNamara in a Gemini-derived 'Manned Orbiting Laboratory' was viewed as an unhealthy development at Boeing, where assembly of the first flight rated X-20 had begun. Roll-out was set for

early 1964, and already a B-52 had started modification to accept the initial drop test trials. Suddenly, on 11 March 1963, the Air Force put a freeze on all X-20 development after the first 12 orbital flights, pending yet another study of possible future uses.

Nevertheless, X-20 development work continued. On 18 September 1963, in support of an Air Force project code-named START, a smaller model of the proposed vehicle was launched on top of a converted Thor missile to an altitude of just over 203,000 ft. On separation, the sub-scale X-20, which was just under 6 ft long and constructed of the same materials as the full-scale version, fired its

X-15-3 moments before touchdown, after achieving an unofficial world altitude record of 354,200 ft with Joe Walker, on 22 August 1963. Note the sawtooth pattern on the aircraft's ventral area showing, in icy outline, the residual liquid oxygen. (NASA)

small hydrogen peroxide jets to set up the correct re-entry altitude. Gliding back through the atmosphere a battery of sensors measured and recorded its behaviour. Aerodynamic controls brought it down on target near Ascension Island. The new heat-resistant materials worked well, and the flight continued to be a success until the little space plane splashed down under its recovery parachute and sank; small flotation bags having failed to deploy.

On 10 December 1963, X-20 was cancelled and all work stopped; semi-completed airframes were scrapped and 5,000 Boeing staff were made redundant. Secretary of Defence McNamara dictated that the remaining X-20 funds should be transferred to the Air Force's new space project, the Gemini-derived Manned Orbiting Laboratory.

X-20 would have been the most advanced project of the nineteen-sixties but was plagued by delays, reappraisals, reorientation and not least, disinterest in official quarters. It was conceived before *Sputnik 1,* at a time when such a project was

ideally placed to satisfy both military and civilian needs for the foreseeable future. But following *Sputnik,* things changed rapidly. The civilian space programme under NASA was committed to ballistics and an American 'man in space soonest'. The subsequent 'race' to the moon caused more and more resources to be spent on ballistic spacecraft 'capsule' research. The advances in that field, although less sophisticated (ie splashing down in the sea under a parachute, fleets of recovery ships, throw away spacecraft and boosters etc) was in line with the new civilian 'moon' goals set up by President Kennedy in 1961. The X-20 could not reach the moon, nor could it play any kind of support role to Apollo, so its direct civilian usefulness was ended. At the same time the Air Force saw in new

generations of NASA 'spacecraft' a means to achieving all their military goals quickly and at a fraction of the development cost of X-20.

Thus by 1963, the only role left for X-20 was in experimentation and flight research, the cost of which no longer justified its existence.

But what of the X-20 pilots? Of the chosen 'six', Major Henry Gordon, Major Russell Rogers and Major James Wood went back to normal Air Force flying duties. Milton Thompson, the NASA pilot, continued with his X-15 duties, whilst Captain Albert Crews Jnr was later picked as an astronaut for the Air Force manned orbital laboratory. Captain William Knight was assigned as an Air Force X-15 pilot in 1965 and in that project was to become both an astronaut and unqualified world air speed record holder.

In June 1963, Captain 'Joe' Engle, part of the third USAF group had transferred to the X-15 programme. In October of that year the USAF X-20 ranks were further depleted when, again out of the third group, Captain Michael Collins (later to fly in Gemini 10 with John Young, and then as command module pilot on Apollo II) and Captain Charles Bassett, left to become NASA astronauts. The rest, for the most part, resumed their military careers.

On 10 February 1964 Dr Eugene Sanger, father of the 'Shuttle', died from a heart attack at the age of 59. Only weeks before he had addressed a major assembly of European Aerospace delegates during which he made a remarkably accurate prophecy.

'When the first successful manned landings on the moon have taken place, the construction of large manned permanent stations in Earth's orbit and routinely-supplied lunar bases, should be considered — undertakings, presumably, of the next decade — then an economic system of space flight becomes essential, even indispensible. If these developments are not yet fully under way in the USA and possibly too in the USSR, then this is because the total intellectual and material resources of these countries are occupied with the actual pioneering efforts, especially with the race to the Moon. As soon as this strain is over, they will devote all their efforts to the next phase of practical spaceflight, the preparatory work of the American aerospace industry shows this quite clearly.

'When, a quarter of a century ago, spaceflight first became technically possible, two fundamentally different directions of development existed. On the one hand was the development of the ballistic missile — like spacecraft, essentially similar to the proposals of Tsialkovski, Goddard, Oberth, and Esnault-Pelterie — whilst on the other hand

lay the aeronautical access to spaceflight, namely the further development of the classical aircraft to include spacecraft capable of cosmic flight velocities — advocated by a group of Viennese scientists, including Von Hoefft, Valier and Sanger.

'More exhaustive work on definitive projects very soon showed that, considering the contemporary state of the art, fewer problems would need solving, and with regard to the low operating frequency the transportation of defined payloads would be more economical in the ballistic mode, (because the absence of wings, undercarriage etc. gave a better payload to gross weight ratio). The high production costs of such ballistic and non reusable transporters were over-shadowed by the far higher development cost, and consequently the economic advantage of the latter was not fully apparent. Because ballistic spacecraft can only be used once, test flights of individual craft are not possible, resulting in a low reliability which, nevertheless, seemed tolerable in view of the projected unmanned military and civil uses. Therefore, the development of ballistic space flight had proceeded during the last decades. This has led to the spectacular first successes, followed by the commercial applications such as communications satellites. The ultimate aim of landing men on the moon, which represents the end of the pioneering phase of spaceflight, already lies near the limit of technical feasibility because of the aforementioned restrictions on reliability. However, in the following years, the continuing demand for large transport volumes is likely to result from a number of tasks, such as the launch and recovery of numerous Earth orbital scientific and commercial satellites; the construction of large, manned space stations for similar uses, and particularly as transit stations between the Earth and the Moon; the provisions of these space stations with the stores necessary for their operation, exchange of crews, transport of visitors and so on; the transportation to the Moon and back of materials and men required to construct permanent lunar bases; and the transportation between different Earth orbiting space stations and between these and unmanned Earth satellites for purposes of control, recovery, assistance, repair, change of orbit etc. ...'

As Von Braun's legacy was the Saturn V moon rocket, so Dr Sanger's was the Space Shuttle. But that was almost 15 years away, and there was still much to be done. The X-15 was, at the time of Dr Sanger's death, the only practical realization of his work in winged reusable spacecraft.

In February 1964, America's newest rocket research aeroplane, the X-15-A2, was turned over to the United States Air Force by North American Aviation's Los Angeles division. The craft had taken 39 weeks and $5 million to complete since the go-ahead was granted in May 1963.

Designed for flight at eight times the speed of sound at an altitude of 100,000 feet, and able to cope with friction-generated air temperatures of

Early supersonic research aircraft pose outside the NACA hangar at Edwards Air Force Base. From left to right: Douglas Skyrocket, Douglas Skystreak, Bell X-5, Bell X-1A and Convair XF-92A.

This unique colour photograph of the X-1A in flight was taken from a chase aircraft during the Mach 2 plus attempt on 12 December 1953. Shortly after, Chuck Yeager was fighting for control of the X-1A after encountering a loss of stability at Mach 2.435. (USAF)

Top left: Joe Walker and X-15-1 separate from the B-52 at the beginning of the programme's first Government flight on 25 March 1960. (NASA)

Bottom left: On 17 July 1962, at 45,000 ft, Bob White prepares to take X-15-3 up to 314,750 ft and establish a new aircraft world altitude record. This photograph was shortly before separation, from the left-hand cockpit window of the B-52. (NASA)

Main picture: The programme's 138th mission completed, X-15-3, with Joe Engle on board, is attended by ground support vehicles as its B-52 'mother' flies past in salute. Whilst a technician removes residual fuel from the tank, others assist the astronaut out of the cockpit. The flight on 29 June 1965 was Joe Engle's first trip into space. (NASA)

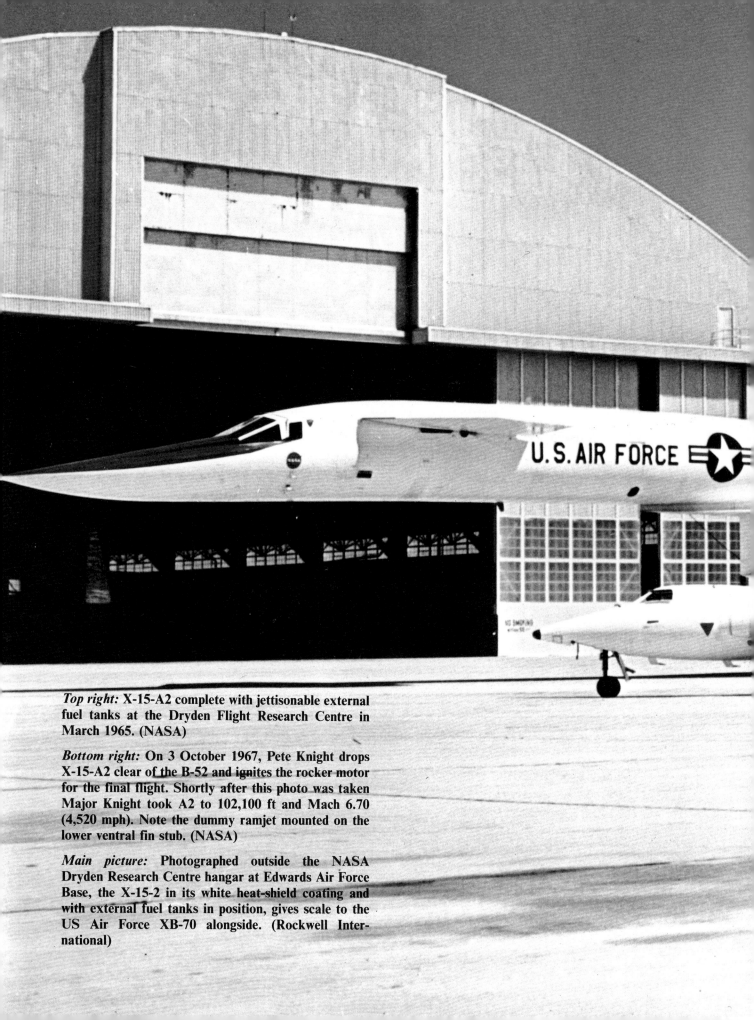

Top right: X-15-A2 complete with jettisonable external fuel tanks at the Dryden Flight Research Centre in March 1965. (NASA)

Bottom right: On 3 October 1967, Pete Knight drops X-15-A2 clear of the B-52 and ignites the rocket motor for the final flight. Shortly after this photo was taken Major Knight took A2 to 102,100 ft and Mach 6.70 (4,520 mph). Note the dummy ramjet mounted on the lower ventral fin stub. (NASA)

Main picture: Photographed outside the NASA Dryden Research Centre hangar at Edwards Air Force Base, the X-15-2 in its white heat-shield coating and with external fuel tanks in position, gives scale to the US Air Force XB-70 alongside. (Rockwell International)

USAF Major William 'Pete' Knight photographed alongside the modified X-15-A2. The new shape windshields were incorporated to withstand the effect of hypersonic flight. (Rockwell International)

over 2400 °F, the new version of the X-15 incorporated many major design changes from the X-15-2, including two large External Tanks containing liquid oxygen and anhydrous ammonia propellants. These extra quantities of propellant were to be used to achieve a speed of 2,000 feet per second at 70,000 feet. At that point, the tanks would be jettisoned and recovered by parachute. Internal propellants would be used to push the rocket plane to 8,000 feet per second in level flight at 100,000 feet. The tanks were 22 feet long and 37.75 inches in diameter. The ammonia tank contained 1,041 gallons (6,000 lb) of NH_3 and the oxygen tank 757 gallons (7,494 lb) of LOX. The tanks were designed to be both recoverable and refurbishable.

Other modifications included: a main gear lengthened to provide 39.5 inches of ground clearance to accommodate the mounting of external ramjets and other experiments on the ventral fin stub; a lengthened nose gear; a 29 inch fuselage extension; liquid hydrogen tanks and plumbing provided for ramjet experiments (the X-15-A2 would provide a hypersonic test platform for the advanced ramjet engines which, up to the advent of this new X-15, could only be tested for limited periods in wind tunnels or on rocket flights. The ramjet, of 36 inches maximum diameter, would remain attached to the truncated ventral fin throughout the flight and landing phase); improved windshield design using a three-pane design with alumino-silicate as a middle pane, and a fused silica panel as the outer pane; a removable right-hand wing tip having a chord at the splice of 80 inches, a span of 41 inches and a tip span of 36 inches (new structural configurations and new materials were to be mounted in this removable tip location for research testing); and access doors, located on the left-hand side behind the cockpit for 'down-looking' experiments and on the right-hand side for 'up-looking' experiments, in conjunction with advanced photographic and optical experiments.

In addition to these changes new heat protection materials were later to be added to the fuselage skin. This material would burn away progressively at around 530 °C and, in doing so, maintain the X-15-A2's structure at less than the 650 °C maximum safety heat level designed into the airframe back in the late nineteen-fifties. Without the ablative coating, X-15-A2 would overheat from atmospheric friction at Mach 8 of temperatures up to as high as 1100 °C and weaken the rocket plane to the point of structural failure.

During the two years immediately following Walker's flight and right up to May 1965, no X-15 was to exceed 196,000 ft nor speeds over Mach 5. Then, on 25 June 1964, almost 19 months after McKay's nearly fatal crash, the new X-15-A2 returned to the programme (though yet to be fitted with the new propellant tanks and its ablative heat shield) and made its first flight in a series of build-

ups to its target of Mach 8.

That successful test flight of X-15-A2 was flown by Major Robert Rushworth and demonstrated that the new vehicle with its new performance was indeed flightworthy. In place of the extended lower ventral fin, X-15-A2 carried on its first flight a prototype 'ram jet' engine aimed at providing hypersonic air-breathing propulsion systems for speeds over 5,000 mph. Data from the 800 lb engine on this flight helped determine the suitability of the A2 as a flying testbed. In addition, the modified A2 instrument bay contained cameras to photograph and record ultraviolet emission from stars, as well as Earth resources experiments and cartography with another standard camera pointed earthwards. It was the beginning of a long series of tests that would establish X-15-A2 as America's most advanced winged flying maching up until the advent of the Shuttle.

In July 1964 X-15-1 was taken, temporarily, out of service so that a Honeywell inertial guidance system, developed for the ill-fated X-20 project, could be installed to control automatically X-15 attitude when required. In addition, two torpedo-shaped wing-tip pods, each approximately 5 ft long were added. The forward section of each pod was designed to collect samples of micrometeorites on six rotary adhesive surfaces. Micrometeorites, being fine, small particles from space, travelling at immense speeds in the upper atmosphere, were a considerable worry to NASA. Calculations had shown that a micrometeorite strike, even if of particles only as large as a grain of sand, could seriously damage the thin shell of a manned spacecraft, given sufficient speed. For this reason information as to the frequency, composition and speed of micrometeorites was very important. The rear part of each wing-tip pod housed a device known as a densitron which measured the fluctuating densities of air at high altitude.

On 29 June 1965, Air Force Captain Joseph Engle became, at 32, the United States' youngest astronaut. He had flown 13 previous X-15 flights and this, the programme's 138th, was the first X-15 astro-flight in nearly two years. As usual X-15-3 was the vehicle, making its 44th flight.

Captain Joe Engle was born on 26 August 1932 in Abilene, Kansas. Graduating from the University of Kansas, he joined the Air Force at 23 with a degree in aeronautical engineering. Before long he had established a reputation of exceptional piloting skills, and became 'top student' during initial flying classes. Joe Engle was sent to serve in Air Force squadrons not only throughout the US, but also in Italy, Spain and Denmark. In 1961 he graduated from the prestigious USAF Experimental Test Pilot School and then, after demonstrating

Space Shuttle

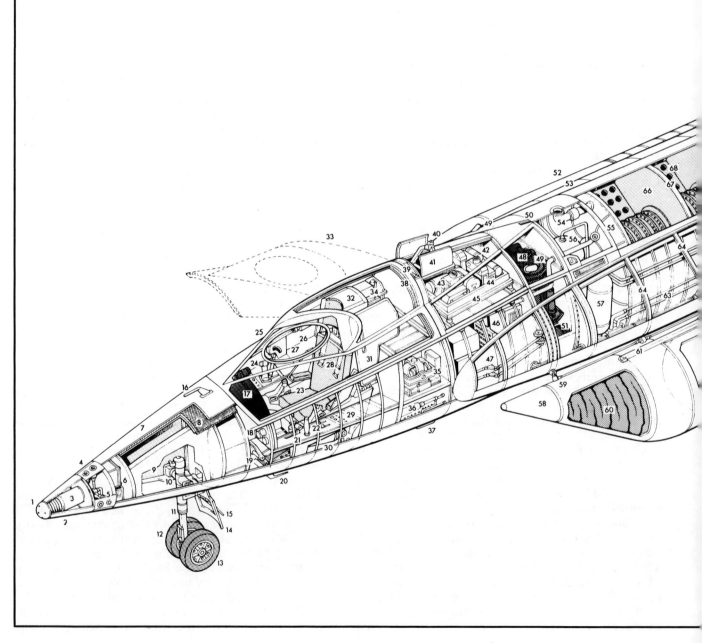

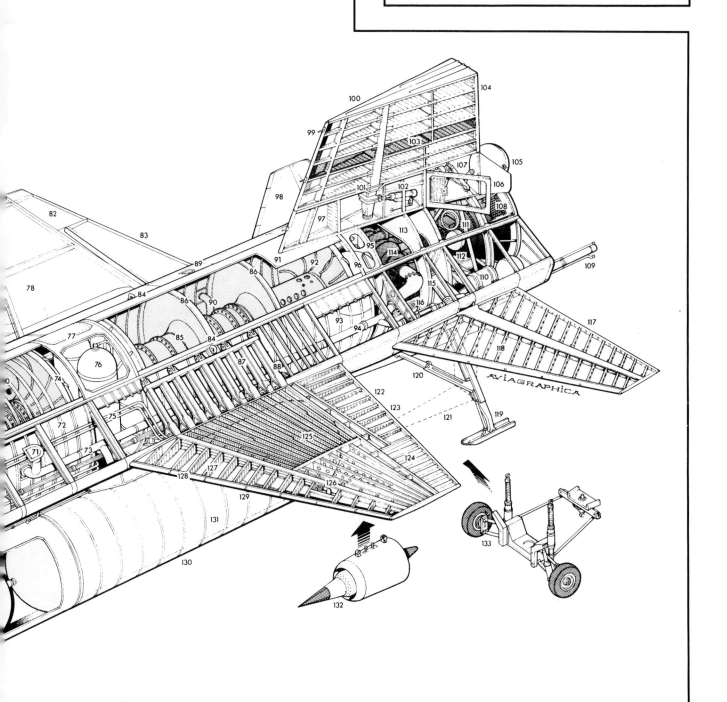

X~15 A2 cutaway

Preceding pages: The North American X-15-A2 (Courtesy Pilot Press)

1 Hypersonic flow sensor
2 Nose cone
3 Power supply amplifier
4 Pitch control reaction jets
5 Yaw control reaction jets
6 Front equipment bay
7 Inconel-X skin plating
8 Heat insulating lining
9 Nosewheel bay
10 Undercarriage leg pivot
11 Nose undercarriage leg
12 Free-fall nose undercarriage
13 Twin nosewheels
14 Nosewheel door
15 Door air scoop
16 Pitot tube
17 Instrument panel shroud
18 Back of instrument panel
19 Rudder pedals
20 Antenna
21 Engine throttle control
22 Ballistic control column
23 Pilot's seat
24 Aerodynamic control column
25 Knife-edge cockpit canopy
26 Fused silica elliptical windows
27 Pilot's starboard side console
28 Safety harness
29 Port side console
30 Telescopic strut for ejection seat blast shield
31 Folded stabilizing vanes
32 Headrest
33 Cockpit canopy open position
34 Rocket powered ejection seat
35 Instrumentation inertia platform
36 Liquid nitrogen cooling system
37 Ventral antenna
38 Canopy insulation
39 Canopy hinge
40 Forward connecting link to NB-52 launcher pylon
41 Sprung doors to connectors
42 Stellar camera platform
43 Two oblique astronomical cameras
44 Two vertical astronomical cameras
45 Camera platform gimballed mounting
46 Systems equipment compartment
47 Control runs
48 Twin General Electric auxiliary power units
49 APU exhausts
50 Cooling system vent
51 Two APU generators

52 Starboard external fuel tank, anhydrous ammonia, 6,006 lb (2,727 kg)
53 Starboard side fairing
54 Liquid oxygen vent
55 Liquid oxygen tank pressure bulkhead
56 Equipment cooling system liquid nitrogen tank
57 Reaction control jet HTP fuel tanks, port and starboard
58 Port external tank nose fairing
59 External tank front attachment
60 Recovery parachute
61 Parachute release link
62 Fuel tank pressurizing helium reservoir
63 Pipe runs in side fairing
64 Side fairing frames
65 Test and recording equipment
66 Liquid oxygen fuel tank
67 Fuel tank compartment bulkheads
68 Tank baffles
69 Welded Inconel-X fuel tank skins
70 Internal stiffeners
71 Liquid oxygen filler cap
72 Welded external tank stiffeners
73 Liquid oxygen supply pipe to engine
74 Liquid oxygen tank rear pressure bulkhead
75 Fuel pipes to roll control reaction jets
76 Liquid hydrogen fuel tank for ramjet engine
77 Access panels
78 Starboard wing panel
79 Roll control reaction jets
80 Interchangeable starboard wing tip
81 Wing tip instrumentation
82 Fixed trailing edge section
83 Starboard landing flap
84 Aft attaching links to NB-52 launcher pylon
85 Anhydrous ammonia main fuel tank
86 Tank dividing bulkheads
87 A-frame wing mounting struts
88 Flap jack attachment
89 Ammonia filler point
90 Ammonia fuel feed pipe
91 Inconel-X welded tank skins
92 Ammonia tank rear pressure bulkhead

93 Welded external tank stiffeners
94 Liquid oxygen feed pipe
95 Access panels
96 Turbopump HTP fuel tank, 64 US gal (242 l)
97 Vertical stabiliser fixed stub section
98 Starboard all moving tailplane
99 Instrumented leading edge
100 Vertical stabiliser upper rudder section
101 Rudder spar pivot
102 Rudder jack
103 Communications aerial
104 Wedge section rudder
105 Helium tank to pressurize liquid nitrogen
106 Air-brake
107 Air-brake jack mechanism
108 Rocket chamber nozzle
109 Liquid oxygen jettison pipe
110 Turbopump lubrication tank
111 Engine mounting struts
112 Thiokol XLR-99 rocket engine
113 Rear fuselage frames
114 Rocket engine turbopumps
115 Tailplane spar pivot
116 Tailplane jack
117 Port all-moving tailplane
118 Inconel-X tailplane construction
119 Port main landing skid
120 Skid lowering hydraulic jack strut
121 Position of wedge section ventral rudder, jettisonable for landing
122 Port landing flap
123 Square section trailing edge
124 Fixed trailing edge section
125 Inconel-X multi-spar wing construction
126 Roll control reaction jets
127 Leading edge construction
128 Inconel-X leading edge heat sink strip
129 Thermal expansion slots in leading edge
130 Port external fuel tank, liquid oxygen, 7,494 lb (3,402 kg)
131 Mylar-tape wrapped insulated tank skins
132 Auxiliary ramjet engine replaces ventral rudder
133 Ground handling wheeled dolly

his ability in X-20 flight research, was selected to fly X-15 in the spring of 1965. His first flight, in X-15-1, took him to 77,800 ft and Mach 4.21.

By 1964, Captain Joe Engle, with a creditable number of X-15 flights behind him, was selected as the 'Outstanding Young Air Force Officer of 1964' by the USAF Association.

On 29 June 1965, he was released in X-15-3 from the B-52 high over Delamar Lake. The subsequent 10½ minute flight achieved a maximum height of 280,600 ft and a speed of 3,432 mph (Mach 4.94) after a total burn time of 81 seconds. The flight included a test of a horizon scanning device later incorporated in Gemini spacecraft, giving invaluable assistance for future space navigation systems.

Captain Engle's next mission, on 10 August 1965, again took him into space in X-15-3, on the programme's 143rd flight. He reached a maximum altitude of 271,000 ft investigating both boundary layer noise and new re-entry manoeuvring techniques. His 10 minute, 3,550 mph flight made him the third man in history to fly into space twice.

Jack McKay had made fifteen X-15 flights since the September 1962 accident which left him ¾ inch shorter and in constant discomfort from his back injury. Nevertheless, on 20 September 1965, he climbed into X-15-3 for a flight to 295,600 ft making him the fifth X-15 astronaut. A total XLR-99 'burn' time of 81 seconds boosted McKay to 3,732 mph during his 12 minute flight. As a result, scientists gained vital research data on re-entry structural loading on the X-15's tail as well as horizon scanner measurements.

On 7 October 1965 a major review of the X-15 programme took place. The accomplishments of the research aircraft were reviewed with respect to progress in areas such as piloting technique, bio-astronautics, aerodynamic heating, vehicle aerodynamics, structural dynamics, advanced systems, test bed experiments and mission simulations. Projected plans and proposed studies were also covered.

By the time of the review, all the studies that were originally conceived for the basic X-15 programme had been essentially completed. In addition, a number of programmes had evolved as the project progressed, and these investigations had either been conducted or were in progress at that time. Paul Bickle of the NASA Flight Research Centre and John S. McCollom of the USAF Aeronautical Systems Division presented the X-15 review team with an indication of future X-15 plans, and approved programmes and several proposals not then approved, but believed to offer the potential for an excellent return on investment.

The major accomplishments of the X-15 programme in terms of piloting represented a significant aspect of the project. Prior to the X-15 there were predictions of how well the pilot might or might not do. Views expressed were either optimistic or sceptical. Solid experience gained served as

2 Wings into Space

the basis for a range of projected hypersonic aircraft applications. Specifically, the pilot had been able consistently to make spot landings for a low lift/drag glider under quasi-operational conditions. The pilot proved his ability to make successful re-entries from extreme altitudes using several types of control system under aerodynamic and acceleration conditions more stringent than those expected in most orbital and sub-orbital re-entries. Because manoeuvrability requirements were much less for the X-15 than for jet fighter aircraft, satisfactory handling qualities were generally obtainable with less control power and at lower damping levels than were required with fighter aircraft.

In terms of bio-astronautics, the review team noted that the X-15's was the first research programme in which the pilot's physiological behaviour was monitored during flight. Doctors reported that the pilot's physiological parameters (heart rate, for example) during free-flight were unpredictably high according to clinical standards; it was soon realised, however, that the norms for the research pilot under stress were significantly higher than had been expected. Post-flight examination revealed no harmful after-effects to the X-15 pilots.

Some of the most enlightening research of the X-15 programme was performed in the area of aerodynamic heating and skin friction. Heat transfer coefficients as much as 35 per cent lower than those predicted by established theories had been consistently evident in flight results. From those results, skin temperatures for any planned X-15 mission could be closely predicted. Skin friction values were consistent with the aerodynamic heating results in that they were also lower than might have been predicted.

The X-15 configuration was originally derived from wind tunnel studies of small scale models. Scale effects on the overall aerodynamic characteristics were generally thought to be small; however, no prior data existed in the mid-nineteen-fifties to confirm this belief for Mach numbers greater than 2. The X-15 programme had, by October 1965, generated extensive aerodynamic data for a wide range of full-scale flight conditions and enabled detailed correlation to be made between the basic stability, control and performance parameters from flight tests and wind tunnel and theoretical predictions.

In the area of structural heating and dynamics research, the thermal-structure problems of the X-15 were generally typified by local failures such as buckles, pulled fasteners and cracks due to repeated thermal loads. All these problems were relieved early in the flight programme by additional expansion joints, local fairings and similar. It should be remembered that were it not for the cautious step-by-step expansion of the X-15's flight envelope, these minor problems may not have been detected in time to prevent major damage to the vehicle. In the area of structural dynamics, a much better appreciation of panel flutter and the mechanism of landing loads associated with skid landing systems was gained as a result of X-15 experience.

X-15 operational experience had provided an understanding of the factors that constitute testing procedures and also the advantages of a step-by-step approach in the qualification of systems and airframe prior to use in a flight programme. The favourable experience of the adaptive control system in the X-15 contributed to the selection of a somewhat similar adaptive system in the F-111 jet fighter and interceptor.

Expansion of the X-15 flight envelope beyond previous research aircraft performance prompted several rather sophisticated ground-based simulations for study of the piloting tasks and control requirements of the aircraft, and for overall flight planning. The effectiveness of the simulations had been evaluated for all phases of the X-15 mission. The simulator, however, was only as good as the information included, and in several cases serious consequences were luckily avoided in actual flight. A six-degree-of-freedom fixed-base simulator with complete cockpit controls and control system hardware had been judged by the pilots to be generally satisfactory for pilot evaluation, familiarization and practice for flights, even for the high acceleration phases.

The October 1965 review outlined detailed new plans and schedules for the three X-15 vehicles. The X-15-1 was committed to test bed experiments, most of which required altitudes of between 150,000 and 250,000 feet. Three of the major experiments were the MIT photographic horizon scanner, the PMR launch-monitor experiments and a study of vapour-cycle cooling systems.

The MIT photographic horizon scanner developed by the Massachusetts Institute of Technology was already being tested on board X-15-1 and was scheduled to continue well into 1967. The programme was in support of an Apollo navigational and stabilization system to provide alignment of an inertial system for mid-course manoeuvres using determinable definitions of the earth's horizon contour. Data obtained at various times of the year provided inputs to the Apollo programme on seasonal, reflectivity (albedo) and day-to-day effects.

The PMR launch-monitor experiments involved the monitoring of missiles launched from the USAF Pacific Missile Range. (Although the timing of this experiment was critical, the flexibility of both programmes, namely the X-15 and the missile Launch, allowed a good chance of success.) A test programme of about six X-15-1 flights to an altitude of 250,000 feet was scheduled to begin in mid-1966. NASA felt it was important to note the similarity of the experiment with the test observations of Pete Conrad and Gordon Cooper during their recent Gemini 5 mission. On that earth orbital mission in the two-man Gemini spacecraft (successor to the Mercury spacecraft), both astronauts remarked on the clarity of ground features such as roads, railways and shipping. They also commented upon the clear visibility of aircraft vapour trails. To the USAF, such observations had a clear military reconnaissance significance.

Vapour-cycle cooling systems capable of sustained operation under weightlessness had been studied and developed in laboratories, and were ready for fabrication and evaluation. For the system to be tested on the X-15-1, photographs would be made through windows in critical component parts, and system performance would be monitored during several flights in extended zero-gravity conditions.

Of all three X-15s, the rebuilt X-15-A2 was certainly the most heavily committed. The A2 had several test bed experiments, of which one, the stellar photography programme to obtain quantitative measurements of the ultraviolet properties of certain stellar objects, was already underway, and would continue into 1966.

A number of flights would first be required in X-15-A2 to obtain experience with the recoverable tanks and then gradually build up flight experience to Mach 8. In the build-up programme, allocated 6 to 10 flights depending on problems encountered, the operational effectiveness of the ablative system would be closely monitored. The problem posed by ablatives depositing on the windshield was of particular concern. In addition, actual aerodynamic data derived from the flight data would be carefully monitored and compared with theoretical wind tunnel results. In October 1965, some thought was being given to the construction of a new wing tip section that would embody the latest aerospace technology advances in lightweight, high-temperature structures for flight testing in the speed range between Mach 6 and Mach 8. The objective of the programme would be to measure pertinent flight qualities and then to test the same flight structure in the new High Temperature Loads Calibration Facility at the NASA Flight Research Centre (Edwards), to determine correlation between the ground facilities and flight data. Once approved, the flight testing would be accomplished prior to the planned ramjet tests for the X-15-A2.

Progress in applying the X-15-A2 as a propulsion-system test bed had taken great strides since the NASA Flight Research Centre feasibility study was completed in 1964. The Hypersonic Ramjet Experiment Project promised to add materially to the state of hypersonic engine development. In 1968 an inert ramjet would be flight-ready, and it was hoped that the actual 'hot' engine tests could be started in 1969. The ramjet experiment would require 12 to 24 months to complete.

The review board decided that X-15-3 would be grounded for the winter of 1965 for three months, at which time an inertial guidance system similar to that currently in use in the X-15-1 would be installed. In addition, a special high-speed digital computer and a new cockpit instrument panel display would be added, permitting a 12-month flight evaluation of various energy management and boost-guidance systems. At the same time, plans were to obtain additional results on heat transfer and skin friction. Longer term plans included a delta wing modification and it was on this project that the programme for the X-15-3 and A2 concentrated.

Much research would have to be done in many areas before definite plans could be made for a manned research aircraft with significantly greater performance than the X-15. In mid-1965 a joint Air Force-NASA ad hoc committee considered a research programme which could ultimately lead to a ramjet-powered research aircraft capable· of flying in the Mach number range of 8 to 12. The programme encompassed theoretical studies, wind-tunnel tests and flight tests. Much of the ramjet development would have been done in actual X-15-A2 flight tests. Three main projects were scheduled for this purpose. The first two projects consisted of unmanned rocket boosted vehicles to take ramjet engines and components to the desired speed and altitude ranges. The third project was the ramjet experiment carried out by X-15-A2. One further proposed flight project, a delta-winged X-15, would precede the hypersonic research vehicle.

The proposal called for the conversion of X-15-3 to a delta wing configuration by the addition of the 75 degree swept wing as well as a new fuel tank section elongating the fuselage by 10 feet. The increased fuel capacity, in combination with the XLR-99 rocket engine uprating at that time planned for X-15-A2, would permit flights to a Mach number of 6.5 without external tanks, or to a Mach number of 8 with a single external fuel tank.

Of course, such expenditure in terms of resources both of time and money had to be justified and NASA, together with the Air Force, made considerable effort to explain the benefits of a delta wing X-15 programme to their government paymasters. First, the flight tests would provide realistic aerodynamic data under fully developed turbulent flow conditions to supplement ground-based research where such conditions could not be achieved. Answers would be obtained to key questions relating to hypersonic aerodynamics of

delta wings, large scale behaviour of flap-type controls, fin-tip interference effects, and handling qualities of a configuration typical of contemporary thinking for a future hypersonic air-breathing vehicle. Aerodynamic research on the delta X-15-3 would be unclouded by propulsion effects inasmuch as most of the data would be taken under glide flight conditions.

Secondly, the delta wing X-15-3 proposal would permit the evaluation in a practical flight application of a hot, radiation-cooled structure, designed for repeated flights at temperatures between 1500 °F and 2200 °F. It would also focus technical effort on a refurbishable hot wing leading edge design.

Overall, the delta wing X-15-3 programme could have established a baseline of confidence and technology from which decisions regarding the feasibility and design of advanced air-breathing vehicles could be realistically made. The proposed time for the delta wing X-15-3 fitted in well with that of an overall hypersonic research vehicle programme, and the cost, NASA maintained, did not appear unreasonable.

The October 1965 X-15 review meeting concluded that the X-15 programme had contributed greatly to the technology of manned hypersonic flight. Furthermore, because the X-15 was such a unique and versatile tool for research it found that, 11 years after the project's initiation, some of the most valuable contributions lay several years in the future. Whereas in 1959 the X-15 was looked upon as America's access to space flight against the Russians, six years later with the 'capsule and missile' astronauts leading the race, it appeared that the X-15 would instead provide much of the information required to bridge the gap from the low supersonic speeds of the nineteen-fifties to the hypersonic cruise vehicle of the seventies and eighties.

On 14 October, X-15-1 made its first flight into space. At the controls and making his third spaceflight was Captain Joe Engle. The flight to 266,500 ft was to be Engle's last X-15 mission. He would return to space a fourth time though, on 12 November 1981 as Commander of Space Shuttle *Columbia* on her second flight. In April 1966 Captain Joe Engle left the X-15 programme and became the first and only NASA astronaut recruit to have previously flown into space.

During October 1965, X-15-3 was withdrawn from service to be fitted out to a similar equipment level which its sister, X-15-1, had received in July 1964. In the meantime, X-15-A2 had also been returned to NAA for the fitting of its two external jettisonable fuel tanks which by then were complete and ready for installation. On 3

November the X-15-A2 flew for the first time with the new tanks in position.

The flight was to be an initial test of the system which, it was hoped, would later give the X-15-A2 a maximum speed of Mach 8. It was also the first of two flights to test the in-flight tank jettison and recovery systems. The two 25 feet long tanks attached to the lower fuselage were empty for this test.

At the controls, Robert Rushworth, by then a Lieutenant Colonel, took the X-15-A2 to 1,500 mph at 70,000 ft before jettisoning the twin tanks at approximately the same speed and altitude that tank separation would occur in operational flights. The jettisonable lower ventral fin was carried in place as a safety measure on this flight to increase the aircraft's stability at the moment of tank jettison.

Unfortunately, soon after separation, one of the two External Tank's 34 feet diameter parachutes failed to deploy and the tank was destroyed on impact with the ground. The other tank was recovered from the target bombing range at Edwards for refurbishing and reuse.

Rushworth left the X-15 programme to become Commander of the Air Force Test and Evaluation Centre. Currently he is Vice-Commander, Aeronautical Systems Division, Air Force Systems Command, Wright Patterson Air Force Base, Ohio.

The USAF had, by the time of Rushworth's flight, reached an advanced stage in the development of their 'Manned Orbital Laboratory', or to be more correct, their manned military outpost. With the X-20 now buried, the MOL, based largely on NASA technology, was to be the first stage of America's military presence in space. The first trained astronauts for this project were selected on 12 November 1965. They were Major Michael J. Adams (USAF), Major Lacklan Macleay (USAF), Captain Richard E. Lawyer (USAF), Captain Francis Neaubeck (USAF), Major Albert H. Crews (USAF and ex X-20), Major James Taylor (USAF), Lieutenant Commander John Finley (USN), and Lieutenant Richard Truly (USN).

The MOL had received President Johnson's official approval on 25 August 1965. The programme called for an initial series of unmanned 'test launchings of a converted Gemini two-man spacecraft with a 'boilerplate' laboratory, on top of a

For ground handling of X-15s, a small trolley was mounted beneath the rear lower ventral fin in place of the standard retractable skids. This photograph was taken shortly before X-15-A2's first flight with the two jettisonable fuel tanks in position. (Rockwell International)

powerful Titan IIIC rocket, developed originally by Martin for the X-20'. The term 'boilerplate' was used by NASA to describe a test article which, whilst outwardly presenting an exact replica of the genuine flight-rated vehicle, lacked all internal instrumentation; in effect, a hollow metal shell.

Once the 'boilerplate' test flights had been successfully completed, five manned Gemini Laboratories would be launched in which USAF astronauts would live, work and carry out reconnaissance and surveillance activity for periods of up to 30 days at a time.

The launches were to take place from the Air Force's Vandenburg, California base, and from Kennedy Space Centre, Florida. Every flight would be under exclusive control of USAF security personnel. Each flight would be conducted under a tight security blanket, and no advance notice of a launch would be made.

The entire $1,500 million project was to be almost entirely military in aspect. The actual laboratory was a cylinder about 40 ft long and 10 ft in diameter. Built by Douglas Aircraft it was divided into two sections of roughly equal space. One houses instruments and equipment, the other, with around 800 cubic feet capacity, was for the crew quarters.

Mounted securely on the forward end of the laboratory by an adaptor section was a modified Gemini capsule in which the astronauts would fly into and out of orbit. Transfer into the laboratory would be made via a hatch installed in the back of the capsule and its heat shield. The laboratory would not return to Earth because only Gemini was capable of re-entry.

Just over a week before the USAF selected its first team of MOL astronauts, on 3 November 1966, the first unmanned MOL test flight took place when a Titan IIIC blasted off from the Kennedy Space Centre, Florida. The Titan was over 50 ft taller than the standard version, with a modified Titan II propellant tank simulating the laboratory, on top of which a reconditioned Gemini capsule combined to give the same launch configuration as the real MOL. This Gemini capsule is officially recognized as the world's first 'reusable' spacecraft. The flight went well, and it seemed that, at last, the Air Force had finally abandoned for good the winged aircraft access route to space.

On 8 June 1966, Edwards Air Force Base was in mourning. Joe Walker, then, at forty-five, NASA's Chief Research Test Pilot had taken off in his F-104 to fly a routine demonstration flight in formation with the second prototype XB-70 Valkyrie, as part of a public relations exercise. For a reason that will never be known, Joe Walker's

F-104 struck the XB-70's tail and both aircraft plunged to the ground, killing the co-pilot of the XB-70 and Joe Walker in the F-104. The pilot of the XB-70 successfully ejected, but his co-pilot did not.

The news stunned everyone at Edwards, and for several months a cloud hung over the X-15 programme. The tragedy was made all the more difficult to bear by the irony that Joe Walker, veteran of so many dangerous test flights, should have died on such a simple, routine mission.

On 17 June, the USAF, spurred on by the first MOL successful test flight, selected a further team of five potential astronauts. They were Captain Robert F. Overmyer (US Marine Corps), Lieutenant Robert L. Crippen (USN), Captain Henry W. Hartsfield Jnr (USAF), Captain Karol J. Bobko (USAF), and Captain Charles Fullerton (USAF).

NASA, in the meantime, was still concerned with the possible effect on a manned space craft of micrometeorites, particularly the increased likelihood of a strike on a long duration mission such as a typical MOL flight. By that time though, a clear pattern of density and frequency was building up indicating that strikes would be an extremely rare occurrence. Still, whilst the opportunity existed to gather even more data, the X-15 tests continued in this area.

Jack McKay flew X-15-1 on three occasions on 28 July and 11 and 25 August 1966 to over 240,000 ft in an attempt to capture some of these elusive particles of 'space dust'. On 8 September, McKay made his last X-15 flight, spoilt by an engine cut-off that prematurely curtailed the mission. His injuries sustained in the 1962 X-15-2 accident finally forced him into retirement soon afterwards. On 27 April 1975, John B. McKay, married with eight children, died from complications arising from the crash.

NASA's preoccupation with micrometeorite collection and astronomical research was extended from McKay's X-15-1 flights to include two flights by William Dana on 14 September and 1 November 1966 in X-15-3.

William Dana was born in Pasadena 3 November 1930. He joined the USAF with a science degree from the Military Academy in 1952, shortly afterwards returning to civilian life to study aeronautical engineering and subsequently to join NASA (then NACA) in 1958. In 1966 William Dana flew five missions in X-15, the last of which, on 1 November in X-15-3, qualified him as 'unofficial' astronaut. It was the programme's 174th flight.

Tasks for this, the X-15-3's 56th, flight, included further micrometeorite collections, precise measurements of altitude and corresponding atmospheric density, and evaluation of wing tip pod acceleration. The flight to 306,900 ft reached a maximum speed of 3,750 mph.

On 30 June 1967, the USAF selected its final four MOL astronauts: Major James A. Abrahamson (USAF), Major Donald H. Peterson (USAF), Lieutenant Colonel Robert Hemes (USAF) and Major Robert Lawrence (USAF).

In the meantime X-15-A2 was ready for the ultimate test for speed. The prime pilot to conduct all the build-up missions and conduct the actual flight was named as USAF Captain William 'Pete' Knight.

Captain William J. Knight joined the USAF at 22 years of age in 1951, soon afterwards graduating from the USAF Institute of Technology with a degree in mathematics. Following a period at the Experimental Test Pilot School, he joined the X-20 project and on 20 September 1962 was named as one of the six prime pilots, in which role he gained valuable familiarization with extreme high-altitude and high-speed aircraft concepts.

When the X-20 was cancelled in 1963, he continued academic studies at the Aerospace Research Pilots School, graduating in 1964 before being assigned to the X-15 programme in 1965, and making his first flight in the vehicle on 30 September of that year. He took over from Air Force Major Robert A. Rushworth.

His flight in X-15-A2 on 18 November 1966 was to be his eighth in total and the first of two record-breaking flights after four familiarization missions on the A2 between 21 July and 30 August.

The flight of 18 November was to be the X-15 programme's 175th. The planned maximum altitude was kept deliberately low to keep all available power to meet the speed objectives. After jettison, Captain Knight ignited the A2's XLR-99 engine and climbed to 98,000 ft, then nosed the A2 down and brought the throttle forward. At just over Mach 2 the two empty external fuel tanks were jettisoned and the X-15 accelerated to break all previous records as it roared through the clear blue sky at Mach 6.33. The A2 had the power to go even faster but Captain Knight knew that this flight was to be just a step towards that ultimate goal. On this flight, engineers were concerned mostly with the A2's handling with the new fuel tanks, filled to capacity for the first time, and how the A2 would react on their separation, how the vital heat dispersing ablative material (increasingly necessary as speed and atmospheric friction increased) would withstand the stresses, and finally how the airflow around the lower ventral fin would behave, again with ramjet testbed implications. Following this, the latest speed record flight, X-15-A2 made one more 'low'-speed mission on 8 May 1967 to verify some final questions before being returned to NAA in the summer for preparation for its all-out speed attempt in the autumn.

As parts of the X-15-A2 could be heated to around 1,100 °C at its maximum speed, engineers at NAA applied a white ablative thermal protective coating to the entire airframe to keep its skin temperature below the design limit of 650 °C. Similar to the material used on the heat shields of ballistic spacecraft, the Martin-developed MA255 silicon material could be sprayed on to the airframe like paint. As it heated up through aerodynamic friction, it would dissipate the temperature build up through ablation (a formation of a 'char' layer would slowly peel off taking with it excess heat) and a lower insulation layer of material next to the aircraft's metal surface. Ideally, after each high-speed flight the charred and scorched material could be scraped off down to the insulating layer, then a new coating could be simply sprayed on. Thickness of the ablative material was 0.70 inch at the wing and lower vertical leading edges and 0.50 inch for other leading edges. On the wings the ablative material varied from 0.10 inch at the forward portion to 0.03 at the trailing edges. On the fuselage the thickness started at 0.25 inch forward to 0.035 inch for the final two-thirds of the length of the aircraft.

The new X-15-A2 emerged from NAA just before August 1967, 300 lb heavier and gleaming white in its new protective shell. As a result of the increased weight, the planned Mach 8 was no longer possible unless further performance modifications were made. NASA opted for a revised Mach 7.2 target.

Captain Knight tested the A2 in its complete configuration during a short, low-level flight on 21 August 1967, reaching Mach 4.94 and 91,000 ft. Engineers, management, and pilot were then satisfied that everything was ready for an all-out speed attempt. In support of the flight's research aims, a dummy ramjet engine was installed on the truncated lower ventral fin, around which sensors were fixed to enable measurements in post-flight analysis of the effect it had on the X-15-A2's handling and performance. Other tests included several relating to sonic 'booms', the dynamics of Mach 7 flight, and not least, the performance of the new heat shield.

Ideally NAA would have liked to rebuild X-15-A2 using the high-temperature materials technology derived from the X-20 project, but costs, and the fact that the record flight would be the 188th X-15 mission out of a planned 200, did not merit such extravagance.

Before the record flight could take place, Captain Knight was to hear the tragic news of the death of his fellow X-20 pilot Major Russell Rogers, when his F-105 aircraft exploded in mid-air near Kandena Air Force Base, Okinawa. Yet another top US pilot had perished on a relatively 'routine' flight.

On 3 October 1967, X-15-A2, under the wing of its parent B-52, took off on what was to prove its final flight and Captain Knight's 12th X-15 mission. High in the sky, the white A2 dropped clear away from the B-52 and the XLR-99 burst

into life causing the rocket aircraft to shoot forward from the B-52 and chase planes like an arrow loosed from a bow. Within seconds, Captain Knight had reached his maximum altitude of 102,100 feet whereupon he levelled off, and with the rocket engine building up full power, he accelerated further still up the Mach scale. At Mach 2 the external tanks fired away, their work done. Captain Knight pressed on, nosing the A2 down. As the machmeter climbed to 3... 3.5... 4... 4.5..., he found it was becoming increasingly difficult to maintain longitudinal control. At Mach 5 rudder effectiveness and aircraft stability were decreasing. Captain Knight had no way of knowing just how well the A2 was taking the increasing punishment and whether the heatshield would stand the sustained high temperatures. At Mach 6, the ramjet mock-up mounted on the lower ventral fin tore itself loose. The tangled lower mounting of the ramjet, pounded by shock waves, was burning up. The temperature on the airframe was reaching 2,700 °F. As the XLR-99 died, its fuel exhausted, Captain Knight had achieved a new record, still unchallenged, of Mach 6.7 (4,520 mph). The flight hit news headlines all over the western world. X-15-A2 was returned to NAA for repair but, as it turned out, it would never take to the air again, its ablative coating and skin damaged beyond reasonable repair. NASA's plans for a ramjet-powered, delta-wing X-15 follow-on had received a major setback. The cost of refurbishing the damaged X-15-A2 was way beyond the programme budget. The maximum speed obtained at Mach 6.7 was not nearly as high as would be needed to conduct a thorough operational test of the ramjet engine and its applications. Only with new, lighter, heat-dispersing materials and extensive XLR-99 engine modifications could engineers start thinking in terms of speeds in excess of Mach 7, but the money was not forthcoming.

Captain Knight added to his speed record the title 'astronaut' just two weeks later when on 17 October 1967, he flew X-15-3 to an altitude of 280,500 ft (53.4 miles) on its 64th flight. By now the X-15 flights were becoming increasingly useful to NASA in a support role to their ballistic manned space programme. Captain Knight's astro-flight again attempted further investigations into micro-meteorites, together with studies of the solar spectrum from 200,000 ft high. The flight also included research on X-15 wing-tip pod deflection rates during the re-entry and an ultraviolet analysis of the XLR-99's exhaust plume, identified as a source of interference during earlier stellar photographic experiments at high altitude.

The X-15 programme had thus far been an unqualified success; it was impossible to underestimate the value of data and learning derived from the programme. Mishaps had been rare, unusually so for such an advanced concept in both airframe and rocket technology. Whilst both Apollo and the Soviet Soyuz programmes had met with tragedy and disaster in 1967, the X-15 had alone maintained public confidence in America's ability in aerospace technology. That was until November. The final flight of X-15-3 was to be a sharp and painful reminder of the constant dangers of flights into space. During the flight a complicated series of equipment malfunctions occurred which led to the pilot (Major Mike Adams) losing control of the X-15 during the aircraft's re-entry into Earth's atmosphere. The result was airframe disintegration due to overstressing, and the inevitable loss of the pilot's life. (A clear understanding of the causes of the crash requires a detailed description of the flight. This, together with extracts from the Accident Investigation Board report conclusion, is given separately at the end of this Chapter. Though technical in nature the account makes clear the causes of the crash, at the same time giving a valuable insight into the problems of flight testing at the limits of knowledge in addition to giving a useful account of piloting the X-15 in particular.)

Mike Adams' death was a blow to the whole X-15 programme, from which it never recovered. With only eight flights left in the programme

X-15-3 was collected and the wreckage returned to Edwards for reassembly and examination.

1967 had been a year of catastrophies. On 27 January Virgil Grissom, a veteran of Mercury and Gemini, together with Ed White and Roger Chaffee, perished when their hastily-built and untested Apollo command module was engulfed in fire whilst undergoing a full pre-flight check-out with all hatches firmly closed. In the oxygen-rich environment the three men did not stand a chance, and while a shocked nation mourned the death of three heroes, three months later the same thing happened to the Russians. Vladimir Komarov, testing the new Soyuz spacecraft, perished when his main landing parachutes failed to deploy properly at 25,000 ft. Strapped inside the Soyuz capsule Komarov was powerless to do anything but wait for impact with the ground. Unlike the earlier Vostok, Soyuz was not fitted with an ejection seat. Back at Edwards, top test pilot Bruce Peterson was severely injured when his M2F2 lifting body crashed on 10 May. At least, it was said at Edwards at the time, both Adams and Peterson had some control over their destiny up to the final moments.

Mercury, Gemini and Apollo astronaut Virgil Grissom had once said in tragically prophetic words: 'If we die, we want people to accept it. We

On 21 August 1967, X-15-A2 was towed out for her maiden flight with her new heat-shield added. The subsequent flight to 91,000 ft and Mach 4.94 (3368 mph) was a dress rehearsal for the next one that would push the X-15-A2 to its design limit. (Rockwell International)

are in a risky business and we hope that if anything happens to us it will not delay the programme. The conquest of space is worth the risk of life. You sort of have to put that [the possibilities of disaster] out of your mind. There is always a possibility that you can have a catastrophic failure. Of course, this can happen on any flight. It can happen on the last one as well as the first one. So you just plan as best you can to take care of all these eventualities, and you get a well trained crew and you go fly.'

As 1968 dawned, cuts in the NASA budget by Congress drew the curtain on the X-15 project, with an allocation of only $3 million left to fund the programme for the year. On 21 January 1968, NASA announced that the final flight, number 200, would take place in the Autumn. X-15-3 was completely destroyed, X-15-A2 was too expensive to repair after its Mach 6.7 flight, and so it fell to X-15-1, the first X-15 to fly, appropriately to conclude the programme.

The next X-15 flight after Mike Adams' crash was on 1 March 1968. William Dana was to check out the electrical system and a new spray-on foam insulation used on the second stage fuel tanks of the Saturn V moon rocket.

On 21 August 1968, X-15-1 made the programme's 13th and final spaceflight. Bill Dana, who with Captain William Knight concluded the final missions, flew to 264,000 ft on his second spaceflight. X-15-1 was by then a veteran of 79 missions and was beginning to show her age.

As the hatch shut tight, securely locking into position, it was to be for the last time a manned, winged vehicle would venture into space for another 13 years. During his brief three minutes of weightless flight Dana busied himself operating equipment that would monitor a simultaneous rocket launch from Vandenburg, the Air Force's Western Test Range. By following the progress of a lift-off some 50 plus miles below, the foundations of military surveillance from space were being laid. Unfortunately, the on-board monitoring equipment failed, but, being X-15, it could of course be recovered to fly again. Another experiment, the Apollo horizon scanner (a navigational aid) was only a partial success. Dana re-entered and touched down after some twelve minutes of free flight.

On 24 October 1968, Dana again flew the last serving X-15 on the programme's 199th mission testing a new (Q-ball) attitude information system housed in the X-15's nose, and an experiment to acquire data on sky brightness at high altitudes. The Q-ball system housed in the X-15, was developed by the Northrop Corporation and was able to sense angles of attack and sideslip during re-entry and high Mach numbers, and report the data to the pilot in such a fashion that he could adopt a flight path and attitude that resulted in an absolute minimum of frictional heat on the airframe. A development of this Q-ball system was to be used on the Apollo launch escape system.

The flight to 250,000 ft reached a maximum

speed of Mach 5.38 and ended without publicity. As Bill Dana came into land he was unaware that, in fact, there would be no more X-15 missions.

The Air Force and NASA had reviewed the X-15 project status and decided to end the programme no later than the end of the year. After ten attempts to launch the final flight, last minute problems continued to set it back until, when bad weather moved in on the 11th try on 20 December, the decision was made to scrub the flight. A few days later Apollo — 8 with Frank Borman, Jim Lovell and Bill Anders — flew around the moon for Christmas. The World was awed and no-one noticed the end of the X-15.

The two pilots who remained in the X-15 programme, William Dana and Captain 'Pete' Knight were re-assigned. William Dana became a research pilot at the Dryden Flight Research Centre at Edwards, later to be assigned to the 'follow-on' lifting body programme of research there. Captain 'Pete' Knight returned to active duty with the Air Force; he is currently the Systems Programme Director, Fighter Attack Systems Programme Office, Air Force Systems Command, Wright Patterson Air Force Base, Ohio.

The entire X-15 programme, spread over almost 15 years from its conception in 1954 cost $300 million, or to put that in perspective the cost of one Apollo moon landing. Each X-15 flight cost around $100,000. The valuable data in high-speed re-entry techniques, unpowered landings, winged flights into space and flight dynamics set the ground rules for the Shuttle Orbiter. In fact, John Young, commander of the first orbital shuttle flight recalled: 'The experience we gained from an aerodynamics stand point, energy standpoint, and basic early rocket technology was the kind of thing that made Space Shuttle possible. The lift to drag ratio of the Shuttle is almost identical to that of the X-15. It was a very similar programme with a good deal of feed-back into the Shuttle, and it really paid off.' The X-15 programme ended with a wealth of data on high altitude flight at hypersonic speed. Its performance was to be predictive of that of the Shuttle Orbiter, on which the X-15 had a crucial design influence.

The X-15 pilots were completely responsible for their aircraft flight profile, without the sophisticated computer aids today's Shuttle pilots enjoy. Each stage of the mission was co-ordinated by the pilot through his instruments, experience and 'feel'. There were few computers, or preprogrammed guidance systems, just a man alone inside a powerful rocket-driven aircraft attempting to confront the unknown in a step-by-step approach at speeds and altitudes never before attained by winged vehicles and stay alive.

As for the surviving aircraft, X-15-1 now resides at the National Air and Space Museum in Washington DC, where it hangs alongside Charles Lindberg's *Spirit of St. Louis,* the Wright Brothers' *Flyer,* and Yeager's Bell X-1. X-15-A2 is now at the USAF Museum in Ohio. After being stripped of its white ablative material down to its metal skin, it remains as it was, after the NAA engineers and technicians left it following its capture of the world's air speed record.

On 10 June 1969, only a few days before the first moon landing, the Air Force's MOL project was cancelled by the Defense Department. The MOL had been delayed in much the same way as its predecessor, the X-20. In 1967 the first manned flight had to be postponed for two years because of technical problems. Instead of 1968, the first launch of an operational station would have been 1970. The financial cost of the war in Vietnam, coupled with the politics of the Johnson and Nixon administrations cut the budget even further. In early 1969, the anticipated first launch slipped to 1971. MOL had outlived its usefulness and was scrapped. From then on, the USAF concentrated their military activities in space to the increasingly sophisticated arena of unmanned reconnaissance

and communication satellites. It was only with the promise of NASA's reusable space shuttle that the USAF, once more, began to look seriously at manned military spaceflight. For the astronauts assigned to the MOL programme it was to be a crushing disappointment. For the second time in a decade a major military space project had been cancelled at an advanced stage of development.

Seven of the Air Force's MOL pilots were, however, assigned to NASA's astronaut programme and an eighth — Lt Col Albert H. Crewes USAF — was assigned to the Flight Crew Operations Directorate at NASA's Manned Spaceflight Centre, Houston, where he is still employed today.

Of those assigned to the NASA astronaut programme, Major Karol Bobko was, at 32, the first United States Air Force Academy graduate to join the astronaut ranks. He joined NASA alongside the 32-year-old Lt Commander Robert Crippen of the US Navy, Major Charles G. Fullerton USAF of Portland Oregon, 35-year-old Air Force Major Henry W. Hartsfield, Major Robert F. Overmyer of the US Marine Corps, Major Donald H. Peterson, a 35-year-old Air Force US

A month after the last X-15 flight, Apollo sent Frank Borman, Jim Lovell and William Anders around the moon. The launch, on 21 December 1968, captured the attention of the world. The Apollo Saturn V rocket was, at the time, the most powerful machine ever built. (NASA)

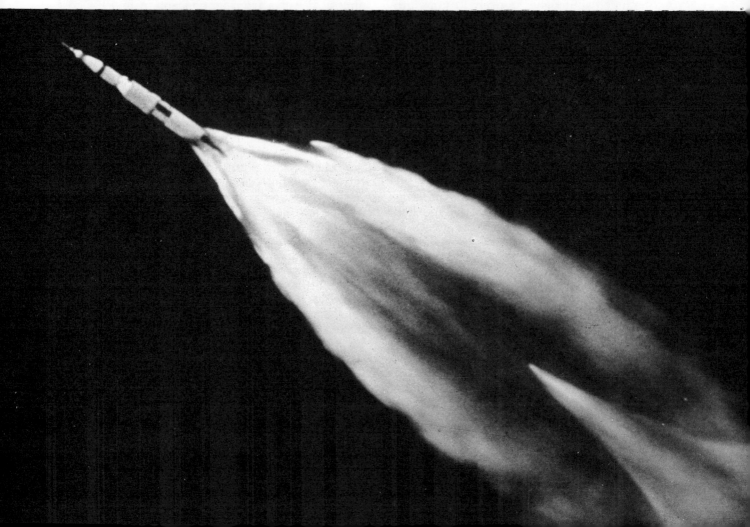

Military Academy graduate from Winoa, Missouri and Lt Commander Richard H. Truly, US Navy, 32 of Meridian, Mississippi.

Three of the group were to complete studies for graduate degrees before assuming their NASA astronaut roles. Major Hartsfield obtained a Master of Science degree at the University of Tennessee, Major Bobko, a Masters Degree in Astrophysics at the University of California, and Major Peterson a Doctorate in Physics at the University of Tennessee.

The seven additions, at that time, brought the total number of 'active' NASA astronauts to 54.

Of the other MOL pilots, Major Robert A. Lawrence of the USAF was dead, killed when his F-104 crashed at Edwards on 8 December 1967. Major Mike Adams had died in the X-15-3 accident in 1967.

Major James Abrahamson became a member of the National Aeronautics and Space Council in June 1969 until its dissolution in 1973. Following a series of Air Force positions, he was assigned as one of the Special Senior Staff support to Management of the Space Shuttle programme at the Johnson Space Centre. He is currently the chief of President Reagan's US Strategic Defense Initiative, or 'Star Wars', programme.

The rest of the MOL team disbanded and returned to their various Air Force and Navy positions.

X-15-3: The last flight

The pilot for the last flight of X-15-3 was Major Michael Adams, USAF. He was born in Sacramento, California on 5 May 1930 and began his flying career in October 1951, joining the USAF the following year. Shortly afterwards, he made 49 hazardous sorties during the Korean war. Obtaining a Bachelor of Science degree in aeronautical engineering from Oklahoma University in 1958, he moved on to become a graduate at the prestigious Experimental Test Pilot School at Edwards, achieving the distinction of number one position in his class.

Joining the Flight Test Operations Division of the USAF at Edwards in 1964, he undertook several test projects on advanced aircraft development, and was one of the few pilots nominated to take part in the tests of the Lunar Landing Simulator — a curious vertical take-off and landing 'flying bedstead' device — over a five month period in 1964.

On 12 November 1965, Major Adams was assigned to the Space Systems Division of the USAF as a possible MOL crew candidate. Prolonged and detailed medical examinations at Brooks Aeromedical Laboratory pronounced him medically fit for spaceflight, particularly in terms of long duration missions such as those envisaged for MOL would demand.

As the MOL project began to falter and follow the path of the X-20, Major Adams volunteered to join the X-15 programme. With a commendation from his superiors, he replaced Joe Engle who left the X-15 programme on 4 April 1966, after being selected as a NASA astronaut. Major Adams started X-15 familiarization in July 1966 and subsequently completed both ground and air training before his first X-15 flight which took place on 6 October 1966.

On that first flight, Major Adams experienced premature engine shutdown soon after ignition which forced him to make his first X-15 landing on an emergency dry lakebed. His performance during this emergency was outstanding and, as a result, he managed a successful landing on an unfamiliar lakebed. It was by no means the first incident in which Major Adams demonstrated his skill and ability as a pilot. Before his participation in the X-15 programme, he was involved in an F-104 jet fighter crash. His sound judgement saved his life when he ejected from the stricken aircraft a fraction of a second after impact with the runway. Though knowing that the F-104 would not survive the impact, he waited until the vertical velocity had stopped as the aeroplane made a hard landing before ejecting. If he had not taken this action, he would certainly have been killed in the ensuing explosion!

Major Adams was selected for the 65th flight of X-15-3 on 5 October 1967, and the flight schedule drawn up on October 13th. Final flight preparations began five days later with the pre-flight work schedule calling for X-15-3's maintenance and minor modification. A leaking hydraulic hose was replaced after its last flight, and a successful leak check carried out. In addition, an RCS 'pitch up' thruster valve leaked helium during a ground gas test. A subsequent leak check using hydrogen peroxide fuel resulted in zero leakage.

The flight plans for the mission were published by NASA on 20 October. Between 12 October and 15 November Major Adams spent 23 hours in the X-15 simulator in preparation for the flight, in addition to over 10 hours in an F-104 of which 8 hours were spent practicing simulated X-15 landing approaches at Edwards, Delamar and Cuddeback Dry Lakes. Major Adams had familiarized himself on the simulator with the X-15-3 instrument panel and flight control system. Emergency procedures were practiced and engine shutdown times established for recovery on emergency lakebeds. Procedures were simulated to extend and retract the on-board experiments that would be carried to high altitudes as well as emergency experiment retraction procedures. As with previous missions, the pilot was involved in the planning of the flight and

The last photograph of X-15-3, taken shortly before the fatal crash of 15 November 1967. With Mike Adams already on board, a ground technician makes final checks before engine start-up on the B-52. (NASA)

in all briefings. It was to be Major Adams' seventh X-15 flight, and his third in X-15-3.

X-15-3's two flights immediately preceding Major Adams' were both high-altitude missions. The first, on 4 October 1967 by Bill Dana, was planned for a peak altitude of 250,000 ft; the second, flown by 'Pete' Knight, reached 280,000 ft. On Major Adams' flight, which was planned to reach 250,000 ft and a velocity of 5,100 ft per second, X-15-3 was to be in the same configuration as it was for the preceding two missions except for the addition to the left-hand upper air-brake of a test panel of Saturn V cryogenic fuel tank insulating material, and a camera mounted on the upper fuselage equipment bay 'bug-eye' behind the cockpit to record data. Another modification was to facilitate the first test of the X-15 bow-shock stand-off measurement (Traversing probe) located on the forward section of the right wing tip pod.

As with the two previous flights, X-15-3 was configured for high-altitude research in line with the programme of activities laid down at the October 1965 review meeting. The experiments to be conducted included a check of the nose gear landing loads which, because of stress problems experienced during earlier flights, involved additional instrumentation mounted on the forward undercarriage assembly. In the lower fuselage equipment bay, a camera in the lower 'bug-eye' would measure wing tip pod deflections during re-entry as a basis for determining the suitability of the pods for future highly vibration-sensitive experiments. Major Adams was also to check the operation of the new boost guidance system. This was an airborne, computer-generated guidance instrument which displayed altitude errors which deviated from pre-set altitude rates of change. Developed at the NASA Ames Research Centre, the boost guidance system would later be used, if successful, during the launch and ascent of future manned spacecraft.

Scientific tasks for the flight involved micro-meteorite collection, located in the forward section of the left wing tip pod; solar spectrum measurement, at altitudes over 200,000 ft, using apparatus atus provided by NASA's Jet Propulsion Laboratory and located in the aft section of the left wing tip pod; and rocket exhaust plume ultra-violet measurements with equipment located in a tailcone box.

After a technical briefing on 27 October and a full crew briefing three days later, everything was set for a flight on 31 October. On that date, however, an engine malfunction, reported by Major Adams shortly before launch from the B-52, caused an abort and return to Edwards. X-15-3 was subsequently detached from its wing pylon, and its

XLR-99 engine removed and replaced with a back-up unit. After further delays caused by bad weather, the flight was attempted again on 15 November.

The B-52 (serial number 008) took off with X-15-3 from Edwards at 9.12 am Pacific Standard Time. Flying out to the launch station over Delamar Dry Lake, Nevada, ground control continued to monitor telemetry between the crew of the B-52 and Major Adams. Slight problems occurred during the ferry flight, a small inspection panel from the B-52 was lost, and the delay in arrival of a supporting C-130 chase aircraft set the launch schedule back several minutes.

As Major Adams made a pre-launch check of X-15-3's RCS rockets, the crew of the B-52 reported a light wisping of residual hydrogen peroxide from a right yaw rocket immediately after the test fire. This was, in fact, a fairly common occurrence resulting from either a leaking valve or a non-zeroing control. Apart from a minor change of his display of precision attitudes caused by a slightly later launch time, everything continued smoothly to launch. The flight was planned so that the PAI attitudes would be nulled at zero degrees in all three axes as he flew 'over the top'. Because of the delayed launch time with resultant changes in sun position, the PAI was changed by Major Adams to 3 degrees nose down in pitch and 2 degrees roll right. These attitudes were needed for the solar spectrum experiment.

Three minutes before B-52 separation, Major Adams threw a switch on the control panel which activated the bow shock stand-off measurement experiment (traversing probe). At just after 10.30 am PST, at an altitude of 45,000 ft and at Mach .78, X-15-3 dropped away from the B-52, ignited its XLR-99 engine and began the first stage of its mission into space, planned to end over ten minutes later with a landing back at Edwards. Within one minute of XLR-99 ignition, however, things had started to go wrong.

An electrical disturbance had begun to affect communications between ground control at Edwards and Major Adams; as telemetry and voice data deteriorated, the B-52 crew assisted by relaying messages to the X-15. With the XLR-99 engine in operation, radio frequency noise was not uncommon at this point on X-15 flights and was not considered critical. Nevertheless, this was later found to be no ordinary interference generated by the engine, but emanated from the bow shock stand-off experiment which was exhibiting abnormal behaviour. As X-15-3 climbed up towards space at 87,000 ft and a velocity of 3,200 fps the disturbance began to affect all systems, particularly the inertial flight data system and the MH96 adap-

tive flight control system. The electrical disturbance caused a partial failure in all three of X-15-3's servo-actuators which in turn caused a reduction of the MH96 gains to less than 50 per cent (as the gains of the MH96 were regulated by servo-activity). As the gains dropped below the 60 per cent level the automatic RCS controls were deactivated. Fortunately, at the start of the electrical disturbance the aircraft was at an altitude where the atmosphere was sufficiently dense that aerodynamic controls were still effective and in those conditions the RCS rockets were not required. When the normal automatic MH96 reaction controls were not armed, the pilot could use manual RCS. Even though Major Adams had sufficient displays and back-up controls to cope with the situation, the problem was sufficient to cause him some distraction on ascent.

As the XLR-99 engine continued to thrust Major Adams and X-15-3 ever higher, all his primary flight guidance information was provided by the Ames Centre's boost guidance experiment. The pitch axis steering commands were displayed on a horizontal cursor (technically termed the 'theta vernier') over the 'floating ball' attitude direction indicator (ADI). This instrument display alerted the pilot to pitch up the X-15's nose when the cursor rose above the horizontal reference centre, and to pitch the nose down when below. The data for this instrument originated from the X-15's inertial flight data system (IFDS), whereupon it was processed in the X-15's digital computer and compared with a separate pre-set trajectory stored in the memory before the flight. This comparison of the actual attitude of X-15-3, together with actual altitude rate-of-change against pre-set stored data, enabled the difference to be relayed to the pilot via the ADI horizontal cursor so that he could make a correct control response pitching the X-15 up or down.

Other information displayed at that stage of the flight included pitch, roll and heading attitudes on the ADI, aerodynamic sideslip angle on a separate sideslip indicator mounted on the instrument panel below the ADI (and also on the vertical cursor of the ADI). Precision heading was shown on the precision heading indicator.

Shortly before shutdown of the XLR-99 engine, at 1 minute 16 seconds into the flight (flight elapsed time — FET), Major Adams reached forward for the engine throttle and either inadvertently put a touch of back pressure on the control column (it was a common occurrence at XLR-99 shutdown), or did so in response to a pitch command from the boost guidance display. The effect was to induce a longitudinal oscillation into X-15-3 which would, nevertheless, dampen out harmlessly twenty seconds and three cycles later.

Immediately before XLR-99 shutdown, at 1 minute 20 seconds FET, the electrical disturbance that continued throughout the boost phase caused the IFDS and the X-15's digital computer to malfunction; as it did so it triggered a relay switch to the warning light on Major Adams' instrument panel. This indicated to Major Adams that all the information presented via the IFDS was subject to a 'lagging' error. Effectively, then, Major Adams was flying this stage of the mission with incorrect information on inertial total velocity, inertial altitude, inertial vertical velocity, and, later, computed angles of attack and sideslip. The IFDS computer was designed to go 'off-line' whenever an electrical power disturbance threatened potential damage to its components. Normally it would recover and reset automatically in either 230 milliseconds or 2.5 seconds, depending on the severity of the disturbance, but in this instance it did not. Indications were that the fault was persistent and the computer was continuously or repeatedly going off-line because of this. With the light continuously illuminated, Major Adams was unaware of the duration of each off-line dump, and of the accumulating errors in the information supplied by the computer, such as inertial velocity and altitude.

With the IFDS computer warning light on, XLR-99 shut-down occurred. The cues an X-15 pilot used for rocket engine shut-down were inertial total velocity and total burn time. Major Adams shut down with an excess burn time of four seconds (eighty-two seconds of burn time, as opposed to a planned seventy-eight), and an excess velocity of 136 fps above the planned 5,100 fps velocity. Major Adams' instruments showed X-15-3 at 5,020 fps! This could be accounted for by the fact that the inertial instruments were lagging because of the disturbance problems, and that at the pre-planned shut-down time Major Adams did not have the proper indicated inertial velocity. He may have waited until the indicated velocity was closer to the planned 5,100 fps before initiating engine shut-down a fraction of a second before fuel exhaustion. This kind of procedure was not unusual in the X-15 programme. In a similar way, his actual altitude of 150,000 ft was a full 10,000 ft above that planned for this stage of the flight, whilst his instruments displayed the 140,000 ft mark! Extra speed also meant that X-15-3's maximum altitude would exceed the planned altitude of 250,000 ft.

With shut-down completed at 1 minute 26 seconds FET, Major Adams immediately switched from the boost guidance steering indicator displayed on the ADI horizontal cursor, to the precision attitude steering commands as planned. As a result of this action the horizontal cursor of the ADI still displayed pitch attitude steering commands, whilst the vertical cursor displayed roll attitude steering commands in the same way that it previously displayed boost guidance and aerodynamic sideslip angle steering commands.

The newly displayed precision attitudes and heading would permit Major Adams to later align X-15-3 and hold the vehicle within the prescribed limits to obtain data from the solar spectrum

experiment located in the rear of the left wing tip pod. With the ADI instrument cursors centred to their pre-set 'null' or centred position, the experiment would be pointing in the correct alignment with the sun. Although Major Adams selected the PAI at this time in the flight he would not need them for the experiment until maximum altitude, and from thence down to 200,000 ft. At the same time as he selected PAI, Major Adams pushed over to a zero degree angle of attack and started a series of planned wing rocking manoeuvres.

At 1 minute 28 seconds FET, Major Adams had been waiting eight seconds for the IFDS computer to reset automatically and the warning light to go out. He had not attempted to correct it manually in the first place, probably because of approaching time for engine shut-down. As it had not reset, he reached forward and attempted to reset the warning light relay switch by pressing it. Despite this attempt and several stabs of the light, it would not go out, indicating that the fault was serious and the computer could not be recovered. As seconds passed, inertial velocity and attitude information, normally processed and supplied by the computer, began to accumulate errors.

With the warning light continually illuminated, Major Adams had no way of knowing that the computer had gone off-line repeatedly no less than 61 times!

Instead of checking his instruments, Major Adams continued the wing rocking manoeuvres initiated during the switch to PAI. Then, after the ground controller's reminder call, he activated the solar spectrum measurement experiment at 1 minute 41 seconds FET, and the micrometeorite experiment a fraction of a second later. The wing rocking was planned to benefit the ultra-violet exhaust plume measurement experiment, which embodied a camera mounted in X-15-3's tail cone, aimed at the starboard horizon. Scientists wanted the line of sight of the camera to sweep up and down across the horizon taking motion picture film of the gases left behind in X-15-3's path.

At this time ground control room staff, monitoring telemetry of the flight, realized something was not quite right with the control of X-15-3. During the wing rocking manoeuvres Major Adams went to either two or three times the bank angles called for in the flight plan, and there was excessive action by the control servos. The wing rocking manoeuvre was planned to be a slow rolling of the aircraft of 10 degrees a second. Ground data received indicated that the rolling rates were generally less than 5 degrees a second, but that the maximum bank angles (roll attitude) on both right and left manoeuvres were greater than 10 degrees.

It was possible that Major Adams knew that the X-15's control response was wrong, based on the hours spent in the simulator as part of his training for the flight. The MH96 RCS was not operating at this point in its normal 'automatic' mode.

Instead of waiting for the RCS jets to engage automatically, Major Adams could have manually selected the RCS 'on' mode switch to improve controllability. He could also have used the manual RCS, but did not choose to do so until much later in the flight. This action was later taken to indicate that Major Adams did not recognize he had a control problem at that time. If Major Adams was unaware of the control problems, ground control weren't. Telemetred data received for the position of the MH96 pitch-roll servo-actuators showed that their motions were not normal during wing rocking manoeuvres. The servo-actuator activity during the wing rocking manoeuvre, together with the still continuing electrical disturbances, resulted in the MH96 gains being too low to provide normal RCS at such an altitude where rocket control would normally be available and required for adequate vehicle control.

At 1 minute 51 seconds FET, twenty-three seconds after Major Adams had unsuccessfully attempted to re-set the computer warning light, communications had improved sufficiently for him to radio to the ground, 'Okay, I'm reading you now. I've got a computer and instrument light'. It was the first indication ground control had received of the IFDS malfunction. To them, the powered portion of the flight at least appeared to be normal in so far as the operation of X-15-3 was concerned. Major Adams neglected to inform ground control that he could not 'punch out' and reset the warning light, and the ground controller acknowledged Major Adams' message. Later, at 2 minutes 01 second FET, he advised Major Adams to proceed with a planned display and use of a reselected IFDS computed angle of attack (and computed angle of sideslip) when X-15-3 had reached 230,000 ft.

The normal procedure in reselecting and checking computed angles of attack and sideslip in an X-15 involved flying the aircraft to obtain zero degree of sideslip and noting the angle of attack, both sets of information (sideslip and attack) being obtained first from the 'ball nose' aerodynamic flow direction sensor, and then by pressing the computed angle of attack/angle of sideslip button whilst holding the X-15's attitude. Any change in the indicators was noted by the pilot to determine the correctness of the computed angle of attack/angle of sideslip. This action had to be taken by Major Adams whilst the 'ball nose' aerodynamic flow direction sensor was still accurate.

(The sensor was generally usable up to an altitude of at least 250,000 ft, but its performance progressively degraded as atmospheric density decreased above 230,000 ft.) Angle of sideslip data at high altitude was generally ignored by both X-15 pilot and ground control for this reason, and the pilot instructed to use heading as primary directional information.

As Major Adams started to select his computed angles of attack and sideslip, the MH96 gains increased to the 90 per cent level, thus arming the automatic RCS to provide normal control ability for the first time since X-15-3 had entered its ballistic flight path.

Before attempting to bring X-15-3 around to the correct zero degree sideslip attitude to check the IFDS, the aircraft was flying at almost a zero degree angle of attack and yawing to the right. The bank angle, or 'roll attitude' was to the right and increasing. Major Adams did not need to control or modify the angle of attack so he did not fire the pitch RCS rockets. His first action was to arrest the right yaw rate and the right roll rate. He fired the wing mounted roll control RCS for two seconds with the result of arresting the right roll motion and bringing the X-15 back towards a wing level attitude. The yaw control RCS also arrested the right yaw rate, and started to bring the X-15's nose around to the left. When it reached a zero degree sideslip angle and wings level, Major Adams applied short RCS pulses of right roll and yaw to arrest and hold the attitudes reached. (If he had not done so, X-15-3 would have continued to yaw and roll to the left.)

Unexpectedly, as Major Adams arrested the X-15's attitude change and held the aircraft steady, the MH96 gains dropped once again and deactivated the RCS just as he was completing a firing of the right RCS roll rocket to arrest the left roll. He held the right roll control for a further 8 seconds, but with atmospheric density so low, the aerodynamic controls were degraded and there was no response. Nevertheless, X-15-3 remained steady, with wings level. There was a small residual right yaw rate drifting the nose slowly to the right.

At this point Major Adams was advised by ground control to, 'check your computed alpha [angle of attack] now'. He reached forward and held his hand over the switch for seven seconds before finally pushing it at two minutes fifteen seconds FET. Simultaneously, computed angle of attack and sideslip appeared on the indicator, first showing X-15-3's nose 6-8 degrees to the right, then succumbing to error and going off-scale, nose to the right, after just three seconds!

The instruments going off-scale coincided with a sudden electrical disturbance so severe it caused a fail-safe monitor in the MH96 to disengage the pitch/roll servo-actuators. Simultaneously, two warning lights came on in front of Major Adams, one steady, the other flashing. He noticed them immediately and reset the MH96 to re-engage the servo-actuators. The servo-actuator disengagement would not have been of any consequence apart from the fact that when this condition occurred, for any reason, the MH96 gains restarted at minimum levels to avoid any sudden re-engagement problems. With the gains at minimum, and their being retarded in any case by the electrical disturbance, almost twenty seconds would elapse before the automatic RCS rockets could be armed automatically.

Fortunately, there was no requirement for precise attitude at this point as X-15-3's bank angle remained close to zero, pitch attitudes slowly drifted towards zero, whereas the heading had drifted 14 degrees to the right of the desired heading.

As X-15-3 and Major Adams approached maximum altitude of 266,400 ft, the automatic RCS rockets became armed once more, 2 minutes 40 seconds FET. Ground control radioed to Major Adams that he would, 'go over the top at 266,000 ft' and to 'check the attitudes'. This second call was a cue for Major Adams to begin the precision attitude tracking task for the solar spectrum measurement experiment. In order to obtain the best results, X-15-3 had to adopt a 3 degree nose down pitch, 2 degree right bank, and 232 degree-true heading yaw. With X-15-3 at those attitude coordinates, the ADI horizontal and vertical cursors would be central to their reference 'nulls' set by Major Adams prior to launch. He had a margin of error of ± 1 degree about all three axes.

At the start of the tracking task Major Adams could see the precision heading indicator pegged to the left side, indicating that a left yaw manoeuvre was required to 'null' the indicator at its reference of 232 degrees. This indicator remained pegged, however, for the entire manoeuvre. The precision roll-attitude indicator was almost centred at the required 2 degrees right bank angle. The sideslip angle was pegged to the left, calling for a corrective left yaw manoeuvre. Telemetered data to the ground showed X-15-3 sideslipping to the left at an angle of 19.5 degrees (nose right), whereas the true heading was 247 degrees, i.e. 15 degrees to the right of the reference B-52 launch heading.

With the MH96 armed, Major Adams' first response was to initiate short RCS pulses to control roll! He should have flown pitch on the horizontal ADI cursor, and roll on the vertical cursor. Major Adams had long training in flying vertical cursors as yaw indicators, and this, coupled with what flight surgeons determined as some type of prolonged flight vertigo brought on by weightlessness after the boost phase, may have led Major Adams to forget that the vertical presentation he was flying was roll, and flew it as yaw. Pilots were trained that the only way to overcome this form of vertigo was to fly basic instruments and disregard attitudes suspected by physical senses. Furthermore, his vertigo could have been made worse by the extreme workload imposed on him by the many problems in the flight.

After the pilot initiated manual roll manoeuvre, the MH96 automatic RCS made a response to the slow, drifting nose right yaw and stopped the rate at zero, where it remained for ten seconds. At 5 minutes 53 seconds FET, Major Adams made a further RCS roll central pulse, but, dissatisfied with its response, switched to the dual manual RCS.

Five seconds later X-15-3 had rolled left to zero bank angle because of a slight drift after previous roll RCS pulses. The precision roll indicator then called for the aircraft to be rolled 2 degrees to the right. Major Adams applied manual right yaw RCS, thus starting the aircraft yawing to the right again, and further increasing the heading error. Roll attitude, unaltered, was continuing slowly to the left. This could be seen by Major Adams on the ADI ball (roll attitude indicator) as a slight rotation of the ball. He stopped that rotation with a brief right roll manual RCS pulse which then started X-15-3 rolling to the right!

When the aircraft had rolled 2 degrees, the precision roll indicator centred, leading Major Adams to believe that the right yaw RCS pulse had centred the yaw cursor, which was actually the precision roll indicator.

X-15-3 was by then in a 2 degree right bank attitude which Major Adams saw on the ADI ball and applied three short manual left roll RCS pulses to bring the wings level once more, adding a final right RCS roll pulse to stop the roll at zero. Unfortunately, the pulse was excessive and started to roll X-15-3 back to the right! This problem was compounded by the fact that when Major Adams had made the initial three short manual left roll RCS pulses, the precision roll indicator was moving towards the right, and he executed another right yaw pulse to stop it and bring it back to centre, thus increasing the right yaw rate. In addition, ground control were advising him to check the MH96 system. Unknown to Major Adams, data was received on the ground showing the servos disengaging and engaging rapidly. He could only say at this moment of crisis in the cockpit that as far as he could tell they were 'still on'.

At 3 minutes 23 seconds FET, X-15-3 had yawed 53 degrees to the right of the B-52 launch heading and the yaw deviation was increasing by 5.6 degrees a second. At that extreme angle, tenuous aerodynamic forces began to roll the X-15-3 to the right to such an extent that at 3 minutes 26 seconds FET Major Adams had to apply almost continuous left roll RCS, full left rudder and full left aileron to prevent X-15-3 from rolling off. At 3 minutes 32 seconds FET, X-15-3 had yawed 90 degrees to the flight path and pitched nose down 20 degrees. Major Adams relayed his uncertainty maintaining that the aircraft felt 'squirrelly'. At 3 minutes 45 seconds the traversing bow shock probe in the wing tip pod ceased to operate, and the electrical disturbance it had generated since the first minute of the flight disappeared from the telemetered data received on the ground. Although the operation of all systems on board X-15-3 appeared normal, the IFDS computer had by then accumulated very large errors. For example, inertial altitude displayed in the cockpit was showing more than 100,000 ft above the actual altitude detected by ground radar.

At 4 minutes 01 seconds FET, Major Adams reported he was in a spin, at an altitude of 240,000 ft and a speed of 4,800 fps. The MH96 pitch gain reached a maximum at about the same time as the spin started. The roll gain simultaneously reached maximum, whilst the yaw gain did not reach maximum until 4 minutes 05 seconds FET.

X-15-3 was spinning about a flight path angle from the horizontal that was initially minus 15 degrees, and finally minus 40 degrees. (The fact that the normal acceleration always remained positive indicated that the spin was not inverted even though the flight attitudes had X-15-3 often upside down with respect to the horizon.) Major Adams' report of his spin was met with incredulity at ground control. No one was monitoring X-15-3's heading and were therefore unaware that it had yawed completely around. They could only see very pronounced, slow pitching and rolling motions.

Major Adams knew that there was no recommended spin recovery technique for the X-15 in the pilot's handbook, and nothing was known about a supersonic spin. During design of the X-15 some low speed wind tunnel spin tests had been conducted, but these were inconclusive. Nine seconds after reporting the spin, at 4 minutes 10 seconds FET, the MH96 automatic RCS became armed once more and fired in a series of continuous bursts to oppose the spin rotational rates, assisted by Major Adams using both aerodynamic controls and the manual RCS. For a further 30 seconds he tried every combination of spin recovery technique practicable before managing somehow to break the spin at 120,000 ft and a velocity of Mach 4.7.

As X-15-3 came out of the spin at 4 minutes 30 seconds FET, the MH96 pitch axis began a limit cycle oscillation that prevented the gain changer from reducing the pitch gain as dynamic pressure increased. The aircraft motion it caused would eventually have catastrophic results.

The limit cycle oscillation existed because the X-15's horizontal stabilizers were moving at their rate limit of 26 degrees a second in a 'saw tooth' manner. At the start of the limit cycle the atmos-

pheric dynamic pressure was relatively low so that the stabilizer produced relatively low normal acceleration changes. As atmospheric density increased, and with it dynamic pressure, the motions became more violent, exceeding the X-15's structural limits. Side load structural limits were exceeded first, and resulted in a loss of rudder effectiveness and directional stability. The rolling and yawing oscillation that produced this overload was caused by the MH96 oscillation. With the horizontal stabilizers driven at maximum pitch rate, there was no control capability left for manoeuvring or stability augmentation. X-15-3 was descending at 160,000 ft per minute, with dynamic pressure increasing at the rate of 100 pounds per square foot a second.

At 4 minutes 47 seconds FET, the fuselage buckled, effectively increasing the horizontal stabilizer setting for trim all load limits on the airframe and X-15-3 started to break up at 62,000 ft and a velocity of 3,800 fps. With a dynamic pressure of 1,300 pounds per square foot, Major Adams could not eject; instead, fully conscious, he was making last ditch efforts to control the aircraft logically. By the time X-15-3 disintegrated he was probably incapacitated either by high g-forces, the loss of the canopy, or both. A black mark discovered on the side of Major Adams' helmet suggested that he was struck unconscious by some part of X-15-3 at this stage.

The wreckage crashed down over an area 10 by 1½ miles, northeast of Johannesburg, California. The major pieces recovered were three sections of the fuselage, each wing, and the three control surfaces. The forward piece of the fuselage, with the cockpit that had saved the life of Scott Crossfield during the test bed explosion seven years before, was the largest piece of the aircraft to strike the ground.

Eight months after the crash of X-15-3, the NASA X-15 Accident Investigation Board completed their enquiries and concluded the following:

'The accident was precipitated during the ballistic portion of the flight when the pilot allowed the airplane to deviate in heading and subsequently flew the airplane to such an extreme attitude with respect to the flight path that there was a complete loss of control during the re-entry portion of the flight. Destruction of the X-15-3 resulted from divergent aircraft oscillation that caused the aircraft's structural limits to be exceeded.

The MH96 control system, operating in the adaptive mode and functioning as designed, contributed to the accident by a) allowing the intermittent loss of normal RCS and stability augmentation during the ballistic portion of the flight, and b) sustaining a subsequent control system oscillation (limit cycle) that eventually resulted in the aircraft being forced beyond its structural limits at flight conditions otherwise acceptable to the X-15.

'An electrical disturbance, probably emanating from the traversing-probe experiment, adversely affected the normal operation of the integrated flight data system computer and the adaptive flight control system. These effects were apparent to the pilot as a deterioration of the X-15's response to control inputs, pitch and roll damper trip-outs, inaccurate inertial velocity and altitude indications and inertial computer system malfunction lights.

'Prior to the loss of control, the pilot had essential sub-systems, adequate display informa-

The final three frames from the cockpit camera inside X-15-3 shows the master alarm at the top of the panel signalling urgently to the pilot. The last frame is obscured by light entering the cockpit as X-15-3 began to break up. (NASA)

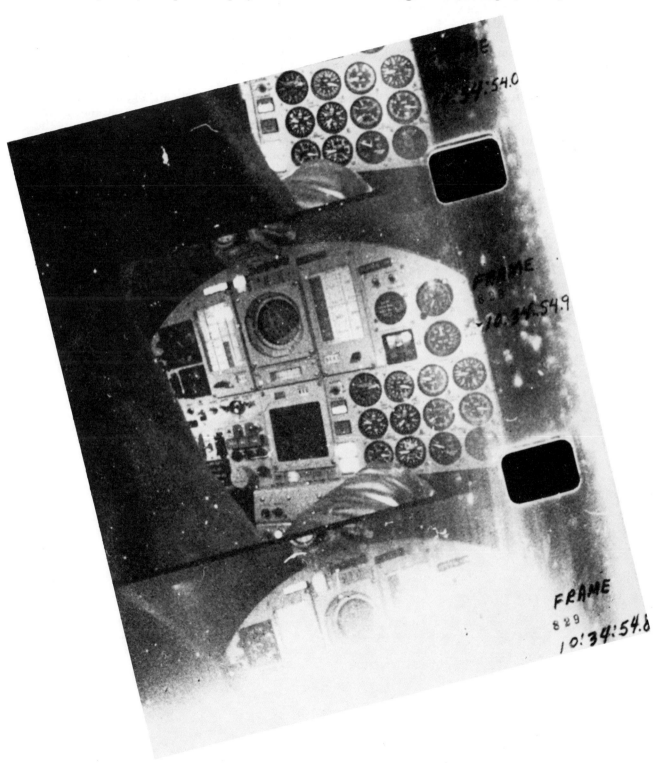

tion and sufficient aircraft control capability. The pilot's improper controlling of the aircraft was the result of some display misinterpretation, distraction and possible vertigo'.

The X-15 Accident Investigation Board made the following recommendations to improve safety on subsequent X-15 flights.

'The telemetered indication of airplane heading should be placed in the X-15 control room where it is visible to the flight controller. The destruction of the only X-15 equipped with an adaptive control system makes detailed recommendations in this area unnecessary. However, there appears to be adequate information available to aircraft designers and operators calling attention to the inherent characteristics of self-adaptive control systems which, under certain conditions, can be detrimental to the operation of an aircraft. Therefore, it is recommended that NASA and USAF engineers publish a report summarizing experience with this type of control system.

'All X-15 pilot candidates should undergo an astronaut-type physical examination, including specific testing for labyrinth sensitivity (vertigo). All experiments and other equipment should be environmentally checked before being placed aboard X-15 and other high-altitude aircraft.

'The following actions should be taken to reduce the possibility of attitude deviations of the X-15 while under predominantly ballistic conditions:

1) The primary attitude indicators and associated vernier functions should be used only in the conventional manner and only for basic flight parameters.

2) Insofar as practical, flights should be kept within the regions where the ball nose aerodynamic flow sensor is usable, and the ball nose information (angle of attack and angle of sideslip) should be continually displayed to the pilot.

3) If higher altitude flights are necessary, a source in addition to the stable platform should be provided in order to maintain redundancy in regard to heading information.'

3 The Lifting Bodies

At the same time as X-15-1 was being assembled at the North American Aviation plant outside Los Angeles, NASA were simultaneously conducting their own independent wind tunnel experiments on various designs of 'lifting bodies' at their Langley and Ames research centres. Before long, combined investigations at these two NASA laboratories began to centre around a number of intriguing, wingless, half-cone shapes that promised to provide sufficient lift for atmospheric flight.

By late 1957, with the 'race into space' firmly established by the launch of *Sputnik 1,* the idea of adapting these half-cone configurations to a one-man space vehicle, capable of both orbiting and re-entering the Earth's atmosphere was conceived by NASA in support of the now famous Mercury programme, then in an early phase of development.

To enable these lifting bodies (as they were called) to survive the extreme temperatures encountered from high-speed entry from space into the Earth's atmosphere, the nose of the half-cone was blunted and heat shielding added, and at the same time larger fins were installed to provide stability. Improved control surfaces were added for pitch, roll and yaw manoeuvrability. It soon became apparent, however, that even with these modifications the problems of designing a craft suited for rocket launching, and also one that would be aerodynamically stable and manoeuvrable from orbital

to subsonic speeds and still capable of horizontal landing was far beyond the technical abilities available at the time. Because of this, and the long developmental programme needed, the beleaguered Space Agency opted for the easier 'capsule' solution for the first American 'man in space' project.

Nevertheless, work on lifting body research continued as it promised several interesting and significant advantages over 'winged' space plane concepts. Unlike the X-15 or X-20 space planes these wingless lifting bodies obtained aerodynamic lift (essential to atmospheric flight) from the shape of the body alone. According to NASA's wind tunnel studies, this type of vehicle would be able to re-enter the Earth's atmosphere, manoeuvre over a wide area to select a landing site and then land like a conventional aircraft all under the control of the pilot. The elimination of wings lessened many of the structural and heating problems encountered by both the X-15 and X-20, whilst in addition reduced significantly the overall weight of the craft. Fins and control surfaces allowed the pilot to stabilize and control his craft and regulate the flight path right down to landing. The 'trade off' came in a steeper re-entry angle and less range of manoeuvrability than a fully-winged space plane.

By the early sixties so much information on a wide variety of concepts had been gained that NASA's Ames Research Centre, under the leadership of its director Paul Bickle decided, on its own volition, to build an experimental, manned, prototype test aircraft embodying all the research results so far gained. The resultant vehicle, coded M2F1 ('M' for Manned, 'F' for Flight), was a strange semi-conical plywood and tubular-steel aircraft over 20 ft long and 13 ft wide with three vertical tail fins. Fitted with an ejection seat, the M2F1 was also equipped with a small solid-fuel rocket engine that would cut in on the landing phase to flatten out an otherwise steep glide approach angle. Controls consisted of rudders, elevons and flaps; the latter two being embodied in the horizontal tapered tail. Landings were to be made on a non-retractable tricycle undercarriage.

On completion of its construction, M2F1 underwent a series of wind tunnel tests at the Ames Centre before being delivered to NASA's Hugh L. Dryden Flight Test Station at Edwards in February 1963.

A civilian NASA test pilot, Milton O. Thompson, was assigned to fly the first tests of M2F1. He was born on 5 May 1926 in Crookston, Minnesota and flew as a Navy pilot during the Second World War in the Pacific conflict. In 1953 he received a BSc in engineering from the University of Washington and was selected for the USAF astronautics course in March 1962 as a Pilot Engineering Consultant.

He was shortly afterwards named as one of the six (and the only civilian) X-20 pilots, in September 1962. When that programme was finally cancelled in 1963 he transferred to the lifting body programme as NASA's Chief Project Pilot, eventually to become the first man to fly a lifting body.

Initially, a Pontiac car was used to tow the lifting body just feet into the air along the runway at Rogers Dry Lake to test the M2F1's controls. The first attempt on 1 March 1963 was a fiasco. The M2F1 bounced from one wheel to the other, hopping into the air for a few seconds then bouncing once more. Film of the attempt looked more like a silent comedy than the first flight of an experimental aircraft. The film, however, did demonstrate two important points, that the M2F1 was capable of only marginal stability and that the slipstream from the Pontiac tow car was upsetting the delicate balance. In addition, basic controls lacked any finesse and Milton Thompson was prone to over-correcting each time the M2F1 bounced around on its tricycle undercarriage. Back in the workshops NASA engineers improved the control mechanics by removing the central fin. Finally, on 5 April, M2F1 climbed off the runway above and behind the Pontiac tow car. Sixty similar subsequent tow tests were carried out with M2F1 reaching a maximum speed of 120 mph with

the assistance of its small, yet powerful solid-fuel rocket engine.

Confident now in the basic flight worthiness of the M2F1, NASA laid plans for the next step in the programme, a series of air-tow flights behind a Douglas C-47 aircraft. Remembering the problems encountered with the Pontiac's slipstream, several experiments were made with a C-47 and a conventional glider to find the ideal tow position for the M2F1 which would minimize turbulence effect on the fragile lifting body.

On 16 August 1963, the first lifting body free-flight took place. The C-47 aircraft lumbered into the air, followed by the M2F1 on tow 1,000 ft behind. The two aircraft continued a circular climb, within the boundary of Rogers Dry Lake just in case the long tow line should accidentally break and Milton Thompson in the M2F1 need an emergency landing ground. At 12,400 ft Milton Thompson released the M2F1, now 150 ft above the C-47, and pulled away to port to avoid hitting any residual turbulence of the C-47 as he fell.

As the M2F1 headed downwards, Milton Thompson made several side-slip manoeuvres together with aileron and rudder pulses and some fixed aileron rolls. Just before starting his landing flare at 2,000 ft he had a worrying moment. As he pushed the M2F1's nose down to a low angle of attack in order to gain speed in pre-flare manoeuvres before landing, it began a 'Dutch Roll'; a condition in which an oscillating roll is accompanied by a cyclic yawing, rather as though the aircraft is wagging its tail. Fortunately he still had enough speed and altitude to effect recovery and within minutes made a perfect landing on Rogers Dry Lake.

It was later found that, apart from flight at certain angles of attack, pilot insensitivity or sudden wind velocity changes could also induce this particularly unpleasant aerodynamic aspect of the M2F1. In future no flight would be permitted in wind speeds greater than 10 to 15 knots. In all, the wooden M2F1 made just under 100 glide flights in this fashion before the programme ended, demonstrating the feasibility of the lifting body concept, and preparing the ground for more definitive designs that would follow.

On 13 June 1963, Milton Thompson was assigned to the X-15 programme also, and between 29 October 1963 and 25 August 1965 he made 14 flights in the aircraft.

Following up the success of the M2F1 lifting body experiment, NASA, in the spring of 1964 invited proposals from the aerospace industry to build two different lifting bodies capable of conducting supersonic, powered, flight tests. Within weeks NAA, Ryan, Northrop, General Dynamics and United Technology Centre had sent in their tenders. In April 1964, Northrop's Norair Division was selected to build a refined and updated version of the M2F1, to be termed M2F2, as well as a new aircraft, designed by NASA's

Langley Research Centre and designated HL-10. (HL stood for 'horizontal landing', and the number '10' meant that it was the tenth lifting body model to be investigated at Langley.) This latter aircraft was, in fact, essentially an upside down M2F1, with a flat underside and rounded top.

Development and construction of the two aircraft was to be made considerably easier and quicker by the use, as far as possible, of existing off-the-shelf hardware. The lifting bodies were not to be subject to the stresses of re-entry and so the airframes were finished in a straightforward lightweight aluminium alloy skin.

On 14 June 1965, the M2F2 was rolled out from Northrop, and sent immediately to NASA, Ames, for an extensive series of wind tunnel tests. It was very similar in size and shape to its predeces-

NASA Dryden Flight Research Centre, California. The lightweight M2F1 (left) and the heavyweight M2F2 were two versions of the M2-series lifting bodies. Both NASA vehicles were part of the lifting body concept being studied for possible future use as manoeuvrable spacecraft capable of pilot-controlled ground landings. (NASA)

sor the M2F1, but very much more advanced. Equipped not only with tail-mounted hydrogen peroxide thrusters of 1,600 lb total throttleable thrust, but also two independent hydraulic systems to power the flight controls in the tail area (elevons, rudders and flaps), and a back-up ram-air turbine to provide power in the event of a battery failure. In case of an emergency during free flight the pilot could eject using a standard F-106 fighter ejection seat. The retractable tricycle undercarriage utilized T-38 jet aircraft components. The M2F2 was delivered with the facility for later installation of an XLR-11 liquid-propellant rocket engine to further boost its performance.

Throughout the rest of 1965 and well into 1966 the M2F2 continued its wind tunnel research programme before being transferred to Edwards and the NASA Dryden Flight Test Centre for its first 'captive' flight under the wing of a B-52 on 23 March.

In the meantime, the other NASA lifting

body, HL-10 was delivered to NASA for ground tests on 18 January 1966. It, too, featured three vetical tail fins to maintain flight stability and control. Movable aerodynamic surfaces included a split rudder and airbrake on the central fin, two 'normal' rudders, elevons and flaps. Standard M2F2 hydraulic systems and back-up power supplies combined with a retractable tricycle undercarriage and an ejection seat for the pilot. As with the M2F2, provision was also made for future installation of an XLR-11 rocket engine.

On 12 July, Milton Thompson made the first

The M2F2 lifting body was an experimental craft flown by NASA's Dryden Flight Research Centre. As a forerunner of the manoeuvrable Space Shuttle of today, the wingless M2F2 was manoeuvred to a glide landing on the dry lake bed. It is shown here during a series of tow tests in preparation for later air-launched flights. The rescue helicopter overhead keeps a watchful eye on pilot Milton Thompson. (NASA)

NASA test pilot Bruce Peterson walks away from the M2F2. Later, he was almost killed flying the same aircraft. (NASA)

flight in the M2F2. Launched in a similar fashion to that employed in the X-15 project, the M2F2 dropped clear of its B-52 parent at just over 45,000 ft, landing a few minutes later on Rogers Dry Lake at 200 mph, after reaching a maximum speed of 452 mph during its descent.

Milton Thompson followed this first glide flight with four others. His last, on 2 September, incorporated a 360 degree turn into approach and landing. Shortly afterwards he left the programme to take up a position as Director of Research Projects at the Hugh L. Dryden Flight Research Centre. He is currently Chief Engineer there. (Milton Thompson made his final X-15 flight on 25 August 1965.)

Taking over from Milton Thompson, NASA's test pilot Bruce Peterson and two Air Force test

Three chase planes fly over the M2F2 lifting body in salute following a successful glide flight in the experimental craft. (NASA)

pilots, Lt Colonel Donald Sorlie and Captain Jerald R. Gentry, continued a further nine systems checkout and handling glide flights. Afterwards, NASA felt confident that the time had finally come to withdraw the M2F2 from service and install its XLR-II engine. This unit, a modified and updated version of the rocket that powered the X-1 and early X-15s, was fuelled by a propellant of ethyl alcohol/water and liquid oxygen, carried internally in two cylindrical tanks.

Exactly a month after the M2F2 was withdrawn for uprating, the HL-10, having successfully completed its ground check-outs, made its début on the glide test trials. The date was 22 December 1966. Air-dropped from a B-52 at 45,000 ft, Bruce Peterson found within seconds of separation that the new HL-10 lifting body had very poor lateral control. At a speed of 456 mph he attempted several turns in which aileron control effectiveness almost disappeared. After a hair-raising flight of just over three minutes, Peterson managed to bring the HL-10 in to land on Rogers Dry Lake. Subsequently, it was grounded for further extensive wind tunnel tests at Ames. These prolonged and detailed investigations discovered a design oversight within the shape of the three vertical fins which had the effect of reducing airflow over the control surfaces. Accordingly, the offending components were modified by the HL-10's next flight which was to be over a year later on 15 March 1968.

With the HL-10 away, the M2F2 once again resumed flying, this time with the XLR-II installed. Its first glide flight in this new configuration took place on 2 May 1967 with Bruce Peterson again at the controls. At the end of the flight the M2F2 had completed a combined total of 15 unpowered descents, and good progress was being made towards its first powered flight. Good progress, that is, until the final planned glide flight on 10 May.

On that occasion Bruce Peterson dropped away from the B-52 parent aircraft wing-mounted pylon at 45,000 ft. Once clear of the B-52's wake he initiated the first of two planned 90 degree turns to test the M2F2's lateral directional characteristics. This task completed he then began a series of S-turns before lining up with the runway centre-line markings on Rogers Dry Lake. Coming out of the final turn the M2F2 began to Dutch roll, a characteristic inherited from its predecessor, the M2F1. The cyclic rolling usually occurred at low angles of attack, for example when the pilot pitched the nose down to gain speed in pre-landing flare manoeuvres or, like the M2F1, when wind gusts changed the angle of attack. Bruce Peterson knew from experience that neither aileron nor rudder application would control this, the only way

out being to increase the M2F2's angle of attack. This done he was faced with yet another problem: it had taken 11 valuable seconds to stabilize the 200 degree-per-second rolls, and he was now off course. The runway markers were a third of a mile to his right and out of sight.

Without runway markings and only the flat, featureless lake bed rushing towards him, Bruce Peterson had no visual clue to altitude. His chase planes had veered off seconds earlier to avoid slip-stream turbulence affecting his Dutch roll recovery attempt. They would normally be alongside, calling-out altitude and speed. Instead, ahead of his flight path, the emergency rescue helicopter hung in mid-air, unaware of the danger it now presented to the M2F2.

With very little time and no further manoeuvring altitude left, Peterson started his landing flare. As the undercarriage was lowered the M2F2 acquired a high sink-rate and stalled into the desert floor. It bounced off the lake bed in a shower of dust, spiralling back up into the air before crashing down again 80 ft from its initial impact point at 217 mph. Slewing to one side it rolled across the ground tearing off undercarriage, tail fins and cockpit canopy, before coming to rest upside down and resting on the twisted stub of the central tail fin and the pilot's head restraint.

Before the dust had settled, the rescue helicopter had swooped in to land nearby and personnel sprinted across the heavily-scored lake bed to the wrecked M2F2. Bruce Peterson was trapped, unconscious, beneath his aircraft. Soon, using every piece of equipment to hand, the emergency services had recovered Bruce Peterson and the helicopter transported him to the Edwards Base Hospital. He had sustained severe facial lacerations, a fractured skull and partial blindness in his right eye. Peterson's injuries necessitated 18 months of surgery to rebuild his face alone. In fact, he was the original 'Bionic Man', and it was film of the spectacular crash that was used in the introduction to the television series 'Six Million Dollar Man', which told the fictional story of an astronaut injured in such a crash and subsequently 'rebuilt' with artificial, 'bionic', limbs. Bruce Peterson had made his final lifting body flight, but nevertheless resumed test pilot duties some time later before taking up a NASA managerial post in 1971.

In May 1967, with Bruce Peterson in hospital, the M2F2 virtually wrecked, and the HL-10 lifting body still undergoing wind tunnel checks, the NASA lifting body programme came to a grinding halt.

There was, however, another lifting body aircraft under development whose roll-out came just two months after the M2F2 crash. It belonged to the USAF and was to begin where their earlier X-20 project had left off.

Back in 1964, the USAF had been keen observers of the old plywood M2F1 flights and were

The wreckage of the M2F2 after the crash of 10 May 1967. The photograph clearly shows the extent of the damage sustained. Bruce Peterson was critically injured, but, nevertheless, was able to return to flight duties after almost two years of surgery and hospitalization. (NASA)

obviously interested in its development as a valuable research tool. So it was that in August of that year the Air Force, freed from X-20 commitments, continued their existing 'Space Technology and Advanced Re-Entry Test programme' (START) by contracting Martin Marietta to build an operational manned lifting body in support of START's final phases which would simulate the projected flight profile of a manned space shuttle returning from orbit.

START was, in fact, a project generated by Robert McNamara at the same time as the cancelled X-20 was under final development, in the hope that it would eventually lead to a more practical form of reusable manned orbital system. START was a relatively low-key three-part operation, the first part of which, in support of the X-20 project, was known as ASSET (Aerothermo-dynamic/Elastic Structural Systems Environment Tests). ASSET initially evaluated a series of X-20 based sub-scale sub-orbital vehicles launched on top of a Thor ballistic missile. Then, when the X-20 was cancelled, ASSET continued with a series of sub-orbital re-entry tests of several different lifting body designs.

Soon after the Air Force had issued their 1964 contract, Martin Marietta conducted an extensive period of wind tunnel tests before deciding on the definitive shape of what was to be the new X-24A lifting body.

Martin Marietta had been engaged with NASA in lifting body research and development since 1960. The X-24A was the direct result of more than two million man-hours of engineering design studies, materials investigations and wind tunnel testing.

It emerged as a rounded, bulbous delta shaped aircraft, built conventionally in aluminium, with a flat base and three vertical fins on the tail. It was approximately 25 ft long and 14 ft wide with two rear-mounted throttleable hydrogen peroxide-powered rocket motors of 500 lb each. In addition the X-24A was equipped with a Thiokol (previously Reaction Motors) XLR-II four-chamber liquid propellant rocket with 8,000 lb maximum thrust. The cockpit was pressurised to 3.5 psi and had a jettisonable canopy together with a zero-zero ejection seat. Conventional aircraft controls operated the control surfaces through powered irreversible dual hydraulic systems.

The X-24A differed from the NASA M2F2 and HL-10 in shape and flight control design. The top of the pilot's canopy was 8 feet above the ground and the vehicle weighed less than 6,000 lb unfuelled (11,000 lb fuelled). The dual rudders mounted in the tail controlled the X-24A's yaw motion. Pitch and roll was controlled by the upper and lower flaps acting as elevons.

X-24A formed the final component of a trio of Martin Marietta aircraft that would complete the second and third stages of START. The other two vehicles consisted of the X-23, an unmanned, sub-orbital, sub-scale version of the X-24A, and an optional turbo-jet powered X-24A 'trainer' aircraft.

The second stage of START would utilize the X-23 sub-scale re-entry bodies and be known as PRIME (Precision Recovery Including Manoeuvring Entry). Earlier ASSET flights in support of X-20 had tested and proved the effectiveness of expanding corrugated alloy heat-resistant airframes and winged vehicle re-entries. PRIME was designed to extend this research into areas of 'wingless' flight handling and control during re-entry and approach, as well as test a new type of heat shielding.

The X-23 shielding was the result of almost seven years of research by Martin who had worked closely in its development with NASA's Langley Research Centre. The new material, a flexible elastomeric silicon filler, was injected into a shaped glass phenolic honeycomb structure which could be made into almost any form to match and be bonded to the X-23 airframe. Like the Apollo and Gemini heat shields this material 'ablates' when heated to extreme temperatures, a process which involves the heat shield forming a charred surface layer which peels off gradually, layer by layer, into the slipstream carrying away with it the frictional heat of re-entry. It had the distinct advantage of a 30 per cent weight saving over the old X-20's corrugated 'super alloys' with accordion type movements which, when under load, were supplemented with 'creeping skin' expansion joints between each airframe panel.

The first PRIME mission included a small X-23 making its first flight on top of an Atlas ballistic missile on 21 December 1966, from Vandenburg Air Force Base, California. The X-23 separated from its SLV-3 Atlas launcher at a speed of 26,000 ft per second, just under that needed for orbit. Simultaneously its small nitrogen gas thrusters aligned it for the correct re-entry attitude. Re-entry began almost immediately. The Martin Marietta heat shield (coded 356OH) and the nose and control fins of moulded phenolic high-temperature materials began to glow with the intense atmospheric friction. The guidance and on-board instrumentation performed flawlessly as the X-23 began a series of pitch manoeuvres using, in unison, its two horizontal hydraulically-controlled flaps.

Hurtling towards splashdown near Kuajalein Island in the Pacific, the X-23's drogue parachute popped out of the tail, followed by the main parachute. Planned recovery involved several US Navy ships and an Air Force HC-130 aircraft fitted with inflight recovery nets. If the air pick-up failed, the X-23 would remain seaworthy using a small flotation bag long enough for a surface recovery to be made.

Unfortunately the first X-23's main parachute failed and the small 900 lb, 7 ft long, 4 ft wide lifting body didn't remain seaworthy, but sank.

The second X-23 flight came on 5 March 1967 and followed a similar flight profile to the first. In addition, however, one attempt was to be made at evaluating its cross-range manoeuvrability to the right and left of its re-entry flight path centre line. While still in the extreme aerodynamic conditions of re-entry the X-23 extended its flaps and altered its course 570 miles before returning to its original flight path. This time the parachutes operated perfectly, but the mid-air recovery failed as did the small flotation bag, and X-23 number two joined its sister at the bottom of the Pacific Ocean.

The third and final X-23 took to the skies on 19 April 1967. This time the X-23 achieved a full 800 mile course deviation on both sides of its flight centre line before returning on course after total cross-range manoeuvres of 3,200 miles. It was recovered in mid-air by the Air Force HC-130 and returned for analysis.

Colonel C.L. Scoville, Director of the Air Force Space Systems Division START Programme, pronounced the entire PRIME series a success.

The new ablative material had neither affected the X-23's stability nor its control. It performed admirably in its role of maintaining an internal re-entry temperature of 400 °F. The X-23 guidance systems were successful, the aerodynamic flaps had worked as designed and the value of ground based terminal guidance had been demonstrated. The shallow re-entry path had also meant a less severe black-out of radio signals than expected. The X-23 proved that an aerodynamically-controlled vehicle could re-enter the Earth's atmosphere from orbital speeds and manoeuvre to a predesignated landing point using a combination of its own internal guidance systems operating aerodynamic control surfaces, with ground-based guidance on the final stages of flight.

In brief, the X-23 had successfully proven the aerodynamic performance of the X-24A shape at orbital speeds, and so, with a man at the controls, the X-24A would begin where the X-23 project ended, exploring the lower regions of the re-entry corridor from space.

In July 1967, the X-24A was rolled out to undergo immediately a series of prolonged tests before it was assigned to fly in 1969.

This newest addition to the joint NASA/USAF lifting body test programme was developed for the Air Force Aeronautical Systems Division at Wright-Patterson Air Force Base, Ohio. In conjunction with Ames and Langley, it was to be the first lifting body shape designed specifically to explore manoeuvring flight through supersonic, transonic and subsonic speeds to conventional landings at between 160 and 240 miles per hour.

The objective of the X-24A programme would be achieved when, carried aloft beneath the wing of a B-52 mother plane, it would be released at an altitude of about 45,000 feet and a speed of about Mach 0.6. The pilot would ignite his XLR-II rocket engine which would boost the X-24A to an altitude of up to 100,000 feet and a speed of around 1,350 mph (Mach 2). From that altitude and speed, the X-24A would be manoeuvred to a landing on Rogers Dry Lake at Edwards Air Force Base, California.

At Edwards, the NASA Dryden Flight Research team wanted to rebuild the wrecked M2F2, then in storage, in order to carry out further research. NASA senior management, however, with the X-24A and the HL-10 soon to arrive in service, was not entirely convinced that such a project was worthwhile. It took a considerable amount of effort by Ames management during the summer of 1967 to convince them otherwise.

On 22 March 1968, NASA, spurred on now by the need for increased levels of research, agreed to finance a partial reconstruction of M2F2, if only to get it in a fit state for transportation to Northrop by the autumn. A week earlier, the lifting body programme had recommenced with the HL-10 making only its second flight in fifteen months. Pilot for that flight was Captain Jerald R. Gentry. After release from the B-52 at 45,000 ft, he checked-out the aerodynamic design changes. Four minutes later the HL-10 landed safely after a flight which reached a maximum speed of 424 mph and set the lifting body programme back on the rails. (After four subsequent flights a new NASA test pilot John A. Manke took his turn to fly the HL-10 on 28 May 1968.)

A diagram showing the flight profile of a typical HL-10 lifting body flight.

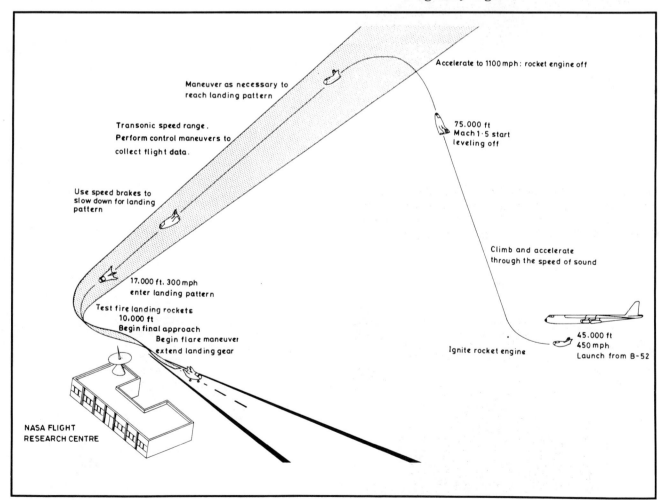

Gliding through 12,000 ft, the HL-10 lifting body prepares to land on Rogers Dry Lake. With its rocket engine, the HL-10 was capable of reaching altitudes of 80,000 ft and speeds of over 1,000 mph to simulate manoeuvring of an actual shuttle craft returning from spaceflight. (NASA)

The HL-10 lifting body begins to climb, leaving behind a white exhaust plume from its rocket engine. Air launched from a B-52 at 45,000 ft, the HL-10 was one of several lifting body concepts tested in the joint NASA/USAF effort to develop a prototype space shuttle craft. (NASA)

The HL-10 lifting body, now alongside the X-1E, forms part of a permanent static museum outside the NASA Dryden Flight Research Centre, Edwards Air Force Base, California. (NASA)

The HL-10 was retired from service temporarily after its ninth glide flight on 21 June, for installation of its XLR-II rocket engine. The complete aircraft was flown for the first time on 24 September by Jerald Gentry, on a glide test flight. A further similar glide flight took place under the guidance of John Manke a week later. The next flight was to be the first under power.

On 23 October 1968, Jerald Gentry was launched from the B-52, at a lower than usual altitude of 35,000 ft for the first powered, lifting body flight. He then ignited two of the four XLR-II chambers. After only a few brief seconds the rocket engine failed and the HL-10 glided down on to Rosemund Dry Lake. It had been hoped that the HL-10 would achieve a height of 45,000 ft, but without rocket propulsion this goal was impossible.

Two weeks later the engine fault had been corrected and this time John Manke took the HL-10 from 35,000 ft up to 42,650 ft after a 'burn' of 186 seconds on two of the XLR-II chambers. It was a success; John Manke was delighted and so was NASA who were satisfied that the engine firing had no adverse effects on the HL-10's stability or control. John Manke had achieved a maximum speed of 523 mph during his brief 6½ minute flight, landing on the same lake bed runway that, the very next day, William Dana would use to complete the final flight of the X-15 programme.

Following Jerald Gentry's further flight in the HL-10, on 9 December 1968, using two of the XLR-II chambers to reach 45,000 ft and 473 mph during his 3½ minute flight time, the lifting body programme was then to take a break from flying until the following April, the début of the X-24A.

With X-15 research completed, it was time to reappraise the goals and objectives of the lifting body programme. NASA had agreed at this point to fund the full rebuild of the M2F2, the finished aircraft to be redesignated the M2F3. The decision was taken in the light of the space agency's affirmed commitment to a winged 'space shuttle' follow-on to Apollo, and the resultant need for further research in support. Supplementing NASA's investigations, the USAF's own X-24A lifting body was also being made ready to fly for the spring of 1969 (after the usual delays caused by funding and continual technical difficulties).

The resumption of the lifting body programme with the X-24A, marked the final series of research flights in the Air Force's START programme and was to be known as the PILOT phase (Piloted Lowspeed Tests). On 17 April 1969, Jerald Gentry made the first of a series of nine successful X-24A glide flights.

Less than a fortnight after the début of the X-24A, a familiar figure climbed aboard the HL-10 for his first familiarization flight with lifting bodies. It was William Dana, astronaut, and veteran of the X-15 programme. His flight on 25 April 1969 was to be the first in a series of signifi-

cant contributions he was to make to the lifting body programme.

Soon after, on 9 May, John Manke cut in the third chamber of the HL-10's XLR-II engine and soared up to Mach 1.13 and 53,300 ft. At nearly seven minutes it was the longest, fastest and highest lifting body flight attempted thus far. The flight returned invaluable data on both its stability and its control.

On 6 June another 'new boy', Air Force Major Peter Hoag, joined the HL-10 programme with a low speed, low altitude familiarization glide flight. All through the summer, as Neil Armstrong set foot on the moon, and the world stood in awe of the incredible Apollo 11, the lifting body programme continued, almost unnoticed by anyone except NASA and the Edwards' staff.

On 6 August, John Manke made the first of a series of HL-10 flights which would examine the projected approach and landing profile of a space shuttle returning from orbit. As the HL-10 dropped clear of the B-52 at 45,000 ft and at 450 mph, John Manke gained full command of the aircraft's controls and ignited the XLR-II rocket engine's four chambers one by one. For the first time in the lifting body programme the XLR-II was at maximum thrust. The HL-10 climbed, accelerated to Mach 1.54, the fuel of ethyl alcohol and liquid oxygen burning to create a long streamer-like vapour trail in the clear blue sky. At 75,000 ft John Manke started to level off, shutting down the XLR-II chamber by chamber, allowing the HL-10 to carry on up under its own momentum to an altitude of 75,800 ft.

Then, turning around, Manke began a descent along a 'corridor' similar to that predicted for a space shuttle returning from an orbital flight. Dropping through the sky, the stubby HL-10 manoeuvred at around 60,000 ft in order to reach the selected landing area near the NASA Flight Research Centre. As the machmeter dropped below 1 John Manke conducted a series of controlled turns to collect flight data.

As the HL-10 passed through 17,000 ft at 300 mph he made final adjustments to his course to enter the landing pattern, then test fired the aircraft's small hydrogen peroxide gas landing rockets. (A standard procedure in case they might be needed to extend the 18 degree final approach beginning at 10,000 ft.) As the Rogers Dry Lake bed runway markings came into view he began the flare manoeuvre and extended the triangular landing gear before making a perfect landing and roll out.

On 3 September, William Dana made a similar flight to John Mankes', in a series of build-ups in the HL-10 that would achieve a maximum speed of

Mach 1.86 on 18 February 1970, with Peter Hoag at the controls, and a maximum altitude of 90,303 ft on the 27th, with William Dana in command. Every flight was planned to explore further the HL-10's flight envelope. In addition, knowledge of lifting body flight characteristics was vital to engineers already drawing up tentative plans for the Shuttle airframe.

William Dana's flight in the HL-10 opened the way ahead for the next phase of lifting body research, that of powered descent and approach phase tests. These would begin in May 1970 and meant that certain modifications would be needed to the HL-10. Accordingly, it was taken out of active service immediately after the flight on 27 February, for four months.

The single 8,000 lb XLR-II rocket engine in the HL-10 was replaced with three 500 lb thrust hydrogen peroxide rocket engines. These new engines could be fired independently by the pilot giving varying degrees of thrust during landing and approach manoeuvres, simulating the shallower landing approaches made by more conventional aircraft. This research would indicate whether or not a space shuttle would need to have a similar system for landing.

In the meantime the final unpowered test glide of the X-24A came on 24 February 1970. Jerald Gentry was at the controls for a flight of just under 4½ minutes which reached a maximum speed of 508 mph and an altitude of 47,000 ft. It tested both rudder and flap settings together with the angles of attack at speeds approximating those expected on the first powered flight.

On 19 March 1970, Jerald Gentry made the first flight of X-24A under power. The seven minute flight was without incident and pronounced a complete success. Shortly afterwards the new M2F3 arrived at Edwards. The task of conducting its maiden flight fell to NASA astronaut William Dana. It had taken three years to rebuild the M2F3 from the wreckage of the M2F2. During the reconstruction it had been given a central fin, a modified lateral control system, a set of small nitrogen reaction control thrusters and improved control and handling characteristics. A first, tentative step towards flight status was made on 22 May when the M2F3 took off and returned under the wing of the B-52 for a systems check-out. The actual first free flight came on 2 June. William Dana brought the M2F3 down from a drop height of 45,000 ft and 468 mph to a perfect landing.

On June 11, Peter Hoag made the first powered HL-10 landing using the hydrogen peroxide thrusters installed earlier, effectively reducing the 18 degree final glide path to 6 degrees in the process. The final flight of the HL-10 came on 17 July. It was the 37th flight of this lifting body, and was flown by Peter Hoag. The flight called for an evaluation of a powered landing approach under ground control, as well as stability and control under such circumstances. It was a success, and the HL-10, having achieved all its objectives, was withdrawn from service and put into storage at the Dryden Flight Research Centre together with the original lifting body, the M2F1. Simultaneously, Peter Hoag left the lifting body programme, leaving Jerald Gentry and NASA's John Manke to fly the X-24A, and William Dana the M2F3.

Meanwhile, the X-24A continued research into aerodynamic lift, drag and stability at progressively higher speeds until 26 August when the first attempt at a supersonic X-24A flight failed. Two of the four XLR chambers would not ignite, despite repeated efforts, and so Jerald Gentry glided back down, unaware that a damaged combustion chamber had caused an engine fire. The post-flight inspection, enquiry and repairs effectively grounded the X-24A until 14 October when, at last, with John Manke at the controls, the X-24A successfully reached Mach 1.18 and 67,900 ft. Objectives for this flight included expanding the X-24A flight envelope to Mach 1.1 and obtaining stability data at supersonic speeds and g-loadings, together with longitudinal trim and lift/drag ratio data.

On 27 October John Manke reached 71,400 ft, the highest that the X-24A would ever achieve, at a speed of 898 mph (Mach 1.35).

Just under a month later, William Dana made the first M2F3 powered flight to 52,000 ft at 534 mph, and of just over six minutes duration. He was to check and report on stability and control reaction control systems and landing visibility. Engineers and designers wanted to be 100 per cent sure that the inherent problems of the M2F2 had been ironed out. All went well during the flight until the XLR-II four-chamber engine cut out before its time. Upon landing, yet another investigation was launched as to why this occurred.

During this time, NASA decided it would be useful to compare lifting body pilot experiences and so on 9 February 1971, Jerald Gentry foresook his X-24A for a ride in William Dana's M2F3. It was hoped that, if there were any quaint similarities between the F3 and F2, having flown both varieties, Jerald Gentry would notice them. After the flight Gentry was satisfied that F2's tendency to Dutch roll had not been inherited by F3; thus, M2F3 could be cleared for the remainder of the flight programme. On 26 February William Dana flew M2F3 to Mach 0.85 on another stability data glide flight. He was to fly all the subsequent M2F3 flights that year.

On 4 February 1971, Air Force Major Cecil Powell joined the lifting body flight programme with a short duration glide flight to familiarize himself with the X-24A controls. On 29 March, John Manke, after a long series of build-up flights

probing even further into the X-24A's capability, finally reached the limit of its flight envelope in a mission to 1,036 mph (Mach 1.6).

Three flights later on 4 June 1971, and having completed its flight test programme, the X-24A was taken out of service and returned to Martin Marietta's plant at Denver, Colorado. Research at the USAF Flight Dynamics Laboratory at their Wright-Patterson Air Force Base in Ohio had indicated much improved performance could be attained from a radically new shape. In particular a redesigned X-24A would have a vastly improved hypersonic lift to drag ratio.

Retaining the basic structure of the X-24A, Martin Marietta removed the rounded 'delta' aluminium alloy skin, replacing it with a sharply-pointed flat under-surface, in essence a narrow triangle flared at the base in a 'double delta' configuration. From 24 ft long the new aircraft was extended to 39 ft, with a similar width extension from 14 ft to 19 ft.

The new lifting body, similar in many respects

Jerald Gentry nurses the X-24A down to a landing on 26 August 1970, after an engine failure and a serious fire. (NASA)

***Inset:* The final X-23 was launched on a sub-orbital flight on 19 April 1967 to prove the vehicle's aerodynamic manoeuvrability during re-entry. The aircraft is shown here in a windtunnel in which the effects are being tested of the roughened, scaly surface gained during atmospheric re-entry at about 17,000 mph. (NASA)**

to the Shuttle Orbiter, was to be known as the X-24B and would investigate how well an airframe configuration designed for Mach 5+ hypersonic flight would perform at supersonic, transonic and subsonic speeds. In particular, a great deal of interest was centred on its approach and landing characteristics.

The X-24B, although shaped to meet the requirements of a Mach 5+ vehicle, could not in actuality achieve anything near that speed, it being very much based structurally on the X-24A. Rather it would open the way for a proposed X-24C by proving that such a vehicle would not, on achieving lower speeds for landing, simply become uncontrollable.

Back at Edwards the M2F3 began, on 23 July 1971, a series of build-up flights designed to expand the aircraft's flight envelope. By August 25, William Dana had taken the M2F3 through the sound barrier to Mach 1.1. He was to make an attempt to exceed even this on 24 September when the mission came close to disaster.

Free from the B-52 William Dana checked the M2F3's flight attitude and started up the four-chamber XLR-II engine. No sooner had he achieved maximum thrust than two of the engine's igniters failed and the M2F3 engine shut down. In an almost exact repeat of Scott Crossfield's third powered X-15 flight a decade before, William Dana began an emergency landing on Rosemund Dry Lake. As he jettisoned fuel, chase planes

The X-24A stands motionless on Rogers Dry Lake Bed after its first supersonic flight on 14 October 1970. (NASA)

spotted a fire around the XLR-II engine's exhaust and the M2F3's tail area. Extinguishing the flames seconds after completing fuel dump, William Dana slammed the M2F3 down on the lake bed for an uncomfortable but 'successful' landing. The flight set the programme back over two months whilst engineers and NASA made checks and modifications to the M2F3's fuel jettison and engine purge systems, identified as the cause of the fire.

The M2F3 made two further supersonic flights before the end of 1971, following which it was again grounded for the installation of additional equipment, until the summer of 1972.

With the M2F3 away and the X-24B under construction there were to be no further lifting

body flights until the M2F3 was ready.

Part of the M2F3's refit included the installation of an electronic automatic fly-by-wire system which would replace the existing hydraulic controls first introduced in the M2F2. This new system, flight tested for the first time on 25 July 1972, was a direct ancestor of a similar piece of equipment installed in each of the Shuttle Orbiters. In a fly-by-wire system the conventional direct linkage, by cable, rod and hydraulics etc., between the pilot's

controls and the control surfaces is removed. Instead, the pilot's actions are converted into electronic signals which are fed to a flight director computer (nowadays in the form of a 'chip'-controlled microprocessor). The flight director interprets the pilot's movements and then transmits control instructions by signal wire to the actuators which operate directly the flying control surfaces. In this way the pilot chooses the change in flight condition, but it is the flight director that administers that change in the most efficient manner by combining commands to flight control surfaces and engine controls.

Once reassigned to flight duties, the M2F3 continued to return handling stability and control data across a wider range of speeds. On 13 December, William Dana made the M2F3's penultimate

flight an all out record speed attempt. It was to be the culmination of ever faster flights that began in July 1971.

At 47,000 ft, William Dana ignited all four XLR-II chambers, and as the lifting body shot forward he climbed, augmenting the 8,000 lb thrust liquid-fuelled rocket engine with the two 500 lb thrust landing rockets. Reaching Mach 1.6, the engines shut down on time and Dana made a few brief checks of the small gas RCS jets before landing on Rogers Dry Lake after a faultless flight.

Finally, on 20 December, John Manke flew in the M2F3 up to a record 71,500 ft. As a final test, he experimented with the RCS during the powered ascent before landing and closing the M2 series on a triumphant note. Shortly afterwards, the M2F3 was donated by NASA to the National Air and Space Museum in Washington, where it now stands on display in the same building as the X-15-1, Apollo 11 command module, X-1 and other milestones of manned flight.

The X-24B began its ground checks soon after

its delivery during October 1972. A jointly funded project between NASA and the Air Force, 30 flights were planned to extend well into 1979. The main goal of the X-24B was to test the handling qualities of a wingless aircraft capable of Earth orbital flight at the low-speed range of its flight envelope. The X-24B would fly no faster than Mach 2, and could gather vital handling, stability and control data down to landing speed.

Both aerodynamically and visually X-24B was the forerunner to the Shuttle Orbiter. In one sense it provided the final evolutionary link between the series of rocket-powered aircraft that began with the X-1 and the Space Shuttle as we know it today. It was on the basis of results gained from this aircraft that the latter's final detail configuration was determined.

The X-24B's propulsion system remained unchanged from that of the X-23A, namely a single Thiokol XLR-II 8,000 lb thrust engine with two Bell 400 lb optional landing rockets powered by hydrogen peroxide. The undercarriage retained the

same triangular layout with the substitution of a new nose wheel from the F-111 jet fighter.

Air launched from a B-52, using an X-15 type pylon, the pilot would sit in a 3.5 psi pressurized cockpit with a jettisonable canopy and a zero-zero ejection seat, which has the capacity of rescuing the pilot from standstill on the ground if needed.

Controls of the X-24B consisted of a pair of upper and lower flaps performing both elevator and pitch trim functions, together with ailerons and dual rudders. These control surfaces were operated via a pair of hydraulic systems and a redundant 3-axis stability augmentation system similar to the unit installed on the M2F3.

A comparative view of the X-24A, the M2F3 (the rebuilt crash-damaged F2) and the HL-10. (NASA)

The whole triangular body with its flat bottom and rounded top was constructed from a conventional aluminium alloy attached to the old X-24A structure. Three vertical fins protruded upwards from the rear of this 'double delta' aircraft.

Not only did the new shape double the lift-generating surface of the X-24A but its cross-range manoeuvrability was over three times that of the X-24A at 1,500 miles.

The most striking feature of the X-24B was its pointed nose. This shape was arrived at for one main reason. The rounded stubby noses of the M2 series and the HL-10 were the best design to combat re-entry atmospheric frictional heating, but were found to have a bad effect on the aircraft's low-speed handling and stability.

Pilots for the first flight tests of the X-24B were named as John Manke and USAF Major Michael V. Love. As 1972 continued, the X-24B made several captive flights and taxi tests under the B-52's wing, returning to the Flight Research Centre with more and more data to inspire confidence in the design.

Back at Edwards, after exhaustive tests of the X-24B, NASA and the USAF were confident enough to allow it to make its first manned free flight. On 1 August 1973, almost a year since its delivery to Edwards, John Manke dropped from the B-52 at 40,000 ft and 460 mph for a 4 minute 12 second flight which consisted of a practice approach during descent to Rogers Dry Lake bed.

Four similar check-out glide flights ensued through the rest of August and during September and October before John Manke ignited the X-24B's XLR engine for the first time in free flight on 15 November. Maintaining a speed of 597 mph, just below Mach 1, the X-24B climbed to 52,800 ft before landing successfully after a total free flight time of 6 minutes and 40 seconds. Confidence in the X-24B was such that NASA and the Air Force agreed to make only one further powered subsonic flight test before going for Mach 1 + on 5 March 1974.

On that day, John Manke cruised the sleek X-24B up past Mach 1 to Mach 1.09 (708 mph) and

The X-24B finally completed the evolutionary trail leading to the Shuttle Orbiter. Seen here after delivery from Martin Marietta to Edwards Air Force Base in late 1972, the X-24B was to make its first flight on 1 August 1973. (NASA)

On 5 August 1975, John Manke and the X-24B made the programme's first attempt at a conventional runway landing, verifying the ability of the Space Shuttle (already under construction) to do the same thing at Kennedy Space Centre. (NASA)

over 60,000 ft. All the data from the aircraft's sensors, coupled with John Manke's observations, indicated that the X-24B was well able to cope, without difficulty, with both transonic and low-speed manoeuvres. A speed build-up series of flights thus commenced to test the full range of X-24B potential.

On 30 April 1974, after three 'scrubs' due to poor weather and difficulties with the B-52 'parent', Major Michael V. Love made his first powered X-24B flight. It was a low, slow flight below Mach 1, meant primarily to give him the experience of handling the X-24B with the engine running. Major Love, as back-up to John Manke, had already made two glide flights in this vehicle. He was able to prove his ability matched that of the experienced John Manke.

The speed of the X-24B was increased progressively flight by flight. Between 24 May and 25 October the maximum speed achieved rose from Mach 1.14 (753 mph), to Mach 1.76 (1,164 mph) at an altitude of 62,100 ft. It is the fastest speed ever achieved by a lifting body.

On 22 May 1975, John Manke achieved another distinction, flying at 74,100 ft, the highest altitude of either X-23A or X-23B.

Around this time, when the X-24B was achieving not only records but invaluable research information for the Space Shuttle, NASA decided that the Shuttle Orbiter should land after each flight on a specially prepared runway at the Kennedy Space Centre, thus cutting the time and cost of transporting the Orbiter across the entire width of the North American continent after each flight. This presented certain unique problems. For example, landing a returning spacecraft in a 'forgiving' area such as Edwards with its miles of flat lake bed surfaces was difficult enough as Bruce Peterson's catastrophic M2F2 flight had demonstrated. Landing a much larger 'space plane' on a single runway strip amidst

X-15 astronaut Bill Dana shares a joke with ground technicians after his first X-24B flight on 9 September 1975, during which he reached 71,000 ft and Mach 1.5 (NASA)

the mangrove swamps and everglade waterways at Cape Canaveral was a completely different proposition!

Without a doubt, if the Shuttle Orbiter was to be scheduled to land and take off from the Florida Spaceport, NASA had to be certain of the lifting body's ability to make a pinpoint landing. So it was that on 5 August 1975, shortly after Apollo 18 linked up with the Soviet Soyuz flight and drew the final curtain on US manned ballistic 'capsule' spaceflight, the X-24B made the first attempt by a lifting body at a conventional runway landing.

John Manke cut the XLR-II engine at Mach 1.23 and 60,000 ft for the long glide down to the Edwards runway. Coming in at a glide angle of 25 degrees he made final course corrections before pulling the pointed X-24B nose up at just over 1,000 ft and making a textbook landing within feet of the touchdown point marked on the concrete runway surface. Major Love followed suit on 20 August. NASA was satisfied, and construction of the runway at Kennedy Space Centre went ahead.

The X-24B was the most successful of the six lifting bodies. It had proved invaluable in the development of the Orbiter. In September 1975,

William Dana took over from John Manke and Major Love making two powered flights. His last, in the 23rd, ended the X-24B research programme and preceded a further six glide flights during October and November 1975. These final, unpowered, missions were introduced in order to familiarize two new NASA test pilots — Einor Enevoldson and Thomas C. McMurtry — together with an Air Force pilot Major Francis R. Scobee, with the handling and control characteristics of the X-24B. At that time a possible X-24C hypersonic lifting body was being considered, so NASA and the Air Force wanted as many pilots as possible familiar with the aircraft which, in a somewhat different

On 26 November 1975, Thomas McMurtry landed the X-24B and brought to a close the lifting body research programme. At the same time across the USA, components of the first Shuttle Orbiter were being assembled. (NASA)

guise, would extend the X-series of rocket research planes into the 1980s.

The X-24C would be half X-24B and half X-15, flying at sustained speeds of over Mach 6 and testing new materials and propulsion techniques. A modified Thiokol XLR-99 engine would boost the X-24C to Mach 7.4 as part of a research programme leading to both a hypersonic civil airliner and a Mach 6 fighter interceptor for the twenty-first century. (Further development still depends on continued government funding and technical capability.)

On 26 November 1975, Thomas McMurtry landed the 36th and final X-24B flight. Soon afterwards William Dana resumed the duties he still performs today, flight testing at Edwards, whilst on 14 January 1978 Francis Scobee was selected as a Shuttle astronaut. Thomas McMurtry was later named as co-pilot for the 'NASA 905' Boeing 747 Shuttle carrier aircraft. The X-24B was shipped to the Air Force Museum in Ohio after a summer show at the 1976 Kennedy Space Centre American Bicentennial Exhibition.

The lifting body flight programme had ended, but the analysis of the data it produced continued. In two years' time the Dryden Flight Research Centre would be host to a vehicle that embodied the results gained from the lifting body and X-15 flight programmes — the Space Shuttle *Enterprise*.

4 The Space Shuttle

In Washington on 28 February 1968, NASA's Associate Administrator for Manned Space Flight, George Mueller, went before the Senate Space Committee to emphasize the importance of a new approach to space flight vehicles for the coming decades.

NASA was at that time busy preparing detailed post-Apollo plans which envisaged the construction of large manned orbiting space stations, regularly serviced by crews of visiting astronauts. Such facilities required a cheap, two-way reusable method of flying into space and back.

Ballistic missiles and 'capsules' were fine for Apollo, with its time-set objectives and open-ended budget, but for the future a new concept would be needed. NASA decided that the time had finally come to build the world's first orbiting aircraft. The X-15 and its predecessors had shown the way. Now it appeared that the entire strength of the Space Agency was set to complete the final step in the programme of development that began in the mid nineteen-forties.

On 31 January 1969, just under a year since George Mueller's Senate address, NASA appointed four US aerospace companies to study the possible configuration of an Integrated Launch and Re-entry Vehicle (ILRV). These contracts, worth half a million dollars each, were awarded to McDonnell Douglas, North American Rockwell, Lockheed and General Dynamics. Together they were to con-

stitute what NASA termed their 'Phase A' Shuttle investigations to run until September 1969 when NASA would appraise the different teams' results. In April NASA's newly formed Space Shuttle task group, formed to co-ordinate the embryonic project, began to look closely for the first time at a two-stage, fully reusable vehicle concept, very similar to the Project Bomi configuration proposed by the USAF and Bell almost two decades earlier. By July all the Phase A companies had aligned their research programme towards the two-stage approach.

By August 1969, with Apollo 11 safely home and the lifting body programme surging ahead, NASA had both fulfilled the goal set by President Kennedy and set into motion the final phases of investigation into their next major space project. The American public was still in a state of euphoria over the space agency's success, and the Nixon administration was looking towards Mars as the nation's next 'giant leap'. In September 1969, interest in the Space Shuttle was gaining ground, and it was not long before Washington and heavy politics became involved. A report by the President's special Space Task Force recommended strongly that America, utilizing the Space Shuttle, should 'embark on a manned flight to Mars before the end of this century'. They gave the President three options on how this could be achieved.

The first option would be a 'crash prog-

Space Shuttle

ramme' launching men to Mars in 1983 with a maximum funding of $9,000 million-a-year, beginning as early as 1980. If this was to go ahead, then a decision to go ahead would have to be taken at the latest by 1974.

The second option, recommended by Vice President Agnew (chairman of the task force) called for a Mars expedition in 1986 with peak expenditure of around $8,000 million-a-year in the early nineteen-eighties. Final commitment to this option could wait until 1977.

The final option would defer any decision on a Mars flight until after 1990 but before the year 2000, and would stretch out funding at the $5,500 million level to 1980, after which funding would increase to around $8,000 million-a-year.

According to Vice President Agnew, what was important was that the three options represented a 'balanced programme' to spread available US resources and abilities over, 'a wide range of manned flights, unmanned planetary expeditions and applications satellites — serving people on Earth and increasing international co-operation in space'.

Clearly such a wide ranging space programme would need the Shuttle's logistical support and so, in addition to the Mars recommendation, the Space Task Group strongly supported further development declaring that the Shuttle would, 'provide a major improvement in cost and operational capability and carry passengers, supplies, rocket propellant, other spacecraft, equipment or additional rocket stages to and from orbit on a routine, aircraft-like basis'.

Larger, Saturn V class, rockets with heavy payload capacity would still continue to supple-

As envisaged in 1969, an expedition leaves Earth for Mars in the mid-eighties. Two nuclear 'shuttle' stages propel the central core containing the Mars Lander on its way. (NASA)

ment Shuttle flights in order to place items such as space station modules and the components of the Mars lander into orbit. In addition, a 'space tug' would be developed; carried into orbit it would perform assembly duties in space and transport equipment from space station to space station.

Whilst these space stations would serve as stepping stones to the first lunar colonies, a nuclear rocket motor called 'Nerva', under development in the late nineteen-sixties, would provide the propulsive power for deep space exploration, and a new generation of orbital based nuclear shuttle craft.

As envisaged at the end of 1969, all of these components — the Shuttle, Space Station, Space Tug, Nerva and Nuclear Shuttle — would come together in an integrated assault on Mars. Initially, three Nuclear Shuttles would be assembled in Earth orbit around a detachable space station body. Space tugs would perform the final assembly, with conventional liquid fuelled Shuttles delivering components from Earth. When complete, the assembly would leave Earth for the 12 month trip to Mars.

4 The Space Shuttle

The Space Station core would house the crew and the Martian Landing Module which would make the final descent to the surface. The three Nuclear Shuttles would be used to provide the necessary propulsion to and from Martian orbit.

After Mars, other explorations in the solar system would follow, with the Kennedy Space Centre, Florida, as the focus of daily manned Shuttle launches into space.

Before any final decision could culminate in a Mars landing, however, NASA had first to develop its fleet of reusable Space Shuttles. On 1 November 1969, in support of this goal, the four Phase A contractor teams from General Dynamics/Convair,

Other ambitious projects included large space manufacturing and research laboratories manned by teams of visiting astronauts. (NASA)

Space Shuttle

Lockheed, McDonnell Douglas, and North American Rockwell (formerly North American Aviation), delivered their proposals for a fully reusable Shuttle. At that time, riding the crest of triumph from Apollos 11 and 12, NASA was increasingly confident of a renaissance in space exploration.

Such were the ambitious plans of NASA at the dawn of 1970. For the most part, however, they turned out to be no more than dreams, for the US economy faltered, public interest in 'space' began to wane, and the money informally promised for these goals was not forthcoming from the Nixon administration. NASA's budget for Fiscal Year 1971, announced in October 1969, was cut back and with it died the momentum of achievement that had carried on from the launch of Sputnik 1. For many it seemed that the solar system and America's future in space had been sacrificed on the paddy fields of Vietnam.

President Nixon applauds the crew of Apollo 11 on their return to Earth. Behind the smiles, however, his administration was preparing a series of cutbacks that would curtail future moon landings and threaten the future of NASA itself. (NASA)

The deeply felt shock of this new realism had its effects immediately, as President Nixon considered his response to the Space Task Force's proposals. On 13 January 1970, NASA's Chief Administrator, Dr Thomas O. Paine, called a press conference in Washington to discuss the implications of a reduced Fiscal Year 1971 space budget. His opening remarks were in stark contrast to the bold speculations of only a few months before. As the assembled audience of media representatives settled in the large meeting room at NASA's Washington HQ, the whole American space programme was about to shift direction as Dr Paine stood to deliver his address. He told them of cutbacks, of changes in the Apollo programme curtailing the final moon flights and of redundancies. Only one project emerged unscathed as hope for the agency — the Shuttle, the only survivor of the manned Mars exploration programme. It was on this programme that NASA was to pin the future of American man in space. When 'NACA' became 'NASA' it entered the big league, and it was now experiencing its first big league problem.

Dr Paine was, despite the setbacks, resolute in his support of the Space Agency. The budget was a crushing disappointment but even in NASA's darkest hour its chief had still to present an outward show of confidence. He told the packed audience:

'A strong space programme continues as one of this nation's major national priorities. How-

ever, we recognize that under current fiscal restraints NASA must find new ways to stretch out current programmes and reduce our present operational base. NASA can move forward strongly while still achieving greater economy in 1971. This is the management challenge which we in NASA face and I am confident that we can meet it. NASA will press forward in 1971 at a reduced level, but in the right direction with the basic ingredients we need for major achievements in the nineteen-seventies and beyond. Whilst we will be reducing our total effort, we will not dissipate the strong teams that sent men to explore the Moon and automated spacecraft to observe the planets.'

'In support of the decisions on the NASA Fiscal Year 1971 budget, I am today taking the following actions...'

Around the hall the media representatives waited, the American space programme hung in the balance.

'We will suspend for an indefinite period production of the Saturn V launch vehicle after completion of Saturn V no 515.

'We will stretch out Apollo lunar missions to six month launch intervals, and defer lunar expeditions during the Apollo Application Programme (Skylab) flights in 1972.

'We will postpone the launch of the Viking/ Mars unmanned lander from 1973 to the next Mars opportunity in 1975.'

What only weeks before seemed almost inconceivable, was happening. America was turning its back on space!

A month later, on 7 March 1970, President Nixon issued a statement that would be as significant to NASA as had been President Kennedy's moon commitment in 1962. He committed further research to the Shuttle whilst, at the same time, dashed all hopes of a manned Martian expedition or any long-term programme beyond Apollo and Skylab. Space was no longer the political winner of the nineteen-sixties. Crucial public support was rapidly waning and, as if to make matters worse, the Russians took every opportunity to express the point that they never intended to go to the Moon anyway, and that there really was never a 'race' at all.

The opening remarks President Nixon made in his speech effectively summed up his administration's 'public' attitude to space exploration.

'Over the last decade, the principal goal of our nation's space programme has been the Moon. By the end of that decade men from our planet have travelled to the Moon on four occasions and twice they had walked on its surface. With these unforgettable experiences, we have gained a new perspective of ourselves and our world.

'I believe these accomplishments should help us gain a new perspective of our space programme as well. Having completed that long stride into the future which has been our objective for the past decade, we must now define new goals which make

sense for the seventies. We must build on the successes of the past, always reaching out for new achievements. But we must also recognize that many critical problems here on this planet make high priority demands on our attention and our resources. By no means should we allow our space programme to stagnate. But — with the entire future and the entire universe before us — we should not try to do everything at once. Our approach to space must continue to be bold, but it must also be balanced.

'When this Administration came into office, there were no clear, comprehensive plans for our space programme after the first Apollo landing. To help remedy this situation, I established in February of 1969 a Space Task Group, headed by the Vice President, to study possibilities for the future of that programme. That report was presented to me in September. After reviewing that report and considering our national priorities, I have reached a number of conclusions concerning the future pace and direction of the nation's space efforts.'

Then followed a blow-by-blow dismantling of the United States programme; piece by piece the enthusiasm and dreams of a decade were cast aside. Repeatedly President Nixon cited 'financial restraint', 'fiscal cut-backs', and 'the competing demands of other national programmes' (Vietnam?), as Apollo was curtailed and missions spaced out or cancelled altogether. NASA's bold space station became 'Skylab', a once-only laboratory in the sky constructed out of a converted Saturn V third-stage fuel tank. President Nixon did his best to emphasize the continuing importance of the US Space Programme seizing every opportunity to preface one rationalization after another with 'bold', 'quest' or 'adventure', but the truth was plain to everyone.

The economies did, however, reaffirm support for the Shuttle. Even so, President Nixon approached the subject with caution.

'We should work to reduce substantially the cost of space operations. Our present rocket technology will provide a reliable launch capability for some time. But as we build for the longer range future, we must devise less costly and less complicated ways of transporting payloads into space. Such a capability — designed so that it will be suitable for a wide range of scientific, defence and commercial uses — can help us realise important economies in all aspects of our space programme. We are currently examining in greater detail the feasibility of reusable space shuttles as one way of achieving this objective.'

Against this backdrop of change and calamity for NASA's fortunes, the Space Shuttle genesis continued.

Following the submission of all the Phase A reports in November 1969, on 18 February 1970 NASA, by that time convinced that the two-stage system was best, issued a request to US aerospace consortia for a further more definitive 'Phase B' study.

Significantly, only the day before, a joint USAF/NASA space transportation committee had been set up to maintain joint civilian and military interests in this new project. From their involvement in the past it was impossible to conceive that the USAF would pass by this opportunity to ride NASA's Shuttle if and when it was developed.

The prospect of gaining a foothold in such a potentially lucrative contract also appealed to all the giants of the US aerospace industry. In response to NASA's requests for proposals on 30 March, the X-20 company, Boeing, joined with Lockheed; North American Aviation went in alone; and McDonnell Douglas formed a consortium with Martin, TRW and Pan American Aviation (whose expertise in maintenance, ground handling and turn around was much needed) to submit their own ideas based around NASA's own two stage reusable Shuttle.

On 12 May 1970, the McDonnell Douglas consortium and North American Rockwell were chosen by NASA from the competition as prime contractors to proceed with Phase B development of a two-stage Space Shuttle. However, no sooner was the ink dry on the Phase B contracts than, reminiscent of the old X-20's 'Phase Alpha' over a decade earlier, on 15 June NASA decided to examine further their basic two-stage concept of the Shuttle by instigating an extension to Phase A to run concurrently with Phase B. The job of investigating alternative Shuttle configurations was given to Lockheed, Chrysler, and a team from Boeing and Grumman.

Under the extended Phase A studies, Grumman and its major sub-contractor Boeing were supervised by NASA's Manned Spacecraft Centre, Houston, and were to study three concepts. Firstly, a stage-and-a-half shuttle, consisting of a single reusable manned spacecraft with an onboard propulsion system and drop tanks to provide supplementary propellants (as X-15-A2). Secondly a reusable orbiter with an expendable ballistic rocket booster. This matched the old X-20 concept, utilizing either an existing expendable booster or a new low-cost first stage fuelled by either solid or liquid propellant. Thirdly, a new approach, a reusable first stage using existing Saturn V J-2-derived rocket engines with solid 'strap on' boosters and a reusable shuttle also powered by a cluster of J-2s.

The $4 million Grumman/Boeing contract was supplemented by a $1 million contract to Lockheed. Managed by NASA's Marshall Space Flight Centre, Lockheed would define an alternative 'stage-ahd-a-half' system including both a winged and a lifting body designed orbiter.

Chrysler was assigned the task of examining another concept — a single-stage to orbit reusable vehicle — and given $750,000 to proceed. Again, Chrysler joined Lockheed in reporting directly to the NASA Marshall Space Flight Centre.

These combined Phase A studies rigorously re-examined the feasibility of technically and economically competitive Shuttle concepts. The results of the investigations, in conjunction with the North American Rockwell and McDonnell Douglas Phase B (definition and preliminary design) contracts ensured that absolutely nothing would be overlooked, and that the final Shuttle configuration would certainly be the most economical and reliable space transportation system.

Back at the Kennedy Space Centre, 1970 had seen only one Apollo flight: Apollo 13. The flight that almost took the lives of astronauts Jim Lovell, Jack Swigert and Fred Haise had attracted the attention of the world, but also delayed the next mission, Apollo 14, by almost a year. The facilities at the Cape were designed for a moon landing programme of up to six moon missions a year, with the simultaneous construction of four Apollo Saturn Vs in the vehicle assembly building (VAB) at any given time. With the severe curtailment of the moon missions through budget cut-backs, such surplus capacity came under the scrutiny of R.H. Curtin, NASA Director of Facilities, who, together with representatives of other NASA centres and the USAF, were looking for suitable launch site and support facilities for the Shuttle.

Aerospace and architectural engineering firms throughout the US had been approached by NASA with a view to submitting proposals on Shuttle ground facilities. The successful contractor would support the new NASA Shuttle Facilities Group which in turn would be responsible to NASA's Director of Facilities in Washington. For 12 months the contractor would develop plans and options for development and compile a master catalogue of facilities including those needed for Shuttle manufacture, assembly, flight testing, engine testing, launch and control.

As the Shuttle developed the contractor would recommend sites that would suit the nature of any testing needed. The final result of the contract would be a 'facilities master plan' encompassing every single stage of the programme.

On 9 September 1970, following on from further financial cutbacks announced in June for NASA's Fiscal Year 1971 budget, Dr Thomas O. Paine announced the cancellation of Apollo moon flights 18 and 19 in order to maintain funds for such programmes as the three-man orbiting space station, Skylab, and the Space Shuttle, to which only $80 million had been allocated by Congress for the next 12 months. Senate narrowly defeated an amendment to the NASA budget which would have withdrawn the $130 million funds of the Phase B work now well under way. The actual count was 28 to 32 votes 'for' with 40 absentees or abstentions. Space Shuttle had survived, just...

The eleven month Phase B programme had, by January 1971, moved into its third and final stage. (The first stage was a three month configuration selection period, followed by a similar period for systems selection. In the final part of Phase B, contractors were to conduct a study of Shuttle design and costing.) It was becoming obvious that the final operating costs of a fully reusable Shuttle would be less than a similar system using off-the-shelf expendable elements. The original development costs, however, of such a fully reusable vehicle would probably, in 1971 prices, have been in excess of $10 billion for two large piloted winged vehicles. NASA realized, in the light of increasingly tight budgets, that this would be more than Congress would be likely to give.

On 19 January 1971, NASA management held an important meeting at Williamsburg, Virginia, to finalize some of the Shuttle's main design points. Influenced heavily both by budget pressures and future USAF requirements, NASA agreed on a delta wing Shuttle 'orbiter' with a high cross-range capability for improved landing site options, and a minimum 65,000 lb payload capacity at 100 miles altitude.

Up to that time two configurations for the Shuttle Orbiter had been considered. One of these had straight, stubby wings and was designed to re-enter the Earth's atmosphere at a high angle of attack. This would reduce the frictional heating but also reduce the Shuttle's cross-range manoeuvrability. The other configuration had delta wings which would enable the Orbiter to re-enter at a lower angle of attack permitting much greater cross-range abilities, but at the expense of greater re-entry heating. It was mainly on the insistence of the DoD with their requirements for different landing site options that the final decision was taken for a high cross-range capacity delta-winged Orbiter.

A search for ways in which a reduction in costs could be made resulted in a smaller Orbiter with external, expendable hydrogen tanks, and the booster's maximum speed was lowered to permit the use of less expensive heat-shielding. These changes cut the prospective costs by around 20 per cent but not enough to satisfy the delegates at the Williamsburg conference. As a result both the liquid oxygen and liquid hydrogen tanks were removed completely from the Orbiter in favour of a single expendable combined tank which would be divided into two sections to carry both propellant and oxidizer. This improvement reduced the Orbiter's size still further, together with its development cost, but not its performance. Having finally settled the baselines for the Orbiter design all that remained was the booster problem.

To meet President Nixon's demands to save money, and also because of concern about the safety of the booster's crew in the event of a launch emergency, plans for a manned booster were scrapped. An unmanned booster presented a choice of either liquid or solid propellant rocket motors. The liquid-fuelled booster engines would operate in what was termed a 'series burn configuration', where the Orbiter's engines would only be ignited after the booster had shut down and separated. Solid rockets on the other hand would be ignited simultaneously with the Orbiter's engines at lift-off and burn in parallel during the first stages of ascent to orbit.

The high price of both liquid and solid fuelled booster systems for the Shuttle meant that, economically, each booster would have to be recovered and refurbished for later flights. The recovery systems would, nevertheless, add further expense and complexity to the prime objective of a cheap access to space. NASA, however, reasoned that whilst the cost per flight would be higher with recoverable solid boosters and (as a cost compromise) expendable liquid fuel tanks, their use would cut by half critical development costs of a fully reusable Shuttle.

On 5 January 1972, President Nixon, speaking from the Western White House at San Clemente, California, announced his decision to continue Space Shuttle development.

'The United States should proceed at once with the development of an entirely new type of space transportation system designed to help transform the space frontier of the nineteen-seventies into familiar territory, easily accessible for human endeavour in the nineteen-eighties and nineties... It will revolutionize transportation into near space by routinizing (sic) it. It will take the astronomical costs out of astronautics. This is why commitment to the Space Shuttle's programme is the right next step for America to take.'

His statement also endorsed the commitment to proceed with either a solid- or liquid-propellant, unmanned, recoverable booster for the Shuttle.

On the completion of the extended Phase A and Phase B studies in early February, NASA's design review team examined the results of the alternative Shuttle and booster configurations proposed by the industry consortia. Of the options, the twin solid booster rockets combined with the Orbiter's own engines came out cheapest by $1,500 million. Consequently, on 15 March 1972 NASA decided to adopt the twin solid rocket booster concept for their Shuttle. Two days later NASA, with the basic concept now almost complete, invited US aerospace industry tenders to build and integrate the Shuttle. Designs and proposals had to be submitted to the Contracting Officer, Space Shuttle Procurement Branch by 1.00 pm Central Daylight Time on 12 May 1972. It was to be the most expensive single aviation contract in history.

Meanwhile, the 1972 NASA budget, announced in February, was even worse than had been expected. Many programmes had been curtailed, postponed or radically altered in the light of a reduced financial outlay.

Whereas Apollos 16 and 17 were safe, alongside the Skylab missions planned for 1973/74, the 'nuclear shuttle' was dropped. Contractor work on 'Nerva' the nuclear rocket engine, almost completed, was also suspended.

The Marshall Centre was to lose a planned 300 staff by June 1972, making a total of 20 per cent NASA staff redundancies since 1966. This was the time of a vociferous 'anti-space' lobby in the US. NASA realised that, if the Shuttle were curtailed, they would no longer have a manned spaceflight capability after Apollo and Skylab. After the success of the moon landings it seemed incredible that the world's richest and most technologically advanced nation was turning its back on space, leaving the door wide open to the Soviets.

On 26 July 1972, NASA selected North American Rockwell as prime Space Shuttle Orbiter contractor and integrator of the total launch system. The contract issued covered the development and manufacture of five Orbiters over about six years. North American Rockwell estimated a total cost of $2,600 million. Glide tests were scheduled for 1976 followed in 1978 by the first orbital flight test.

The selection by NASA of NAR was made after a detailed analysis of all the designs, costings and schedules of NAR and its Phase B counterparts including McDonnell Douglas. The external tank and SRBs were planned to be contracted by NASA when work at NAR had progressed sufficiently to enable NASA to gain firm proposals from other US aerospace companies.

NASA's facilities department had selected the Government-owned rocket assembly plant at New Orleans for tank construction; the same place that Saturn V stages were assembled. In contrast to the NASA redundancies, employment generated by the Orbiter development in the Shuttle project was estimated at around 15,000 by 1976, decreasing gradually thereafter as work was completed.

The Air Force had always maintained an interest in the Space Shuttle definition study phases, and were to monitor closely NAR's development of the Shuttle in their position of potential future users.

William F. Rockwell Jr, Chairman and Chief Executive Officer of NAR said: 'The United States

and the world have entered a new era of space exploration, one that we expect to be highly instrumental in delivering the benefits of practical space utilization.

'Scientists and Universities can now direct their efforts to space research projects that were previously prohibitive because of cost. The Shuttle is tangible evidence of the transition in the space programme from the dramatic to the pragmatic.

'We appreciate the fact that North American Rockwell has been given great responsibility as a result of this award. But we are also confident that the experience gained by the company as prime contractor for the Apollo programme combined with the talents of our scientific, technical and engineering professionals, will enable us to fulfil that commitment. We look forward to the challenge.

'Our job, one which we have accomplished before, is to build a quality product, at the lowest possible cost, and deliver it on time — and that we will do.'

Certainly, with the experience of X-15 and Apollo, NAR were in a prime position to exploit this new project. Robert Anderson, President and Chief Operation Officer of NAR, announced the commitment of 9,000 staff to the Shuttle.

The major portion of Shuttle work would be centred at NAR's Downey, California, plant on the outskirts of Los Angeles; assembly of components would take place at their Palmdale factory close to Edwards AFB, where drop tests of the first Orbiter would commence.

NAR were to sub-contract much of the Shuttle work, and in October, after two years of gestation, the Space Shuttle concept as we know it today was born. On 7 November NAR issued requests for sub-contract work on the Orbiter's wings, central fuselage and vertical tail. By March 1973 NAR had changed its corporate name to Rockwell International and had awarded four major Orbiter subcontracts. Grumman Aerospace Corporation were to build the double delta wings of the Orbiter, Convair Aerospace Division of General Dynamics the mid fuselage, Fairchild Republic the vertical tail fin and McDonnell Douglas the 'Orbital Manoeuvring System' (OMS).

Simultaneously, NASA issued McDonnell Douglas, Boeing and Martin Marietta with a request for their proposals for external tank design, development and production. The successful contractor would co-ordinate and build this massive fuel tank which would feed the Space Shuttle's main engines right up until the combination almost reached orbit when it would fall back to Earth and burn up. The Thiokol Corporation were to build the Solid Rocket Boosters (SRBs) based on their experience with similar boosters on the Air Force Titan IIIC.

On 14 December 1972, the Apollo 17 lunar module left the lunar surface as President Nixon had relayed a special message to the crew: 'This

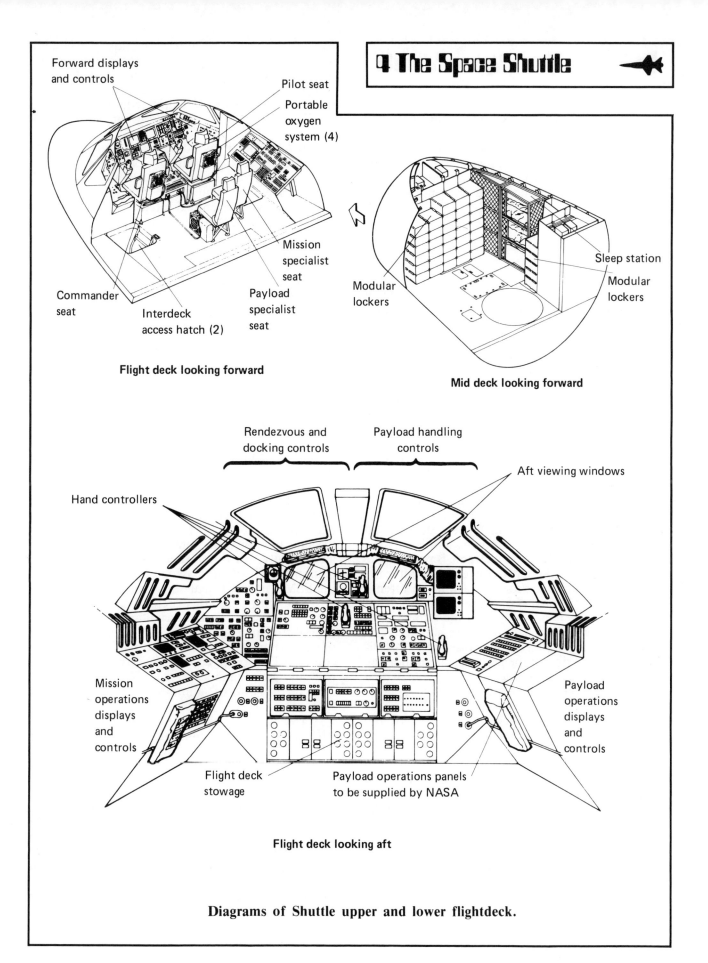

Forward displays and controls

Pilot seat

Portable oxygen system (4)

Mission specialist seat

Commander seat

Interdeck access hatch (2)

Payload specialist seat

Flight deck looking forward

Modular lockers

Sleep station

Modular lockers

Mid deck looking forward

Rendezvous and docking controls

Payload handling controls

Hand controllers

Aft viewing windows

Mission operations displays and controls

Payload operations displays and controls

Flight deck stowage

Payload operations panels to be supplied by NASA

Flight deck looking aft

Diagrams of Shuttle upper and lower flightdeck.

may be the last time in this century that men will walk on the Moon. But space exploration will continue, the benefits of space exploration will continue, the search for knowledge through the exploration of space will continue, and there will be new dreams to pursue based on what we have learned.'

The Orbiter

The Shuttle Orbiter emerged as the single most complex machine ever built by man, with 49 rocket engines (including RCS jets); 23 antennas for communications, radar, and data links; 5 computers; separate sets of controls (developed from the X-15) for flying in both space and in the atmosphere, and electricity-producing fuel cells. NASA's Orbiter is just over 122 ft long, 78 ft wide, 57 ft high and weighs 160,000 lb empty. Its payload bay, mounted amidships, is 60 ft long by 15 ft wide and is capable of transporting up to 65,000 lb of cargo to between 230 and 690 miles in altitude. The Orbiter can return payloads of 32,000 lb from space and, with a supplementary power source, carry out a variety of space missions lasting up to 30 days.

Unlike the X-15 whose airframe was constructed of a nickel alloy over a titanium and stainless-steel frame (and other very-high-speed aircraft, all of which also use heat-tolerant materials in their manufacture), the Orbiter's airframe is remarkable in that it is built, like most conventional aircraft, mostly of aluminium, protected from the intense heat of re-entry by layers of reusable surface insulation (RSI). The main sections of the Orbiter consist of a forward fuselage and pressurized crew cockpit; the payload bay at mid fuselage with full-length overhead doors; the aft fuselage supporting the main engines; and a lower body flap which controls the Orbiter's pitch attitude in atmospheric flight and shields the main engine 'bells' from the heat of re-entry. Other characteristics include the double-delta wings and the tailplane with split air brake/rudder.

Like the rest of the Orbiter the forward fuselage is largely constructed from aluminium alloy panels and bulkheads for lightness. Window frames for the pressurized cabin are attached to the structural panels and frames. There is a total of ten windows, six forward, two in the roof and two overlooking the payload bay. The crew module is divided into three areas: an upper flight deck containing the flight controls; a lower or 'mid deck' with a side hatch for normal crew entry and exit, together with an airlock for access to the unpressurized payload bay; and an equipment subsystem bay below the lower deck floor. The

forward fuselage also houses the nose wheel landing gear, its undercarriage bay doors, the forward mounted RCS thrusters, various items of electronic equipment and three avionics bays. Ports in the airframe outer structure facilitate equipment such as air data booms and star tracking sensors for navigation.

Behind the forward fuselage and cabin, the mid fuselage acts as a primary load-carrying structure between the crew compartment and the aft engine assembly. The outer skin is, once more, aluminium with machined integral stiffeners and a truss-structure central section. The upper half of the mid fuselage consists of the two long cargo bay doors which are hinged right along each side and split along the top centre line. The doors, made out of a graphite-epoxy composite, also incorporate freon loop radiators which are exposed to space when the doors open soon after launch to dissipate excess heat from electrical equipment in the Orbiter and its payloads.

The aft fuselage structure carries the main engine thrust loads to the mid fuselage and, during the first phase of launch, to the External Tank. Because of the extreme stresses, the aft fuselage is covered in machined aluminium panels over a truss-type internal structure of 28 titanium struts reinforced with boron epoxy. The aft fuselage consists of three main sections: a primary thrust structure which supports the Space Shuttle main engines (SMME), their turbo pumps and the connections between the Orbiter and its External Tank; a secondary internal structure of titanium and aluminium alloy to support the tail, Orbital Manoeuvring System and the 136 square foot rear body flap; and, finally, an outer shell that contains all the equipment aft of the payload bay and forward of the SSME nozzle's heat-shielding bulkhead.

The wings are constructed with a corrugated spar and truss-type rib internal arrangement and a skin of stiffened aluminium alloy. The trailing edge of each wing incorporates a two-part hydraulically-controlled elevon to control the Orbiter's pitch and roll in aerodynamic flight. The elevons are constructed out of aluminium honeycomb and titanium.

The vertical tail is a two-spar multi-rib, stiffened skin box of aluminium alloy bolted to the aft fuselage on the two main spars. The combined rudder and split air-brake assembly is constructed out of aluminium honeycomb panels for lightness and strength.

The rudder/split air-brake is locked into position for launch flush with the tail, the air-brake only becomes operational during the final phases of re-entry and landing at speeds below Mach 10. The rudder can be activated only at speeds below Mach 5.

Extensive use of aluminium in the Orbiter's construction (rather than more specialized heat-resistant metals) calls for an extremely efficient form of heat shielding. The type of thermal protection used on the X-20 was rejected early in the Orbiter's development because of weight and complexity. Ablatives as used on X-15-A2 were also discounted because NASA insisted on a material which would last for at least 100 flights before replacement. Such a material would also have to be effective enough to protect the Orbiter's aluminium skin for 500 missions! The answer came after lengthy investigations as an insulation material the heat conducting properties of which are so poor that when one side is heated to white heat the other side is cool enough to touch with bare hands. Four types of insulation were developed to cover the airframe of the Orbiter. One comes as blocks of silica fibre with a glassy coating, another as flexible sheets of nylon felt coated with silicon. The 'tiles', which are generally around 1 inch thick by 8 inches square, protect the aluminium skin from temperatures up to 650 °C; the flexible insulation only 371 °C. This latter coating gives the upper part of the Orbiter its white colour which also serves to reflect solar radiation. The third type of insulation is a high-temperature variation of the tiles described above, with a different coating to protect both the bottom of the spacecraft and leading edges of the tail plane up to 1260 °C. The higher temperature tiles are instantly recognisable by their semi-gloss black finish. In total more than 32,000 tiles are used to cover the surface of the Orbiter. The nose and leading edge of the wings which receive the greatest frictional heat during re-entry are covered with a reinforced carbon material (carbon cloth impregnated with additional carbon, then heat treated and coated with silicon carbide) that protects them from temperatures as high as 1650 °C.

Each of the Orbiter's three main engines, developed by the Marshall Space Flight Centre and built by Rockwell's Rocketdyne Division, is an advanced oxygen/hydrogen-fuelled rocket engine designed specifically to meet the requirements of the Space Shuttle programme. Burning the propellants at a high pressure (3,000 psi) provides maximum thrust within a compact unit. The Space Shuttle Main Engines (SSME) each develop twice the thrust of the J-2 engine, which powered the second and third stage of the Saturn V/Apollo vehicle. Unlike early rocket engines, which were used only once, each SSME is designed for seven and one half hours of operation over a life span of one hundred missions. Maintenance performed between flights uses techniques similar to those employed by commercial airlines to lower the cost per flight. Fourteen feet tall and eight feet in diameter at the flare of the nozzle 'bell', each produces 375,000 lb of thrust at the rated power level used for most launches and 470,000 lb of thrust in the vacuum of space. The thrust can be varied from 65 to 109 per cent of rated power to meet the different requirements of the launch from ground to orbit.

Mounted on the Orbiter's aft fuselage in a tri-

angular pattern, the three engines can swivel 10.5 degrees up and down and 8.5 degrees from side to side during flight to change the direction of thrust, with the two SRBs assisting during the first two minutes of flight. The SSME's continue to burn for six minutes after SRB jettison, each minute drawing about 47,000 gallons of liquid hydrogen and 17,000 gallons of liquid oxygen from the expendable External Tank.

The liquid propellants react with an igniting device to burn in two stages. In the first stage of ignition the fuel is only partially burned, at a relatively low temperature in 'pre-burners', and at the second stage completely burned at high temperature in the main combustion chamber or nozzle of each engine. The propellants (liquid hydrogen and liquid oxygen) are fed to the igniters under high pressure by turbine pumps driven by hot gases from the pre-burners. The operating pressure on the main combustion chamber is 3,000 psi, four times that of the Saturn V first stage engine, as it burns at 3515 °C.

Each SSME is controlled through a primary and back-up computer that monitors its operation. They compare the SSME's actual performance with its programmed performance fifty times a second. The computers automatically correct any problems or, failing that, shut down the engine. In addition they also receive commands from the Orbiter's guidance and navigation computers for engine start, throttle changes and shut down.

In addition to the SSME's, two smaller, 6,000 lb thrust, Orbital Manoeuvring Engines (OMEs) in external pods to the left and right of the upper main engine, accelerate the Orbiter to orbital velocity after the SSME's shut down and the External Tank drops away. They also provide the necessary thrust to change orbits, rendezvous with other spacecraft and slow the Orbiter down for a return to Earth. Unlike SSMEs the OMEs burn monomethyl hydrazine as a fuel and nitrogen tetroxide as an oxidiser, which ignite on contact when mixed, the technical term for this type of fuel being hypergolic. Propellants are force fed to the engines from separate pairs of tanks in each pod, by pressure derived from a tank containing gaseous helium.

The two OMEs can be fired separately or together and can be swivelled plus or minus 8 degrees to control the Orbiter's direction. They are designed to be reusable for 100 missions and are capable of 1000 starts and fifteen hours of continuous firing.

Small RCS thrusters in the Orbiter's nose and on each Orbital Manoeuvring System (OMS) engine pod near the tail provide both attitude control in space and precision velocity changes for the final phases of rendezvous and docking in orbit. As with the X-15, the RCS also combine with

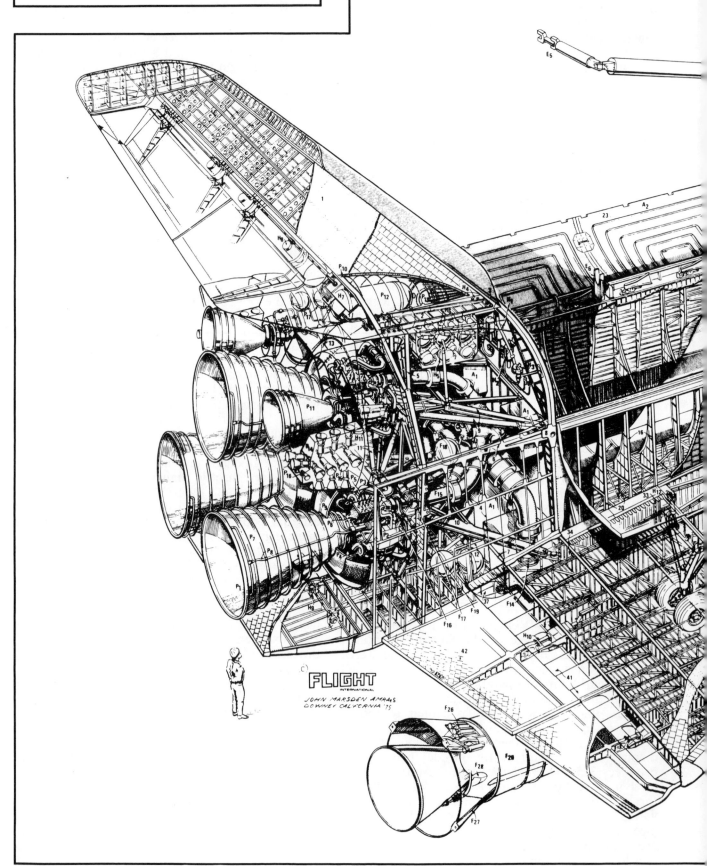

FLIGHT
INTERNATIONAL

JOHN MARSDEN AMRAeS
DOWNEY CALIFORNIA '75

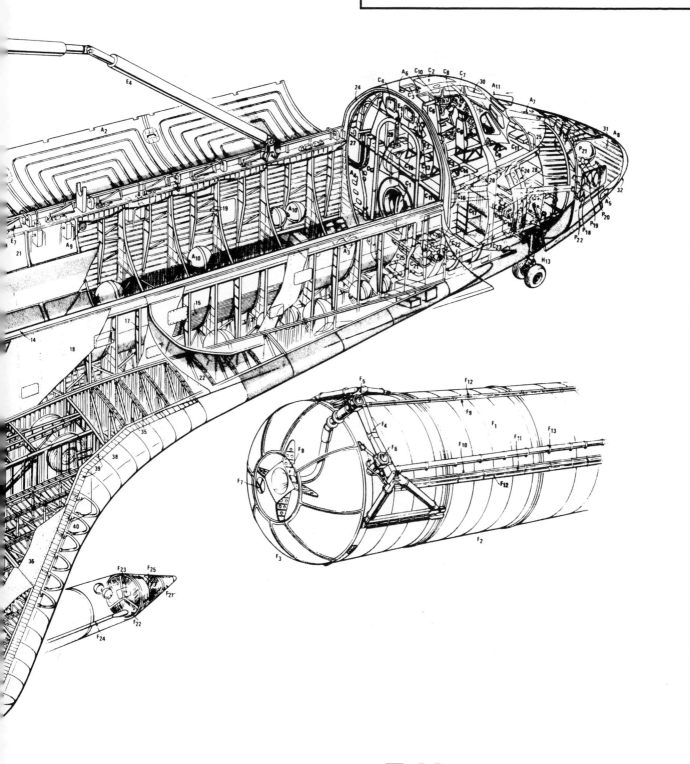

Orbiter cutaway

Preceding pages: A cutaway of the Orbiter, Solid Rocket Boosters and the External Tank, showing the STS in an early development stage. (Courtesy of Flight International) 4/13

Structure and general

1 Two-spar fin torsion box, integrally stiffened skin panels
2 Fin base rib, integrally machined
3 Multi-bolt fin/fuselage attachment fittings
4 Engine support/thrust structure
5 Main engine thrust and fin support canted frame, integrally machined
6 Shoulder longeron
7 Wing spar carry-through structure
8 Upper fuselage attachment fitting, also used for hoist attachment
9 Upper thrust beams, titanium machined with boron epoxy-reinforced welded-on end fittings
10 Lower thrust beams
11 Machined and diffusion-bonded titanium bracing structure
12 Keel beams
13 Aluminium honeycomb heat-shield, thermally insulated
14 Mid-fuselage payload bay shoulder longeron
15 Electrical cable tray
16 Machined, integrally stiffened frames
17 Between-frame machined skin stiffeners
18 Integrally stiffened aluminium skin panels
19 Truss bracing
20 Payload bay wing carry-through structure
21 Payload bay lining insulation panels
22 Payload-bay door, conventional skin and stringer construction (two doors, four panels)
23 Radiator panels (two per side)

24 Forward fuselage crew module
25 Integrally stiffened machined frames and skin for inner cone (crew module is self-contained unit, housed in aerodynamic shell)
26 Cabin support links, total 12
27 Rear pressure bulkhead
28 Forward pressure bulkhead
29 Crew entry door
30 Machined window frames and thermal-resistant transparencies
31 Forward unpressurized nose section
32 Reinforced carbon-carbon nose-cap
33 Wing/fuselage multi-bolt attachment fittings
34 Corrugated-web wing spars
35 Built-up, multi-braced and capped wing ribs
36 Rivetted stringer, upper and lower wing-skin panels
37 Wing/fuselage 'stub' structure (electrical and hydraulic connection panels)
38 Detachable leading-edge structure, reinforced carbon-carbon skin panels
39 Leading-edge access panels (upper and lower)
40 Heat-resisting surface insulation along entire leading-edge spar, with built-in thermal barrier
41 Sliding elevon shrouds, also give access to elevon controls and jacks
42 Entire structure covered in HRSI and LRSI tiles

Environmental control and life support

C1 Access door to payload bay or Spacelab when carried

C2 Emergency exit, first two Orbiters only
C3 Upper observation windows
C4 Rearward-facing observation windows
C5 Commander's station
C6 Pilot's station
C7 Flight control panels (automatic control and manual override)
C8 Hand controller, both sides
C9 Rudder pedals, both sides
C10 Air-brake 'thrust' controller (both sides)
C11 Avionic consoles
C12 Toilet and hygiene
C13 Galley
C14 Access via floor hatch to lower deck, both sides
C15 Airlock
C16 Ladder to lower deck
C17 Four-berth sleeping bunks
C18 Cabin heat-exchanger and water separator
C19 Fan
C20 Waste-water tanks
C21 Drinking and domestic water tanks
C22 Avionics-bay heat-exchanger and fan
C23 Avionics and instrument cooling ducts
C24 Return-air ducts to cabin fans
C25 Capsule and payload-bay venting ducts (nitrogen purged, vented rearwards)

Fuel system

F1 Hydrogen tank (oxygen tank forward)
F2 Integrally stiffened aluminium skin structure supported on frames
F3 Machined end dome
F4 Rear External Tank/Orbiter attachment cradle
F5 Hydrogen-fed pressurization line

F6 Oxygen-feed pressurization line
F7 Manhole cover
F8 Anti-vortex baffle
F9 Hydrogen tank pressure line
F10 Oxygen tank pressure line
F11 Oxygen recirculating line
F12 Electrical conduit
F13 External pipe support, sliding ball on Teflon-coated surface to accommodate shrinkage
F14 Orbiter oxygen pull-off umbilical connector (hydrogen on other side)
F15 Hydrogen main fuel-feed pipe
F16 Oxygen umbilical panel (hydrogen on other side)
F17 Oxygen tank fill and drain pipe (hydrogen on other side)
F18 APU fuel tanks (three)
F19 Helium tanks (four) used for pneumatic systems, valve-actuation and tank-purging
F20 Solid-fuel rocket booster, one each side
F21 Ribbon-type drogue chute (four)
F22 Recovery parachute (three)
F23 Navigation stowage and thrust-vector system access
F24 Cable tunnel
F25 Forward separation motors, 15,000lb thrust each
F26 Rear separation motors, 15,000lb thrust each
F27 Rear skirt and launch support cone
F28 Contoured expansion nozzle, 8 degree omni-axial gimbal capability

Payload-handling equipment
E1 Payload-handling station
E2 Rendezvous and docking system
E3 Payload specialist's station
E4 Payload manipulating arm
E5 Mating adaptor
E6 Manipulator arm rest
E7 Payload retention guide, electrically actuated
E8 Payload mounting trunnion

Propulsion, main engines and orbital manoeuvre system
P1 Rocketdyne liquid-propellant, throttleable main engine, one of three
P2 Gimbal actuator (two per engine) ± 10.5° pitch, ± 8.5° yaw
P3 Low-pressure turbopump (liquid hydrogen) mounting
P4 High-pressure hydrogen turbopump
P5 High-pressure oxygen turbopump
P6 Engine controller
P7 Thrust nozzle
P8 Nozzle cooling pipes
P9 Heatshield
P10 Orbital manoeuvring system engine packs (both sides inter-connected)
P11 OMS main engine (6,000 lb thrust in vacuum) one of two, electro-mechanical gimbal-actuated
P12 OMS propellant tanks containing nitrogen tetroxide and monomethyl hydrazine
P13 Helium bottle to pressurize OMS propellants
P14 Orbiter reaction-control system (RCS)
P15 Primary bipropellant thrusters (879 lb in vacuum), 12 per side
P16 Vernier thrusters (25 lb in vacuum), one each side
P17 RCS propellant tanks containing nitrogen tetroxide and monomethyl hydrazine
P18 Forward RCS propulsion units (three)
P19 Fixed thrusters (total 14)
P20 Vernier thrusters (total 2)
P21 RCS forward propellant tanks
P22 Ground servicing receptacle

Avionics, electrical and radio
A1 Rear avionics bay, one of three
A2 Electrically deployed payload-bay doors and radiators
A3 Orbiter electrical fuel cell (total three)
A4 Crew module electrical connecting panels to payload bay
A5 Static and temperature probes (normally retracted except for approach and landing)
A6 S-band antenna
A7 L-band antenna
A8 Ku-band antenna
A9 Floodlight (three per side)
A10 Hydrogen/oxygen fuel cells
A11 Transparency cover for star-tracker

Hydraulics
H1 One of three hydraulic reservoirs serving three independent systems
H2 Pump (three) 3,000 lb/sq in variable delivery
H3 Sundstrand APU (one of three)
H4 APU exhaust ducts
H5 Water boilers and coolers (one of three)
H6 Boiler blow-off outlets
H7 Rudder/air-brake actuator unit
H8 Rotary actuator (one of four)
H9 Body-flap actuators (total three) − 11.7° + 22.5°
H10 Eleven actuators (two per side, total four) − 40° + 15°
H11 Main engine gimbal actuating jacks (two per engine) and control valves (three)
H12 Hydraulically actuated anti-skid device, main under-carriage, and up-lock (all three legs of free-fall design)
H13 Nose undercarriage, hydraulically steered

the Orbiter's own aerodynamic control surfaces to control its flight attitude during re-entry into the atmosphere and at high altitude. In the nose of each Orbiter are 14 primary RCS jets, each of 870 lb thrust, and two vernier engines of 25 lb thrust for fine tuning. Aft in each of the two OMS pods, 12 primaries and two verniers share a similar location to the OMS engine. Their propellants are the same as the OMS engines, and although the aft 12 thrusters have their own tanks, they can also draw, if needed, on those of the larger engines. Each of the primary RCS engines is designed for 100 missions, 50,000 starts and 20,000 seconds of cumulative firing, each vernier engine for 100 missions, 500,000 starts and 125,000 seconds of firing. To assist instruments on board the Orbiter's payload bay that require precision pointing to study stars or Earth features, the Orbiter's own computers can fire the vernier RCS thrusters to maintain a pointing accuracy of within half a degree.

The internal power for the Orbiter is generated by electrical and hydraulic systems. Hydraulic power is generated by three Auxiliary Propulsion Units (APUs) driven at 74,160 revolutions per minute by the decomposition of hydrazine fuel as it passes over a catalyst bed. Hydraulic actuators move the elevons (wing flaps), body flap, rudder/split air-brake, main engine valves and swivelling mechanisms, landing gear, wheel brakes, nose wheel steering gear and devices that disconnect the propellant lines from the external tank to the Orbiter on separation.

Electricity is generated by three fuel cell power plants. Developed during the two-man Gemini programme, fuel cells generate direct current through the electrochemical reaction of hydrogen and oxygen. Electrical power needed may vary from 20 to 30 kilowatts during the ten minute launch phase and the half hour or so of re-entry and landing.

The Shuttle's electricity-producing fuel cells work on the 'Hydrox' (hydrogen/oxygen) principle. Ordinary Hydrox batteries, when on charge, work by decomposing water in a cell. The resultant hydrogen and oxygen is then chemically 'fixed' by coatings on the cell plates. Under discharge conditions the electric current produced is a result of the recombination of hydrogen and oxygen into water.

The fuel cell eliminates the 'on charge' phase. Liquid hydrogen and liquid oxygen is fed via preheaters, which warm the hydrogen and oxygen from extremely low temperatures to 40 °F or higher, to the electrodes (negative cathode and positive anode). There, in contact with an electrolyte and a catalyst, the creation of a difference in potential between the electrodes yields an electric current. The two gases combine to form water as a useful by-product of the reaction.

Amongst the major consumers of electrical power on board the Orbiter are the experiments carried aloft in the payload bay. This bay, with payload attachment points along its full length, is able to accommodate up to five unmanned satellites or experiments of various shapes and sizes on a single mission. The Orbiter supplies them with electrical power from its own fuel cells together with heating and cooling, data transmission or storage and displays for the payload specialists on board and communications with ground stations.

Using radar the Orbiter can rendezvous from 350 miles away with an 'active' satellite, or from about 12 miles with a 'passive' one.

Voice communications, television signals and scientific and engineering data is transmitted from and received at the Orbiter via between 17 and 23 antennas (depending on the mission).

Satellites can be lifted out of the payload bay, or captured and returned therein by means of a manipulator arm controlled remotely from the rear of the Orbiter's flight deck. The story of the RMS arm began in 1969, when representatives of the Canadian government met NASA officials to discuss their nation's involvement in the field of space technology. Following a Memorandum of Understanding signed by both parties in 1974, Canada was assigned development of this vital component of the Shuttle space transportation system. Under the financial and administrative auspices of the National Research Council of Canada, a consortium of companies led by Spar Aerospace Products Ltd was contracted to proceed with development and construction of the RMS.

Designed to work in a weightless and airless environment, much of the RMS development and testing had to rely on accurate computer models of its performance, and simple testing in two dimensions only over a frictionless air-cushion flat floor.

The RMS arm is 50ft long, and has six rotating joints each with six independent electric motors, and is attached to the Orbiter by a 'shoulder' joint. It is protected from the heat of direct sunlight exposure by gold covered mylar film, and a white thermal blanket. Heaters keep the motors warm when the RMS is in the shade.

Inside the flight deck the RMS operator controls the arm's movements via two hand controls. The left control, mounted below the right-hand (facing rearwards) payload bay window, moves the RMS arm forward or back, or to either side. A right hand control maintains the speed of operation when moved from left to right, and when pushed forward or back moves the RMS arm up or down. A button beneath the right hand control activates the grapple 'end effector' which can grasp or release a satellite either in the payload bay, or floating outside. Progress is relayed to the operator via the windows (line of sight) and by two TV monitors above his (or her) head.

The Solid Rocket Boosters stand just over 150 ft tall from nozzle to nose and 12 ft in diameter. These two rockets are attached during the Shuttle's first launch phase to the external tank (which is slightly taller and over twice as wide) which in turn is attached to the underside of the Orbiter. The SRBs are the largest solid fuelled rockets in the world and the first designed for reuse. They are assembled from seamless segments of half-inch thick steel lined with heavy insulation by McDonnell Douglas Astronautics Company of Huntington Beach, California, who besides manufacturing the casings also check and refurbish the structures after launch and recovery. The casings are filled with propellant with a hollow central core at the Thiokol Chemical Corporation's plant, Brigham City, Utah, and then shipped in segments on railway trucks to the Vehicle Assembly Building (VAB) Kennedy Space Centre, Florida, for assembly.

The propellant for each SRB is a mixture of aluminium powder as fuel, aluminium perchlorate powder as an oxidizer, iron oxide as catalyst to speed up the burning rate and a polymer that serves as both a binder and fuel. The final compound will only ignite under extreme heat and is not sensitive to static, friction or impact. This is a strict requirement of NASA from a safety point of view, with regard to assembly and storage.

The segments which make up each SRB are filled with this hard, rubber-like fuel from individually processed batches of raw materials in order to minimise any possible thrust imbalance between a pair of SRBs on any one Shuttle flight. In this manner SRBs are essentially manufactured in pairs.

At launch, once the SSMEs have ignited and run up to full power, the Orbiter's computers verify their correct operation before a small rocket motor inside each SRB fires to ignite the 1,100,000 lb of propellant in each booster. In under 0.15 second flames spread up the hollow insides of each booster across the exposed inner face of the propellant. As it burns at over 3,200 °C hot combustion gases are forced out of the exit nozzle thrusting the SRB upwards. The combined thrust of the two SRBs (5,200,000 lb) supplement the Orbiter's own 1,125,000 lb thrust SSME engines, the hold down clamps on the launch pad are released and the Shuttle lifts off.

At just over a minute after launch the Shuttle enters a period known as 'Max q' which signifies maximum dynamic pressure. To reduce the stresses on the structure at this point the SSMEs throttle back. At the same time the SRB propellant, which is shaped to reduce the thrust briefly at 62 seconds into the flight, assists the Shuttle during the critical transonic period of maximum aerodynamic force.

Changes to the Shuttle's flight path attitude can be accomplished by swivelling or gimballing both the SSMEs and the 12 ft diameter SRB nozzles on commands from the Orbiter's own guidance computer. The SRB nozzles can be gimballed hydraulically up to 6.65 degrees.

The outer casing of each SRB is covered with a layer of white insulation to protect it from aerodynamic frictional heating during launch, and the plume of the SSME's exhausts once jettisoned. At that point, with their fuel exhausted the SRBs are severed from their connections with the External Tank by electronically detonated explosive bolts. A clean break is assisted by eight small SRB separation thrusters, four near the nose of each booster and four just above the nozzle, operating after separation from the Shuttle. The two SRBs continue to climb under their own momentum following a parabolic trajectory before falling back to Earch once more. Almost four minutes from ignition, the SRBs reach a speed of 2,900 mph before atmospheric drag slows them down sufficiently to allow deployment of drogues at 3 miles altitude, followed by three main parachutes each 115 ft in diameter. Fired from the nose of each SRB on a signal from a barometric pressure switch the parachutes enable the SRBs to descend to a splashdown at 60 mph.

As the empty SRB casing hits the water nozzle first, air is trapped in the nose to float it upright until one of two special NASA recovery ships, summoned by a radio beacon and flashing light, attaches tow lines and tows it back to Kennedy Space Centre. Then the booster is once more dismantled into segments and sent back via rail to Thiokol and McDonnell Douglas. There the SRBs are cleaned out, inspected for cracks, pressure tested, relined, reloaded with fuel and sent back to Kennedy Space Centre.

When the SRB nozzle and combustion 'throat' have been relined with ablative insulation, the parachutes washed and repacked, the complete booster is ready to fly again. The main structural casing, directional controls and electrical systems are designed for twenty flights, the parachute systems for ten.

Made of 2 inch thick aluminium alloy, the giant External Tank is the second element of the Shuttle system to be jettisoned on ascent to orbit, and the only significant part to be used only once.

Built by Martin Marietta of Denver Colorado, the External Tank contains the liquid hydrogen and liquid oxygen that fuels the Shuttle's three SSMEs. The External Tanks are assembled at NASA's old Saturn V plant near New Orleans, from where they are shipped by barge across the Gulf of Mexico to the Kennedy Space Centre.

Essentially the External Tank is two propellant tanks connected by a cylindrical ring that houses its control electronics. The tip of the tank curves up towards a pointed lightning rod, necessary in view of the frequent thunderstorms around

An External Tank (this one destined for use by *Columbia*) being hoisted from the VAB transfer aisle to its check-out stand in hig-bay number 2. (NASA)

Cape Canaveral. The uppermost tank is loaded with 140,000 gallons of liquid oxygen at a temperature of −147 °C and weighs 1,330,000 lb at launch. The lower, larger, tank contains 380,000 gallons of liquid hydrogen at −251 °C. This weighs only 223,000 lb because liquid hydrogen is 16 times lighter than oxygen.

The External Tank's outside surface is insulated from the sub-tropical climate of Florida with a spray on polyurethane foam that reduces heat build-up in the tanks that would otherwise cause evaporation of the propellants. The insulation also helps prevent the build-up during pre-launch preparations of ice that could break off in flight and damage the thermal tiles on the Orbiter's underside. In addition, a layer of ablative material protects the tank from heating during the Shuttle's journey into space.

Horizontal baffles in the oxygen tank prevent sloshing that could, if unchecked, throw the Shuttle out of control, while anti-vortex baffles, shaped like propeller blades, in both tanks prevent the formation of whirlpools that could let gases, rather than liquid propellants, into the 17 inch diameter pipes that carry 64,000 gallons a minute to the engines. Propellants are fed to the engine pumps by the pressure of gases formed by controlled boiling of the super-cold liquified fuel in the tanks and, during flight, by vaporized propellant gases routed back from the engines into the tanks. To save costs, most of the propellant controls and valves are located in the Orbiter rather than the expendable External Tank.

After the SRBs have burnt out and separated at 31 miles altitude, the Orbiter with its SSMEs still firing, carries the External Tank to near orbital velocity at just over 70 miles above the Earth. Then, eight minutes after lift-off, the empty tank is jettisoned to re-enter the atmosphere in a planned trajectory ending in the Indian Ocean. Venting of unused liquid oxygen during descent controls the rate of tumbling to prevent 'skipping' of the tank as it hits the tenuous upper level of atmosphere, and ensures that the bulk of the External Tank will break up and fall within designated ocean areas clear of regular shipping lanes.

In case a serious problem should occur during the launch phase, contingency procedures have been devised to get the Orbiter, its crew and payload back safely on the ground.

If a failure occured during the first four minutes the Shuttle would continue on up to an altitude of 60 miles. There the atmosphere would be sufficiently thin to enable the Orbiter and External Tank to 'about turn' and execute a Return to Launch Site (RTLS) manoeuvre. This would be the most dangerous of the abort options. With its main

The X-24B was one of the attractions at the 1976 American Bicentennial exhibition at the Kennedy Space Centre, Florida. Seen here behind the launch control building, the red tower in the background is the top of a Saturn V mobile launch tower.

As the lifting body research programme continued, the Summer of 1969 saw NASA's moon landing goal fulfilled as Apollo 11 achieved the objective set by President Kennedy in May 1961, 'to land a man on the moon and return him safely to the Earth'. (NASA)

From a pilot's point of view, a conventional landing was infinitely preferable and more dignified than a splash-down at sea.

America's first scientist astronaut Harrison 'Jack' Schmitt seen here on the moon with the US flag and the Earth in the background. He was, in effect, the forerunner of the Shuttle mission- or payload-specialist. (NASA)

The Apollo moon landing flights ended with the spectacular night launch of Apollo 17 in December 1972. (NASA)

The Skylab space laboratory, placed in orbit in 1973 on top of the last Saturn V, was visited by three crews of astronauts until abandoned in 1974. Three of the men who flew Skylab – Paul Weitz, Owen Garriott and Jack Lousma – were to remain with NASA to fly later Shuttle missions.

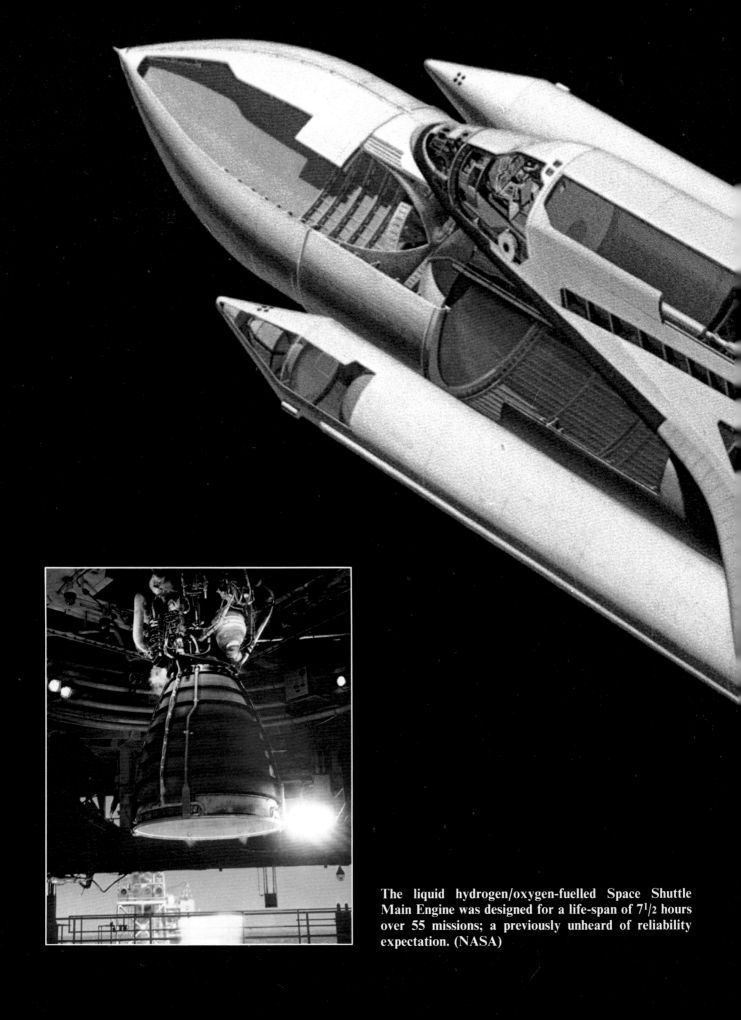

The liquid hydrogen/oxygen-fuelled Space Shuttle Main Engine was designed for a life-span of $7\frac{1}{2}$ hours over 55 missions; a previously unheard of reliability expectation. (NASA)

By mid-1972 the basic design of the Shuttle system has been agreed, with twin solid rocket boosters, external expendible fuel tanks, and a high cross-range winged orbiter attached. (Rockwell International)

The Apollo II Service Module burning-up as planned during re-entry. This sequence highlights the more acceptable economy of a Shuttle concept in which a reusable vehicle returns safely to Earth. (NASA)

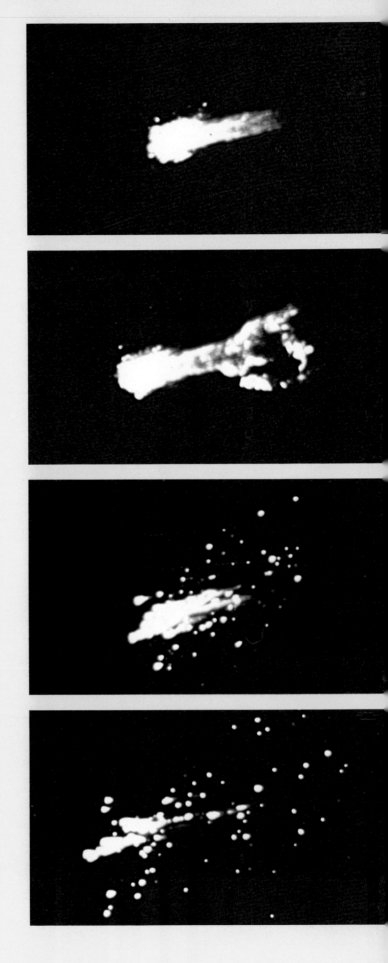

engines still firing, the disabled or damaged Orbiter would slow its 'tail first' velocity to zero, then accelerate nose first back towards Kennedy Space Centre. At a point where the Orbiter had gained enough energy to cut-off its engines and make a glide approach, the SSMEs would be shut down and the External Tank jettisoned into the Atlantic. A contingency computer 'abort guidance programme' would control critical energy management manoeuvres until the pilot and commander took over for landing on the Kennedy runway almost twenty minutes after launch.

Alternatively, the Shuttle could continue out over the Atlantic and make an emergency landing at Rota Naval Air Base in Spain, one of several such sites across the world equipped with Orbiter recovery facilities and a long runway. In a mission aborted during the last half of the launch phase, there would be enough momentum to power the Orbiter in a sub-orbital trajectory to land at either Edwards or White Sands Missile Base in California.

The three-level crew compartment of the Shuttle is constructed from aluminium alloy plate, with integral stiffening stringers and internal framing welded together to create a fully pressure-tight vessel for the crew. The compartment has a mid deck side hatch for normal entry and exit before launch and after landing, a hatch into the airlock from the mid deck, and a hatch through the aft bulkhead into the payload bay for extra-vehicular activity (EVA) and payload bay access.

Redundant pressure window panes are provided in the windshield, and in the overhead aft viewing and side hatch windows. The left-hand upper window provides for an emergency exit route. The 300 or so openings in the pressure module that form the crew compartment are sealed during manufacture with plates and fittings. A large removable panel in the aft bulkhead provides access to the crew compartment interior during initial fabrication and assembly, and provides for subsequent airlock installation and removal. Equipment supported in the crew cabin includes the environmental control life support system (ECLSS), avionics, guidance and navigation (G & N), displays and controls (D & C), navigation startracker base, and crew accommodation for sleeping, waste management, seating and the galley.

The pressurized crew compartment is supported within the forward fuselage at only four attachment points, to minimize the thermal conductivity between them. The crew compartment is covered in several layers of gold-covered mylar insulation also for this purpose. The two major attachment points are at the aft end of the crew compartment at the flight deck section floor level. The vertical load reaction link is on the centreline of the forward bulkhead. The lateral load reaction links are on the lower segment of the aft bulkhead.

The crew compartment is configured to

accommodate a crew of four on the flight deck and three in the mid deck. (The crew cabin arrangement consists of a flight deck, mid deck, and lower level equipment bay.)

The crew compartment is pressurized to 760 plus or minus 10 millimetres of mercury (mm Hg) (14.7 plus or minus 0.2 pounds per square inch) and is maintained during normal flight conditions at an 80 per cent nitrogen and 20 per cent oxygen composition by the ECLSS, which provides a shirt-sleeve environment for the flight crew. Total volume with the airlock installed in the mid deck is 2,325 cubic feet. If the airlock is mounted outside in the payload bay the crew compartment cabin volume is 2,625 cubic feet. Temperature during flight is maintained at around 70 °F. Humidity is automatically regulated and carbon dioxide continually filtered out along with other airborne impurities.

The 67 cubic feet flight deck is the uppermost compartment of the crew compartments. The commander's and pilot's work-stations are positioned side-by-side in the forward portion of the flight deck. These stations have controls and displays for maintaining autonomous control of the vehicle throughout all mission phases. There is a conventional pilot/co-pilot arrangement of forward facing seats for the Shuttle commander (on the left) and pilot (in the right-hand seat). TV-like displays, and duplicate sets of hand controls, pedals, levers and switches enable either astronaut, if needed, to fly the Shuttle alone.

The Shuttle's flight is controlled by what aerospace engineers call 'fly by wire'; unlike the X-15, there are no direct rods, cables or hydraulic linkages at all. Instead, movements of the pilot's hand controls and pedals are converted into electronic signals and routed through computers. There is, by implication, no 'feedback' from the flight control surfaces to the astronaut via his controls, although the controls are spring-loaded to be self-centering. The computers relay the signals to the engines and attitude thrusters during launch, orbital operations and re-entry, or to the hydraulic actuators that operate the eleven flaps, rudder and air brake during descent and landing. Data on the Orbiter's performance, attitude, position, acceleration and directional headings pass through the computers to the cockpit TV displays and instruments from rate gyros, star-trackers, thrusters, inertial measuring units, accelerometers, air-speed probes, radar altimeters, and air navigation and microwave landing systems.

Four computers process the combined data simultaneously, whilst a fifth back-up computer stands by waiting to cut in if any one of the other four should fail. Each computer compares its computations with those of the others and agreed-upon commands are sent to the appropriate flight control actuator. If there is a disagreement between the computers they carry out a 'vote' and commands from the out-voted computers are ignored.

Directly behind and to the sides of the commander and pilot centreline are the mission and payload specialists' seats. The mission specialist station is located on the right-hand side of the Orbiter and has controls and displays for monitoring systems, communications management, payload operation management, and payload/Orbiter interface operations. The payload specialist station is located on the left-hand side of the Orbiter and contains further controls and displays. At this station there is a removable panel section for instrumentation that can be fitted prior to launch to meet the peculiar requirements of certain payloads. A caution and warning display alerts the crew members to malfunctions in the payload components.

In addition to the mission and payload specialist stations, there are two others facing back into the payload bay with two windows. Facing into the payload bay on the left of the flight deck is the Orbiter's rendezvous and docking station, a position usually occupied by the commander, containing radar displays and controls for precision manoeuvring the Orbiter to another spacecraft. To the right, still facing the payload bay, is the payload handling station, with controls to manipulate, display, release and capture payloads. The pilot would normally occupy this station to open or close the payload bay doors, deploy cooling radiators, operate the RMS arm and also the payload bay lights and TV cameras. Two TV screens to the upper right display live pictures from any one of the cameras outside.

The forward flight deck, including the centre console and seats, is approximately 24 square feet in area, and with the side console and displays added another 3½ square feet can be obtained. The aft flight deck is of approximately 40 square feet area.

The commander and pilot seat system has controls for electrically adjusting the seat forward, backwards, up and down, and for support during vertical launch and horizontal flight and 'tilt' for back angle positioning. (For the first four engineering test flights both commander and pilot would use static, non-adjustable ejection seats.) Each seat also has an inertia reel restraint which allows the astronauts mobility for performing tasks, and capability for locking. The seats accommodate mounting of a rotational hand controller, and stowage of in-flight and emergency equipment. The seats have removable cushions and pads.

Mission and payload specialist seats are not adjustable, but do have mounting provision for emergency equipment, communication, biomedical monitoring, and controls. A mechanism is provided to release the seat from the flight deck or mid deck for stowage during zero-g orbital flight. The specialist seats have restraint devices and controls to lock and unlock the seat back for tilt change, and removable cushions and pads. These seats can be folded down for stowage in flight to 11 inches in height.

Directly beneath the flight deck is the mid deck. Access between the mid deck and flight deck is achieved through two inter deck hatches 40 inches square. A ladder attached to the left inter deck access hatch allows easy passage between the two levels in 1g conditions. The mid deck provides crew accommodation, and three avionics equipment bays. The two forward avionics bays utilize the complete width of the cabin and extend 39 inches into the mid deck from the forward bulkhead. The aft bay extends into the mid deck 39 inches from the aft bulkhead on the right-hand side of the airlock (looking towards the 'nose'). Just forward of the 'waste management system', or toilet, on the left-hand side of the airlock is the side hatch. The mid deck completely stripped has approximately 160 square feet of floorspace, of which 100 square feet can be usefully employed by the astronauts with their equipment.

The side main hatch in the mid deck is used for normal crew entrance and exit and may be operated from within the crew cabin mid deck or externally. The pressure-tight hatch is secured to the cabin access tunnel, which extends two ft from the outer airframe of the Orbiter to the crew compartment inside. Employing hinges, torque tubes and support fittings, the hatch opens outwards 90 degrees 'down' with the Orbiter horizontal (or 90 degrees sideways with the Orbiter vertical). This main hatch is 40 inches in diameter, and has a 10 inch diameter clear view, three-pane window in its centre. The main hatch has a pressure tight seal which is compressed by the hatch latch mechanism when closed. A thermal barrier of Inconel wire mesh spring with ceramic fibre braided sleeve is installed between the reusable surface insulation tiles on the forward fuselage and the side hatch. Total weight of the hatch is 129 lb.

Four sleep stations (three horizontal, one vertical) and a galley (or a payload in lieu of a galley), can be installed on the mid deck; in addition, three seats can be installed on the mid deck floor of the same type as the specialists' seats on the flight deck. These seats are normally removed once in orbit and stowed during flight operations. Three further seats can be installed on the mid deck for rescue missions to another Orbiter stranded in space if the sleep stations are removed.

The galley includes an oven, hot and cold water dispensers for preparing freeze-dried foods, storage for seventy-four kinds of 'conventional' food and twenty beverages (excluding alcohol, expressly forbidden by NASA), places for drinking cups and eating utensils, a shelf for dining trays, a water tank and rubbish bins. Meals on board the Shuttle have been planned to be both pleasurable and nutritious. Experience gained during Mercury, Gemini and Apollo flights, with various kinds of food stuffs dispensed via toothpaste-type tubes, had led NASA to decide upon more tasty and attractive food for the Shuttle crews. NASA was no longer dealing with seasoned test pilots who would tolerate unattractive, bland and repetitive meals on a mission. Instead, a new breed of civilian astronaut who would be involved, to whom good food was important for both physical and mental wellbeing. As Skylab demonstrated in the early nineteen-seventies, the longer the flight, the more important mealtime becomes as a pleasurable interruption of the daily chores.

A typical daily menu on board the Shuttle could be — breakfast: sweet roll, scrambled eggs and sausages, fruit, cocoa or orange juice; lunch: soup, ham and cheese sandwich, stewed tomatoes, fruit, biscuits and tea; dinner: shrimp cocktail with dressing, steak, broccoli au gratin, strawberries with cream, biscuits and cocoa.

All the meals are planned so that an individual crewmember can have a different menu for six successive days. On the seventh day the cycle begins again. Dining can be either at a table fixed onto the galley, or from a food tray held in the lap or fixed to any convenient surface prepared with a velcro fastener. The 'toothpaste tubes' of Apollo are now replaced by conventional knives, forks and spoons. Surprisingly, even in zero g these utensils work almost as well as on earth, the food tending to stick to the utensils rather than floating about.

It is possible for a crewmember to assemble a meal for four in about five minutes, and to prepare it in an hour. Washing-up is accomplished using 'wet wipe' cloths.

Five types of food are carried on the Shuttle, they include: thermostabilized, heat-processed foods, canned or packaged in laminated foil pouches such as cheese spread, beef with barbeque sauce and tuna; intermediate moisture foods preserved by controlling the available moisture, such as dried fruit and cereals; freeze dried foods with all water removed such as strawberries, shrimp and bananas; rehydratable foods reconstituted with water, such as scrambled eggs, noodles and beverages; and finally, 'off the supermarket shelf' foods such as biscuits, fresh fruit, nuts, cakes etc.

On the delicate subject of lavatory facilities on board the Orbiter, NASA has introduced a marked improvement over the messy plastic bags and plumbing arrangements of early Apollo and Gemini spacecraft. For operational missions each Orbiter will carry aloft in its mid deck what amounts to a conventional lavatory, which differs in the substitution of a downwards air flow for the action of water and gravity. Facilities for male and female crew have been provided, and the entire

waste management facility is screened off from the rest of the mid deck for reasons of hygiene and privacy.

Sleeping arrangements on board operational Shuttle flights consist of four (maximum) cubicles in the mid deck. Sleeping bags are attached inside each cubicle, together with a privacy screen, reading light, air circulation fans and audio facilities. Although many astronauts, particularly those on board the Skylab space station of the early nineteen-seventies, found sleeping to be no problem ('just close your eyes and float', according to one astronaut), many preferred the security of being attached to a fixed point, eliminating the risk of bumping into static objects in the night!

Working in zero-g has several advantages. First, for engineers designing cabin layouts, it means that the walls and ceilings areas for stowing additional equipment and experiments. Secondly, moving heavy objects around becomes a simple task in zero-g, although mass remains the same and this must be remembered when an object is in motion and coming towards you! A zero-g workshop can also be more spacious, as crewmembers are no longer confined to the floor area for mobility. Against these advantages it must be remembered that objects cannot simply be placed in one area and remain in place, under the influence of gravity. If a tool or experiment is not attached it will simply float around and (invariably) get lost! The psychological importance of a visual 'up and down' reference must be retained in cabin design, as well as adequate hand holds, and air filters to remove floating particles from the breathed air.

Anna L. Fisher demonstrates the versatility of the Shuttle sleep restraints during mission 51A. Also pictured in this photograph are the mid deck stowage lockers. (NASA)

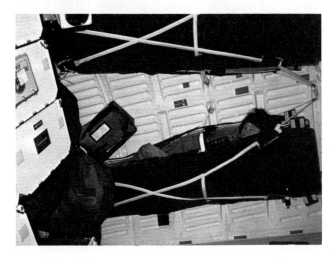

In the event of an in-flight emergency on board an Orbiter, crew transfer to the rescue ship can be accomplished in the following manner. The rescue astronaut will, using a Manned Manoeuvring Unit (MMU), transfer from the station-keeping 'rescue' Orbiter to the payload bay airlock of its crippled sister. Inside, non-spacesuited astronauts will, one at a time, climb inside a one-man pressurized ball-shaped personal rescue enclosure. Each PRE contains breathing equipment for the brief 10 minute flight back to the rescue ship in the safe custody of the rescue astronaut with his MMU. Several trips will be made depending on the number of crew to be rescued. Each PRE is pressurized by normal oxygen/nitrogen cabin air, which eliminates the need for pre-breathing pure oxygen. A rescue Orbiter will, prior to launch, have had its sleeping bunks removed in favour of additional seating facilities.

The mid deck areas also provide the crew with a storage volume of 140 cubic feet. Accommodations are included for maintenance, exercising, and data management. The floor of the mid deck contains removable panels that provide access to a 30 cubic feet third crew compartment level wherein the ECLSS equipment is located. This unit incorporates all the necessary fans, ducting, and lithium hydroxide air cleaning and revitalization equipment needed to keep the Orbiter's cabin environment healthy for the crew. Extra stowage space is also provided beneath the mid deck floor in the equipment bay. An opening in the forward ceiling of the mid deck provides access to the Orbiter's inertial measurement units.

Modular stowage lockers are used to store the flight crew's personal gear, mission necessary equipment, and experiments. The lockers are made out of sandwiched panels of Kevlar/epoxy and a non-metallic core. This reduces the weight by 83 per cent compared with all-aluminium lockers. This is a reduction of approximately 150lb. There are 42 identical boxes, 11 by 18 by 21 inches which can be used for storage.

A cylindrical airlock is located at the rear of the mid deck. This airlock has two air-tight hatches, on opposite sides to each other. Together with the airlock they permit the crew to conduct space-walks, or extra-vehicular activity (EVA). Flight crew members can transfer from the mid deck crew compartment into the payload bay via the airlock without depressurizing the entire Orbiter crew compartment. Normally, two space-suits, or, to be more precise, 'extra-vehicular mobility units' (EMUs) are stowed in the airlock. Each EMU is an integrated pressure assembly and life support system which provides the capability for a flight crewmember to leave the pressurized Orbiter crew compartment and work outside in the vacuum of space.

The Shuttle EMUs are significantly different from space suits used in Mercury, Gemini and Apollo. The upper torso section is constructed out of a rigid aluminium shell with jointed flexible arms. The lower section of waist, legs and feet attaches to the torso section at the waist with a pressure-sealing locking slip ring. Gloves and helmet are put on after the upper and lower sections of the suit. The EMU's life support system is an integral part of the upper torso section. A status display panel is permanently attached to the front of the torso section which continuously shows the astronaut the function of the EMU. In addition to the status display, an emergency oxygen supply is also carried on the chest section of the EMU.

Astronauts enter the airlock and don their respective EMUs. They then pre-breath pure oxygen to purge all the nitrogen from their bloodstream (a precaution against the 'bends' in the reduced pressure of the EMU). Once the pre-breathing has been completed, the astronauts close the mid deck airlock hatch, vent the air out into space, and open the second hatch to the payload bay.

The airlock is just under seven feet high and has an inside diameter of 5ft 3 inches. Hand rails, hand holds and foot restraints at various locations in the cabin, airlock and payload bays help the weightless astronaut to work and move about.

EMUs come in three different sizes — large, medium and small; sizes to suit the heaviest and tallest marine, right down to the most petite female scientist astronaut.

5 Enterprise

On 17 September 1976 the first Space Shuttle Orbiter, vehicle number 101, was rolled out from Rockwell's Palmdale assembly building to be christened *Enterprise,* the first of a proposed fleet of five space vehicles.

On hand to welcome *Enterprise* were NASA, State and Congressional officials together with guest celebrities. Following the ceremonies which attracted a great deal of media attention, *Enterprise* was moved by road trailer to the Hugh L. Dryden Flight Research Centre on 31 January 1977. The journey of just over 48 miles followed the same route taken by X-15-1 in its delivery journey almost two decades earlier. After years of development and testing, *Enterprise* was ready to prove to the world that the Shuttle really could fly.

Enterprise was to begin a series of glide flight drop tests in early 1977, carried aloft from the Dryden Flight Research Centre by a converted Boeing 747 airliner. The Boeing 'Shuttle Carrier Aircraft' (SCA) was purchased by NASA from American Airlines in the summer of 1974 and subsequently modified at the manufacturer's plant in Everett, Washington. The 231 ft long, four-engined jet aircraft was stripped of its seats and standard passenger accommodation, this being replaced by banks of equipment and instruments needed to monitor the two aircraft's performance during test flights. The Boeing's upper fuselage was reinforced around the three Orbiter attach-ment points to compensate for the *Enterprise's* weight and induced stresses. Three struts (or pylons), two aft and one forward, were added to the 747 SCA (now designated the NASA 905, or simply the 905 for short) these would connect to the *Enterprise's* underside at points close to its three undercarriage doors. Explosive bolts would enable a quick and clean separation at the right time. In addition to its role in the 'Approach to Landing Tests' (ALT) of *Enterprise,* the 905 would serve as a future ferry craft to transport the Orbiter fleet from the assembly and landing sites across the USA to the Kennedy Space Centre.

To install *Enterprise* on top of the 905, the giant Orbiter was moved into a specially construc-ted Mate-Demate Device (MDD). This gantry-like structure was one of three, the other two being at Kennedy Space Centre in Florida and at the USAF Base at Vandenburg, California. A lattice work of steel girders supported three 43 ton capacity hoists which would lift *Enterprise* off the ground and on to the 905's back. On 8 February 1977 two of the hoists were attached to the rear of *Enterprise's* fuselage, and the third above the Orbiter's nose. Slowly *Enterprise* was raised inch by inch off the ground. At four yards its undercarriage was retrac-ted, and then, at its maximum height, the 905 was rolled in underneath and *Enterprise* was lowered onto its three attachment points. The two aircraft were ready.

NASA had selected the first two *Enterprise* crews some time earlier. The commander of the first crew was Fred Haise, a civilian. He was selected by NASA for the astronaut programme as far back as April 1966, and served subsequently as back-up lunar module pilot for Apollos 8 and 11. Had the crew of Neil Armstrong, Edwin Aldrin and Mike Collins been replaced, for whatever reason, Fred Haise would have been the second man on the moon. Instead he became lunar module pilot on Apollo 13, the flight that had to be aborted when an oxygen tank exploded in the Apollo's Service Module and threatened the lives of Fred Haise and his fellow astronauts Jack Swigert and and Jim Lovell. On return to Earth, Fred Haise was assigned as back-up commander for Apollo 16.

Fred Haise's pilot was Charles Gordon Fullerton of the USAF. Since joining NASA from the abandoned Air Force Manned Orbiting Laboratory in September 1969 he served as a member of the support crew of both Apollo 14 and 17.

Assigned to command the second crew was X-15 veteran Joe Engle, then a Colonel in the USAF. After joining NASA in April 1966 he became a member of the Apollo 10 support crew, and the back-up lunar module pilot for Apollo 14. His crew mate on the ALT programme was Richard Truly, a NASA astronaut and a Commander in the US Navy. Truly was another ex-Manned Orbiting Laboratory crew man who transferred to NASA in September 1969. He was a member of the support crew for all three manned Skylab missions between 1973 and 1974.

The four NASA *Enterprise* astronauts had begun training for the test flights over a year earlier on board two highly modified NASA Grumman Gulfstream II aircraft.

The Gulfstream Shuttle Training Aircraft (STA) had been altered in such a way as to produce up to 16,000 lb of drag, simulating the flight characteristics of *Enterprise* on final approach. In addition, the left-hand crew position had been fitted with working replicas of the Orbiter's instruments and controls. The passenger cabin was removed and the furnishings and partitions replaced with a computer and a third seat for another astronaut trainee.

An STA simulation of *Enterprise*'s landing profile began at around 35,000 ft with a 24 degree flight path downwards resulting in a drop of 12,000 ft per minute. The training Shuttle pilot 'touched

The flight deck of *Enterprise* under construction. The seats and some instrumentation are yet to be installed. It is interesting to compare this early 'prototype' layout with the more developed Columbia flight deck. (NASA)

down' 22 ft above the runway, thus enabling his instructor in the Gulfstream's conventional right-hand seat to disengage the simulated Shuttle controls and fly the STA either to a normal landing or to climb away for a second approach and landing simulation.

After initiating a Shuttle landing profile at 35,000 ft the instructor would lower the STA's landing gear to simulate the action of *Enterprise's* air brakes. The engines would then be simultaneously throttled back to a minimum flight power level, whilst thrust reversers in the jet engines produced an effect deemed predictive of the Orbiter's aerodynamic drag.

After these initial adjustments had been made the STA's auto-pilot would be engaged, together with the simulation computer which maintained Orbiter-like responses to the left-hand seat controls and also maintained an automatic throttle control on the jet engines to maintain the correct airspeed and rates of descent.

During final approach to land, the computer would activate the STA's flaps, and the flaperons that replaced the original aircraft's spoilers, to give direct lift and roll control, together with 'turn vanes' added beneath the mid fuselage to give side to side control.

As February 1977 drew to a close, final preparations were being made at the Dryden Flight Research Centre for the first of the six planned 905/*Enterprise* 'captive' flights. There would be

subsequent progression from just take-off and landing tests to long duration trials of the 905/ *Enterprise* combination. *Enterprise* would be un-manned for these first six flights, until May 1977. Then, the first of a series of five 'captive-inactive' tests would provide the opportunity for manning, powering-up equipment, and testing the flight controls of the Orbiter whilst anchored in the air to the 905.

Soon after the successful completion of these tests the first of eight manned free flights would begin. On these occasions *Enterprise* and 905 would take off and climb up to 24,000 ft then turn in line with the runway selected for the Orbiter's landing. At a height of 28,000 ft, with all the checks completed, at just over 30 miles from the runway's threshold and around 55 minutes from take-off, the 905 would pitch its nose down for a shallow, 9 degree, dive and release *Enterprise* at 250 mph and 22,000 ft. It was predicted that, once

When *Enterprise* was moved from Rockwell at Palmdale to Dryden, a number of obstructions along the desert highway had to be moved back or temporarily taken down to allow her to pass. (NASA)

free, the Orbiter would pitch up 6 degrees from the 905 and then bank away for landing around five minutes later.

These tests would verify the airworthiness of the Orbiter, and confirm its equipment operation, glide approach and landing techniques and qualification of the automatic landing systems. It would also allow investigation of performance and handling response over differing weight and centre of gravity configurations. Most significantly, the ALT programme would qualify the 905/Orbiter configuration as prime carrier for delivering Orbiters from the production lines in California to the launch site in Florida, and of returning Orbiters to the launch site when they had returned from space and landed some distance away from the launch centres.

Enterprise would make all of its ALT flights without any of its main, orbital, or reaction control engines. Instead, in their place, wooden, glass fibre and metal mock-ups would be installed to simulate the weight and the effect of airflow over the real things. In addition, the thermal protection tiles were simulated by simple plastic plates, whilst the leading edges of the wings and tail plane were clad in a glass fibre shell.

Protruding from *Enterprise*'s nose, like a long lance, was mounted an instrumentation boom. On board, electricity-generating fuel cells would power the electrical circuits, the fly-by-wire controls and instruments. Standard aircraft-type ejection seats were fitted to *Enterprise*'s flight deck, each providing the two-man crew with a method of escape in the event of an in-flight catastrophe. The ejection system had been developed from those employed on the Lockheed SR-71 aircraft and would be standard for both *Enterprise* and the first spaceflight-rated vehicle, Orbiter 102. The escape system had been carefully tested and developed at Holloman AFB in New Mexico. There, a 'dummy' astronaut was propelled along a rocket powered sled, strapped into the ejection seat. At 278 mph the ejection seat was blasted away from the mock-up Orbiter cabin mounted in the sled and the dummy recovered intact.

Less drastic, but equally effective, methods of escape from *Enterprise* whilst stationary on the ground would involve the jettisoning of the two ejection roof panels in the cabin, followed by the development of two 60 ft long ropes down which the crew could clamber to safety. Alternatively, the side hatch could be opened which could serve as both a platform and a mounting point for a folding boom from which a 45 ft long nylon rope could be lowered. Each crewman would descend to the ground using a 'hook and clutch' system. A rapid escape from the 905 could also be made via a chute from the flight deck down to a hatch in the lower fuselage.

On the initial flight tests of *Enterprise* the stubby tail of the Orbiter with the protruding engine bells would be shrouded in a tailcone device designed to streamline the Orbiter and minimize turbulence on the 905's tail plane which was already augmented by the addition of two vertical fins attached to the horizontal stabilizers. On later tests it was planned to dispense with this so that the airflow across the tail of an Orbiter returning from space could be precisely simulated.

The 905 crew included two pilots, Thomas C. McMurty and Fitzhugh L. Fulton jr, and two flight test engineers, Victor W. Horton and Thomas E. Guidry jr. Of these, McMurty had for long been a project pilot on NASA's aeronautical design programmes and had flown the X-24B many times. Horton had been a test engineer on earlier lifting body drop test experiments, Guidry had participated in the zero-g training flights of C-130 aircraft, and Fitzhugh Fulton had performed many drop test flights as B-52 pilot with the X-15.

Heading the team, and co-ordinating the ALT programme was ex-Mercury astronaut Donald 'Deke' Slayton. An astronaut since 1959 Deke Slayton had been grounded shortly after selection because of a minor heart murmur. This did not, however, restrict him in his duties as NASA's Director of Flight Crew Operations, nor did it prevent him from making his first (and only) space flight in the last Apollo during the 1975 link-up with the Russians. At the time of the ALT programme he was the only remaining member of the original 'seven' still active with NASA.

After a short period of ground vibration tests with what Fitzhugh Fulton called 'the world's largest biplane', the assembly was ready for the ALT programme to commence. Before the Orbiter could take to the air, however, the combination's general handling characteristics had first to be evaluated in a series of high-speed ground runs along the concrete runway. As usual, the step by step approach to test flying prevailed. On each occasion the 905/*Enterprise* would avoid the dry lake bed as both aircraft would almost certainly suffer damage from debris thrown up from the surface under the combined weight of 584,000 lb!

On 15 February 1977 the 905's four uprated Pratt and Whitney JT9D-3A engines whined into life and the combination sped down the Rogers Dry Lake Runway 22 for the first of three high-speed taxi tests at 75, 120 and 135 mph respectively. On the second run of the day, Fulton and his three man crew made a further test of the 905's braking capability and raised the 905's nosewheel briefly into the air before coming to rest and turning to commence a third and final taxi run at a speed just below that needed for the combination to take to the air. On completion of these tests, Fitzhugh Fulton and the ALT team were confident of achieving a 'first flight' on 18 February.

On that date, at 8.30 am local time the 905 together with the Orbiter *Enterprise* roared 6,000 ft down the Rogers Dry Lake Runway 04 heading in a north easterly direction, accompanied by a Cessna T-37 and three Northrop T-38 chase aircraft. In common with all the planned ALT flights in the series, an early start was made to avoid the daily build up of atmospheric turbulence. At 184 mph the combination cautiously left the ground for the first time. Fitzhugh Fulton radioed calmly, 'We are airborne'. The flight plan for this first airborne mission called for the 905/*Enterprise* combination to remain very low at first, with the 905's undercarriage and flaps down. The two aircraft would 'feel' the atmosphere in a series of gentle manoeuvres until they passed the end of the 14 mile emergency runway overrun extension. Then the 905's undercarriage was retracted and its flaps raised as the aircraft climbed slowly to 16,000 ft. Fulton manoeuvred the world's biggest flying machine at speeds of between 150 and 260 mph to check its handling behaviour during a flight that lasted just over 2 hours. Touchdown on Runway 04 at 143 mph followed an approach made on a standard 3 degree glidescope. Throughout the flight, engineers Horton and Guidry constantly monitored the stresses on the 905 airframe through their respective flight deck instruments.

In the post-flight debrief session Fitzhugh Fulton was evidently delighted with the aircraft's performance, declaring to the assembled media and officials that the flight, 'went exactly as planned,' and that, 'most of the time we couldn't even tell that the Shuttle was up there'. NASA manager William Anderson was likewise inspired with confidence, and with it the team felt that the first flight, 'had gone so well that the testing can proceed on schedule'.

The 905/*Enterprise* combination made a second successful flight on 22 February. Taking off at 8.32 am the two aircraft needed a shorter run because of a strong north easterly wind. This, the longest flight in the ALT programme, lasted 3 hours 13 minutes achieving a maximum height of 23,000 ft. By the time the second flight was over, the crew of the 905 had performed 30 tests so successfully that 'Deke' Slayton, the ALT manager, announced the cancellation of the sixth planned captive flight if the next three performed as well as the first two.

The third flight, on 25 February 1977, was planned to investigate the effects of airframe flutter and stability during shallow dives that would simulate the portion of later flights just before 905/*Enterprise* separation. Immediately after take off the 905's outer starboard engine was throttled back to idle and the remaining three engines strained under the increased load-share to take the aircraft up to over 4,000 ft, at which point the fourth engine was again brought up to full power. This experiment simulated the effect of an engine failure at the critical stage of climb-out. As

the crew began a series of speed tests Fitzhugh Fulton noticed increasing amounts of buffeting on the tail of the 905 caused by the slipstream of *Enterprise*. No sooner had he reported this fact than one of the T-38 chase planes confirmed a visual 'ripple' effect on *Enterprise*'s tail cone fairings. Nevertheless the 2½ hour flight continued and investigations afterwards gave ground engineers the confidence that no problems would ensue from this effect on later missions. Deke Slayton confirmed that the sixth captive flight would be cancelled. All the time confidence in the new space plane and its carrier aircraft was increasing.

The fourth captive flight took place on 28 February at 8.00 am on the dot, and consisted of a complete test of the 905/Orbiter's flight characteristics and a test of emergency procedures.

At around 23,000 ft the combination began a series of 'dives' during which spoilers were put out from the 905 to check the drag and handling performance on the mated configuration. The two aircraft then climbed back to 28,600 ft when the combination began yet another shallower dive down almost 10,000 ft for further spoiler tests and then an emergency descent test with all four of the 905's engines cut back to flight idle. Holding the 905's nose up 5 degrees as it fell, Fulton checked the rate of descent as best he could until the giant aircraft reached just over 12,000 ft in line with Runway 22. The flight ended with a test of the emergency landing abort or 'go around' procedure under full power. On its second run in to land the combination touched down and immediately started to apply brakes. The objective was to achieve as short a landing as possible, to demonstrate that the mated aircraft and spacecraft could stop well within the distance allowed at NASA's Marshall Space Flight Centre runway at Huntsville, Alabama. (At that site after completion of the ALT programme, *Enterprise* would be air-lifted to complete a series of ground-based vibration tests in a specially prepared facility.)

The fifth and final captive flight of the 905/*Enterprise* took place just two weeks after the first on 3 March.

This final captive-inactive flight would be conducted to simulate fully two different altitude separation profiles.

Shortly after take off the two aircraft climbed up to over 25,000 ft then Fulton pushed the 905's nose down 5.7 degrees below horizontal flight and into a shallow dive. Just as in the future separation flights, the countdown commenced as he throttled back the 905's four Pratt and Whitney jet engines and deployed the converted airliner's spoilers. As planned the countdown stopped just seconds before the explosive bolts linking the two vehicles

Enterprise and the NASA 905 take to the air for the third captive-inactive Orbiter/905 flight, which was to test stability and explore minimum flying speed for heavy and light gross weight conditions at several 747 flap settings. (NASA)

After a last minute crisis before take-off, the first captive-active flight took off on 18 June 1977. This photograph shows well the cross-section of the Orbiter's 'boat-tail' engine fairing, and the 905's additional 'end-plate' vertical stabilizers on the tail plane. (NASA)

were due to release. The 905 then climbed back up to an even greater height for a similar test.

At the end of the flight another successful short landing inspired further confidence in a landing at the Marshall Space Flight Centre runway. The Dryden Centre found no problems on any of the five captive-inactive missions. All the tests had resulted in data falling within levels set during both sub-scale simulations and extensive wind tunnel tests. One of the most important pieces of information was that concerning the upward force *Enterprise* would experience at the point of separation from the 905. Too much would cause *Enterprise*'s nose to pitch up, the vehicle would then lose speed instantly and crash back on to the 905's tailplane with catastrophic results. Too little force would be insufficient to separate the two vehicles with similar consequences. 0.8g was deemed sufficient by designers, and, after flight tests, 0.8g was the force encountered and recorded by instruments aboard the 905.

After just five out of a planned six captive-inactive flights, Phase One of the ALT programme had proved the soundness of the 905/*Enterprise* airworthiness.

NASA was delighted that after much careful planning the two vehicles had demonstrated aerodynamic handling qualities superior even to their most optimistic estimates. As Phase One proceeded so well, it had been accelerated in pace so that the four waiting astronauts could, in their simulator training, benefit from all the engineering and aerodynamic data gained through those first five flights.

During February Joe Engle, Dick Truly, Fred Haise and Charles Fullerton had spent countless hours 'on board' the computer controlled Orbiter ALT Simulator based at NASA's Johnson Space Centre, Houston. Every day more and more actual flight measurements were added to the computer and mathematical model predictions on the performance of the combination. As a result the simulator responses became more and more like the real thing would be.

Such improvements were certainly welcomed by the astronauts, but in speeding up Phase One to such a rate several important certification schedules for *Enterprise,* including tests of on board equipment, were missed out. Before Phase Two of the ALT programme, designated 'captive-active' could be carried out, more equipment had to be added to *Enterprise*. The 'captive-active' phase would be the first with *Enterprise* 'live' and with a two-man crew.

On 3 March 1977 the combination was towed to the mate/demate structure where the complex system of cranes and hoists lifted *Enterprise* off its

tripod mounting on to the back of the 905 to commence a month of work preparing *Enterprise* for its first manned captive-active flight.

Engineers replaced *Enterprise*'s elevon actuators and devised a method whereby the Orbiter's undercarriage could be retracted or deployed whilst in a mated configuration with the 905. After installation of the auxiliary power units, computers and hydraulics a further 15 days of testing followed in order to clear the vehicle for flight. A 'hot fire' series of ground tests followed the installation of components. During this period the Orbiter's auxiliary power units, fuel cells and computers were activated as they would be in actual flight. These tests were the final acceptance requirements in preparation for the mated manned captive flight test phase.

By May, Deke Slayton and the ALT project team had decided on a reduction of captive-active flights from five to four. The first, to be flown in mid-June, would follow a race-track course for a period of around 49 minutes. Flutter checks would be made, the Orbiter's air-brake/split rudder would be tested and the Tactical Air Navigation System (TACAN) evaluated. The second flight would simulate a pre-separation manoeuvre, last for 60 minutes and follow a longer race-track course. The third captive-acitve flight would be a repeat of the second but would additionally check out every aspect to be encountered as if an actual separation were to be made. The fourth flight, the final one in this phase, would be the same as the third in every respect apart from an additional final Orbiter undercarriage deployment on the run after touchdown.

At this stage with plans drawn up, systems checked and the astronauts trained and ready, everything was going well for the Shuttle. As has been seen in previous programmes, however, the unexpected can happen.

On 17 June, a day before the first captive-active flight, coupling links that secured the overhead ejection seat roof panels would not locate properly, one of the three on-board inertial measurement units that assisted in maintaining the Orbiter's flight attitude failed, and two of the four primary flight control computers also packed up in sympathy.

Early in the morning of 18 June 1977, Fred Haise and Charles Fullerton crossed the desert airstrip and boarded *Enterprise*. Shortly afterwards Fitzhugh Fulton, Thomas McMurty, Victor Horton and Thomas Guidry climbed aboard the silver 905 and, together with the two astronauts, began the long pre-flight checks.

As the sun appeared over the horizon, the pilots on both aircraft were discussing a last minute change of runways from 04 to 22 because of strong cross-winds. Slowly the 905/*Enterprise* combination was being eased backwards out from the mate/demate device. By this time Fred Haise and Charles Fullerton had activated all of *Enterprise*'s systems. All the problems of the previous day had been solved apart from the inertial measurement unit (engineers had decided, nevertheless, to go on the remaining two).

Quite without warning, toxic ammonia gas found its way from the Orbiter's exhaust into the 905's flight deck and suddenly the four men were choking and reaching for oxygen masks. Fitzhugh Fulton soon realized what had happened. The gas had escaped from *Enterprise*'s ammonia 'boiler' vent tubes and entered the ventilation system of the 905 below. In the cramped flight deck the leak could easily have been disastrous, but quick reaction by the crew soon purged the poisonous air from the system and the two aircraft continued under tow to the ramp for engine start-up at 7.00 am.

At 8.06 am the assembly began to roll, slowly at first, then picking up speed along Runway 22. Above, the T-38 chase planes which had taken off minutes earlier, matched speed with their charge as it climbed slowly up into the clear morning air. By now flight control had switched from Dryden to Houston, Texas, and the Johnson Space Flight Centre. Fourteen minutes after take-off the combination had manoeuvred into the same position it would have been in had take-off from Runway 04 gone as planned. At a height of just under 15,000 ft the 905 set a 10 degree flap position to compensate for its low (185 mph) speed. In *Enterprise* Fred Haise and Charles Fullerton were busy trying to

vent their cabin atmosphere to two-thirds sea level pressure. A faulty valve had prevented the operation being performed automatically. That done, the two *Enterprise* pilots conducted a series of Orbiter flight control system checks which were found to have no serious effect on the two vehicle combination's stability. No effect, that is, until Fred Haise opened *Enterprise*'s split rudder air-brake to its fully deployed position.

Fitzhugh Fulton was well aware that the air-brake test on *Enterprise* would have to be accompanied by extreme vigilance on the part of himself and his three-man crew. What he did not expect was the severity of the total drag effect induced by *Enterprise* in this configuration. As soon as the Orbiter's air-brake reached a full 100 per cent opening, providing the panels with a 90 degree angle to each other, Fulton saw the airspeed fall away sharply. Before a stall could set in, he opened

In preparation for the captive-active part of the ALT programme, Charles Fullerton, pilot of the first ALT crew, is seen in the Shuttle Procedures Simulator in Building 35 during Shuttle ALT training at the Johnson Space Centre, Houston. (NASA)

all four engines to maximum climb throttle, even so he was barely able to maintain level flight. Having undoubtedly proved the air-brakes' effectiveness the panels were closed. The twin aircraft came into land after 55 minutes 46 seconds after achieving 14,970 ft maximum altitude and a maximum speed of 208 mph.

Following the flight, improvements to both aircraft were made to eliminate the possibility of a recurrence of the gas leak problem which nearly halted the first captive-active mission. Examination of all the other aspects of this flight proved so encouraging that the ALT management team decided to drop the planned fourth captive-active

flight, combining flights two and three into one to take place on 28 June 1977, followed by the third and final captive-active flight on 8 July.

The *Enterprise* crew for the second captive-active flight was to be Joe Engle and Dick Truly. As the giant combination rolled down the runway for take off at 7.50 am on 28 June there was no shortage of people who observed that, over a decade earlier, the same men had flown the B-52/X-15 combination from that same flight centre.

This flight consisted of a 1 hour 2 minute mission to a maximum altitude of 22,030 ft. As with the first captive-active flight all the Orbiter's on-

A T-38 photographer took this unusual photograph of the 905/*Enterprise* combination during the first captive-active flight. Note the drogue and line extending back from the top of the 905's tail to indicate any turbulence in that area. (NASA)

board systems were activated prior to take off. During the initial climb out, low-speed flight control system tests were performed by the crews. These low-speed tests were performed with the Orbiter's flight control surfaces activated first, then with the 905's control surfaces operating in conjunction with the mated *Enterprise* for a flutter test at 259 mph.

Following these experiments the Orbiter's airbrake was again opened in stages to 60, 80, and 100 per cent deployment. The combination lost speed at the 60 per cent setting and its climb stopped altogether in the fully-open position.

Closing the air-brakes once more the Engle/Fulton crews performed a second series of flutter tests before nosing the combination down to pick up speed before yet another series of *Enterprise* air brake evaluations.

The final manoeuvres before landing involved tests of the auto-landing device using a microwave scanning beam landing system (MSBLS). This system would be used to guide *Enterprise* to touchdown on the future 'free' glide tests, and later in the final stages of landing on return from orbit.

The flight went so well and subsequent modifications were accomplished so quickly that the third and final captive-active flight was moved forward to 26 July.

At 7.47 am on that date the 905/*Enterprise* combination took to the air with Fred Haise and Charles Fullerton once more at the Orbiter's controls for a dress rehearsal of the first release, or free flight of the ALT programme. Again, the Orbiter's auxiliary power units, hydraulic, coolant, and electrical systems were all powered-up and active as the combination climbed into the clear blue sky above Edwards.

All went well until, during the initial stages of the climb up to 27,000 ft, Fred Haise and Charles Fullerton saw the caution and warning display on their console flash urgently. The number one auxiliary power system's exhaust had become dangerously overheated. Almost straight away, in line with the mission rules, Fitzhugh Fulton shut down the number one auxiliary power unit. For several minutes the flight hung in the balance before Houston confirmed a faulty heat sensor as the cause of the alarm.

Continuing its climb the combination tested *Enterprise*'s avionics, flight control systems and deflection of the flight control surfaces. In addition TACAN tests were conducted. The TACAN system, using a system of ground sited beacons, already employed by the military for many years, was to be used to track future Orbiters returning from space down to the 10,000 ft mark where the MSBLS would take over for landing.

At 25,905 ft, less than 48 minutes after take off, the 905/*Enterprise* combination pitched nose down and began a shallow dive along a flight path identical to that which would be used on the next, free, flight. At the precise point of simulated separation the assembly was just under 17 miles to the right of Runway 17, exactly the point it would be on the next 'free' flight test. The 905 entered a steep dive which matched as nearly as possible the rate of descent of *Enterprise* once free of the 905. Following a preset approach to Runway 17 the combination levelled off at just under 3,000 ft, continued on over the runway and then made two wide left turns before swooping in to Runway 22. No sooner had the 905's main wheels touched down than Fred Haise and Charles Fullerton lowered *Enterprise*'s landing gear for the first time in the ALT programme, qualifying the system for use on its next flight, the first Phase Three flight. The 905's nose wheel finally came down to the runway and the combination taxied back to the starting point.

NASA wanted *Enterprise* refurbished and ready for orbital flight alongside vehicle 102 in early 1981. It would take two years to refurbish the first Orbiter to full orbital status after the ALT programme. For this reason Deke Slayton and the project team wanted to complete this last phase of the tests as soon as possible. The original plan called for five 'tailcone on' drop flights, one captive-active 'tailcone off' flight to check aerodynamic stability, then three 'tailcone off' drop flights. Deke Slayton insisted that only three of the five planned 'tailcone on' flights would be necessary, and one 'tailcone off' free flight. NASA agreed, subject of course to the continued progress of the programme.

Enterprise's free-flight phase would verify the Orbiter's pilot-guided approach and landing capability and demonstrate the Shuttle's subsonic 'terminal area energy management' (TEAM) autoland and approach capability. In addition, the free flights would check out the Shuttle's subsonic airworthiness, its integrated systems operation and its manual control in preparation for the first manned spaceflight scheduled for vehicle number 102, then undergoing final assembly back at Rockwell's Palmdale facility.

12 August 1977 had been scheduled as the date for the first 'free' flight of *Enterprise*. The first time that a space shuttle would take to the air on its own, 30 years to the day almost since Charles Yeager had taken the X-1 past the sound barrier over that same desert airstrip.

For this, as with all previous 'captive' flights, *Enterprise* flew with its streamlined tail cone on to prevent any turbulence buffeting the 905's tail during critical separation manoeuvres.

On 11 August, the normally quiet roads leading to the Dryden Flight Research Centre at Edwards Air Force Base were packed with cars, trailers and campers. Thousands of visitors from

During the final captive-active flight, the landing gear of *Enterprise* was deployed for the first time. (NASA)

The third and final ALT captive-active mission on 26 July 1977 qualified *Enterprise* for her first 'free' flight. Once again, Fred Haise and Charles Fullerton were at the Orbiter's controls. (NASA)

all over the world were arriving, some to camp overnight, in order to witness the event. Long before the Southern Californian night began to turn into the early dawn of 12 August, miles of waiting vehicles led across the desert to the opened main security gates. By 5.30 am over 65,000 people had passed through to watch the proceedings.

Away from the parking area, at the red lattice-work mate/demate tower, the final countdown was underway. At 6.00 am dawn was breaking with a typically beautiful burst of colour across the distant horizon as Fred Haise and Charles Fullerton climbed into *Enterprise* via the hatch in its lower deck, and made their way up into the cockpit. Shortly after, Fitzhugh Fulton led his flight crew into the 905 and the preparation began. The Orbiter's fuel cell reactant was transferred from gound supply, that had powered the units up, to liquid reactants stored in the cavernous cargo bay. At 7.00 am the 905 and *Enterprise* were slowly backed out from the mate/demate tower and towed across the dry lake bed to the Dryden start up ramp. At 7.30 am the combination taxied across Runway 04 under its own power. High above the 905's cockpit, Fred Haise and Charles Fullerton looked down and ahead at the long dusty desert runway as they performed last minute control system checks from the Orbiter flight deck. T-38 chase planes were already in the sky, wheeling around waiting for the world's largest flying machine to join them. At a distance, crowds of onlookers gathered at every vantage point, cameras at the ready, binoculars and telescopes trained, as reflected sunlight on their lenses glinted like thousands of stars across the desert horizon.

At 8.00 am precisely, the 905's specially-rated jet engines built up to a deafening roar as thousands of people stopped talking and watched. Releasing its brakes the combination trundled slowly at first, then building up speed down the concrete runway. Five T-38 chase planes followed it into the sky as the noise of the engines thundered across the flat desert landscape.

It was an unusually hot early morning at Edwards, and high atmospheric temperatures meant that the heavy 905/*Enterprise* combination would need an extra 180 seconds to reach 'push over' height of 22,800 ft above ground level (25,100 ft above sea level). Forty seven minutes after take-off, with *Enterprise's* cabin pressurized to two-thirds sea level and all its power and flight controls activated, the 905 entered a shallow dive of nearly 7 degrees. The countdown to separation began, relayed to thousands of spectators over ground public address systems. Fitzhugh Fulton then throttled back the four Pratt and Whitney engines to flight-idle speed and extended the giant

Boeing's spoilers. At 18,300 ft above ground level the 905 was in the correct 'high drag' configuration necessary to prevent *Enterprise* from creeping backwards relative to the 747 after separation and crashing into the latter's tail fin.

As the countdown reached zero Fred Haise, after receiving the 'launch ready' call from the pilot of the 905, reached forward and pressed a button on *Enterprise's* control panel that detonated the explosive bolts holding the two craft together. On the ground, the announcement of separation was greeted by tumultuous applause as eyes strained into the heat haze for the first glimpse of the Shuttle.

The break was clean and smooth. Fred Haise and Charles Fullerton waited for the 905 to move carefully away to the right to avoid turbulence before initiating a practice landing 'flare' manoeuvre which decreased *Enterprise's* speed whilst evaluating its flying qualities. They then pitched the nose down once more, accelerated and initiated the first of the two 90 degree left turns which would align *Enterprise* with Runway 17.

Two minutes after separation *Enterprise* entered its landing approach phase, but was approaching much too fast. As soon as Fred Haise saw the runway ahead, he realized something was wrong, *Enterprise* was too high and building-up speed rapidly.

On the ground spectators watched the 905, a tiny speck in the clear blue sky alongside which a tell-tale contrail marked the descending progress of *Enterprise*. The black and white dot at the head of the white line was growing rapidly larger, and within minutes had taken on the familiar form of the Orbiter.

Fred Haise deployed *Enterprise's* air-brake to 40 per cent to slow the Orbiter down and lose height, but it was not enough. The spaceplane continued to accelerate as it soared down to the lake bed runway in front of thousands of onlookers. He extended the brake to 50 per cent holding on to the original landing point marked on the runway, but knowing all the time that the landing flare would carry them far beyond. The expected rates of drag and lack of lift of *Enterprise* were wrong. It was a much more lift efficient vehicle than had been anticipated. On this flight the maximum air-brake setting had been set at 50 per cent so there was nothing either Fred Haise or Charles Fullerton could do but hold off until the speed and height fell away. At over 245 mph *Enterprise* flew over the pre-determined touchdown point on the runway with a roar of slipstream until its speed fell below the 210 mph safety limit of the tyres and under-carriage. Eventually the main wheels touched down in front of a trail of dust, followed seconds later by the nosewheel. Rolling 9,000 ft along the 13 mile long runway *Enterprise* came to a halt as the 905 and chase planes flew overhead in formation; a salute to the Orbiter's maiden flight. The crowds cheered and all over the world the first free flight of *Enterprise* was headline news, in contrast to Yeager's X-1 flight exactly three decades earlier.

The total free flight duration was 5 minutes 21 seconds. Fred Haise was delighted, describing the flight as 'super slick'. Pilot Charles Fullerton said *Enterprise* was, 'a very stable airplane'.

Analysis of data gained on the first free flight and a change of NASA schedules moved the planned second free flight forward from 30 to 26 August. Then the weather that had been so good to the test programme turned bad. The rains moved in and flooded the dry lake beds at Edwards moving the second flight back to September when they had dried out sufficiently to support further Shuttle flight operations.

Free flight number two was another 'tail cone on' mission, on 13 September 1977. The flight commander was to be Joe Engle and pilot Richard Truly.

The second flight differed from the first in that *Enterprise*'s flight control systems were to be tested in a series of complex manoeuvres at both high and low speeds. In addition, *Enterprise*'s first left roll turn after separation was designed to subject the Orbiter to a 1.8g force which would

The crews of both 905 and *Enterprise* disembark after landing. The method of leaving the Orbiter was not suited to those without a head for heights. (NASA)

provide valuable information to be used in TEAM during later Earth orbital missions.

The 905/*Enterprise* combination left the ground at 8.00 am local time and began its 'push-over' manoeuvre prior to separation 48 minutes later at 28,000 ft and at over 250 mph. A minute later, Joe Engle and Dick Truly were flying free and picking up speed as *Enterprise,* once more, nosed down to land. On the way down, Joe Engle made a number of control stick movements to assess the response of *Enterprise* before entering the crosswind leg of the journey by pulling a 1.8g left-hand turn and placing the greatest aerodynamic load yet experienced on the airframe. He made further stick movements whilst opening the Orbiter's split rudder air-brake to 50 per cent for a few seconds to test its effectiveness. Although the flight plan had only called for one large rudder movement afterwards to assess *Enterprise*'s directional stability, Joe Engle and Dick Truly managed three before touchdown.

Climbing down the steps alongside the exit hatch Joe Engle was visibly delighted with the 5 minute 28 second flight, describing *Enterprise* as 'performing superbly'. Pilot Dick Truly called

it, 'an excellent-handling machine'. The maximum height reached on this second free flight was 30,500 ft.

The third free flight of the Space Shuttle *Enterprise* was described by Commander Fred Haise as, 'a busy, enjoyable flight in a very good vehicle'. Pilot Charles Fullerton stated that *Enterprise* was 'absolutely smooth' during the 45 second auto-land portion of the flight. This mission on 23 September 1977 began at 8.00 am and lasted 5 minutes 34 seconds from 905 separation at 22,400 ft to touchdown. Maximum altitude was 29,500 ft.

Following the third glide flight, *Enterprise* was to be prepared for the final phase of the ALT programme. The rear fuselage tail cone was removed and dummy exhaust nozzles fitted to the rear bulkhead to duplicate exactly the mass and aerodynamic characteristics of a 'real' Shuttle returning from orbit. It had finally been decided to make two free flights in this configuration.

Glide flight number four, 12 October, was the first 'tail cone off' flight. As such the flight path glide slope of *Enterprise,* once free of its carrier, was much steeper in comparison to the previous 'tail cone on' flights, due to the increase in aerodynamic drag. The flight path glide scope was between 18 and 28 degrees in comparison with the 10 to 14 degrees in the 'tail cone on' flights. As a

In preparation for the first free flight, the Orbiter attachment points are armed with explosive bolts to achieve a clean break. Shown here is the rear port attachment point surrounded by a temporary platform. (NASA)

part of the test programme the descent of this fourth flight was steeper than that predicted for a return from space.

The 905/*Enterprise* combination left the Dryden Flight Research Centre runway at 7.45 am, *Enterprise* separating 1 hour 5 minutes later at 22,400 ft. During descent Joe Engle and Dick Truly carried out a planned series of pitch and roll manoeuvres before touching down again at 8.52 am after a free flight of 2 minutes 34 seconds.

The increased drag caused by the exposed engine nozzles gave the crew much less time for any tests than in the three previous flights. *Enterprise* was accordingly released from a position downwind of the landing area so that it could glide straight in without having to make 'U' turns or any other major manoeuvres before touchdown.

As before, the crew, Joe Engle and Dick Truly, were full of praise, calling *Enterprise* a 'great machine, flies good', and that the 'handling characteristics were similar to the 'tail cone on' flights except for the deceleration and speed decrease due to increased drag'.

The final glide flight came next on 26 October and lasted 2 minutes 1 second. The 905/*Enterprise* combination left the ground at 8.00 am with Fred Haise and Charles Fullerton at the Orbiter's controls. The two aircraft reached 20,000 ft in 50 minutes, almost exactly the time expected. The separation point for the combination was a few miles south-west of the airbase and directly in line with the previous *Enterprise* landing runway, Runway 22. 'Push over' followed by separation came at 17,000 ft.

During this 'tail cone off' flight, the flight path glide slope was not as severe as in the fourth flight. The flight path glide slope in this mission was between 20 and 26 degrees in comparison with the 18 to 28 of the 12 October flight. *Enterprise* followed a straight in approach to Runway 04 following separation from the 905, with its centre of gravity moved aft of the centre line, the same as it would be for the first orbital test flight.

Without the drag reducing tailcone, and with its air-brakes fully deployed, the descent path was still very steep compared with conventional aircraft. After only 85 seconds of free flight *Enterprise* was down to 2,000 ft altitude and beginning its flare to arrest a rate of descent of over 10,000 ft a minute. Although the microwave landing system was switched on, the crew took manual control of the vehicle throughout final descent.

The landing of the spacecraft at over 200 mph on the 15,000 ft long concrete runway at Edwards AFB demonstrated that the Shuttle could be stopped within a safe distance on a similar runway at both the Kennedy Space Centre in Florida and Vandenburg AFB in California, on return from Earth orbital missions.

The landing, however, was not as smooth as predicted on this final flight, as *Enterprise* bounced several times and veered across the runway as assembled observers held their breath. The rough landing resulted from, of all things, a better than expected lift/drag ratio. The previous flight test, as Orbiter project manager Aaron Cohen explained, had suggested that *Enterprise* minus tail cone had a higher lift to drag ratio than predicted. Even bearing this in mind, Fred Haise still found the *Enterprise* flying faster than anticipated as he approached the runway. 'He came in a bit hot and lowered the elevons at touchdown to get the nose down. The increased lift from the elevons lifted *Enterprise* into the air again.' Crabbing to the right of its landing path Fred Haise tried to correct, only setting up an oscillation in the process! Immediately he relaxed the controls and *Enterprise* settled down again on the runway as the speed fell away. The completion of this free flight brought to a close the ALT Shuttle glide flight programme.

For the final captive flight of the ALT Programme *Enterprise*'s hydraulic systems were drained and purged, the tail cone reinstalled along with special locks on the elevons. To reduce the drag on the two aircraft the forward mounting strut on the 905 was replaced with a shorter version bringing the two fuselages into parallel.

The final four flights would evaluate ferry flight performance of the mated configuration. These took place on 15, 17, and 18 November 1977. Upon completion *Enterprise* was removed from the 905 and rolled into the main Dryden Flight Research Centre hangar where it underwent a series of modifications to prepare it for the next phase of the test programme: the 'ground vibration trials' at the Marshall Space Flight Centre, Huntsville, Alabama.

In all, the nine month long ALT programme at NASA's Dryden Flight Centre, Edwards, proved that the Space Shuttle could fly. America's newest spacecraft had gained her wings appropriately at the exact location of many of her forerunners. Soon after the programme ended, Fitzhugh Fulton, pilot of the 905, was named 'Pilot of the Year' by the US Society of Experimental Test Pilots, and pronounced winner of the 1977 Iven C. Kincheloe Award.

By the beginning of 1978, NASA were faced with yet another acute money shortage and were forced to consider a new approach to their Orbiter delivery schedules which would disqualify *Enterprise* as a space-worthy shuttle, in favour of a cheaper 'uprating' of the prototype Structural Test Article (STA) Orbiter to flight standard. The STA was being assembled right next to Orbiter 102 at Rockwell's Palmdale factory. Structurally identical to production Orbiters it was to be used for loading and structural fatigue testing from January to May 1979. The new schedule called for by NASA would mean that the STA would only be tested to 120 per cent of design load instead of the 140 per cent originally planned, leaving it acceptable as the second production Orbiter in favour of *Enterprise*. Orbiters 103 and 104 would, in the plans of early 1978,

be making their first flights in June and December 1983 respectively, six months later than originally scheduled.

With the plan to upgrade the STA approved, *Enterprise* would be the fifth operational Orbiter entering service in January 1985. NASA expected to save approximately $100 million by realigning their plans in this way. If *Enterprise* were to become the second flight vehicle, deliveries of 103 and 104 would have to be delayed and possibly cancelled altogether.

On 10 March 1978 *Enterprise* began a long journey across the USA to the Marshall Centre at Huntsville, stopping for the weekend at the 'home' of American manned spaceflight, Houston. By that time *Enterprise* was so far below the engineering standard required for production Orbiters that it would never make a flight into space. *Enterprise* was overweight, lacked many critical pieces of equipment, and had so many alterations made that NASA could not justify the money and man hours needed to bring this space plane up to Orbital flight standard. *Enterprise* would be nothing more than a working mock-up destined eventually, perhaps, for the National Air and Space Museum.

The Orbiter's airworthiness had been proven, but there were two increasingly difficult problems to overcome in its development. The engines and the heat shielding development were falling behind.

The final problem that the Space Shuttle had

The traditional pre-launch breakfast was provided for Fred Haise and Charles Fullerton on the morning of the first free flight, 12 August 1977. (NASA)

to meet and overcome, after the successful completion of its glide tests, came through further budget reductions. The provisionally-scheduled first orbital flight in March 1979 depended on the first Orbiter, *Columbia,* being delivered from Rockwell to the Kennedy Space Centre no later than August 1978. Funding shortages delayed this move. (Even if NASA had made an all-out effort to meet the March launch date against a later delivery from Rockwell, reduced funds would still have threatened Shuttle's later operational flights.)

Apart from budgetary problems, NASA's Orbiter was experiencing problems with its main propulsion systems and its thermal insulation tiles, which in the case of the latter had cost NASA more

than $120 million so far. Twice in 1977 an SSME caught fire while under test and threatened to delay the engine test schedule by several months.

The Fiscal Year 1979 budget submitted to Congress at the end of January 1978 by President Carter effectively removed from the flight schedule a fifth orbiter. As a result NASA rearranged their plans eventually to include four orbiters for their own and Department of Defense missions. Orbiter serial number 099 *(Challenger)* which was the refurbished STA, together with Orbiter 102 *(Columbia),* 103 *(Discovery)* and 104 *(Atlantis)* would comprise America's Space Shuttle fleet. By the second week in May 1978, the US House of Representatives and the Senate decided to allocate $4

For the fourth and penultimate free flight, on 12 October 1977, the streamlined 'boat tail' covering the three simulated engine bells on *Enterprise* was removed. (NASA)

million to keep a fifth Orbiter option open. Against President Carter's wishes, there were still some people of influence who recognized the possible future needs for another Orbiter.

A month later 35 new NASA astronauts joined the 27 already on flight status at the Johnson Space Centre, Houston. The newly-selected astronauts included 14 civilians and 21 military officers. 15 were in the pilot category and 20 were taken on as potential mission specialists. Six of the chosen astronauts were women. Those selected in January 1978 were:

Civilians

Anna Fisher	(mission specialist)
David Griggs	(pilot)
Terence Hart	(ms)
Stephen Hawley	(ms)
Geoffrey Hoffman	(ms)
Shannon Lucid	(ms)

Ronald McNair	(ms)
George Nelson	(ms)
Judith Resnik	(ms)
Sally Ride	(ms)
Margaret Seddon	(ms)
Kathryn Sullivan	(ms)
Norman Thagard	(ms)
James Van Hoften	(ms)

Military

Lt Cdr Daniel Brandenstein, US Navy	(plt)
Major Guion Bluford, USAF	(ms)
Major James Buchli, US Marines	(ms)
Lt Cdr Michael Coats, US Navy	(plt)
Major Richard Covey, USAF	(plt)

Lt Cdr John Creighton, US Navy	(plt)
Lt Col John Fabian, USAF	(ms)
Lt Dale Gardner, US Navy	(ms)
Lt Cdr Robert Gibson, US Navy	(plt)
Major Frederick Gregory, USAF	(plt)
Cdr Frederick Hauck, US Navy	(plt)
Major Michael Mullane, USAF	(ms)
Lt Cdr John McBride, US Navy	(plt)
Captain Stephen Nagel, USAF	(ms)
Captain Ellison Onizuka, USAF	(ms)
Major Richard Scobee, USAF	(plt)
Captain Brewster Shaw, USAF	(plt)
Major Robert Stewart, US Army	(ms)
Captain Loren Shriver, USAF	(plt)
Lt Cdr David Walker, US Navy	(plt)
Lt Cdr Donald Williams, US Navy	(plt)

The new '35' were the first group of astronauts to be selected by NASA since the MOL transfer in August 1969. The gap represented the diminished scale of US space effort during the early-to-mid nineteen-seventies.

Soon after NASA had recruited their latest batch of pilot and scientist astronauts, the Space Agency confirmed that the first orbital test flight of the Shuttle would be no earlier than June 1979. Budget problems combined with developmental difficulties with the SSME had forced the move which hailed the first of many subsequent delays. In addition, preparative work both on the External Tank and SRBs was also behind schedule. NASA hoped to announce a firm launch date commitment by October 1978, but that depended on the outcome of SSME test firings which would show the extent of the engineering problems to be overcome.

By the summer of 1978, Space Shuttle *Enterprise* and its External Tank were undergoing a series of 'ground vibration' trials at the NASA Marshall Space Flight Centre in Alabama. Suspended inside the test facility both the Orbiter and the External Tank were subjected to stresses applied to the airframe, simulating the dynamic forces of the atmosphere expected during the launch phase. At a later date these tests would also include the two SRBs attached to the *Enterprise* and External Tank to demonstrate the Shuttle system's ability to withstand the shock of SRB separation. (Tests on the *Enterprise* were due to be completed in January 1979.)

On completion of the Ground Vibration Tests in April 1979 NASA was pleased; the tests had been completed on time and showed no major deficiencies in design. *Enterprise* then left Alabama and flew atop the 905 to the Kennedy Space Centre, Florida, where its final role would be as a test orbiter for the NASA facilities there, checking out the giant Vehicle Assembly Building structures and the mobile launchers, and ground handling and check out procedures before the first flight-rated Shuttle arrived.

Back at Lockheed's Palmdale factory, Orbiter vehicle 099, the Structural Test Article, was being similarly tested, although to a lesser degree and excluding the External Tank and SRB. Loadings applied to the fuselage and wings of 120 per cent design proof (instead of the 140 per cent originally planned) enabled engineers to gain the information they needed to qualify the design for operation, whilst allowing 099 later to be refurbished, for space mission as *Challenger* the second delivery flight-rated Shuttle Orbiter. Not far away, at the Rockwell plant, Orbiter 102 (*Columbia*) was nearing completion. During the summer *Columbia* underwent several successful 'power-on' checks of electrical systems. At NASA's White Sands, New Mexico, test facility the forward RCS system to be fitted to the Orbiter had completed its firing tests. Meanwhile, engineers at Rockwell's Rocketdyne plant were continuing to investigate the constant SSME developmental problems. Despite efforts to begin NASA's flight qualification of these three main engines, repeated problems pushed the first orbital launch date back until well into 1980.

The constant delays in flight certification of the SSMEs was simply due to the fact that they were the most complex propulsion system ever built. Repeated failures in the high pressure turbopumps, hot gas manifolds, and metal fatigue under punishing thermal and dynamic loads in the engine structure took their toll in development time. It seemed that as soon as one problem had been solved, another arose. Time and again the Santa Susana Test Facility overlooking California's San Fernando Valley echoed to the roar of clustered SSME test firings. Several thousand miles away at the Mississippi Test Facility, further tests were underway. Rockwell's Rocketdyne subsidiary was working 'all out' to solve the SSME problems.

The pressure on NASA to 'get things right' was increasing. The USAF was constructing their own launch facilities at Vandenburg Air Force Base, California, and was planning a series of military missions for the Shuttle. In Europe, Ariane, the commercial, expendable launcher (ie a conventional rocket), was approaching launch readiness (it would compete against Shuttle as a satellite launcher) and in the Soviet Union reports were emerging of a new Soviet Space Shuttle. This, in terms of defence, economics, and national prestige, meant an early launch was critical.

Vandenburg, the Air Force's third largest base in the world, was chosen as their Shuttle launch site both because of its existing missile launching facilities, and because of its strategic location. Launches from Vandenburg would enable Orbiters to reach polar orbit, impossible from Kennedy without flying over densely populated areas which was expressly forbidden. Polar orbits were ideal for space reconnaissance satellites. The 'Space Launch

Complex 6' (Slick 6) would be used to assemble Orbiters with both External Tank and SRBs as well as to install payloads in strictest secrecy.

Intelligence reports from Russia indicated that their 'shuttle' would in fact be very similar in design to the X-24A lifting body, but slightly larger. Development flights had been of unmanned, sub-scale models, but no one was prepared to be complacent. America had underestimated the Soviets once before!

Even as engineers were struggling with the SSMEs, the SRBs successfully completed their test and development programme on 17 February 1979. Although 'flight proven', three more SRB firings were later carried out at Thiokol's test range near Brigham City, Utah.

On 24 March 1979 *Columbia* arrived at Kennedy Space Centre after a stormy flight from Dryden, California, on top of 905. On its arrival it was discovered that some of the temporary tiles installed had fallen off during the flight. NASA had elected to bring *Columbia* to Kennedy before Rockwell had installed the final 10,000 tiles. It had been hoped that this would speed up flight readiness. Temporary 'filler' tiles were fixed onto the *Columbia*'s aluminium skin with tape and glue; however, most of these were lost by the time the combination reached Kennedy. It was the first encounter Kennedy Space Centre staff were to have with a problem that was to cause increasing concern over the coming months.

Shortly after arrival, *Columbia* was installed in the Orbiter Processing Facility behind the Vehicle Assembly Building (VAB). She was joined some weeks later by her sister, *Enterprise*.

Enterprise was to undergo a series of tests on Orbiter ground handling facilities at the Cape which would involve mating all three components of the Shuttle system (Orbiter, External Tank and SRB). Once assembled *Enterprise* was transferred to launch pad 39A, to check all the equipment and procedures to be used later in the roll out of *Columbia*. By using *Enterprise*, valuable time, lost on extra tiling work, could be partially regained. The only simulation *Enterprise* could not perform would be the actual fuelling of the External Tank. That would be a task assigned to *Columbia* before her maiden flight.

By July 1979, *Columbia* was still short of almost a quarter of her thermal insulating tiles. Installing a single tile was a lengthy process; involving first applying a layer of felt insulation to the Orbiter aluminium alloy skin; this base material allowed for a certain amount of movement between the metal and tile itself. The installation of a contoured tile to the felt was accomplished with the use of an epoxy adhesive. During the 6-7 hour setting time each tile had to be held in place under carefully controlled pressure. With 10,000 tiles to go, the weeks rolled into months, and NASA was becoming increasingly concerned about the rate of installation.

5 Enterprise

After an intensive period of engineering development *Columbia*'s first flight-rated SSMEs were fitted to the Orbiter in early August 1979. NASA hoped to have the *Columbia*, complete with External Tank and SRBs, assembled and in the launch pad by the end of November for a pre-launch test. It was not to be.

In January 1980 NASA was confident of a first flight before the end of the year. Tiling had delayed the project still further, but extra staff were working around the clock to get things right. Then, just when the job was almost completed, tests on almost 40 per cent of the tiles revealed a weakness. The bonding was not good enough to withstand NASA's safety margins. In consequence, hundreds of tiles had to be carefully removed, re-treated and re-applied.

Throughout 1980, launch dates were scheduled then moved back. At the end of the year, first flight was scheduled for March 1981, two years later than planned. NASA had by then solved all of the tile problems and the SSMEs had been flight ratified.

In Houston's Johnson Manned Spaceflight Centre, John Young and Robert Crippen, the crew of *Columbia*'s maiden flight stepped up their training programme.

NASA had named the two astronauts to fly STS 1 (Space Transportation System, Flight One) as far back as the beginning of 1978; anticipating then a launch in early 1979. Both John Young and Robert Crippen, although NASA astronauts, were also serving members of the US Navy.

John Watts Young was born on 24 September 1930 in San Francisco, California. After a distinguished Navy career he joined the ranks of NASA astronauts on 17 September 1962, as part of the space agency's second group of astronauts; the first being the original Mercury 'seven'. He became the joint-seventh American to fly into space as pilot of Gemini 3 on 23 March 1965. Commander of that flight was Gus Grissom. On return to Earth Young was assigned as back-up pilot for Gemini 6, then prime commander of Gemini 10 during its flight between 18 and 21 July 1966. His pilot for that flight was astronaut Michael Collins, later to become Command Module Pilot for Apollo 11.

In May 1969, after serving as a back-up Command Module Pilot for Apollo 7, John Young became the first man to fly 'solo' around the Moon during Apollo 10. Whilst *Snoopy*, the lunar module, descended to within a few miles of the Moon's surface with astronauts Tom Stafford and Eugene Ceman on board, John Young remained alone in *Charlie Brown*, the Command/Service Module, awaiting their return. Back on Earth once more John Young was assigned as back-up commander for the ill-fated Apollo 13, before finally making it to the moon's surface as commander of Apollo 16 in April 1972. On that flight he spent over 71 hours on the Moon, during which time he was told of America's commitment to the Shuttle. Less than a year later John Young was assigned as chief of the astronaut group assigned to the Space Shuttle. On the retirement of Deke Slayton in 1978, John Young became Chief of the Astronaut Office, a position he retained on assignment as commander of STS 1.

John Young's pilot on *Columbia*'s maiden flight was seven years his junior.

Robert Crippen had never flown in space before, he had transferred to NASA's astronaut ranks from the Air Force's X-20 follow-on MOL project on its cancellation in 1969. Since that time Robert Crippen had served in a key support role to the final Apollo flights and later the Skylab, and Apollo-Soyuz Test Project.

The two reserve crewmen for STS 1 were X-20 and X-15 veteran Joe Engle as commander and pilot Richard Truly.

On 24 November 1980, at 6 am Eastern Standard Time, *Columbia* left the Orbiter Processing Facility after a stay of almost 18 months, and transferred to the adjacent VAB. Once inside the VAB, *Columbia* was lifted off the floor under several cranes attached to her at four points. Her undercarriage was retracted, and the Orbiter was hoisted to a vertical position ready for mating with the External Tank and SRBs.

On 29 November 1980 *Columbia* completed a seven hour, two mile journey from the VAB to launch complex 39A. Although *Enterprise* had paved the way, checking out *Columbia*'s ground support systems, it did not have the facility to allow propellant loading out on the launch pad. NASA was therefore loading Shuttle liquid propellant for the first time, and many people anticipated further snags or delays before 'test' fuelling had been accomplished. Their doubts were to be confirmed after the External Tank's insulation began to crack and peel off close to its uppermost attachment point to *Columbia*. Subsequent repairs delayed the flight until April.

On 20 February 1981, *Columbia*'s three SSMEs ignited for a 20 second test fire. Martin Marietta, on examining the External Tank afterwards, found it to be in sound condition. The SSMEs had functioned perfectly. *Columbia* was ready; the countdown to launch began.

***Enterprise* stands on the desert airstrip after her fifth and final free flight. This orbiter would never again fly alone, but serve as a test bed for her space-rated sisters to follow. (NASA)**

6 Columbia

Several days after *Columbia*'s flight-readiness firing, on 30 March 1981, President Reagan was shot in an attempted assassination. Around the world memories of the death of President Kennedy were reawakened and America's image suffered a terrible blow. Television pictures repeated again and again the distressing scenes of bloodshed as the President, severely wounded, was bundled into his car by security men and rushed to hospital.

STS 1

The first flight of *Columbia,* scheduled for 10 April, was not only going to demonstrate that the Space Shuttle could perform as everybody had hoped, but would also regain some of the nation's faith and self respect. John Young was, by 1981, a national hero, and his fellow astronaut Robert Crippen was no less admired for the fact that he too had flown this, the most important spaceflight since Apollo 11, and the most dangerous in the history of NASA.

Mercury had made numerous unmanned launches before it was qualified as safe for a man to ride in. Gemini had made two flights and Apollo six; but the Shuttle was to carry two men on its first attempt to reach orbit. There was a tension at Kennedy Space Centre never before encountered, which built up almost to breaking point in the early hours of 10 April 1981. The whole future of America's 'man in space' hung on the outcome of this flight.

At a pre-launch press conference Bob Crippen described his approach to the flight of STS 1. 'It is a test flight, and that basically is what this entire 54 hour 37 orbit mission consists of, to make sure we can get up into orbit properly, and don't have any problems, that we can make sure all the systems on the vehicle function as they should, and we'll go through a systematic check-out of basically everything that's aboard, and make sure that we can fly re-entry like we planned. If we can just get up and get down, even if we had to do it all in one day, that would satisfy 95 per cent of the objectives of the flight.

'One of the most significant things that we'll be doing, especially the first time we come over the States after launch, is opening up our payload doors. The two payload bay doors are those which we open to expose the cargo bay of the Orbiter, which is 60 ft long and 15 ft wide, and those doors have a complicated set of latches on them and we're going to make sure that they do unlatch and function properly, and that they'll be able to close down properly once we do get them open. We'll also be testing out the environmental control systems, the cooling systems on board the spacecraft — we will even be doing mundane things like checking out the potty we've got on board!'

Both John Young and Robert Crippen were

woken early, at 2.00 am Eastern Standard Time, to begin the well established routine of breakfast and suiting up. Out on launch pad 39A, *Columbia* stood fuelled and ready. Over one million people had travelled to Cape Canaveral to witness the launch, whilst out at sea the liner *Queen Elizabeth II* was moored at a safe distance, to give her crew and passengers the best view of the lift off.

John Young was outwardly confident: 'It's gone through a multitude of tests, the tile system is designed to be in most areas four to five times

the NASA public affairs commentator announced a hold in the countdown:

'We do have a problem that we are working on at the present time. We have had a light come on which is a red-line indication that the ph [acid] level in fuel cell 3 is at an improper level. At the present time that problem is being analysed to determine whether or not to pick up the count at the normal time, or whether there is a 'fix' that has to occur, or what is the next course of action.'

Whilst launch control tried to find out what was wrong with fuel cell number three, another failure occurred, this time in one of *Columbia's* five general purpose computers.

'This is Shuttle Launch Control at T minus 9 minutes and holding, at the present time we are in

stronger than it needs to be. The engines have come through a rigorous test and they have had a lot of problems and they've fixed them. Last engine test was successful, if there is a vehicle we can have confidence in I believe it's the *Columbia*.'

With the crew aboard at 5.00 am EST, the countdown proceeded smoothly as dawn broke over the Cape. Then at T (lift off) minus 9 minutes,

The crew of STS 1: (left) John W. Young, Shuttle commander, and (right) Robert L. Crippen, Shuttle pilot. (NASA)

the process of 'dumping' the programme which has been the back-up flight computer's software, and we are going to re-enter that programme into the computer. We had thought that this particular

156

problem had gone away but it currently has not.'

Hours passed and *Columbia* remained Earth-bound. NASA's commentator continued to give updates to the massive audience.

'This is Shuttle Launch Control. At this present time we are reconfiguring the countdown clock to the 20 minute hold point. The countdown clock has been moving; however, it is just part of the procedure for recycling the clock, and it has nothing to do with the counting down in the countdown. We do not as yet have an estimated lift-off time, we are in the process of trying to calculate that. We have a number of constraints; the propelants which are on board are not a constraint; we can hold that as long as necessary.'

Unfortunately engineers could not overcome *Columbia's* difficulties and shortly before mid-day the launch attempt for 10 April was ended.

'The Launch Director George Page and Centre Director Dick Smith have just announced that we will scrub the launch attempt for today. We will stop the clock probably at the T minus 9 minute point, and send out a crew to open the hatch of the Orbiter, and take the crew back to the astronaut quarters. The earliest time in which we could possibly reschedule the launch will be for Sunday morning at 6.50 am EST.'

John Young and Bob Crippen had been on board the Orbiter *Columbia* for 6 hours. The veteran commander responded to the cancellation announcement, 'what a pity on such a lovely day'.

STS 1 Flight Plan

Mission elapsed time   Activity

hr	min	sec	
00	00	00	Solid Rocket Boosters ignition and lift-off
00	00	53	Mach 1
00	00	54	Maximum aerodynamic pressure on the vehicle
00	02	12	Solid Rocket Booster separation
00	08	32	Main Engine cut-off
00	08	50	External Tank separation
00	10	00	Orbital Manoeuvring System engine, burn 1 (Orbit 130x55 nautical miles altitude)
00	14	00	OMS burn 2 (orbit 130x130 nautical miles altitude)
01	20	00	Begin payload bay door test
02	45	00	Inertial Measurement Unit (IMU)/Startracker tests

03	15	00	Fuel cell purge
03	35	00	Crew remove emergency ejection suits
04	00	00	Activate *Columbia* orbital systems
05	00	00	Meal
06	22	00	OMS burn 3 — (orbit 150x130 nautical miles altitude)
07	05	00	OMS burn 4 — (orbit 150x150 nautical miles altitude)
07	30	00	Flight Control System check including IMU alignment and RCS jet tests
09	20	00	Television broadcast
09	50	00	Meal
11	00	00	IMU alignment
11	55	00	Fuel cell purge
12	15	00	Rest period
20	50	00	Wake up call
21	35	00	IMU alignment
22	20	00	RCS test
22	45	00	Meal
24	00	00	Television broadcast
26	00	00	RCS test
26	30	00	Close payload bay doors
27	22	00	RCS test
27	35	00	Cabin air test
28	15	00	Payload bay doors opening
29	00	00	Meal
30	15	00	IMU alignment
30	45	00	Emergency Ejection Suit checkout
32	40	00	RCS test
33	40	00	Meal
34	45	00	Carbon dioxide absorber (cabin air) replacement
35	40	00	IMU alignment
37	13	00	Rest period
44	50	00	Wake-up call
46	00	00	IMU alignment
46	15	00	RCS test
46	25	00	Meal
47	25	00	Stow equipment and prepare for re-entry
49	25	00	Put on Emergency Ejection Suits
50	30	00	Close payload bay doors
51	15	00	Meal
52	00	00	IMU alignment
52	30	00	Strap into seats
53	28	00	De-orbit OMS burn
53	56	00	Begin re-entry
54	28	00	Landing

Sunday 12 April 1981 was the twentieth anniversary of Yuri Gagarin's first manned spaceflight. At just after 2.00 am, John Young and Bob Crippen were awakened to begin again the same pre-launch preparations of two days earlier. The earlier problems had been corrected and *Columbia* was ready to 'Go'.

As John Young and Bob Crippen shook hands and bade farewell to the launch technicians out in the 'white room' on top of launch pad 39A, and entered *Columbia,* the countdown was proceeding normally. The two crewmen entered the Orbiter through its side access hatch, then, wearing their bulky rust-brown-coloured Emergency Ejection Suits (EES), clambered across the 'wall' of the lower deck and up onto the flight deck. There astronaut Loren Schriver assisted the two men into their seats. John Young, as commander, sat on the left, Bob Crippen, pilot, on the right. With *Columbia* pointing upwards to the sky any movement inside the cabin was extremely difficult. Loren Schriver, wearing only engineer's overalls, was in a far better position to plug in and secure the astronauts' many communication interconnections than John Young or Bob Crippen.

Before Loren Schriver could leave *Columbia* a problem arose. NASA's commentator relayed the problem to the million plus audience at the Cape. There were no 'secrets', if anything went wrong; everyone should know. As Schriver later recalled:

'After the crew had entered the cabin, when we tried to hook up their air hoses to their helmets, it was discovered that they were not getting air properly at their helmets. It turned out that the

Columbia's aft flight deck station in final assembly at Rockwell's Palmdale facility. It is from this station that the RMS is operated, viewing through the two lower windows into the payload bay and through the flight deck 'roof' windows. (Rockwell International)

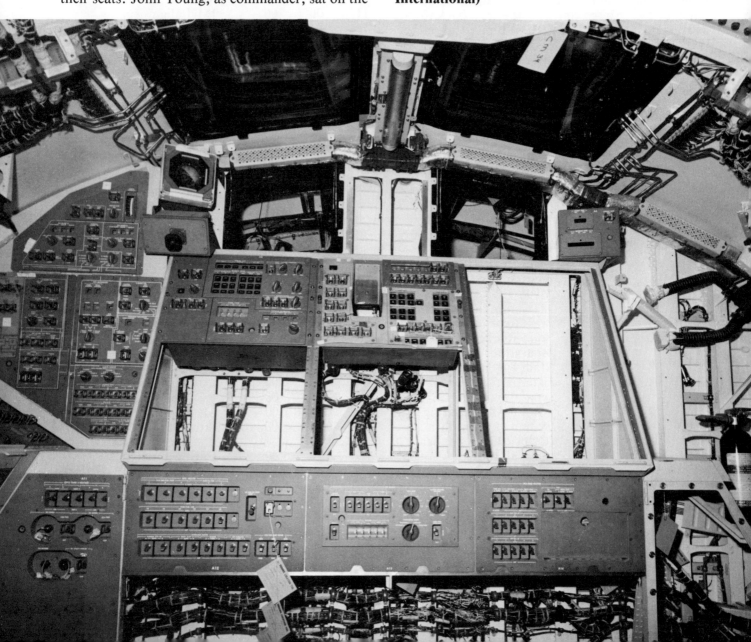

problem was in what is called a 'quick disconnect', it's a connection that is located underneath the ejection seats which is used for connecting the hose that goes to the helmets. The 'quick disconnect' was not quite in the proper position and a locking pin was not in place.'

With the crew of *Columbia* securely in place, strapped in, and connected up Loren Schriver left the vehicle. The technicians closed *Columbia's* side-hatch securely, locking it in position, then began evacuating the launch pad. The countdown proceeded normally, passing without a murmur the 9 minute mark reached two days earlier. At T minus 5 minutes the access arm and 'white room' swung back inside the protective cocoon of the launch gantry. Then *Columbia's* APUs started up to power her control surfaces and engine gimbal actuators. *Columbia* was now alone and beginning the final seconds to launch.

This moment was the culmination of aviation achievement which started with the Wright Brothers' first heavier-than-air flight in 1903; it was the final justification of the investment of

inspiration, energy and cash that resulted in Chuck Yeager's Mach 1 flight in 1947, the X-15 and Bob White's first winged flight into space, the X-20 that almost made it, and the almost forgotten lifting body programme. If only Dr Eugene Sanger could have lived to witness the launch of the 'Silver Bird' he prophesied almost half a century earlier in Vienna! The weight of historical significance was overwhelming, enhanced by the appearance of *Columbia,* who, with her white External Tank and Solid Rocket Boosters, stood out from the mangrove swamps and waterways around Cape Canaveral like a national monument.

The aft flight deck station is used also for rendezvous manoeuvring using hand controls and the attitude indicator shown in the bottom left of the picture. (Rockwell International)

For those watching, any nostalgia for the past was soon to be forgotten in the awe inspiring events to come. NASA's public affairs commentator marked off the final major events to launch, his voice echoing from numerous loudspeakers situated around the launch site. The weather was perfect, a typically hot, humid Florida day.

'T minus four minutes and counting; as preparations for main engine ignition the main fuel valve heaters have been turned on. T minus 3 minutes 57 seconds and counting; the final fuel purge on the Shuttle Main Engines has been started in preparation for engine start. The liquid oxygen replenish system has been turned off in preparation for pressurization of the tanks for the launch. T minus three minutes 35 seconds and counting; the elevons, speed brake and rudder are being moved through a preprogrammed pattern to ensure that they will be ready for use in flight. T minus 3 minutes 20 seconds and counting; the Shuttle is now on internal power; however, the fuel cells are still receiving their fuel from the ground support system for one more additional minute. Coming up on T minus 3 minutes. T minus 3 minutes and counting; the engine gimbal, or movement, check is underway to ensure that they are ready for flight control. T minus 2 minutes 52 seconds; the liquid oxygen valve on the External Tank has been closed and pressurization has begun. After the tank is pressurized the 'hold' capability is limited to 3 minutes 36 seconds. T minus 2 minutes 40 seconds, and counting; the fuel cell ground supply of hydrogen and oxygen has been terminated and the vehicle is using its on board supply. T minus 2 minutes 25 seconds and counting. T minus 2 minutes 15 seconds; the pressure in the liquid oxygen tank is at flight pressure. Coming up on just 2 minutes away from launch: T minus 2 minutes mark, and counting; the liquid hydrogen vent valve has been closed and its flight pressurization is underway. T minus 1 minute and 50 seconds and counting; Chuck Hannon has just said, "Smooth sailing, baby", to astronauts John Young and Bob Crippen. T minus 1 minute and 35 seconds and counting. T minus 1 minute and 10 seconds and counting; liquid hydrogen tank is at flight pressure. T minus 1 minute, mark, and counting. The firing system for the sound-suppression water system will be armed at just a couple of seconds from now. It has been armed. T minus 45 seconds and counting. T minus 40 seconds and counting; the development flight instrumentation recorders are on. T minus 35 seconds; we are just a few seconds away from switching on the redundant sequence. T minus 27 seconds; we have gone for redundant sequence start. T minus 20 seconds and counting. T minus 15-14-13, T minus 10-9-8-7-6-5-4- we've gone for main engine start. We have main engine start.'

The commentator's voice was drowned in the howling roar of Columbia's three SSMEs as clouds of smoke and steam billowed up and around pad 39A. Seconds later the two SRBs kicked into life and shook the very ground itself for miles around.

'Lift-off. Lift-off of America's first Space Shuttle — The Shuttle has cleared the tower!'

Bob Crippen's heartrate soared to 130 beats a minute, the veteran John Young's only to 85.

Over a million people cheered, waved, shouted or wept as the pounding shock waves of six and a half million pounds of thrust thundered across Cape Canaveral. Slowly, the white Shuttle vehicle rose from the ground, the brightness of her engines like a second mini sunrise. Pressmen and photographers looked and cheered, their cameras and notebooks forgotten as Columbia rose higher into the blue sky, a long billowing trail of exhaust in her wake.

In the cockpit, John Young and Robert Crippen monitored equipment and instruments as Columbia began its long sweeping arc out across the Atlantic. Through Mach 1 at 50 seconds into the flight, all the engines reduced thrust for a moment to relieve the tremendous strains on the structure. The entire cabin was illuminated by the light of the engines far below. The flight deck forward windows were being hit by pieces of ice from the External Tank, the sound of multiple impact lost in the low hard roar of the engines almost 80 ft behind. For the two astronauts every second that the flight continued normally brought them nearer orbit. Abort contingency times came and went as Columbia soared even higher. It was soon apparent that engineers had underestimated Columbia's power, climbing a full 5 degrees steeper than had been planned. At just under 132 seconds from lift-off the SRBs, their fuel exhausted, shut down and fired away. On the ground onlookers could clearly see the flash of pyrotechnics that accompanied SRB separation. A loud cheer went up; across the waterways, launch complex 39A smouldered from the intense heat of the launch, the power of the Shuttle had scorched and blackened parts of the structure.

Communications between Mission Control's capsule communicator or CAPCOM and the Orbiter's crew interspersed the NASA Public Relations commentary.

Houston: Press for MECO [*Columbia* to continue on up to main engine cut-off]

Columbia: Rog — press to MECO

NASA (PR): Mark 4 minutes 8 seconds

Houston: *Columbia* stand by for negative return

NASA (PR): Mark 4 minutes 25 seconds; that call up from CAPCOM Brandenstein, *Columbia* now committed to space travel, Young and Crippen can no longer turn around and return to the launch site.

Houston: Columbia-Houston, we're showing both OMS, PC transducers off scale high.

NASA (PR): Mark 4 minutes 45 seconds, the

	flash evaporators activated on board to cool *Columbia*.
Columbia:	We're showing the transducers off scale low here.
Houston:	Roger stand by will keep an eye on it.
NASA (PR):	Mark 4 minutes 56 seconds; *Columbia's* lofting early in the second stage has now been taken out of the trajectory as programmed, *Columbia* now 74 nautical miles in altitude, 181 nautical miles down range.
Columbia:	Everything's on the nominal — what a view! — what a view! [*Columbia* had just pitched over so that the crew could see the horizon].
NASA (PR):	Mark 5 minutes 15 seconds; *Columbia* now 75 nautical miles in altitude, 202 nautical miles down range velocity now reading 11,000 feet per second.
Houston:	Status check in Mission Control by flight Director Neil Hutchinson. Columbia-Houston you are go at 5.30, MECO 8 plus 34.
NASA (PR):	Mark 5 minutes 40 seconds; that call up from CAPCOM Brandenstein says *Columbia* trajectory navigation and engine performance look good.
Columbia:	How do you read us Houston?
Houston:	Columbia-Houston, reading you loud and clear.
Columbia:	OK, your signal's a little weak.
Houston:	Columbia, we just switched over Bermuda, voice should be getting better in a second.
Columbia:	Roger — Okey-doke that's good.
NASA (PR):	6 minutes, *Columbia* now 76 nautical miles, 280 nautical miles down range, velocity now reading 13,000 feet per second.
Houston:	Columbia-Houston, could we have the cryogenic reading please; and Columbia you are single engine Rota.
Columbia:	Roger.
NASA (PR):	Mark 6 minutes 25 seconds; that call up from Capcom Brandenstein says that if two engine failures occur, *Columbia* is capable of an emergency landing at Rota Naval Air Station, Spain. Mark 6 minutes 40 seconds, *Columbia* pitching over

	now, diving to increase velocity, decrease altitude giving *Columbia* her most favourable altitude, *Columbia* now 72 nautical miles in altitude, 373 nautical miles down range, velocity now reading 16,400 feet per second. Standing by for single engine press to MECO from Capcom Brandenstein.
Houston:	Columbia you are single engine press for MECO.
NASA (PR):	Mark 7 minutes 20 seconds; that report says that Young and Crippen can achieve orbital insertion even if two engines go out. Mark 7 minutes 30 seconds; *Columbia* now 67 miles in altitude, 485 nautical miles down range g-forces building for Young and Crippen now — up to 3gs. Mark 7 minutes 45 seconds; *Columbia's* main engines slowly being throttled back now, should be throttled at 65 per cent at 6 seconds before main engine cut-off status check at control centre.
Houston:	Columbia-Houston, you are go at 8.
Columbia:	Looking good.
NASA (PR):	Mark 8 minutes 4 seconds; *Columbia* now 63 nautical miles in altitude 606 nautical miles down range. Mark 8 minutes 15 seconds *Columbia* now 63 nautical miles altitude 650 nautical miles down range. Standing by now for main engine cut-off.
Columbia:	MECO! 25,670 up at 220 feet per second!
Houston:	Roger *Columbia,* MECO!
NASA (PR):	Confirm shut-down, *Columbia,* the gem of this new ocean now in space, not yet in orbit, standing by now for External Tank separation.
Houston:	Roger we confirm the separation *Columbia.*
NASA (PR):	Confirming Tank Separation, *Columbia* now performing an evasive manoeuvre moving below and beyond, and translating to the north of the External Tank. Young should see it moving away outside his window.

NASA (PR): 9 minutes 40 seconds; Go/No-Go status check in mission control for the first OMS burn — given a Go.

Houston: Columbia-Houston, you are 'Go' for nominal OMS 1, and APUs shut down on time.

Columbia: Roger that.

NASA (PR): Mark 9 minutes 55 seconds; *Columbia* now manoeuvring to its OMS 1 burn altitude. Using the two 6,000 lb thrust engines OMS 1 will be posigrade moving *Columbia* forward and higher on her flight path, placing *Columbia* in orbit. Standing by for ignition 10 minutes 22 seconds.

The twin OMS engines ignited, thrusting *Columbia* into a stable orbit. John Young commented, 'The view hasn't changed any — it's really something else!' Bob Crippen replied, 'I tell you; John has been telling me about it for three years, but there is no way you can describe it!' On the ground Launch Director George Page was ecstatic, 'It was a great job. I think the feeling there [in the Launch Centre] was just fantastic. We got off on time, apparently everything worked well, we had very few problems in the minus count — what more can I say? We are thrilled and proud today.' Neil Armstrong was a guest at the launch, and he said, 'It was a beautiful sight and we are delighted it's gone so well. I understand that there is nothing wrong at this time and that's always a great surprise; you usually expect a few things going wrong.'

As John Young and Bob Crippen settled down in orbit, the first major task was to open, close and then open again one of the two payload bay doors. With this test completed, both doors were opened, and the first problem of the flight became obvious: John Young commented on the TV pictures being

Columbia's starboard payload bay door is checked prior to installation on the Orbiter, and addition of the heat-dispersing radiators. (Rockwell International)

relayed live to Earth, 'We do have a few tiles missing off both of them [OMS pods] — off the starboard pod basically — what looks or appears to be three tiles and some smaller pieces; and off the port pod it looks like I see one full square and looks like a few little triangular shapes that are missing, and we're trying to put that on TV right now. From what we can see of both wings and leading edges, all those are fully intact.' Houston commented for the benefit of concerned viewers: 'These are not critical tiles, these tiles that are missing represent no hazard to the vehicle or the crew — the worst that can happen is that after landing a small patch of skin underneath the tiles may have to be replaced.'

Despite these assurances the non-specialist press continued in an attempt to sensationalize the missing tiles, concentrating for the rest of the flight on this one aspect whilst everything else performed flawlessly. Within hours of the discovery of miss-

The long and laborious task of installing *Columbia*'s heat-resistant tiles was one of many jobs to be completed at the Kennedy Space Centre before launch. Shown here is a part of the Orbiter's underside. (Rockwell International)

ing tiles on the OMS pods, NASA had photographed the underside of *Columbia* from secret high-resolution ground-based Air Force cameras. Confident that there were none missing on the critical underside, the flight continued. The payload bay's doors had been opened successfully and her heat dispersing radiators were functioning well. With a good 'Go' for orbit, both crewmen took off their bulky Emergency Ejection Suits and stowed them in favour of blue lightweight flight overalls.

The next major item to be tackled was the first alignment of *Columbia*'s Inertial Measurement Units. This device enables the Orbiter's computers to establish an accurate 'fix' on *Columbia*'s position at any given moment. The IMUs provide a gyroscopically-stabilized platform which is 'fixed' in space, and around which the space vehicle's movement can be gauged. The movement information is recorded and interpreted by a guidance computer which transmits the information to the crew via flight deck instruments. Regular checks of

specific star locations through an adapted telescope in the mid deck allow continual astro-navigational correction to IMU drift. The crew would make three alignments of the IMUs each 'day' in space to compensate for minor drifts in the IMU system. Each time, the crew would set the IMUs up against known star positions through a 'star-tracker' device mounted in *Columbia's* nose section.

Following a purge of *Columbia's* fuel cells, in which all accumulated impurities were flushed out, the crew ate their first meal in space, then turned on the TV cameras for a broadcast to Earth. The first pictures showed John Young at work in the left-hand (commander's) seat, wearing glasses and going through the checklist. He was full of praise for *Columbia*. 'We've done every test we're supposed to do, and we are up on the timelines, and the vehicle is performing beautifully; much better than anyone ever expected to do on its first flight. No systems are out of shape and, to give an example, we did three star-tracker alignments in less time than it takes to do one star-tracker alignment in the mission simulator. All the RCS jets have been firing and the vehicle is just performing like a champ. Really beautiful, it's delightful up here!'

Bob Crippen added his comments: 'OK we're switching over to the aft camera here and showing the aft deck — how does that picture look to you?' Hank Hartsfield, astronaut and Capcom for STS 1, replied: 'Coming in real good.' Bob Crippen continued, 'OK Hank, I'd like to echo John's words, as I usually do. I guess that being a so-called 'rookie' on this flight I had a thrill from the moment of lift off all the way up to what we're doing now. It has really been super; the spacecraft has worked as advertised all the way along, a few little minor nuisance problems but nothing of significance. I guess the major one you guys are working on down there is dealing with some of our instrumentation, but I think we have got something that's really going to mean something to the country and the World. This vehicle is performing like a champ, like all of us who have worked so long in it knew that she would'.

The TV transmission ended the first 'day' in space and the crew prepared to turn in for the night. On this flight the crew slept strapped into their flight deck ejection seats. The space provided for bunks on the mid deck had been taken up by additional flight test equipment. Bob Crippen closed day one on an optimistic note, 'We are looking forward to working with you guys and looking forward to landing at Edwards just over a day from now — unless you've got some questions for us Hank, I guess that does it.' 'Oh, that's good timing,' said Henry Hartsfield, 'I guess you must

have practiced, we're just about to lose you at Goldstone'.

Columbia flew out of range of Goldstone ground station, and into another period of communication 'black-out'. On board, John Young and Bob Crippen, who had been awake for 18 hours, enjoyed a few minutes sightseeing before they put up the window blinds and turned in for what was to be a restless night. During the night the cabin temperature dropped and the constant noise on the flight deck made sleep almost impossible. *Columbia* was a noisy vehicle, and although both John Young and Bob Crippen had acoustic blankets which they fastened to the floor to lessen the 'hard' resonances in the cabin, the noise, coupled with the day's excitement, made sleep difficult. By morning (if that definition can be used in space!) John Young and Bob crippen had managed to snatch only a few hours of rest between them.

At 3.43 am EST, as *Columbia* flew over Ecuador, Capcom Daniel Brandenstein woke the crew with a Country and Western song specially written for the occasion; the lyrics were particularly apt:

Now many man hours went into
this thing,
A job well done by the Shuttle space team,
We can't say that she's sleek and lean,
But I'll tell you right now she's a mean machine.
The Columbia!

Daniel Brandenstein followed with a call up 'Morning *Columbia,* welcome to day two.' John Young responded with 'Alright'. Intrigued as to how well the astronauts slept, Daniel Brandenstein asked, 'You guys shivering up there, or is the temperature pretty good?' 'Well,' said John Young, 'it certainly got a little bit chilly last night. We were about ready to break out the long undies!'

As Daniel Brandenstein relayed procedures to the crew to 'warm up' *Columbia's* cabin, the two astronauts began the major pre-breakfast task of testing the spaceship's RCS thrusters. They also allowed *Columbia* to 'drift' on several occasions, to see how stable she would remain without the RCS thrusters maintaining attitude. Breakfast on board *Columbia* on this test flight would be much like those 'enjoyed' by astronauts on Apollo and Skylab. The deluxe galley for *Columbia's* lower deck had not yet been installed, and so John Young and Bob Crippen had to make do with rehydrated food for their three meals a day. To relieve the monotony NASA had arranged for a variety of conventional items such as tea, coffee and assorted snacks to eat between meals if they wanted.

After breakfast the crew of *Columbia* continued testing the RCS and then made a further closing and opening test of the payload doors. Engineers were concerned at the possibility of warping of the doors after prolonged space exposure. As it turned out their fears were to be dispelled as the doors closed perfectly, and opened again two hours later. Later, with *Columbia* passing over Kennedy Space Centre, Capcom Joe Allen, who had taken over from Daniel Brandenstein, made a call to *Columbia* saying, 'Columbia, if you look down you'll see Cape Kennedy perhaps, there was a tremendous launch from there yesterday, which you may not have seen.' Bob Crippen entered into the spirit of light-hearted banter, 'Oh, we saw it! Oh! Let's see, we're coming over. Oh! There we go, I've got the runway and the VAB in sight.' 'Very good,' said Joe Allen, 'it's exactly twenty-four hours ago. You've been there for one day now.'

The other activity before lunch on the second day was a live TV broadcast during which American viewers could see both John Young and Bob Crippen working at the payload bay and RCS controls, surrounded by notebooks and the leads connecting their communication headsets to the flight

consoles. These leads were a source of constant nuisance to the crew as one remarked: 'It's like swimming around in a sea of spaghetti.'

After lunch on the second day, at just after 3 pm EST, Vice President Bush, standing-in for President Reagan (who was still in hospital) made a congratulatory speech to the crew of *Columbia* during the second TV broadcast of the day. Once the broadcast was over and all the PR work done, John Young and Bob Crippen set about a dress rehearsal for the next day's landing. John Young

Flight status information is provided by three CRTs controlled by the computer console at the bottom of the picture. (NASA)

and Bob Crippen took turns in putting on their respective Emergency Ejection Suits and climbing into and out of their ejection seats on the flight deck.

With their Emergency Ejection Suits once more stowed away, the crew of *Columbia* made an attempt to repair a faulty data recorder located beneath the floor of the lower deck. The attempt had to be abandoned as Bob Crippen found that the screws which secured its panel cover had been torqued in too securely. He told Houston, 'We can't get enough leverage to break them. I'm not sure if I was in 1g I could break them. I'm just not sure this is going to be productive because we are going to end up spending at least four or five hours trying to do it.'

By 7.00 pm EST, John Young and Bob Crippen had returned to the flight deck and strapped themselves into their seats for the second night in space.

On the ground the crowds were gathering at

This view of the uncompleted forward section of the lower deck gives a good indication of the complexity of the electrical and electronics system within the Orbiter. Much of the equipment represents back-up components for primary systems. (Rockwell International)

NASA's Dryden Research Centre, Edwards AFB for *Columbia*'s return. Meanwhile, NASA was becoming increasingly annoyed at the media's continued questions and enquiries about the *Columbia*'s missing OMS pod tiles. Despite their continued reassurance that everything would be fine, the media still pressed this point. At one conference a woman reporter asked, 'What would be the worst possible thing that could happen during re-entry with these tiles missing?' The Flight Director looked at her squarely and said, 'Nothing'. The press conference erupted in laughter. The next searching question was, 'Why does John Young wear glasses?' Exasperated, ex-Skylab astronaut Dr Joe Kerwin explained, 'Astronauts have been carrying sunglasses around for years, not necessarily prescription, so the provisions were already there, and what he's got on is a pair of reading glasses to enable him, in the occasionally dim light of the cockpit, to read the fine print of the check-list.'

John Young was awake early for 'day' three. Their second night had been more comfortable than the first, albeit broken by a systems alarm when one of *Columbia*'s APUs began to experience a temperature drop. The problem was dealt with by the crew and they soon resumed their rest. As Bob Crippen slept, John Young made a few systems checks before disappearing down to the lower deck to brew some coffee and heat-up some breakfast. Below at Edwards, the weather was perfect for landing, the skies were clear, and the wind merely a breeze.

The official wake-up call to the crew came at 3.40 am EST, during *Columbia's* 31st orbit of the Earth. The morning was filled with activities related to de-orbit, re-entry and landing. The RCS thrusters were checked, the APUs powered up, all *Columbia's* movable aerodynamic controls flexed, and her cockpit avionics tested. At 8.20 am EST came the final TV transmission of the flight. Whilst the cameras relayed spectacular views of Earth to millions of Americans, John Young and Robert Crippen prepared to put on their Emergency Ejection Suits for the final time and close the payload bay doors.

Whilst this activity was taking place John Young and Bob Crippen also found time to load a software package called OPS-8 into *Columbia's* computers. OPS-8 was a self-checking diagnostic programme which would help the computers to function without reference to the ground telemetry during re-entry 'blackout'.

At just after 11.30 am EST, the final, starboard, payload bay door was closed and the crew 'dumped' data from *Columbia's* guidance computers to Mission Control so that they could verify that the information and stored data was correct.

At 12.45 pm EST, John Young made a final IMU alignment before closing the star-tracker port doors on *Columbia's* nose section. Bob Crippen purged the fuel cells, and the two men strapped into their seats for re-entry and put on their helmets. The flight data recorder was switched on. During the de-orbit 'burn' John Young would maintain a check on *Columbia's* attitude via the attitude direction indicator on the flight deck instrument console. Simultaneously, Bob Crippen would monitor the OMS engine pressures.

By 1.54 pm EST *Columbia* was turning 'tail first' to her flight path in preparation for the burn of her two 6,000 lb thrust OMS engines. They would slow the 100 ton spacecraft down sufficiently for the pull of Earth's gravity to overcome the outward pull of centrifugal force. The burn came at 2.21 pm and lasted for just under 160 seconds. It was perfect; *Columbia* had effectively slowed down by 298 feet per second and was on her way, the first time a manned, winged vehicle had returned from space since Bill Dana brought X-15-1 home in August 1968.

Just before radio black-out, 'Capcom' Joe Allen called, 'Nice and easy does it, John; we're all riding with you.' 'Roger that,' said John Young, 'we'll see you at Mach 12.' Behind Joe Allen at Houston Mission Control was Joe Engle, recalling no doubt the last time he flew back from space, in X-15-1 in October 1965. He said about flying the Shuttle down to landing:

'I think the vehicle is exciting to fly, I don't think it will ever become a bore to learn to fly the

John Young logs time in the Shuttle mission simulator in preparation for STS 1. (NASA)

The two Orbiter Processing Facility buildings (with the VAB behind), prior to receiving *Columbia* on her delivery from Rockwell International. (Author)

Columbia arriving at Kennedy Space Centre on 24 March 1979 on board the 905 for what was to be two years of preparation for her first flight into space. (NASA)

Shuttle. It's a demanding airplane to learn to fly and it requires a great deal of aggressiveness to keep ahead of the airplane, so I don't think that you'll ever want to put a pilot in the airplane who does not think and is not capable of acting and performing aggressively and with very short notice.

'The vehicle has some subtle characteristics that require a little different type of technique in landing. The aerodynamic flight controls are some 80 feet behind us and they go up and down while we sit generally still, while they change its attitude and the angle of attack to generate more lift. If you can imagine coming in for a landing and deciding that you want to descend or get down a little lower to the runway because your airspeed's a little low, you push forward on the stick. The first thing the back end does is come up, the elevons go down and you don't feel anything, so you don't realize that you've changed attitude at first. Then as you start coming down, you see that you have, and perhaps it's too much! You want to arrest that sink rate, so you come back on the stick and the reverse thing happens! Your elevons go up and you dump lift,

Whilst *Columbia* was made ready for flight, *Enterprise* (flown into Kennedy Space Centre) checked out the ground handling procedures and launch pad structures. (NASA)

the back end drops down, but you are not aware of anything for almost a full second. So the Shuttle has some characteristics that do require getting used to.'

At around 2.50 pm EST, John Young and Robert Crippen could see bright flashes of colour appear out of their forward-facing flight deck windows, the tenuous upper atmosphere reflecting the short bursts of *Columbia*'s OMS pod-mounted RCS thrusters. At 400,000 ft and Mach 25, *Columbia* was flying in a 'nose-up' attitude of 40 degrees, held steady by the nose- and rear-mounted RCS thrusters. At 335,000 ft, the air outside began to thicken and *Columbia*'s aerodynamic controls began first to supplement, then later replace altogether, the thrusters. At 330,000 ft *Columbia* was still in the Earth's night-time shadow. A pinkish glow began to illuminate the outside of the spacecraft, then a deeper shade of orange. The crew felt themselves forced down into their seats as the g-forces returned. Suddenly *Columbia* broke into sunrise, and all the colours disappeared. Her automatic systems handled every aspect of the flight

Lift-off. The launch of America's first Space Shuttle on 12 April 1981. (NASA)

The moment of ignition of both SRBs. (NASA)

control and energy management flawlessly. At 263,000 ft and Mach 24 *Columbia* began the first of a series of 'S' turns to dissipate speed and energy.

As *Columbia* re-entered the Earth's atmosphere, the computers conducted complex calculations matching her remaining energy with remaining distance, altitude, weather conditions etc. Because the Orbiter is a glider it is essential that sufficient energy is in hand at any moment of the approach phase to allow the runway to be reached. At the same time, the energy remaining must be dissipated with precision so that little is left at the runway threshold.

As *Columbia* roared high across the Pacific, her computers banked the spaceship 80 degrees to the right. In their enthusiasm they overshot to 85

Launch Complex 39A; in the foreground is parked one of the mobile launchers. (Author)

degrees and *Columbia* rolled to the left as the error was corrected. Still in radio blackout, the temperature of her leading wing edges climbed to 2,700 °F. At 220,000 ft, *Columbia* rolled to the left at Mach 18. Below them John Young and Bob Crippen could see the coast of California rushing up to meet them, after almost 15 minutes of radio silence they tried to contact Houston once more.

At 1.08 pm EST, John Young called, 'Hello Houston, Columbia here.' 'Hello Columbia, Houston here,' responded Joe Allen, 'You've got perfect energy, perfect ground track.'

By the time *Columbia* had slowed to Mach 9 she was at 155,000 ft altitude and beginning her third roll, once more banking to the right. 'What a way to come to California,' said John Young as *Columbia* roared across the Californian coastline at Mach 6. Above Edwards, four T-38 chase planes moved in ready to follow *Columbia* down. TV cameras had, by then, tracked the returning spacecraft which looked like a white dart as it streaked across the sky. Although the automatic systems were performing perfectly John Young took over manual control at 115,000 ft and Mach 5. Engineers were not sure just how well the Orbiter shape

would behave at speeds from thereon down to Mach 2, and if there were to be any unexpected 'quirks' during her final banking manoeuvres they wanted an experienced test pilot, rather than a machine at the helm. At Mach 3, the crew were relatively safe. Joe Allen called-up and announced that they could, if an emergency occurred, use their ejection seats from then on.

At 85,000 ft altitude, both astronauts were being forced forwards into their seat harnesses by *Columbia's* deceleration. By the time they reached Mach 2 John Young had made his final manual banking manoeuvre and had switched back control to automatic. There were no unexpected surprises in *Columbia's* handling. During the transonic zone between Mach 2 and Mach .8, however, the crew felt the spaceship vibrate and buffet before smoothing out five minutes before landing.

On the ground thousands of people peered into the blue sky for their first glimpse of *Columbia,* whose arrival was heralded by the distant thunder of a double sonic boom. At 50,000 ft, *Columbia* streaked in from the west and over Rogers Dry Lake bed before making a 210 degree turn to port to line up with Runway 23. John Young once

more assumed manual control. This phase of landing involved flying around a planned 40,000 ft diameter circle to lose any remaining excess speed. Spiralling down from 35,000 ft to 12,000 ft, *Columbia* left the circle and straightened out her flight path on a direct heading for Runway 23.

Around her, the T-38 chase planes closed-in to call out the final altitude and speeds. John Young was now in full control of *Columbia* as they descended rapidly to the lake bed below. At 1,750 ft, he raised *Columbia's* stubby nose to bleed-off the remaining speed as the lake bed threshold passed beneath them. At 400 ft and 211 mph he lowered the landing gear. For a few seconds *Columbia* held off touchdown as she flew above the dusty runway, then, with a puff of dust, the main wheels made contact followed by the nose-wheel. 'Welcome home, *Columbia,'* said Joe Allen, as Mission Control erupted into applause. 'Do you want me to take it up to the hangar Joe?'

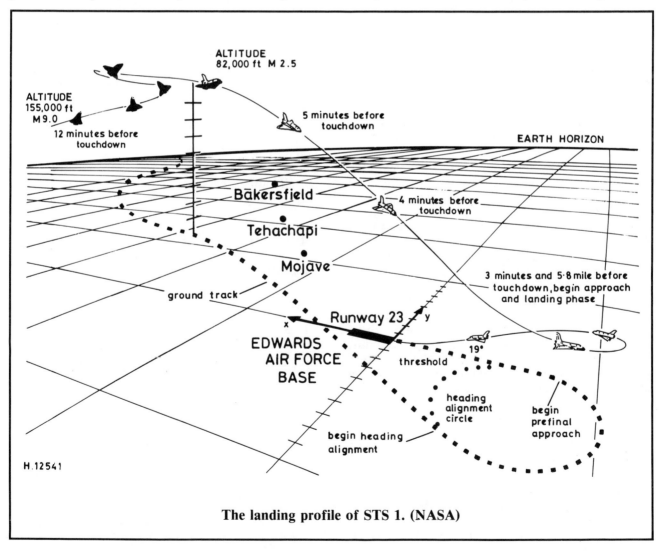

The landing profile of STS 1. (NASA)

said John Young as if he has just returned from a brief weekend hop. 'We're going to dust it off first!' Joe Allen replied.

As *Columbia* rolled to a halt, NASA and America knew that they had not only regained the lead in spaceflight, but had established the start of a whole new era in space exploration and exploitation.

Over the airwaves between Houston and *Columbia* the banter continued. Joe Allen said, 'There are lots of contractors with smiles on their faces.' John Young replied, 'You can tell them we are preparing the cheques.'

As John Young bantered with Houston, a convoy of twenty specially-equipped service vehicles closed around *Columbia* which was still hot from the frictional heat of atmospheric re-entry. Technicians, wearing protective 'Self Contained Atmosphere Protection Ensemble (SCAPE) suits, began to sample the air around *Columbia* to test for toxic emissions from her RCS exhaust nozzles. With the 'all clear', an air conditioning unit was towed up to *Columbia* and connected to an umbilical panel just below the port OMS pod. This mobile unit fanned cold air through *Columbia,* whilst another unit alongside began to pump liquid coolant around heat sensitive Orbiter electronics. If these measures were not taken within 15 minutes of an Orbiter's landing, residual heat from re-entry might have a chance to 'soak' through the outer structure and cause severe internal damage.

Whilst work outside continued, inside the cockpit John Young and Bob Crippen began a sequence of operations to 'power down' and 'safe' *Columbia's* flight systems; a job they completed before the ground crew had brought up the Orbiter Hatch Access Vehicle. It was clear to mission control that the crew was impatient to leave Columbia. John Young, in particular, wanted to inspect the spacecraft that had taken him and his fellow astronaut 1,074,567 miles and 37 times around the Earth.

Over an hour after touchdown, John Young left *Columbia,* still in his Emergency Ejection Suit, dashed down the steps leading from the hatch and set about the ground crew, shaking hands, slapping backs, obviously delighted with the flight. Five minutes later Bob Crippen joined him. The two men were national heroes.

STS 1 returned with all the main objectives of the flight achieved. Six hours after touchdown *Columbia* had been towed to the special Orbiter gantry at Dryden, so that her residual fuel could be off-loaded in preparation for her ferry flight back to the Kennedy Space Centre, where she arrived on 28 April.

Immediate post-flight inspections revealed damage to 300 of *Columbia's* tiles of which almost 230 had been affected during launch, with many others scored and chipped by debris thrown up during the lakebed landing; those being mostly concentrated around the rear body flap.

As John Young and Bob Crippen began extensive de-briefing session in Houston, Joe Engle and Richard Truly were getting ready to prove that *Columbia* could fly again, on STS 2.

With the successful completion of STS 1, NASA announced the names of nineteen new pilot astronauts and mission specialists. Out of the total, thirteen had strong military back-grounds, a clue to future potential uses of the Space Transportation System. The group of 1981, NASA's ninth (the first being the original Mercury 'seven'), were:

Military

Lt Col John Blaha, USAF	(plt)
Major Charles Bolden, US Marines	(plt)
Lt Col Roy Bridges, USAF	(plt)
Major Guy Gardner, USAF	(plt)
Major Ronald Grabe, USAF	(plt)
Captain David Hilmers, US Marines	(ms)
Lt Cdr David Leestma, US Navy	(ms)
Major Bryan O'Connor, US Marines	(plt)
Lt Cdr Richard Richards, US Navy	(plt)
Captain Jerry Ross, USAF	(ms)
Lt Cdr Mike Smith, US Navy	(plt)
Major Sherwood Spring, US Army	(ms)
Major Robert Springer, US Marines	(ms)

Civilians

Dr James Bagian	(ms)
Franklin Chang	(ms)
Mary Cleave	(ms)
Bonnie Dunbar	(ms)
Dr William Fisher	(ms)
John Lounge	(ms)

STS 2 Flight Plan

Mission elapsed time   Activity

hr	min	
00	10	OMS burn 1
00	42	OMS burn 2
01	25	Payload bay doors test
02	20	IMU alignment
03	30	Crew suit removal
04	00	OSTA 1 activation
05	00	Meal
06	21	OMS burn 3 — (incorporating simulated engine failure)
07	09	OMS burn 4
08	00	Main propulsion system de-activation
10	00	Meal
11	55	Gas sampling in crew compartment

13	00	Sleep (8 hours)
21	50	Hydraulic circulation test
22	40	Meal
23	50	Hydraulic circulation test
24	15	RMS test
27	50	Meal
28	40	Reaction control system test
29	35	Suit donning and testing
33	00	Crew exercise period
33	20	Gas sampling
35	00	Cabin noise level test
37	00	Sleep (8 hours)
46	10	Hydraulic circulation test
47	30	RMS — manual test
51	20	Hydraulic circulation test
52	00	Meal
54	10	Communications test
55	00	Crew exercise period
56	35	Tail jet tests
59	25	Gas sampling
60	45	Sleep (8 hours)
69	25	Star navigation test
72	30	Payload bay door open/close test
74	30	Crew exercise period
75	50	Meal
77	00	RMS test automatic
78	05	RMS test unload simulation
78	50	RMS test back-up system
79	30	RMS test data check
82	00	Meal
83	00	Gas sampling
84	00	Sleep (8 hours)
95	00	Star navigation test
96	05	RCS test firing
97	30	RCS translation test
98	00	OMS engine power up
100	00	Spacesuit/airlock test
103	00	RCS nose jets test
104	00	Window observations
104	30	Meal
107	45	Sleep (8 hours)
117	40	OSTA 1 de-activate
117	50	Stowage for re-entry
118	25	Flight control systems check
120	05	Crew don spacesuits
121	05	Payload bay doors close
122	55	Crew strap into seats
123	12	De-orbit OMS burn
124	38	Atmospheric re-entry
124	55	Landing Edwards AFB

STS 2

The crew of *Columbia's* second journey into space were confirmed as late as April 1981. Commander was to be Joe Engle, pilot Richard Truly.

Since leaving the X-15 programme and partici-

6 Columbia

pating in the Approach and Landing Test of *Enterprise,* Joe Engle had concentrated on his new role as back-up commander of STS 1 and prime commander of STS 2. Richard Truly too, had, since leaving the *Enterprise* Approach and Landing Tests been assigned as 'back-up' to STS 1 as pilot. STS 2 would make him the second ex-MOL astronaut to reach space (after Bob Crippen).

For this second flight of *Columbia,* scheduled to last over 124 hours or just over five days, the two crewmen would carry out further engineering tests on the Orbiter, in addition to a series of scientific tasks.

The first scientific payload in the Shuttle programme was in the form of five pallet-mounted experiments out in the cargo bay. Code named OSTA 1, they would be controlled by the astronauts via the flight deck. These first experiments consisted of MAPS, a device to measure carbon monoxide gas in the Earth's lower atmosphere; OCE, to trace and follow the migration of shoals of fish; FILE and SMIRR, to test remote sensing equipment; and SIRA, to test geological survey mapping work using a form of radar.

STS 2 would also be the first flight to carry the Canadian built RMS, or Remote Manipulator System arm. This arm would later be used to lift satellites out of the cargo bay for deployment, or rescue them for return to Earth. Essentially a general purpose tool, the RMS would form a mechanical extension to the operator's own arm, as he manoeuvred it via controls in *Columbia's* aft upper flight deck. Almost as long as the payload bay itself, this multi-jointed arm with a grappling device as a 'hand' was later to prove the most important accessory to the Shuttle operations.

Launch of STS 2 was delayed for several weeks because a slight spillage of *Columbia's* RCS fuel during filling damaged 379 of her thermal tiles. By the time engineers had replaced them, lift off had been rescheduled for 4 November.

Arriving from Houston two days before scheduled launch, Joe Engle and Richard Truly held an impromptu press conference. Joe Engle told the assembled audience, 'We're mightly glad that we are getting this close to flying, and Dick and I are both anxious. We've been looking forward to it for a long time and we're ready to go, — we're going to trim up and polish up tomorrow with the STA [Shuttle Training Aircraft] out on the strip, and the day after tomorrow we're going to do the real thing'. Dick Truly added, 'I'd just like to say that the *Columbia's* ready to go and we're more than ready!'

On 4 November 1981, *Columbia* stood fuelled and ready for her second trip into space. One hour and fifty minutes before launch the crew crossed over from the launch gantry to the flight deck and joined in the countdown. Then, thirty one seconds from the launch, data from *Columbia* indicated that a fuel cell oxygen tank was below pressure and the launch was held. No sooner had the hold been announced than one of the *Columbia's* APUs began to operate abnormally. Almost five hours elapsed before NASA, with the weather closing in, decided to scrub the launch.

Whereas the problem with the fuel cell was minor — and the computers had over-reacted by halting the launch sequence — the APU problem was more serious. Once technicians had managed to get to the unit some time after *Columbia* had been 'safed', they found that two of the three APUs had their lubricating oil contaminated with

The crew of STS 2. X-15 veteran astronaut Joe Engle, and his pilot, Richard Truly. (NASA)

hydrazine fuel. This fuel powered the APUs so that they could provide the power for *Columbia's* control surfaces and engine gimbals.

By 12 November *Columbia* had been repaired and was once again nearing lift-off. A computer malfunction earlier in the countdown had been rectified and all looked set for launch. The crew, prior to boarding *Columbia,* had held a second public appearance in which Joe Engle announced, 'We're really going to go this time — I don't think there was anybody more surprised than Richard and I when we heard we had to call a scrub last time because we were thoroughly convinced that we were just about ready to lift-off! We've just got this feeling that we are really going to do it this time! We've even got the weather good for us again!' Dick Truly added, 'We've just got to stop meeting out here like this! I'm going to say it one more time: the *Columbia's* ready and Joe and I are ready and we are going to do it this time.'

At the pre-launch breakfast the crew were guests of honour for a surprise birthday for Dick Truly. It was his 44th birthday and the launch team had prepared a special *Columbia*-shaped cake for

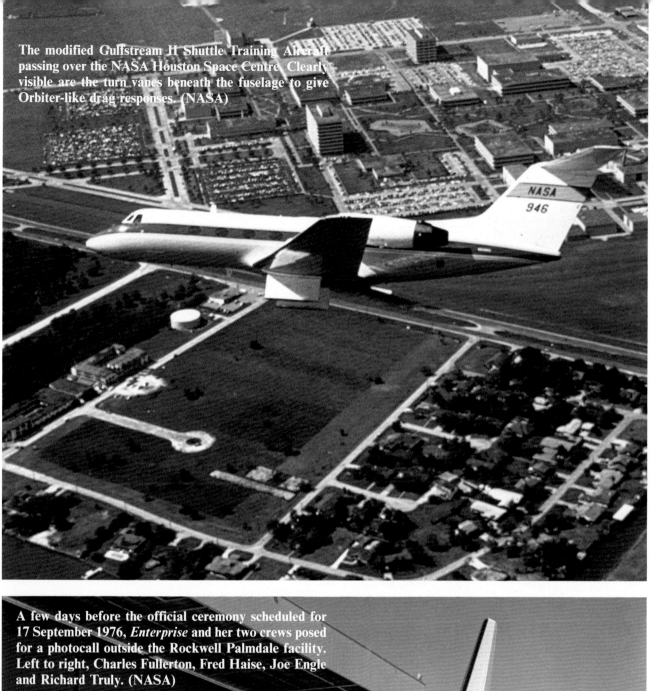

The modified Gulfstream II Shuttle Training Aircraft passing over the NASA Houston Space Centre. Clearly visible are the turn vanes beneath the fuselage to give Orbiter-like drag responses. (NASA)

A few days before the official ceremony scheduled for 17 September 1976, *Enterprise* and her two crews posed for a photocall outside the Rockwell Palmdale facility. Left to right, Charles Fullerton, Fred Haise, Joe Engle and Richard Truly. (NASA)

This sequence of photographs shows *Enterprise* during the captive-active part of the ALT programme at various stages in flight from release from 905 to landing.

1. Escorted by T-38 chase planes, preparation is made for separation.
2. Separation is achieved and *Enterprise* clears the 905's tail plane.
3. The craft manoeuvres before entering the landing phase of the flight.
4. The flare occurs with the nose sufficiently high that the main wheels touch down first, at over 200 mph.
5. *Enterprise*, still flanked by the T-38s, drops her nose wheel onto the runway and is brought slowly to a halt. (All photos NASA)

Top left: In a repeat performance of the ceremony that marked the end of Joe Engle's first space flight in X-15-3 in 1965, the 'mother' aircraft and chase planes fly over *Enterprise* and crew Joe Engle and Richard Truly, in salute to the successful completion of the third free test flight. (NASA)

Top right: The 905/*Enterprise* captive-active flight of 18 June 1977 was controlled from NASA's Houston Johnson Space Flight Centre. Here flight controllers monitor progress via TV pictures relayed from T-38 chase planes. (NASA)

Bottom: Facilities on a part of the huge Edwards Air Force Base in the desert of Southern California form the backdrop for *Enterprise* as she heads for a landing during the fourth free flight. (NASA)

Orbiter 102 *Columbia*, in March 1979, some weeks before transferring from Rockwell in California to the Kennedy Space Centre, Florida. (NASA)

The flight deck and instrumentation of *Columbia* during final assembly. As in a conventional aircraft, the primary flight controls and instrumentation are duplicated for pilot and commander. (Rockwell International)

Each contoured tile was numbered and had its own place on the outer skin of *Columbia*. Here technicians carefully check and double check correct positioning. (Rockwell International)

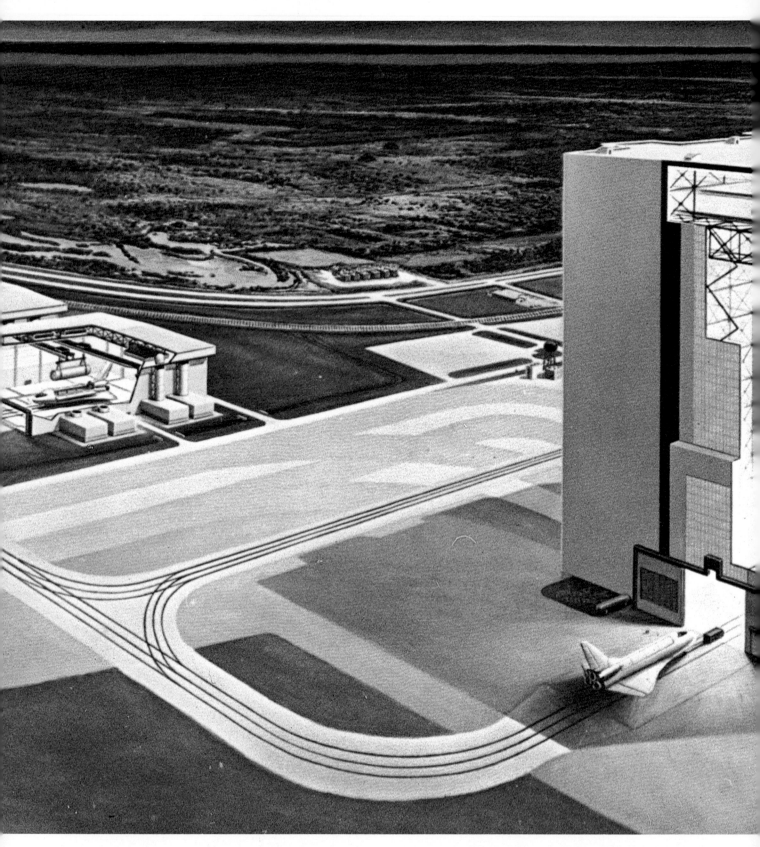

At Kennedy Space Centre, preparations were under way to facilitate regular flights of the Shuttle. In this artist's impression, Orbiters are transferred from the two low Orbiter Processing Facilities in the background, where payloads are installed and systems checked, to the Vehicle Assembly Building (VAB) for integration and assembly with External Tank and Solid Rocket Boosters. From the VAB the complete Shuttle is transported by the mobile launcher to the launch site over 2 miles away. (NASA)

him. A chorus of 'happy birthday' was followed by a message from Shuttle Launch Director George Page: 'To ensure your satisfaction we have thoroughly checked your engines, filled your fuel tanks, charged your tyres. Please have a safe, enjoyable, and trouble free trip — we like to have repeat customers.' It was signed 'Big George' and Company.

Later, on the pad, with Joe Engle and Richard Truly safely aboard *Columbia,* the final seconds passed to launch. NASA's public affairs commentator called out the final launch events:

'T minus 2 minutes 15 seconds; the main engines have been gimballed to their start positions and the pressure on the liquid oxygen tank is at flight pressure; coming up on the 2 minute point. T minus 2 minutes and counting; the liquid hydrogen vent valve has been closed and flight pressurization is underway. T minus 1 minute 50 seconds and counting; the gaseous oxygen vent arm is almost fully retracted. T minus 1 minute 40 seconds and counting. T minus 90 seconds away from launch of STS-2. T minus 1 minute 15 seconds and counting; the liquid hydrogen tank is at flight pressure. Coming up on the 1 minute point in the countdown, everything going smoothly. T minus 1 minute and counting. T minus 50 seconds; the firing system for the ground suppression water is armed. T minus 40 seconds; development flight instrumentation recorders are on. T minus 37 seconds we are about a few seconds away from switching control of launch to the computer sequencer. We have control of the — the countdown is now being conducted by the launch sequencer on board the Orbiter. T minus 20 seconds and counting; SRB hydraulic power units started, the SRB nozzles have been moved to the start position. Coming up on 10. T minus 10-9, we are go for main engine start; we have main engine start. T minus 3-2-1 we have ignition, we have ignition of the Solid Rocket Boosters and lift-off. Lift Off of America's Space Shuttle and the Space Shuttle has cleared the tower.'

Amidst applause and the thunder of her engines, *Columbia* rose into the sky on a pillar of flame.

NASA (PA): Houston now controlling, mission control reports the roll manoeuvre started. 20 seconds; thrust looks good. 25 seconds; roll manoeuvre completed. 30 seconds; *Columbia* now one nautical mile in altitude. 35 seconds; data check in Mission Control by Flight Director Neil Hutchinson gives a 'go' at 40 seconds.

Houston: Columbia-Houston, you are 'go' at 40.

Columbia: Roger, go at 40, — master alarm on.

NASA (PA): 48 seconds throttling the engines down for Max Q.

Houston: Roger, ignore the master alarm, *Columbia.*

Columbia: Okeydoke.

NASA (PA): Coming up a period of maximum aerodynamic pressure on the vehicle; mark 1 minute. *Columbia* now 5 nautical miles in altitude, 23 nautical miles down range, velocity now reading 2,300 ft per second. 1 minute 8 seconds; passed through Max Q. Looking good throttling up the engines back to 100 per cent. Mark 1 minute 20 seconds; *Columbia* now 9 nautical miles altitude, 6 nautical miles down range, velocity now reading 3,000 ft per second. Mark 1 minute 35 seconds.

Houston: Columbia-Houston, you can expect an evap-C&W.

NASA (PA): 1 minute and 45 seconds coming up now on negative seats, where altitude is too high for ejection seat's use.

Houston: Negative seats.

Columbia: Roger, negative seats.

NASA (PA): Mark 1 minute 55 seconds; *Columbia* now 21 nautical miles in altitude, 18 nautical miles down range, velocity now reading 5,000 ft per second; standing by now for Solid Rocket Booster separation confirmation.

Columbia: Roger, copy PCII-50.

NASA (PA): Confirms the Solid Rocket Booster separation.

Columbia: Smooth as glass, Houston.

NASA (PA): 2 minutes 25 seconds; on board guidance is converging as programmed, *Columbia* is now set up, steering for its precise window in space for main engine cut-off (MECO). *Columbia* now 35 nautical miles altitude, 40 nautical miles down range.

Columbia: OK, Houston, the engines are coming down and looking good.

Houston: Roger Columbia — thank you.

NASA (PA): Mark 2 minutes 45 seconds; *Columbia* now has two-engine landing capability at Rota Naval Air Station Spain; 2 minutes 54 seconds; we have a go from Mission Control at 3 minutes.

Houston:	Columbia-Houston, you're looking good at 3.
Columbia:	Roger copy, looking good at 3.
NASA (PA):	Mark 3 minutes 8 seconds; *Columbia* now 46 nautical miles in altitude, 66 nautical miles down range. Three main engines continue to run smoothly, Engle and Truly really moving out now, velocity now reading 6,700 ft per second. Mark 3 minutes 30 seconds; *Columbia* now 52 nautical miles altitude, 85 nautical miles down range. Velocity now reading 7,000 ft per second. [Already Joe Engle had exceeded the maximum altitude he had reached in X-15-3 over a decade and a half earlier.]
NASA (PA):	Return status check in Mission Control by Flight Director Neil Hutchinson — Engle and Truly given a 'go' to continue. Mark 3 minutes 55 seconds; *Columbia* now 58 miles altitude, 112 nautical miles down range, velocity now reaching 7,900 ft per second. 4 minutes 8 seconds; standing by for negative return.
Houston:	Mark negative return.
NASA (PA):	With that call up, Engle and Truly now committed to space travel, they can no longer turn around and return to launch site.
Houston:	Columbia-Houston, you are press to ATO. [Abort to Orbit]
Columbia:	Roger, press to ATO, over.
NASA (PA):	4 minutes 34 seconds. For the first time *Columbia* has forward abort to orbit capability on two engines by throttling two engines up to 107 per cent. 5 minutes; *Columbia* now 68 nautical miles altitude, 189 nautical miles down range, velocity now reading 10,300 ft per second.
Houston:	Columbia-Houston, you are go for normal throttle.
Columbia:	Copy that, go for normal throttle.
NASA (PA):	5 minutes 14 seconds. That call up from Capcom Brandenstein says that Engle and Truly now capable of abort to orbit on two engines without throttling up *Columbia's*
	engines. 5 minutes 20 seconds; *Columbia* now 68 nautical miles in altitude, 228 nautical miles down range. Mark 5 minutes 40 seconds; standing by for press to MECO — really smooth. 5 minutes 55 seconds — the press to MECO call from Capcom Brandenstein says that should *Columbia* lose but one engine she can press on and keep flying forward, *Columbia's* engines have enough energy to achieve normal altitude.
Houston:	Columbia-Houston, you're single engine Rota and everything's looking good.
Columbia:	OK, we have single engine Rota and looking good here.
NASA (PA):	Mark 6 minutes 18 seconds; that report from Capcom Brandenstein indicates that should a two-engine failure occur, *Columbia* is capable of an emergency landing at Rota Naval Air Station Spain. Mark 6 minutes 30 seconds; now 68 nautical miles in altitude, 346 nautical miles down range, velocity now reading 14,900 ft per second. Mark 6 minutes 50 seconds; *Columbia* now 67 nautical miles in altitude, 397 nautical miles down range. *Columbia* pitching over now to increase velocity and decrease altitude giving *Columbia* her more favourable altitude. 7 minutes 5 seconds, standing by for single-engine press to MECO.
Houston:	Columbia-Houston, single engine press to MECO.
Columbia:	Roger that, single engine press to MECO, looking good here.
NASA (PA):	7 minutes 20 seconds; that report says that Engle and Truly can achieve normal engine cut-off targets even if two engines go out. Mark 7 minutes 30 seconds; *Columbia* now 64 miles altitude, 511 nautical miles down range, velocity now reaching 23,000 ft per second. 7 minutes 43 seconds; g-forces building for Engle and Truly coming up to 3g. *Columbia* now 63 nautical miles altitude, 562 nautical miles down range. Mark 8 minutes.
Houston:	Roger Houston you are 'go' at 8.
NASA (PA):	*Columbia's* main engines slowly throttling back now to 65 per cent at 6 seconds before main engine

cut-off; *Columbia* now 63 nautical miles altitude, 645 nautical miles down range, velocity now 24,000 ft per second. 8 minutes 28 seconds standing by now for main engine cut-off.

Columbia: OK, Houston, we've got a good MECO.

Houston: Roger, we copy *Columbia*.

NASA (PA): Confirmed shut-down. *Columbia* returned to space, not yet returned to orbit, standing by now for external tank separation.

Houston: Columbia-Houston, you can ignore the IMU byters.

Columbia: Roger Houston, and we have ET sep.

NASA (PA): 8 minutes 58 seconds, confirmed External Tank separation.

Columbia: Roger, ET sep and the rates are good.

NASA (PA): *Columbia* now performing an evasive manoeuvre moving below and beyond the External Tank. 9 minutes 15 seconds; standing by for the first OMS burn.

The final 1 minute 30 second burn of the two 6,000 lb thrust OMS engines accelerated *Columbia* to the orbital speed of 25,700 ft per second. Joe Engle, Richard Truly and *Columbia* had made it into orbit. It was, said Dick Truly, the best birthday present he could have hoped for.

Orbital insertion was as accurate as anyone could have wished, the speed being only 1 ft per second below the target, and within four hours *Columbia* had opened her payload bay exposing the vital heat radiators to space. This task was delayed somewhat so that Joe Engle and Dick Truly could check any distortion along the inside of the doors whilst in the closed position.

Soon after the payload bays had been opened, trouble hit *Columbia*. One of her three fuel cells was behaving abnormally. First indications came in the form of an increased electrolyte alkaline level in fuel cell 1. As problems mounted with the 200 lb cell, situated just behind the crew cabin, NASA officials at Mission Control began to look seriously at a shorter duration mission than the five days originally planned.

The flight controller decided that fuel cell number 1 should be shut down if its performance fell below a set level. There were fears that some of the excessive water being produced by the cell might have caused an explosive mixture of hydrogen and oxygen, and that the electrolyte (potassium hydroxide) might leak and contaminate the drinking water.

Daniel Brandenstein, the STS 2 Capcom, in-

structed Dick Truly on the contingency procedure. Truly responded, 'OK, when fuel cell pressure is less than 10 [psi], will stop the fuel cell and delete step three. Do you think we can recover the fuel cell later?' Daniel Brandenstein replied dejectedly, 'I don't believe we can'.

Mission rules dictated that if only two fuel cells were functioning then the flight would be cut short. This was necessary because STS 2's mission would involve a complex series of aerodynamic manoeuvres at Mach 24+ during re-entry. These manoeuvres would need the power of at least two cells (24 kilowatts maximum). Despite this, and the fact that NASA was renowned for flying by the book, the Flight Director, Neil Hutchinson, decided that for the time being STS 2 would continue its nominal mission with regular reviews of the fuel cell status. Taken mainly in response to pressure to maintain a favourable image of Shuttle reliability and performance, this decision was rescinded by day two and the decision made to go for a flight of two days instead of five.

Whilst Mission Control was making up its mind whether or not to curtail the flight, the two astronauts had completed their first night's rest-period and were awake to start the next phase of STS 2 work with the OSTA pallet, and testing of the RMS arm. Almost 23 hours since *Columbia* lifted off from launch complex 39A, Dick Truly began to deploy the RMS arm, slowly raising it from its cradle alongside the port side of the payload bay. Both manual and automatic operations were tried as the RMS-mounted TV cameras provided American audiences with spectacular views of *Columbia* in space. As one of the TV cameras focussed on the payload bay facing the cabin window, Dick Truly held up a sign which read 'Hi Mom'. As the arm was being stowed the crew was jubilant in that, so far, apart from the fuel cell problem, the flight had been a great success.

Capcom for this phase of the mission was Dr Sally Ride, one of NASA's scientist astronauts and shortly to be named as America's first woman in space. Joe Engle described the TV views to her.

'OK, Sally, we've got the arm secured right now. We are just getting ready to activate the SIR-A [Shuttle Imaging Radar — an Earth geological mapping device stored in the payload bay]. We've got the power on and we are getting ready to turn it on.' 'OK sounds good,' said Sally Ride. 'You sound mighty good, too!' retorted Joe Engle, continuing, 'It's a little cloudy down there Sally, it's a good thing the SIR-A sees through that.' Pictures of the *Columbia*'s payload bay with the Earth as a backdrop were relayed around the world. 'OK,' said Sally Ride, 'be advised that we are looking at a

The launch of STS 2 is reflected off one of the many waterways that cut through the marshlands around Kennedy Space Centre. (NASA)

great picture, from what looks like camera Delta, of the [RMS] arm and the Earth.'

Later, President Reagan dropped into Mission Control to chat to the astronauts. 'I told them when I came in,' said the President, 'this was a rare experience for an old horse cavalry officer! Say, could you pick me up and take me out; I haven't been to California since last August!' (*Columbia* was scheduled to land at Edwards) — 'We'll be glad to sir.' — 'Thank you very much. Let me just say I'm sure you know how proud everyone down here is, and how the whole nation, and I'm sure the world, but certainly America, has got its eyes and its heart on you.' Joe Engle replied, 'Mister President; we thoroughly do appreciate that you are taking the trouble to show all the people working on the Space Shuttle how much you care — it makes us mighty proud!'

The call from the President was a morale booster after Sally Ride's earlier communication when she had told the crew of the curtailed mission. 'OK, and first the bad news; our plan is that we are running a minimum mission and you'll be coming in tomorrow.' — 'Oh boy! I'll tell you what,' said Joe Engle, 'you are garbled and unreadable there, Sally.' — 'OK, you get to hear the bad news one more time then. We are running a minimum mission and you'll be coming in tomorrow.' — 'Oh!' said Joe Engle, clearly disappointed, 'that's not so good.' Sally Ride did her best to soften the blow. 'Think of it that you got all the good OSTA data and all the RMS data and you just did too good a job — we are going to bring you in early.'

The day of re-entry began for Joe Engle and Dick Truly with a call up from Houston. A quick chorus of patriotic naval music was followed in lighter vein by a prerecorded message from characters in the popular TV series *The Muppets*. Two astronaut muppets spoke to the crew: 'We wish the *Columbia* happy landings. We will be staying here in the outer reaches of space — because we don't know how to get down!! Oh! Joe — Dick — which button do you press? Help — give us a break!'

An hour before the planned re-entry de-orbit burn of the twin 6,000lb thrust OMS engines, John Young was in the air over Edwards Air Force Base checking the landing conditions. Plans for the return of STS2 included a touchdown with moderate crosswind to simulate the expected conditions of a landing at Kennedy Space Centre. Half an hour after the 'all clear' for Runway 15, John Young reported that the crosswinds had exceeded the safety limit and a last minute change to land into the wind on Runway 23 was made. The relevant approach details for both runways had already been input into *Columbia's* guidance com-

puters, and a change could be accomplished by the astronauts merely resetting the computer commands.

During her return, *Columbia* was to perform no less than 19 sets of aerodynamic manoeuvres as part of her flight test programme. At 137 miles in altitude Joe Engle and Dick Truly ignited the OMS engines for a 2 minute 55 second burn which slowed them down for re-entry. As *Columbia* streaked across the Pacific sky at Mach 25, Joe Engle manually performed a series of manoeuvres using *Columbia's* aerodynamic and reaction controls to gather data on her hypersonic handling.

Coming out of re-entry blackout on course for landing at Edwards, Mission Control monitored the final minutes of the flight.

'We have you on TV, at 100,000 ft Mach 3.6, you are positive seats.' — 'Houston, you are a little garbled there,' said Joe Engle, 'say again your last.' 'Positive seats,' repeated Houston [Ejection seats could be used if there was a problem], '90,000 ft at a range of 74 miles, Mach 2.9.' Chase planes began to move into position around *Columbia's* predicted flight path. 'Houston this is Columbia, everything looks good on board.' — 'Roger, we're looking at it,' responded Houston. 'Columbia-Houston you can take the air data.' — 'Roger,' said Engle, now manually flying *Columbia*. — '82,000 ft Mach 2.5,' Joe Engle was switching control to automatic and then back to manual performing a series of tests before flying around the approach circle manually and then onto automatic control for the first part of the approach and landing phase. 'And Houston, PTR 5 Mark.' — 'Roger. Everything is looking right on the money there Joe, and we have a wind update for you and a weather update. You've got a very thin layer at 25,000, the winds airborne are as briefed, and on the ground 220/18 knots gusting to 24. Altimeter is 30.07 inches. You've got 60 miles visibility underneath over.' — 'Oh! good. It sounds like a good old Edie [Edwards] day!' Joe Engle was reliving in many respects, his X-15 astro-flights of over 20 years previously. — 'Yes sir, now at 68,000.' — '39 miles range, Mach 1.5,' called Houston, — '60,000 ft.' — 'Columbia this is Houston. At your convenience transfer the state vector from the pass to the B55,' — 'You're almost unreadable Rick say again please.' — 'Roger. 50,000 ft — Mach 1 — Range 27 miles.' — 'Roger you're tracking right down the line'. — '*Columbia* approaching the heading alignment circle now.' — '42,000 ft Mach .8, 22 miles range.' — 'Columbia-Houston, we show you intercepting the track and a reminder you got the strong winds out from the west. Now at 13,000 ft.' *Columbia* entered into the alignment circle for approach. Cameras on board the chase planes monitored the returning space plane as it entered a long left hand turn. Once out of the turn *Columbia* would be lined up with the runway. 'OK we got a little bit of PTI Zero in but not too much'. — 'Roger'.

Edwards' Runway 23 was ready and waiting. Landing was originally scheduled for Runway 15 to try a landing in a crosswind, but as winds increased to exceed the safety margin a last minute switch to lakebed Runway 23 was made.

'*Columbia* making a wide sweeping turn now to get lined up with the runway.' — '25,000 ft'. Tenuous contrails streamed back from *Columbia's* wing tips. 'Columbia, this is Houston. 3,000 ft low now out of 24,000 ft.' — 'Roger that.' — 'We're showing 290 at 20,000.' — 'Check body flaps to manual.' — 'Roger; body flaps on manual.' — '480 knots at 18,000 ft.' Chase planes closed in on *Columbia*, checking all around her for signs of damage. — 'OK, speed brakes start now.' — 'Roger, still just slightly low on the altitude, looking OK.' The final test of the flight involved airbrake evaluation. — 'Still slightly below glide scope.' — 'You are slightly below the glide scope you have a 'Go' for auto-land.' — 'OK, thank you sir.' Autoland was a development of the microwave terminal phase guidance system used so effectively in the lifting body programme. The autoland system was scheduled to take over at 18,000 ft using information supplied by the Microwave Scanning Beam Landing System (MSBLS). Autoland would be maintained to flare at 2,000 ft, but then Joe Engle would take over to land *Columbia* manually. — '9,230 — set speed brake auto.' — 'Roger, speed brake and body flap auto — everything auto, thank you!' Joe Engle called in as *Columbia* entered a 20 degree glide. Speed [air-] brake to auto helped Joe Engle maintain the correct airspeed of around 265 knots. 'About a minute away from touchdown.' The chase planes closed in nearer, they would call out the last tens of feet to touchdown and confirm *Columbia's* airspeed to Joe Engle. '3,500 ft — 250 knots.' — 'OK, 2,500 ft speed brakes are closed we're 270 knots.' — 'Chase converse.' — '*Columbia* clear to land lakebed 23 whenever you're ready.' — 'OK.' — '100-50-30-20-10-5-3- touchdown. Nose gear 15-10-10-5-3 touchdown. Welcome home!' — 'Thank you, Chase,' said Joe Engle as applause broke out at Mission Control. 'This is Shuttle control, the unofficial touchdown time and mission elapsed time is 2 days 6 hours 13 minutes 10 seconds.' — 'OK, *Columbia* has rolled to a stop and we are in to the post landing.' — 'OK Joe,' said Houston, 'It's a great day for the "Ace moving Company". Welcome home!'

In one sense the flight of STS 2 forged the final link between the X-15 and the Shuttle. Joe Engle, having flown both spacecraft, was in a unique position to draw comparisons. On looking back he said: 'The techniques and flight control systems, the manner in which we fly and manoeuvre re-entry from space back into the atmosphere, manage the energy, terminating in a conventional landing — on a lakebed now, but eventually on a runway — that technique which we are using on the Space Shuttle was pioneered, and is in fact very

similar to, the same technique that we used on the X-15, twenty years ago. We've got that knowledge and know-how, and the confidence to do it.'

STS 3

Whilst the damage to *Columbia's* heat shield was less severe after STS 2 than on its maiden flight, the repairs needed to NASA's first Orbiter were nevertheless substantial and well above that which NASA had expected. Tiles had been damaged by debris during the launch and landing, moisture had penetrated critical seam areas and an umbilical lanyard had lashed some other areas.

In total over 3,750 tiles needed repair and 471 replacement. In addition, APUs and fuel cells were removed and tested and, in the case of the former, replaced with new units.

At the beginning of January 1982 NASA announced that STS 3, the third test flight of *Columbia*, would be flown by Skylab veteran Jack Lousma as commander, and Charles Fullerton from the ALT programme as pilot. The more likely commander of this mission, astronaut Fred Haise, Charles Fullerton's commander on the *Enterprise* Approach and Landing Tests, had resigned from NASA in June 1979 to join Grumman Aerospace Corporation, Bethpage, New York, as vice president for space programmes. Before he left he had been assigned alongside Charles Fullerton to command one of the Space Shuttle early orbital test flights. NASA also confirmed that the mission would last seven days and that the *Columbia* would carry into space OSS 1 (The Office of Space Science experiment). The third test flight was scheduled for 22 March.

In the meantime, the ground handling experience gained on the first two flights was beginning to pay off; for example, on 2 February it took just 18 minutes to transfer *Columbia* to the VAB from the Orbiter Processing Facility (where it had been checked out following STS 2 and, on 10 January, had had the OSS 1 pallet installed in its cargo bay). Within days *Columbia* had been mated with SRBs and the ET and was ready for roll out.

Columbia reached pad 39A on 16 February 1982, the two mile journey having taken 6 hours. The gleaming white ET of STS 1 and 2 had then been replaced by an orange, unpainted, variety saving 594 lb in weight. Countdown was to begin on 18 March. As *Columbia* prepared for launch, NASA announced the names of the crews for STS 4, 5 and 6. They were, in flight order, Commander Thomas Mattingly, pilot Henry 'Hank' Hartsfield (STS 4); Commander Vance Brand, pilot Robert Overmyer and mission specialists Dr William

Columbia clears the launch tower at Kennedy Space Centre launch Complex 39A during STS 3's launch on 22 March 1982. The External Tank is unpainted for the first time. (NASA)

6 Columbia

Lenoir and Dr Joseph Allen (STS 5); and STS 6, the first planned flight of *Challenger* would be another four-man crew commanded by Paul Weitz with Karol Bobko (pilot) and Dr Story Musgrave and Donald Peterson riding as mission specialists.

STS 1 and 2 were relatively short duration 'up and downers'. Now *Columbia* would, on her third flight, extend the time spent in space with all the thermal and reliability problems involved. In addition, STS 3 would, for the first time, use the RMS to pick up and use a gas leak detector and probe around the outside of the *Columbia* whilst in space to track down any out-gassing from the space plane's many systems.

Launch was scheduled for between 10.00 and 13.16 Eastern Standard Time on 22 March. Touchdown, if all went well, would occur at 13.36 EST on Runway 23, Edwards AFB.

As it turned out, the launch was delayed a full hour because of a malfunction in the ground-based fuel loading system. Launch control counted down

the final seconds as water flooded down onto the pad, protecting it from the intense heat to come, 'T13-12- we're "Go" for main engine ignition.' A flash preceded the ignition of the three main engines that howled into life, pitching the entire shuttle stack over one foot in the direction of the External Tank. '8, 7, 6, — we have main engine ignition'. The solid rockets burst into life and *Columbia* lifted off the pad. 'Houston now controlling, mission control confirms roll started — 20 seconds, thrust looks good'. *Columbia* climbed skywards on a pillar of white exhaust and into the low cloud, completely lighting up the cloud

Of the two crewmen assigned to STS 3, only one had been in space before. Commander Jack Lousma is seen here seated on the left after splashdown of Skylab 3, in 1973. Next to him is Owen Garriott (later to fly on STS 9), and Alan Bean who had also walked on the moon during Apollo 12. (NASA)

as it flew out of sight from the ground. All that remained was the sound of the Shuttle's engines, the power of six and a half million pounds of thrust.

Apart from a single APU failure, the entire flight was pronounced a success and on the seventh day the crew were preparing for landing when problems started to occur. Edwards AFB was waterlogged, the vast expanse of lake bed was undergoing its annual rejuvenation and was covered with several inches of water. Not willing to subject *Columbia* to a concrete runway landing, NASA opted for the White Sands landing site 1,000 miles south in New Mexico. The dry, powdered, gypsum lake bed was ideal for landing, but on the flight's seventh day the weather was bad. High winds and blowing sand were a hazard. Nevertheless, John Young took off into the overcast sky to check the weather conditions. It would be his decision whether or not *Columbia* would land. Only one hour before the planned de-orbit John Young radioed in, 'I think we ought to knock this off'. NASA replied, 'OK — we concur'. The landing was postponed for 24 hours.

The following day, 30 March, the small New Mexico town of Truth or Consequence echoed to the double thunder of sonic booms as *Columbia* soared overhead on its final approach to land. From 147 miles high and after a flight of four and a half million miles Jack Lousma and Charles Fullerton were coming home. At 253 mph *Columbia's* main undercarriage touched down sending up clouds of white gypsum dust. Slowly the nose wheel came down until it was barely a foot from touchdown. Then, to everyone's surprise, the blunt nose of *Columbia* began to rise once more, higher and higher as onlookers caught their breath. A slight over-opening of the air-brake had caused the Shuttle to pitch upwards before the pilot's lightning reflexes caught the movement and brought the nosewheel down firmly onto the ground. Finally, over 13,730 ft from initial touchdown *Columbia* rolled to a halt in the shimmering haze of Runway 17, White Sands Missile Base.

STS 3 was an astounding success story. It was discovered later that the faulty APU which provided, along with its counterparts, *Columbia's* hydraulic power, overheated because of a frozen cooling system. All three APUs nevertheless performed faultlessly when they were turned back on again for re-entry a week after launch.

The long orbital flight had no ill effect whatsoever on *Columbia*. The Orbital Manoeuvring System rocket engines were test-fired successfully after prolonged hot and cold 'soaks', and the Canadian manipulator arm performed excellently.

A number of thermal protection system tiles were lost during launch. Film taken from the ground showed that some, at least, came adrift immediately after the first shock of engine ignition, but their loss was not significant. Only one final test remained, after which, if all went well, the Shuttle would be pronounced operational.

STS 4

Before *Columbia* had returned from her third trip into space, the astronauts assigned to her fourth and final test flight, STS 4, had reached an advanced stage in their training. Commander Thomas Kenneth Mattingly and Pilot Hank Hartsfield would spend seven days in space conducting tests and scientific experiments before returning to Edwards Air Force Base in California.

Ken Mattingly was a distinguised NASA veteran. Born in Chicago in 1936, he became an astronaut in 1966, serving on the support crew for Apollos 8 and 11. He was later assigned as prime Command Module Pilot for the ill-fated Apollo 13 mission until exposure to German Measles meant that he had to stand down in place of his back-up, Jack Swigert, just three days before launch. Ken Mattingly was then reassigned as prime Command Module Pilot for John Young's Apollo 16 mission, during which flight he made a single EVA in deep space returning from the Moon, to collect film and data stored in the Service Module. During the Skylab flights he was made the 'Chief of Shuttle Support, Astronaut Office'. He served as back-up commander for STS 2, and for STS 3, being named as prime commander of STS 4 in December 1981.

Hank Hartsfield was one of the 1969 ex-MOL group of astronauts. Prior to his MOL work he had been an instructor at the renowned USAF Test Pilot School at Edwards Air Force Base. Before being assigned as back-up pilot for STS 2 and 3 he had undertaken a number of support duties for Apollo and Skylab missions as well as assisting with Shuttle simulator and flight systems hardware development. He was 49 years old.

Launch, on 27 June 1982, followed an almost faultless countdown and within minutes *Columbia* was back in space for a fourth time, at over 180 miles altitude. Soon after *Columbia* reached orbit NASA announced the loss of her two SRBs. Apparently their parachute system had failed to deploy and they splashed down in the Atlantic and sank.

Because of the success of the previous three Shuttle flights NASA decided to reduce the engineering checks of *Columbia* on STS 4 in favour of an extended payload: a military satellite called DOD 82-1, about which NASA and the Department of Defense imposed a strict information black-out. No pictures of its deployment would be released, and the crew were forbidden to discuss any aspects of its size, weight, or function.

NASA's own public affairs chief, Brian Duff,

explained that the space agency would still maintain its 'open door' policy for all aspects of Shuttle operations, apart from, 'Defence payloads and other customers who would prefer not to divulge the nature of their equipment'. The DoD spokesman, Brigadier General Richard Abel (USAF), however, complicated matters by adding, 'All military payloads assigned to launch by the Shuttle, will be secret regardless of whether or not the cargo itself is generally classified. This will eliminate anyone pinpointing the truly vital secret manifest'.

Whereas the DoD payload had been described in detail by several leading aviation weekly magazines (and even the Soviets had freely obtained blueprints), the DoD remained tight-lipped. On the other hand no-one could discover any detail whatsoever about *Columbia*'s other payload, a medical drug-producing unit developed by Johnson and Johnson. Observers commented wryly on the fact that US industry was better at keeping secrets than the DoD.

During deployment of DOD 82-1, the crew talked directly to Air Force Satellite Control, bypassing Mission Control Houston for the first time.

STS 4 continued to run smoothly. Both Ken Mattingly and Hank Hartsfield soon settled into a professional and organized pattern of work in space. Soon after launch Mission Control instructed the crew to fly *Columbia* 'upside down' to dry her underside off. Apparently several hundred of her lower insulating tiles had been scratched by a severe hailstorm which occurred on the day before launch, penetrating the Scotchguard waterproofing layer on the tiles. Concerned that the tiles may have absorbed water, which, once in space, might freeze and loosen the tile fixing, NASA decided to point the affected tiles at the sun for around 19 hours to dry them out.

Later in the flight one other minor problem occurred. The RMS arm's hand, or to use NASA's description 'end effector', would not work. Mission Control traced the fault to an incorrect computer programme and set matters aright.

STS 4 ended at Edwards on 4 July 1982, only five minutes earlier than planned. *Columbia* had been well proven and the Shuttle was pronounced operational.

On 1 July, *Challenger*, the second flight-rated Shuttle, was rolled out at Rockwell's Palmdale facility to be towed via road to Edwards Air Force Base. From there it would be transported to Kennedy Space Centre on top of the 905. When STS 4 landed, observers were able to see, for the first time, the two Orbiters side by side. *Challenger* made its way back to the Kennedy Space Centre first, arriving on 5 July.

STS 5

Scheduled for launch on Armistice day, 11 Novem-

ber 1982, the fifth, and first operational, flight of the Shuttle would carry a four-man crew into space, as well as launch two satellites.

During the flight, the two mission specialists, Joseph Allen and William Lenoir, were destined to make America's first space walk for almost nine years, whilst commander Vance Brand and pilot Robert Overmyer monitored their activities from inside *Columbia*'s flight deck.

Columbia had returned from Edwards on top of the 905 on 15 July, whereupon she was taken directly to the Orbiter Processing Facility to undergo extensive refurbishment for her first operational flight. To enable *Columbia* to carry an additional two crew members, two extra seats were installed together with necessary communications and ancillary equipment. One seat was installed on the flight deck between and to the rear of the two pilot seats, whilst the other was secured down below on the lower deck. Both mission specialists' seats were foldable and could be stowed away once in space to allow more space on both decks.

As a matter of ethics the commander's and the pilot's ejection seats were deactivated for STS 5. On completion of the mission they would be removed altogether and replaced with conventional seats at Rockwell's Palmdale facility.

The 900 lb remote manipulator system (RMS) arm would not be needed on STS 5 and so it was removed. Many sensors and instruments that formed part of *Columbia*'s 'Development Flight Instrumentation' were repositioned, removed, or integrated in *Columbia*'s operational instrumentation.

STS 5 would be a much shorter mission than STS 4, so one oxygen and hydrogen tank providing fuel to the electricity-producing fuel cells was deleted. While modifications to *Columbia*'s tiles, APUs and RCS thrusters continued in bay one of the Orbiter Processing Facility, in bay two her sister, *Challenger*, was being checked out for her first flight, on STS 6.

During the second week in September *Columbia* was towed to the VAB when she was once more mated with her External Tank and solid rocket boosters.

Vance Brand, commander of STS 5, was born in Longmont, Colorado in May 1931. Serving as a US Navy fighter pilot he graduated from the Navy Test Pilot School in 1963 to work on F-104 Starfighter development. In April 1966, after spending a period working with the Lockheed Aircraft Corporation, Brand was selected as a NASA astronaut. Initially specializing in the Apollo Command Module, he was named as back-up Command Module Pilot for Apollo 15 and prime CMP for the cancelled Apollo 18 lunar mission. With the end of the Moon landings, Vance Brand served as a back-up commander for the second and third mission to Skylab, eventually making his first and only space-flight on the Apollo Soyuz Test Project (ASTP) in July 1975 as Command Module Pilot.

Robert Overmyer was five years younger than Vance Brand and had a background in the US Marines. In August 1965, he entered the Air Force's Test Pilot School at Edwards, graduating into the second group of MOL astronauts and transferring to NASA in 1969. Subsequently Robert Overmyer served as a member of the support crew to both Apollo 17 and ASTP. Later he flew as the prime T-38 chase plane pilot on *Enterprise* ALT flights.

Joseph Allen, flying on board *Columbia* as mission specialist, was yet another nineteen-sixties NASA astronaut. Born in Indiana in 1937, Joe Allen's first role with the Space Agency was as a mission scientist for Apollo 15 the first of the extended Apollo moon flights.

After a sabbatical during which he served on the President's Council on International Economic Policy, Joe Allen became heavily involved in Shuttle science programmes. His voice became known to millions as 'Capcom' for STS 1. Joe Allen's colleague on STS 5 was William Lenoir. Selected by NASA in 1967, Lenoir had waited almost fifteen years to make this, his first space-flight. He had served as back-up pilot for the second and third manned Skylab flights before being assigned to the Shuttle project.

As *Columbia* rolled out of the cavernous VAB en-route to launch complex 39A, *Challenger* came one step nearer to her first flight, with the installation at the Orbiter Processing facility, of her Orbital Manoeuvring engines. On 18 October *Columbia*'s two satellites, the Satellite Business Systems communications satellite, SBS 'C', and the Canadian Anik C-3, were loaded into her payload bay from the 'clean room' on pad 39A's rotating service structure.

Finally, in the early morning of 11 November, the astronauts Vance Brand, Bob Overmyer, William Lenoir and Joe Allen boarded *Columbia* to start her fifth flight into space. For this and all subsequent flights each crew member wore a blue coverall and, for lift-off and re-entry, a white, oxygen-fed helmet. This new garment replaced the ejection suits worn on all previous flights. A lower-body g-suit would nevertheless be worn over the blue coveralls for re-entry.

The final countdown went smoothly, and precisely on time *Columbia* lifted off the pad and thundered her way upwards towards the heavens. Within hours her payload bay doors were open and the two mission specialists, William Lenoir and Joe Allen, were getting ready to deploy the first of

Columbia's two satellites, SBS 'C'.

Just over eight hours from lift-off the 'Ace Delivery Co' as the crew of STS 5 dubbed themselves, first put *Columbia* in the correct attitude. SBS 'C' atop its PAM 'D' booster stage then began a 'spin up' at 50 rpm on a turntable within the payload bay launch platform. Like most modern satellites SBS 'C' was spin stabilized. By obtaining a spin rate of 50 rpm the optimum gyroscopic stability can be achieved. All was well with the satellite and the astronauts fired explosive hold-down bolts freeing the clamps, and powerful springs pushed SBS 'C' clear. Thirty hours from launch on day two of the mission, Anik C-3 was successfully deployed in much the same way.

On day four, preparations began in *Columbia*'s payload bay for a spacewalk by Joseph Allen and William Lenoir. Using the new space suits stored in *Columbia*'s airlock, they were to practice the use of tools that would be needed on later satellite repair missions. Three and a half hours had been allocated in the flight programme to the Extra Vehicular Activity (EVA), preceded by a similar period of 'oxygen pre-breathing' in the spacesuits. *Columbia*'s cabin was filled with a mixture of oxygen and nitrogen at 14.5 psi. The suits, operating at only 3.5 psi, and pressurized by pure oxygen, would leave the astronauts susceptible to the bends had they not purged all excess nitrogen from their bloodstreams beforehand.

As things turned out, both Joe Allen and William Lenoir began putting on their spacesuits during *Columbia*'s fourth day in space. This was a little later than planned in the flight schedule because William Lenoir was suffering from recurring bouts of space sickness. By the time the two astronauts had completed suiting-up William Lenoir's suit began to malfunction. A faulty regulator appeared to be preventing a correct internal oxygen pressure being maintained. No sooner had this problem surfaced than Joe Allen's suit began to misbehave. His motor-driven oxygen circulator fan and water cooling pump was not working properly. As in the past Mission Control and the astronauts were not going to give up without trying to 'fix'. Several different switch settings on each suit were tried, and even a partial depressurization of the airlock occurred in an attempt to jolt William Lenoir's pressure regulator into action. It was to no avail, however, and reluctantly NASA had to concede defeat for this flight's EVA.

At 11.25 am Eastern Standard Time *Columbia* touched down at Edwards Air Force Base after a flight lasting 5 days, 2 hours and 14 minutes. STS 5 had been only a partial success, but the Orbiter *Columbia* had once again proven herself equal to her task.

As a result of STS 5, NASA implemented a more rigorous spacesuit testing programme. The new procedures and ground rules applied mainly to the manufacturer, Hamilton Standard.

7 Challenger

STS 6

One of the problems that the Space Shuttle system faced from the very beginning of the programme was that of achieving constant ground-to-space communication links. During each 90 minute orbit around the Earth a Shuttle could only be in range of ground stations for just over a third of that time.

In order to maintain continuous communication with the Shuttle NASA developed three Tracking and Data Relay (TDRS) satellites, each one of which would be launched by the Shuttle into geosynchronous orbit spaced 120 degrees apart. In such a configuration the Shuttle would always be in contact with at least one TDRS and, therefore, would be in constant uninterrupted communication with Houston. This system would eventually mean the end of the costly and inefficient ground-based systems.

The first mission of *Challenger* would not only prove this second Shuttle's flight capability, but would also launch the first of the three TDRS satellites, as well as conducting the EVA aborted during STS 5.

Of the *Challenger*'s crew, only one had been in space before: Commander Paul Weitz had spent 28 days in space back in 1973 as pilot of Skylab 2. The others, making their first flight, were pilot Karol J. Bobko and mission specialists Donald H. Peterson

and Story Musgrave. Karol Bobko was one of the seven ex-Air Force Manned Orbiting Laboratory astronauts who transferred to NASA in 1969. Since then he had gained valuable experience as a member of the support crew for the joint Russian American Apollo Soyuz Test Project in 1975 and also in a support role for the *Enterprise* Approach and Landing Tests at Edwards in 1977. Don Peterson, too, was an ex-MOL astronaut who had served as back-up crewman for Apollo 16. Both Karol Bobko and Don Peterson had been waiting fourteen years to make their first space flight.

Following a two month delay in the launch caused by several tiny leaks of hydrogen being discovered in the *Challenger*'s main engine, *Challenger* was ready for launch at 1.30 pm Florida time on 4 April 1983. The countdown had gone so smoothly that Lieutenant General James Abrahamson (ex-USAF MOL astronaut and now NASA Associate Administrator for Manned Spacecraft) publicly announced that the launch team was getting bored.

As the countdown reached its final hours, earlier doubts about the weather cleared as astronauts Weitz, Bobko, Musgrave and Peterson enjoyed their traditional pre-launch breakfast. Like everything else concerning flight crew management the pre-launch breakfast is carefully planned; it consists of 'low residue' foods so that use of the lavatory at an impractically early stage of the flight (for instance, when fully suited-up) is avoided. Soon after, wearing blue NASA flight overalls, the four men crossed over to launch complex 39A, up the launch gantry and into the flight deck of *Challenger*.

With the crew safely aboard, the countdown settled into its final seconds. Launch Control marked off the time to SSME ignition until, with a cloud of steam and smoke, the main engines burst into life.

'3-2-1-zero and lift-off. Lift-off of the Orbiter *Challenger* and the sixth flight of the Shuttle programme.' Across the marshland, onlookers watched as the combination rose in eerie silence up past the launch tower as Commander Weitz called out, '*Challenger* is under way, and we've got a roll programme'. No sooner had Paul Weitz's voice echoed from the public address system than the first pounding, howling shockwaves of sound

Paul Weitz, commander of STS 6 (seen here second from left) at the end of his flight to the orbiting workshop Skylab in 1973. With him on that mission were Dr Joseph Kerwin (centre) and Commander 'Pete' Conrad (second from right). (NASA)

rocked the very ground itself as the hot, humid Florida air became a wall of deafening thunder.

For over two minutes onlookers could watch *Challenger* climb ever upwards into the cloudless blue sky, leaving a winding vapour trail in its wake. A flash of light at 2 minutes 11 seconds signalled SRB separation. *Challenger* was on its way; the launch was perfect.

Main engine cut-off came at 8 minutes 20 seconds into the flight. Soon after, the giant External Tank fell away to burn up in the atmosphere far below. Finally in space, orbiting at 240 miles altitude above Earth the crew commenced their first task of the mission: opening the cargo bay doors and exposing both the Shuttle's radiators and the bulk of the TDRS satellite. TV cameras relayed the operation to ground observers, but as the doors opened they revealed a worrying sight. Reminiscent of STS 1, the view that greeted the four astronauts was one of a damaged heat shield. The starboard orbital, manoeuvring system pod's new 'Flexible Re-usable Surface Insulation' was torn loose during launch exposing the vulnerable skin of *Challenger* like an open wound. According to NASA, however, this area was a 'low re-entry heat zone' and would not be a hazard. Nevertheless, it gave rise to a few worrying moments so early in the flight.

The launch of the TDRS was to be the main objective of a first, busy, day in space aboard *Challenger*. After completing vital systems checks

of the Orbiter, all four men turned their attentions to the satellite. Story Musgrave, who was chiefly concerned with this particular operation, supervised checking of both the TDRS and its rocket booster needed to place it in the correct orbit above the Earth, to be joined at a later date by its two sisters.

By the time the first stage of launch had been reached *Challenger* was flying in the Earth's shadow, floodlights in the cargo bay illuminated the scene as the TDRS pivoted upwards from its stowed position until it was a full 90 degrees vertical to the cargo bay. It was shortly after 11.30 pm Florida time when Story Musgrave flicked a switch on *Challenger's* aft instrument panel which sent the TDRS on its way, against the backdrop of a waning half moon. For a while the astronauts watched the satellite drift away further and further before Paul Weitz and Karol Bobko nudged *Challenger* away from the satellite a greater distance still, to avoid the plume of engine exhaust when TDRS climbed up into geosynchronous orbit. At just after midnight the engine ignited and TDRS was on its way.

It had been a busy day filled with activity and there was much work still to do over the next few days. Paul Weitz, Karol Bobko and Don Peterson unstowed their sleeping restraints and turned in. Story Musgrave could not sleep, however, and so he drifted over to the airlock in *Challenger's* lower flight deck to do some checking of the space suits to be used later in the flight. As the 'night' moved in *Challenger* continued its 17,500 mph glide silently through space.

On the ground things were not so peaceful. Something had gone wrong with the TDRS. All communications had been lost with the 35ft long satellite, and the last data received had indicated that it was spinning out of control. Through the night, ground-based engineers attempted to make contact with TDRS. By early morning an atmosphere of gloom had settled over TDRS controllers at the White Sands, New Mexico tracking station. Talk was circulating of a board of enquiry to be set up and lengthy investigations into what was seen as a catastrophic loss. Morale dropped to a low ebb, then, at around 8.20 am EST, TDRS came alive. Data streamed in and it appeared that during the night it had stopped itself spinning, separated from its rocket stage and deployed its solar wings. The satellite, however, was in a wrong orbit, and it soon became apparent that its 'Inertial Upper Stage' Booster had suffered a catastrophic failure.

When the crew of STS 6 woke at 10.40 am on 5 April, they were unaware of the night-time drama. NASA control at Houston soon filled them in, assuring them that at no time did either their, or the *Challenger's* actions, cause the problem. Somewhat relieved, the crew settled down for breakfast and a day of scientific research activities. Day two in space sent all four astronauts from one console to the next flicking switches, pressing buttons and

taking pictures. Plans for *Challenger's* second day in space involved a simulated rendezvous manoeuvre, in which Paul Weitz and Karol Bobko performed a sequence of burns using the RCS and OMS engines to circularize its orbit at 236 miles altitude. Don Petersen and Story Musgrave began work on *Challenger's* experiment cargo. Principally, they included three 'Getaway Special' experiments located in three cannisters in the forward payload bay. The Getaway Special (GAS) experiments were scheduled by NASA as cheap research facilities that needed an absolute minimum of crew attention during the mission. Those carried on this mission included the Monodisperse Latex Reactor (MLR), which was designed to produce perfect latex spheres for medical and industrial precision measurements; the Night-time/Daylight Optical Survey of Lightning, a weather monitoring experiment; and the Continuous Flow Electrophoresis System (CFES) drug-making experiment. Finally, at twenty three minutes past midnight on 6 April, the crew turned in to sleep once more. *Challenger* continued to behave virtually perfectly on her maiden flight.

The following day Paul Weitz and his crew beat the early morning call from Houston at 11.30 by a full hour, the time being usefully spent tidying the Orbiter and preparing for the morning's first task: firing the *Challenger's* reaction control motors in order to make circular the somewhat elliptical orbit. This done, at 10.45 the crew enjoyed a breakfast before commencing the day's work. Once more the two decks of *Challenger* assumed the environment of both a busy office and a research laboratory. By 2.00 pm Don Peterson was working the 'continuous flow electrophoresis system' (CFES), a device for producing space-processed medicines down on the lower deck. Paul Weitz was taking photographs of thunderstorms over the Gulf of Mexico; Story Musgrave, the eager EVA man, was checking out his spacesuit; and Karol Bobko interspersed scientific research experiments with periods of in-flight exercise.

With proper regard to this being *Challenger's* maiden flight, a full systems check was made just before 5.00 pm. Naturally the main part of this task fell to Paul Weitz and Karol Bobko. The one hour test of *Challenger's* flight control system involved a brief 'power-up' of one of the three APUs to provide enough hydrualic power to conduct a check on all *Challenger's* aerodynamic control surfaces. Whilst Paul Weitz and Karol Bobko were busy, the two mission specialists turned on the TV cameras for a 'prime time' broadcast of life in space for the American networks. Starting on the flight deck the camera focused on both commander and pilot busy at their stations, then moved downstairs to the mid-deck where, for the benefit of viewers, Don Peterson explained the function and future benefits to be derived from the medical experiments he had been conducting earlier in the day.

By six that evening, Don Peterson and Story Musgrave had finished their TV 'special' and were down to the serious work of inspecting their space suits for use the next day. So anxious were both the astronauts and NASA to have a successful EVA on this flight that the evening was spent conducting a complete dry run of every event leading up to depressurization and exit from the air lock. NASA had learnt from STS 5 not to rush things and it paid off. The dress rehearsal had gone smoothly and just after 8 pm, both mission specialists had removed their suits and stowed them for tomorrow.

All four men finished their evening meal early and both Story Musgrave and Don Peterson went straight to bed. Paul Weitz and Karol Bobko elected to stay up a while longer to tidy up and spend a while at the windows and reflect as they watched the Earth roll by.

It had been over twenty years since Bob White faced a host of unknowns as he flew X-15-3 to the fringe of space, thirty-six years since Charles Yeager broke the 'sound barrier' in the sleek X-1, and fifty years since Dr Eugen Sanger first proposed the concept of a winged space plane. Now, over 170 miles above the Earth, the 100 ton Shuttle *Challenger* and its four-man crew were playing their own part in the story. High up in the remote silence of space it was difficult to imagine the troubles on Earth, but the evidence of man's folly became only too clear as *Challenger* flew over the Middle East where an enormous oil slick in the Persian Gulf blotted the crystal blue sea. Paul Weitz and Karol Bobko photographed the evil spillage before returning to their sleep restraints.

Day four in space aboard *Challenger* began at just after 10.00 am EST on 7 April with a musical call-up from Mission Control, Houston. Breakfast was brief, as the EVA planned for the next few hours was eagerly looked forward to.

At 11.30 both Story Musgrave and Don Peterson climbed into *Challenger*'s airlock, mounted in the bulkhead between the lower flight deck and the payload bay. The space suits were mounted on the wall of the airlock chamber and were each in two parts, a lower 'trouser' section and upper 'torso' section which was complete with arms and backpack. The suits, manufactured by Hamilton Standard, joined together at the waist with an airtight locking ring. As the two mission specialists donned their suits pilot Karol Bobko assisted as best he could in the operation.

By lunchtime the two space-suited astronauts had completed their checks and with helmets and gloves on began slowly to purge from their suits all of *Challenger*'s cabin air, replacing it gradually with pure oxygen. This process was to take a full 3½ hours before all traces of nitrogen gas could be removed from their bloodstreams. Too rapid a change over could cause the astronauts to suffer from the bends. Meanwhile, Paul Weitz and Karol Bobko continued with their Shuttle housekeeping chores.

With the pre-breathing completed, Story Musgrave's and Don Peterson's suits were disconnected from *Challenger*'s power and oxygen supply as they began breathing oxygen and using power from their own backpacks. The airlock door on the cabin side was closed and the air vented slowly from the chamber. No-one on the ground knew exactly what was happening at this point, for *Challenger* was in one of its orbital 'black out' points out of range of ground stations. By the time they linked up with the Guam tracking station, the outer airlock hatch was open and Story Musgrave was leaving *Challenger*. As he moved cautiously about in the airlock hatch, attaching the end of one of his two tape-like tethers to the reel on his suit, he made way for Don Peterson to join him. Each astronaut was fully independent from the Shuttle with regard to power and oxygen. *Challenger* was flying with its base 'upwards', the open payload bay pointing towards Earth. As Story Musgrave looked down the length of *Challenger*'s bay, the clouds and continents of Earth drifted by above. The first and most important aspect of the EVA was for Story Musgrave to tether himself to one of two slide wires that ran the complete length of the payload bay alongside each payload bay door hinge. Handrails adjacent to the lines enabled an astronaut to clamber along the bay to perform any number of tasks required. Story Musgrave began to ease his way back along the bay whilst Don Peterson watched his progress from above the airlock door.

By now the TV cameras, mounted at strategic points in the cargo bay, were transmitting live pictures of the activities to American audiences via the Hawaiian tracking station. Across the USA people stopped to watch Story Musgrave manoeuvre around the aft end of *Challenger*'s payload bay; the diminutive figure giving scale to the size of the Shuttle Orbiter. Soon he was joined by Don Peterson who had attached his tether to the port slide line and made his way back in a similar fashion to Story Musgrave. The TV cameras captured the most dramatic scenes of manned spaceflight seen since the first moon landing, but outside the US the events were given scant coverage. Both men were obviously enjoying their work, and Story Musgrave, with his gold plated mirror-like visor stowed, could be seen smiling and laughing as he waved at the camera lens, with Don Peterson doing graceful pirouettes in the background.

The EVA was not to be all fun, however, and soon both men had returned to the forward payload bay bulkhead. On the way back Story Musgrave had performed a task which would demonstrate how well an astronaut could work in the centre of the payload bay. With the assistance of Don Peterson, he attached his second tether to an opposite (port) handrail and then stationed himself midway in the open payload bay secured to both sides. NASA concluded that in such a position an astronaut could rely on remaining securely in one place whilst working inside the bay.

Back once more at the forward end of the payload bay the two space walkers began to unstow tools that would be needed during the remainder of the EVA.

The next task in the flight plan called for a simulation of procedures for levering back down into the bay a stuck satellite launching platform. If, for example, the platform that launched the TDRS had remained in its 90 degree tilt position, it would have been impossible to close the payload doors and *Challenger* would not have been able to return to Earth. In the event of such an emergency

the platform could be winched back down into its correct position using a combination of ropes and pulleys operated by a winch crank on the payload bay aft bulkhead. It was this procedure that Story Musgrave and Don Peterson were to simulate. Although the operation went according to plan, the EVA was exhausting and on one occasion Don Peterson's spacesuit alarm went off indicating an oxygen leak. In fact, the suit had misinterpreted Don Peterson's high oxygen consumption as holed fabric and flashed up the warning.

Following this another emergency contingency

While *Columbia* was making repeated flights into space, her sister ship, *Challenger*, was being prepared at Rockwell's Palmdale facility. Thermal tiles are being installed in this photograph. The yellow lattice-work on the payload doors facilitates ground handling. (Rockwell International)

to be simulated was that to be adopted should the payload bay doors themselves not close. A rope, pulley and crank device was employed, similar to that used for a faulty launching platform. Although it was hard work the astronauts proved that such emergency procedures would work in practice.

Two further major outside items remained to be tested. First the 'Payload Retention Device', which would secure any stray pieces of cargo in the bay prior to re-entry and, secondly, the 'Massive Article Translation'. In effect, this latter glorified name really meant 'could an astronaut carry a heavy tool kit or object successfully from one end of the bay to another?' The two men proved it could be done, and then tired and happy they returned to the airlock. The EVA, the first by American astronauts for nine years, had lasted 3 hours 32 minutes. Within a few hours the crew had removed their suits, tidied up and gone to sleep.

The final full day in space was kept deliberately low-key by NASA, aware that the crew were now very tired after the previous day's activities. It was also a time for levity. By lunchtime US Vice President George Bush put in a call to the crew who were assembled on the lower deck in front of the TV camera. To most people's surprise, every astronaut was wearing spectacles which prompted Vice President Bush to comment on the seniority of the crew. The astronauts responded in good spirit by holding up a card saying '111 years of aviation experience'. Closing down transmission Paul Weitz cracked, 'This programme has been brought to you by the Geritol Bunch'.

Apart from housekeeping and preparation for re-entry the only other major task of the day was undertaken by Don Peterson. During launch, the crew had heard a loud crack and a tearing noise in the cabin and on the final full day they found the cause. The mounting bracket holding two TV monitors in position had broken under the strain of lift-off. Under instruction from Houston, Don Peterson removed the screens, wrapped them up in the pillows used at night and taped them to the floor of the lower deck out of harm's way.

For a maiden flight, STS 6 had gone about as well as anyone could have dared hope. So Mission Control Houston said goodnight to the crew, *Challenger* entered into radio blackout away from the ground station, and the astronauts prepared to sleep.

Suddenly, the tranquility was broken by the urgency of *Challenger's* alarm system. General Purpose Computer (GPC) Number Two had failed. It was serious but not critical. The crew attempted to find out what had gone wrong. As soon as they reached contact with the next tracking station Paul Weitz relayed the problem to Houston. Mission Control decided to close down GPC2 and fly the rest of the mission on one of the three remaining back-up computers.

The next day, 9 April, Edwards Air Force Base was in prime condition for *Challenger's* return. Up early, chief astronaut John Young was aloft in NASA 903 (a T-38 jet) surveying the weather along *Challenger's* final flight path. With scattered cloud and a 10 knot surface wind the weather was ideal. Rogers Lake Bed was flooded, the hard flat surface was now a sea of salty mud. As a result STS 6 was scheduled to land on Edwards' concrete Runway 22.

After 80 orbits of the Earth, flying over Senegal, *Challenger* was given the 'Go' for the de-orbit burn. The 62 second ignition of *Challenger's* OMS engines slowed it down to begin the long re-entry path to California on the other side of the world. Paul Weitz jokingly asked his crew if they didn't 'want to go around one more time'. 'And,' he said, 'all I got was a blank look. Nobody wanted to do that'. Before *Challenger* entered re-entry black-out the Houston communicator Roy Bridgers replied, 'Maybe we can get you another flight real soon. I think that's a better way to go'.

Minutes later *Challenger* was back in communication. Soon Houston and America could see on TV a small, distant yet familiar shape appear, growing steadily larger until there was no mistaking the double delta wings of *Challenger* as she flew home to Edwards. Cameras on board the T-38 chase planes gave startling close-ups of the Shuttle as it completed its final approach. For the last few minutes Paul Weitz took over from the autoland system and using the new 'head-up display' (a system that projects critical flight instrument readings onto the windscreen, allowing the pilot to see the approaching runway and his instruments at the same time) he lowered the undercarriage and brought *Challenger* home after 5 days, 23 minutes, 42 seconds.

It was not long after *Challenger's* return that engineers from NASA had given it a thorough post-landing checkout and pronounced it to be in better condition than *Columbia* had been after any of its previous five flights. *Challenger* had encountered only 22 minor problems during its flight, compared with 27 on *Columbia's* fifth and 82 on its first flight. NASA was delighted; their newest spacecraft had passed her first test with flying colours and everyone was looking forward to STS 7 scheduled for the second week in June.

STS 7

The second flight of *Challenger* was to be the most demanding of the entire Shuttle programme so far. STS 7 would launch two satellites, ANIK C-2 (Telesat F) and Palapa B-1, a communications satellite. In addition *Challenger* would carry into space an international experiment coded OSTA -2, which would experiment with the manufacture of

This photograph shows clearly that the insulated crew module is quite separate from the remainder of the airframe. This assists in preventing loads and heat from being transmitted from the outer shell. (Rockwell International)

unique materials in a zero-g environment.

A free-flying experiment SPAS-01 would be deployed from *Challenger*'s cargo bay during the

week-long flight, and then be recovered before return to Earth. This would give the crew a chance to practice station keeping in space with another space vehicle.

The crew for STS 7 was commanded by Captain Robert Crippen. The other four were pilot Fred Hauck, and three mission specialists, Dr Norman Thagard, Colonel John M. Fabian (USAF) and, for the first time in an American spaceflight, a woman, Dr Sally Ride, whose speciality was the Remote Manipulator System (RMS).

On 18 June 1983, STS 7 lifted off the pad into a glorious sunshine-filled sky at 6.33 am Eastern Standard Time. The launch, like the weather, was perfect. It was a textbook start to what was to be NASA's most ambitious flight to date. No sooner had *Challenger* and her crew arrived in space than the payload doors were opened and orbital preparations began.

The first major task for Day One in space was the deployment of the Canadian satellite Anik C-2. After checking out *Challenger*'s systems, at around 2.15 pm EST, Sally Ride and John Fabian began the pre-deployment checkout of both Anik and its PAM-D booster rocket system. Twenty minutes before the planned launch time, the crew opened the satellite's sun shield cover and immediately began spinning Anik C-2 in its launch cradle. Anik C-2 would continue to spin on deployment because, like a gyroscope, it relied on centrifugal force to keep it in a stable attitude in space; in addition, the delicate solar panel segments around its circumference would soon melt if continuously exposed to harsh, unfiltered, sunlight.

For the remainder of the countdown, Sally Ride and John Fabian watched Anik C-2 from the rear-facing payload bay windows on the upper flight deck. As it span it flashed sunlight from its reflective solar panels. At just after 4.00 pm EST, small explosive charges fired, the hold down points released, and Anik C-2 sprang out of *Challenger*'s payload bay into the void of space. The crew were jubilant, fully living up to their flight motto 'We deliver'. Deployment, at 17,500 mph, was just over 200 yards away from the optimum position.

With a full day's work behind them and a busy schedule ahead for the coming days, the crew of STS 7 made a final systems check, ate dinner and turned in. Day Two in space began at 3.30 am EST. Breakfast on board *Challenger* was followed by several housekeeping chores before the main task of the day, launching Palapa B-1, was undertaken.

Launched in almost exactly the same fashion as Anik C-2 a day earlier, the 'spin up' was completed on scedule under the control of Sally Ride and John Fabian. Norman Thagard was at hand with

TV and video camera to record the event for later transmission to Mission Control. Whilst preparations for launch were underway, Bob Crippen and Fred Hauck carefully manoeuvred *Challenger* to a proper flight attitude to make sure that Palapa would be launched, like Anik, in precisely the right direction. At just after 8.30 am EST Palapa sprung out of the payload bay on the next leg of its journey up to geosynchronous orbit above the Earth. STS 7 had successfully delivered both its commercial payloads on time and with incredible accuracy. Anik had been deployed within 300 yards of the scheduled position and within 0.085 degrees of its planned pointing angle. Palapa had been deployed with similar accuracy, whilst *Challenger* flew at 17,500 mph.

Lunch was preceded by an impromptu TV broadcast during which, in true NASA astronaut tradition, the usual exchange of banter and in-house jokes were made. To outsiders the initials TFNG on the pilot and mission specialists' own unofficial tee-shirts meant very little; in fact, it stood for 'thirty five new guys' with reference to the 35 NASA recruits in 1978 of which they were a part. Below the letters TFNG was a cartoon Shuttle stuffed with thirty five astronauts attempting to do around seventy operations simultaneously!

The 'afternoon' of Day Two in space was spent testing the RMS and in activating the free flying SPAS-1 pallet ready for its role in Day Five's operation. The RMS was Sally Ride's speciality. Working from a position in the rear of the upper flightdeck, and looking both at the TV monitor, relaying pictures from the camera on the end of the arm, and through the payload bay window, Sally Ride could control the RMS with total precision. RMS would be used to pick up the SPAS-1 free flyer, deploy it in space next to *Challenger*, then pick it up later and replace it for return to Earth. The arm, controlled via a hand controller inside *Challenger*'s flight deck, had all the dexterity of a human arm and, in fact, was designed to be an extension of the mission specialist in performing complex tasks outside, not demanding the inconvenience of a full EVA by the crew. STS 7 would prove to NASA that the RMS was capable of handling with precision an article of hardware such as SPAS-1.

After several hours of testing, both SPAS-1 and the RMS were found to be in good shape for Day Five, and the crew once more began a well-earned eight-hour sleep period.

Challenger's third 'day' in space was mostly taken up with an experiment relating to EVA. During STS 6, NASA began to contemplate seriously the problems of the 3½ hour oxygen pre-breathing needed to clear each astronaut's system of nitrogen before going outside in a low pressure oxygen-filled spacesuit. One solution, at least partially, to alleviate this problem was to lower the Orbiter's cabin pressure from sea level (14.7 psi) by 75 per cent for around 30 hours. If this could be done successfully it would mean that on future EVA flights of the Shuttle, astronauts would only have to 'pre-breathe' oxygen for an hour or so.

Other tasks for the third day included test-firing *Challenger*'s RCS thrusters; trimming the orbit from eliptical to circular, and conducting experiments mounted on the SPAS-1 pallet whilst still inside the payload bay. Whilst Sally Ride, John Fabian, Bob Crippen and Fred Hauck were busy, Dr Norman Thagard was continuing his medical research into the space sickness syndrome encountered by astronauts ever since the early days of spaceflight. On Apollo and Skylab several astronauts had been almost incapacitated for days by sickness, but always a cause and a cure had eluded doctors. To Dr Norman Thagard's frustration not one of the STS 7 crew were suffering from space sickness at all! Not to be defeated, he turned his medical skills to an analysis of the question — 'Why not?'

As the third 'day' wore on one of the flight's few failures occurred, when one of the pilot's flight deck TV screens failed. These screens conveyed data to both commander and pilot during launch, re-entry and landing. For a while the crew considered a 'fix', by unscrewing the faulty screen and replacing it with another from the rear of the cockpit. Mission Control, however, was not so enthusiastic about tinkering, particularly because the screen was adjacent to a 'live' emergency escape hatch operating handle that, if knocked, would fire explosive bolts and punch a massive hole in *Challenger*'s flight deck roof! Weighing-up the risk, Mission Control decided that STS 7 should continue to fly using the other panel-mounted screens.

The fourth day in space for *Challenger*'s crew on 21 June 1983, began on a troublesome note. Instruments left on overnight, mounted within the SPAS-1 pallet, had begun to overheat. Accordingly, not wishing to take any chances with damaging the pallet before its free flight, Mission Control ordered it to be shut down until Day Five. Sally Ride then began work on the McDonnell Douglas 'CFES' drug-making experiment assisted by John Fabian; the commander and pilot tried to fix faulty headset communicators, while Dr Norman Thagard continued his investigations into motion sickness.

By the close of Day Four's activities, Bob Crippen and Fred Hauck had once more brought *Challenger*'s oxygen/nitrogen atmosphere back to normal sea level atmospheric pressure after a successful trial. The way had been cleared for easier EVA's from the Shuttle.

The next day was the most demanding of the STS 7 flight and would involve a complex series of proximity manoeuvres with the free-flying SPAS-1 pallet. Shortly after breakfast, John Fabian began to power up the SPAS-1 free flyer, whilst concern was mounting about the possible temperature-rise experienced during its first activation on day four.

Mission Control decided to abandon the test if the SPAS-1 equipment's internal temperature exceeded 102 °C. Within an hour of operation, SPAS-1 temperature began to climb steadily upwards, much to the concern of Bob Crippen, the flight commander. The temperature began to level off just below the red line as John Fabian began to operate the RMS arm lifting it out of its stowed position. Slowly, he brought the mechanical arm across to the payload bay and latched its end onto a probe on the SPAS-1. Then the SPAS-1/Orbiter umbilical was disconnected and John Fabian cautiously removed the mini spacecraft from the payload bay and positioned it high above *Challenger*. To test the RMS arm's ability to deploy and recover, Mission Control gave him the 'go' to initiate a quick release/grab test in which he let the SPAS-1 free for 60 seconds before once more catching it with the RMS arm. The test was successful and marked the first time a Shuttle payload had been removed from the cargo bay, released and recaptured by the RMS arm. The second test would establish a distance between *Challenger* and SPAS-1 of several hundred yards. At its furthest point away from the Orbiter, SPAS-1's TV camera relayed spectacular video of *Challenger* far below, gliding above the continents of the Earth, payload bay doors open, and the RMS arm left by the crew in the shape of the number seven, a symbol of the flight. At its furthest distance away from *Challenger* the small robot SPAS-1 had its own RCS thrusters turned off by Sally Ride in *Challenger*. SPAS-1 would be allowed to drift for a while as delicate experiments were undertaken. Just before 5.55 am EST, Sally Ride turned its thrusters back on as Bob Crippen began to move back in for a pick-up. Cautiously, Bob Crippen closed on SPAS-1 using *Challenger*'s attitude thrusters. Extreme caution was needed to avoid damaging SPAS-1 with gas from the small jets. At 7.30 am EST the free-flying pallet was grabbed once more by the RMS arm: the second phase of the test completed.

One final test remained before lunch, and that was to deploy SPAS-1 a third time and attempt to recover it whilst it was spinning. This was a necessary task if future recoveries of spin-stabilized satellites were to be made regularly. Again the test was a complete success, indicating the faith NASA had placed in the RMS performance as Shuttles' most important tool.

After lunch, in order that each crew member could gain as much experience as possible in handling the RMS/SPAS-1 test tasks, Sally Ride and John Fabian swapped responsibilities. For the next few hours John Fabian would assume command of SPAS-1 whilst Sally Ride would operate the RMS.

Space Shuttle

At the same time, Rick Hauck would fly *Challenger* whilst Bob Crippen kept a watchful eye on Orbiter systems. Dr Norman Thagard was continuing his medical experiments.

In contrast to the previous deployment, SPAS-1 was now to take a battering. NASA wanted to know how direct impact from *Challenger's* thrusters could affect the small robot flyer. Each time, at varying distances, Rick Hauck fired the *Challenger's* thrusters SPAS-1 could be seen on TV clearly to wobble and sway, its own gas jets struggling to keep it level and under control. Repeated blasts rocked SPAS-1 before Mission Control decided that enough was enough. Bob Crippen was full of admiration for the amount of punishment SPAS-1 could take. The final recovery of SPAS-1 was made testing *Challenger's* rendezvous radar at difficult approach angles.

Eventually SPAS-1 was taken back on board and safely stowed once more in the payload bay. The crew ended their fifth day in space on a triumphant note proclaiming, 'On Flight Seven, we pick up *and* deliver!'

The final day in space was spent tidying up in preparation for landing back at Kennedy Space Centre, marking the first time any space vehicle had ever returned from space to its launch site. As the crew began to complete all the outstanding onboard experiments and tests, however, the weather around the eastern Florida seaboard began to close

As proclaimed by the notice in the foreground, when working on the Orbiter, jewellery must be removed or taped to the skin; eye glasses must be tethered when working above ground level; all items must be removed from upper pockets when working above ground level; and tools, clamps and loose tool components must be tethered (when required). Working on *Challenger's* fuselage, all staff were subject to strict working rules. (Rockwell International)

in. Heavy rain clouds and thunderstorms around the Cape had worried Mission Control planners to such an extent that they were considering keeping *Challenger* aloft several days longer until conditions had improved. This was accepted by the crew who were keen to stay up, 'as long as it takes'.

Edwards Air Force Base was clear, but NASA was keen to try out the Kennedy Space Centre's runway facility if possible. In addition, a landing at Kennedy would reduce the turn around time to STS 8 by about a week, and save the time and expense of ferrying *Challenger* back across the USA on top of the 905 carrier aircraft. As things turned out *Challenger* herself made the final decision as to when the flight should end.

As part of the re-entry and landing checks Bob Crippen and Rick Hauck powered up the third APU for a quick check of *Challenger*'s aerodynamic control surfaces. No sooner had the APU started up than it shut down.

Despite checks no one could find out why. Rick Hauck started the APU up again and it worked perfectly, but Mission Control was not confident at all. It was the kind of situation that NASA disliked. Shortly afterwards the decision was made not to extend the mission but land at Edwards if poor weather at Kennedy persisted.

The rest of the last day in space was taken up with a final captive test of SPAS-1 and RMS arm, during which *Challenger*'s thrusters were fired once more to see the RMS's tendency to sway as the Orbiter manoeuvred. Finally, with SPAS-1's batteries exhausted, it was replaced for the last time in the cargo bay and the RMS stowed.

On 24 June, the day of the landing, the foggy pre-dawn air clinging to the mangrove swamps at Kennedy Space Centre was stirred by the muffled exhaust of John Young's T-38 jet aircraft as he flew low around the 'spaceport' checking conditions for landing. Banking in from the sea off Cape Canaveral he tried to make out the Shuttle runway, shrouded in mist, but could see nothing. As dawn broke, John Young had landed and taken off again — this time in the Gulfstream II Shuttle Training Aircraft — to practice some Shuttle landings. Alongside him in a T-38 Joe Engle watched John Young make several aborted landing attempts before advising STS 7 flight director to cancel any plans to land at Kennedy. Several 'alternate' landing sites had been preprogrammed into *Challenger*'s flight computers, so a last-minute change presented no problem from the flight guidance point of view.

To all intents, Edwards was devoid of all but essential staff to deal with a returning Orbiter, the bulk of the Shuttle's support equipment having been returned to Kennedy Space Centre! So it was with a quiet reception that STS 7 came to an end after a flight of just over 6 days 2 hours. As *Challenger* came to rest along Lakebed Runway 15, Mission Control radioed, 'We have some good news and some bad news. The good news is that the

beer is very cold this morning. The bad news is that it's 3,000 miles away.' Bob Crippen replied, 'That's what I was afraid of!'

The use of such an alternative landing site as Edwards presented more of a logistical than a technical problem. Essential servicing equipment needed to maintain a returned Orbiter was always on hand, as was a team of trained technicians to carry out the first important post-landing checks. What was inconvenient was that *Challenger* would have to be ferried back across the entire width of the United States on top of the 905 aircraft with all the cost, delay and potential damage during transit that would entail.

At the post-flight conference, Shuttle Manager Lt General James Abrahamson announced that only twenty-one problems had been encountered during the flight. Amongst these none was considered likely to cause a delay of the next flight, STS 8.

STS 8

Several hours before dawn at Kennedy Space Centre, on 30 August 1983, amidst a driving tropical rainstorm, a small convoy of vehicles left the crew checkout building en-route for launch complex 39A. On board the white transfer van, taking the route followed by many space-bound crews in the past, were Commander Richard Truly, Daniel Brandenstein, Dale Gardner, Guion Bluford and Dr Bill Thornton.

Richard Truly was making his second space flight since STS 2. Truly's pilot for STS 8 was Daniel Brandenstein, who was selected as a NASA astronaut in 1978 and named as STS 8 pilot in April 1982. Before joining the Space Agency he had served as a pilot with the US Navy in Vietnam. In addition Daniel Brandenstein held a B.Sc. in physics and mathematics, gained in 1965. He was 40 years old.

Dr Bill Thornton was, along with John Young, one of NASA's oldest astronauts. Joining NASA in 1967 he had waited 16 years to fly in space. As a specialist in aerospace medicine he was to study the effects of space sickness.

Both Dale Gardner and Guion Bluford had been selected for the NASA Shuttle project in 1978, and were both scientists with a background of military flying.

Before the difficulties encountered with the TDRS satellite's inertial upper stage booster on *Challenger*'s first flight, STS 8 was to have taken aloft its sister, TDRS-B. However, engineers were still attempting to find out why signals had been lost for vital hours during the first satellite's deployment, and were not happy about launching another until they had isolated the problem concerning its booster stage, which had left TDRS-A desperately short on fuel, since it had to rely on its own manoeuvring engines to reach a proper orbit. As a result STS 8 was to carry, in place of TDRS-B, a variety of individual experiments and commercial payloads. One of these was a 'Payload Flight Test Article'. Essentially a massive dumbell structure over 15 ft long, it was designed to test the RMS arm's ability to move heavy objects around in space. This would be necessary in future if large satellites were to be deployed and recovered in space.

STS 8 was also to use fully the TDRS-A satellite, then in operation, to check the satellite's ability to handle high volumes of data in preparation for the next flight, STS 9, which would carry the European Space Lab. Only one satellite would be depoloyed on STS 8, the Indian satellite named INSAT 1-B. It was this satellite, and the need to deploy it in orbit at a precise point, that meant the launch of STS 8 had to be scheduled for pre-dawn. This, in turn, meant that the landing would have to be made at night also, for each time *Challenger* passed over Edwards, it would be in darkness. Both Richard Truly and Daniel Brandenstein had put in extra hours in the Shuttle Training Aircraft and Shuttle simulator so that they could face any of the problems they might encounter. Chief of these was the 'Return to Launch Site' abort. If anything went wrong just after lift-off *Challenger* would have to fly out over the western Atlantic to gain altitude, then do an about turn and drop the external tank and solid rocket boosters and come back down to Kennedy Space Centre. This manoeuvre was considered extremely difficult even in daylight.

NASA, nevertheless, had been looking at the possibilities of launching more Shuttle missions at night, because the weather in Florida tended to be more benign after sundown. Ironically, as the crew of STS 8 crossed from the transfer van to the launch gantry, the rain was driving down in torrents and lightning flashed across the leaden skies. Once aboard *Challenger* the crew strapped in and began the final checks to lift-off. As the Shuttle swayed in the wind, out of the cabin windows the crew watched the clouds above swirl and the rain lit by lightning. It was beginning to look as if STS 8 might have to be postponed. Back in 1969, Apollo 12 had been struck by lightning shortly after lift-off and only quick reactions by Pete Conrad and his crew had saved America's second moon landing. NASA was certainly not going to risk a recurrence of that incident.

Nine minutes from launch, *Challenger*'s countdown was 'held' for ten minutes as planned, during which time the skies began to clear and the thunderstorm died. By 1.23 am EST, the countdown resumed. *Challenger* was clearly visible for miles around, illuminated by high-intensity xenon searchlights mounted around the launch pad. As the final seconds passed, the three main engines flexed in readiness for ignition.

'10-9, we have main engine ignition.' The clouds of exhaust billowed out from the flame trench, the solid rockets kicked into life and *Challenger* lifted off the pad like an enormous flare, so bright against the night-time sky it lit up Cape Canaveral like day. As this man-made sun rose higher into the sky and its thunder echoed across the everglades, the crew were surrounded in the cabin by an eerie orange glow. Almost nine minutes after lift-off *Challenger*, by now no more than another star in the heavens, was on a perfect course for orbit. Not since Apollo 17's final, night time launch to the moon had Kennedy Space Centre witnessed such a spectacle.

Once in space the crew began orbital operations, with live TV coverage of the payload bay door opening. In a display of patriotism, as both doors opened sunlight burst in upon a huge 'Stars and Stripes' flag painted on the PFTA.

Down on *Challenger*'s lower deck, Air Force Lt Col Guian Bluford, America's first black astronaut, and a mission specialist on STS 8, was activating a new experiment in which, it was hoped, new super-pure drugs and vaccines could be manufactured. Alongside Guion Bluford, fellow mission specialist Dr Bill Thornton had started to set up his experiments which would closely examine the causes of space sickness. Before the end of their first day in space, the crew of STS 8 were well into their stride and had, significantly, tried and tested communications with the TDRS-1 satellite and found it working perfectly.

After a good eight hours of sleep, the crew of *Challenger* awoke to commence the deployment of INSAT 1-B. At just before 3.00 am EST the small Indian satellite sprang out of the payload bay on its way to a perfect orbit. The Indian Government was delighted, and for the crew the next task was a live chat with President Reagan. The President made great play on the significance of America's first negro astronaut, and the age of Dr Bill Thornton, at 54 the oldest man in space. President Reagan joked that perhaps he too might at some later date make a flight into space!

Following the third day's successful manoeuvers with the RMS arm and the PFTA/dumbell, the crew continued with numerous complex scientific experiments. Among these were some engineering tests on *Challenger* and her systems. On Day Five, Dale Gardner used the RMS arm's TV camera to inspect the *Challenger*'s underbelly tiles, a useful procedure which made inspection by EVA unnecessary. Further, final, tests were made with the PFTA, then the crew settled down together on

Challenger's lower deck for an in-flight press conference, relayed live on TV via TDRS-1. Predictably, the main question centred on how Guion Bluford felt about being America's first black astronaut, how Richard Truly and Daniel Brandenstein felt about a night landing, and what Dr William Thornton had learnt about space sickness. It was, of course, not possible for Bill Thornton to announce a solution there and then to the problem that had dogged most manned spaceflights since the nineteen-sixties, but he had 'learned more in the first hour and a half [of investigation] than I have in all the previous years that I've put in'.

Day Six in space saw the completion of inflight experiments and tidying up on *Challenger* in preparation for the next day's night time landing at Edwards.

On 5 September 1983, Edwards Air Force Base was ready for *Challenger*'s return. It was a clear, starry night out in the desert as Runway 22, illuminated by a battery of powerful xenon searchlights, stood out as a bright strip along the Rogers Dry Lake. Without landing lights of her own, *Challenger* would be visible to onlookers only as she flew over the runway before landing. Suddenly, against the backdrop of a clear sky came the thunder of double sonic booms, echoing across the flat desert. *Challenger* appeared like a white spectre gliding silently above the ground. Seconds later she was down. The flight had been an unqualified success, and had lasted for 6 days 1 hour 19 minutes.

When technicians had a chance to examine *Challenger*, they found all her tiles to be in place with hardly a mark on them. NASA's second Orbiter had completed her third flight with credit.

Meanwhile, in California, on 5 November 1983, the latest Shuttle, *Discovery,* was taken by road from her assembly plant at Rockwell's Palmdale facility to Edwards Air Force Base. It was a traditional route, followed not only by the X-15 but also by *Discovery*'s sisters, *Columbia* and *Challenger*.

The roads were crowded on each side by sightseers, as *Discovery* and her trailer passed through the town of Lancaster, the Orbiter squeezing through between telegraph poles with just inches to spare. Through the crowded streets, past restaurants, barbers' shops and banks the world's most advanced aircraft crawled along at walking pace. John Sheerwater, a resident of Lancaster, remembered coming out of the supermarket and being confronted by *Discovery* as she headed East. 'I just could not believe it,' he said, 'there was I, with a bag of groceries in one hand climbing into my 1978 Chevy on a perfectly ordinary day, when right in front of me was *Discovery*! I'm 78 years old now, but I cannot remember a time in my life when I was more proud of being an American. Just looking at that spacecraft made my eyes misty and seeing the Stars and Stripes up there — well I was just about choked!'

The earlier roll-out of *Discovery* coincided, almost to the day, with the 25th anniversary of the formation of NASA from the old NACA. As the latest Orbiter first saw the light of day at Palmdale, Rockwell International's final-assembly site, it was exactly 15 months (exactly on schedule) behind that of her sister *Challenger*, which had just completed her third mission, STS 8.

There were few major differences between *Discovery* and *Challenger*; each possessed the same 122 ft of black and white sleekness, but internally *Discovery* was a little lighter because of a manufacturing weight reduction programme first started with *Challenger*. The weight savings were achieved through the use of graphite-epoxy structural members in place of heavier aluminium, and the removal of several flight engineering test data instruments. Also, a new heat shield material was being used. *Discovery*'s on-board systems were of a more advanced construction, and there was an improved galley in the lower deck of the crew compartment.

Externally there was a noticeable cosmetic difference. The 8 inch by 8 inch white-coloured, low-temperature tiles along the spacecraft's mid-fuselage, sides, and the upper portion of the double-delta wing structure had been removed. In place of these tiles was a lighter blanket type material known as AFRSI (Advanced Flexible Reusable Surface Insulation).

Initially, approximately 5,000 low-temperature white tiles were installed on both *Columbia* and *Challenger* to protect against re-entry friction temperatures of up to 1,200 °F. Over 2,200 AFRSI blankets were used on *Discovery* in place of the tiles. The blanket material consisted of low-density matting made from high-purity silica fibres. Apart from the weight-saving benefits of the new blanket material, it would also be easier to maintain, quicker to install and less prone to damage than the fragile tiles.

STS 9

On 16 August 1983 *Columbia* completed a major hurdle in her return to flight status. Spacelab 1 was loaded into *Columbia*'s payload bay at the Orbiter Processing Facility, Kennedy Space Centre.

Built by the European Space Agency, Spacelab 1 consisted of a habitable research module and an external experiment-carrying pallet. Astronauts from Europe and the USA would carry out scientific experiments within the pressurized crew module, and control Spacelab's pallet-mounted instruments from a 'shirt-sleeve' environment. Originally, NASA had scheduled STS 9 for 28 Oct-

Finally, after months of intensive effort, the finishing touches are made to _Challenger_. Artists proudly add the Stars and Stripes to the fuselage sides and wings. (Rockwell International)

ober 1983 but, after STS 8, technicians discovered a flaw in the SRBs which, until it could be put right, would halt all further Shuttle operations.

The thrust chamber or 'nozzle' of each SRB on STS 8 had eroded much faster than engineers had anticipated. The carbon-carbon lining of each nozzle was designed to wear, but one of the SRBs recovered from STS 8 had suffered severe pitting. At one point only 5mm of lining remained, which, combined with its glass-fibre and metal backing, would have held for only another 14 seconds of ignition. Failure of an SRB chamber would be catastrophic; the resultant thrust imbalance would send the entire Shuttle assembly into a cartwheel across the sky before it broke up under atmos-

pheric and dynamic forces. It was soon found that faulty materials used on the STS 8 SRBs were to blame, and so _Columbia,_ which by then had been mated with her External Tank and SRBs and rolled out to pad 39A for launch, was returned to the VAB once more. As _Columbia's_ SRBs were replaced, NASA knew that, by delaying STS 9 for a further month, some of Spacelab's experiments would be compromised by unfavourable earth observation conditions. To overcome this problem NASA dropped one of the Shuttle Atlantic abort targets to allow for a more northerly (57 degree) launch angle. This would allow high-resolution photographs, with low sun angles, to be taken of Europe for map-making purposes. Normally the Shuttle would be launched at a 28.5 degree northeast inclination.

Whilst _Columbia_ was receiving last minute attentions, the crew of STS 9 were going through their final training. STS 9 was to be the last space flight of the legendary John Young. As Chief of the Astronaut Office he also became commander of _Columbia's_ six-man crew.

Pilot for STS 9 was Brewster Shaw. Another graduate of the USAF Test Pilot School at Edwards, he acted as both instructor and test pilot there from 1975 until his selection as a NASA astronaut in August 1978. Owen K. Garriott was the senior mission specialist. Then 53 years old, Garriott had spent a lifetime specializing in electrical engineering, gaining a Ph.D. in 1960, and becoming an associate professor in 1961. Selected as a scientist astronaut by NASA in 1965, he made his first spaceflight on board Skylab 3, the second manned mission in that programme. On his return, Owen Garriott became Director of Science and Applications at the Johnson Space Centre, Houston, before being selected as mission specialist for the first Spacelab flight in August 1978.

The three other mission specialists included Robert Parker, Byron Lichtenberg and Ulf Merbold. Robert Parker was another long-standing NASA astronaut, selected by the agency in August 1967 as a scientist astronaut. Between 1974 and 1978 he was Chief of Scientist Astronauts, before being assigned to fly the first Spacelab flight in 1978. Dr Byron Lichtenberg made up the fifth and final United States crewman on board STS 9. A former Vietnam fighter pilot he was also a biomedical engineer. Dr Lichtenberg joined the NASA ranks in 1977.

For the first time in a US space mission a non-US National was aboard: Dr Ulf Merbold, a 42-year-old physics scientist from West Germany. He was selected by the European Space Agency for Spacelab 1 in 1977, having his place on the first flight confirmed in September 1982.

The flight of STS 9 was to be the most politically significant of all the flights so far. For the first time two principal components of the Space Transportation System were together — the Shuttle and Spacelab. It was of little surprise then to find Commander John Young leading such a distinguished crew out to pad 39A for launch on 28 November 1983.

A few moments after 11.00 am EST *Columbia* lifted off the launch pad and thundered into space. John Young (whose first flight had been on 23 March 1965), together with his crew of five, climbed towards orbit, crossing over the eastern USA, Europe and the Soviet Union in only 30 minutes. It had been a perfect launch, both SRBs performing flawlessly.

Once the payload doors had been opened with their critical heat-dispensing radiators, Houston Mission Control confirmed *Columbia* as 'Go' to stay in orbit. Not long after, the crew began entry into the pressurized Spacelab module out in the payload bay. It was connected by a long pressurized tunnel which began at the *Columbia*'s lower deck airlock and ran back to Spacelab in the bay. Owen Garriott, Ulf Merbold and Byron Lichtenberg drifted along to their laboratory in the sky. As the TV pictures relayed to Earth showed, the three men had congratulated each other warmly. On the ground, it was not so much elation at a successful launch, but more that they had just overcome a problem that could have been an acute embarassment to NASA — the hatch connecting *Columbia* to the Spacelab tunnel had jammed shut; it took all six men to prise it open!

With Spacelab open for business, the crew slipped into the two-shift pattern of work that would continue until re-entry. To maximize the returns from Spacelab, both NASA and ESA wanted it manned and operating 24-hours a day. The 'blue' team, consisting of Brewster Shaw, Owen Garriott and Byron Lichtenberg, would operate for 12 hours between 9.00 am EST and 9.00 pm EST whilst the 'red' team of John Young, Bob Parker and Ulf Merbold would work from 9.00 pm to 9.00 am. All six had prepared for the mission weeks in advance by adjusting their normal sleep/awake patterns to suit.

NASA, with the experience of the 'three men at a time' Skylab flights of the early seventies, was interested to see whether or not such an arrangement would be feasible. Could, for example, three men sleep whilst three others worked around them? To minimize any disturbance of the resting crew, either the *Columbia*'s pilot or commander would remain at his flight deck station, whilst the mission and payload specialists would occupy Spacelab. This would leave the lower deck of *Columbia* free from activity.

Before the end of the third day in space things were beginning to go wrong. Equipment functioned well, but the crew were getting increasingly frustrated about the tight schedules of work to which they were being subjected. It appeared that NASA and Mission Control had learnt nothing from the similar problems aboard Skylab almost a decade earlier. On that project's last 84-day mission, a fully-fledged row developed between

astronauts and ground control over the sheer quantity of work expected of them. Now, on Spacelab, the mission and payload specialists were being asked to do two or three jobs at once. It was too much. Bob Parker, in the midst of working on an experiment with Ulf Merbold, was being harassed by the Payload Operations Control Centre adjacent to Mission Control, Houston. Things got to such a pitch he cut in on their instructions with: 'Just wait! Would you guys please tell us exactly what you want done when, and we'll forget about what else we're doing at the present time!'

Suitably admonished, ground controllers relaxed the work schedules. In the event *Columbia* had performed so well that the flight was extended a further day to complete tasks delayed in solving some minor technical problems with Spacelab. On the eighth day in space, the political side of STS 9 was to be demonstrated at an international press conference. Statements prepared by President Reagan and West Germany's Chancellor Helmut Kohl, were to be read to the crew before the press could fire their barrage of questions. Unfortunately, of the six astronauts, only John Young, Byron Lichtenberg and Ulf Merbold were allowed to take part. Even then, they had been carefully primed with a detailed manuscript from the White House so that they would have, in advance, the answers to many questions. As the TV cameras came on for testing before the conference, the crew switched transmissions to show the three other crewmen making their protest in the form of a 'hear no evil — see no evil — speak no evil' three-monkey act. Bob Parker covered his ears, Owen Garriott his eyes, and Brewster Shaw his mouth. The demonstration did not change the plans for the conference, but effectively floored the pretence of an 'open' press interview. Try as they might, even after almost a quarter of a century of spaceflight, there was no way government or media could upstage the astronauts!

By the tenth day in space, *Columbia* was preparing for her last full day in space before re-entry. It had been her longest flight to date, and the pre-landing checks continued flawlessly. *Columbia* had performed so well on STS 9 that, when a problem did occur just before the de-orbit manoeuvre the next day, it came as a complete shock to everyone concerned. At 5.15 am EST on 8 December 1983, John Young fired *Columbia*'s nose-mounted RCS jets as part of the alignment for re-entry burn schedule. As John Young recalled, '[there] was a loud bang and the whole spacecraft shook — my stomach turned and my legs turned to jelly'. At the same time as the 'hard' RCS burn, one of *Columbia*'s four general purpose computers stopped functioning. A few minutes later a further 'hard' burst of the RCS knocked out a second computer. 'Hard' RCS burns were an extremely rare phenomenon, usually the result of impurities in the RCS fuel supply, or induced by transient mechanical faults within the RCS system. As Mission Control called-off the landing for four more orbits to gain time in which to investigate the problem further, one of *Columbia's* three Inertial Measurement Units (IMUs) failed. Hours of effort by ground-based teams failed to reproduce the sequence of events leading to the failures. Mission Control and the astronauts were sure that the problems had been caused by the shock generated by the hard RCS firing. A 'Go' for de-orbit was given. On her 166th orbit around the Earth, *Columbia* fired her two OMS engines for 156 seconds. Soon after, *Columbia* re-entered the atmosphere and within minutes was soaring in towards Edwards, flying over China, the Gulf of Alaska and San Francisco. Finally, just before sunset, *Columbia* was picked-up by the chase planes which accompanied her in to a perfect touchdown on Runway 17. As *Columbia's* nosewheel thumped down, GPC2 failed once again confirming the failure due to shock theory.

As *Columbia* rolled to a halt after a flight of 10 days, 7 hours 47 minutes, TV monitors showed smoke pouring from one of her OMS pods. Investigations soon after, revealed that two of her three APUs had leaked hydrazine fuel shortly before touchdown. This highly volatile fuel had ignited wiring and surrounding equipment. The area around two of the APUs was badly charred. Had

the fire occurred during re-entry, and the third APU suffered similarly, with no power to control her flaps and air-brakes, *Columbia* would certainly have crashed; all as a result of the failure of two rubber 'O' rings in the hydrazine fuel lines which perished, causing the fuel to leak and catch fire around the hot APUs. As with the test bed explosion of X-15-2 all those years ago, the lesson was once more brought home — watch out for the simple things! In future technicians would check the conditions of the APU's 'O' rings after each flight.

Columbia 'flew' back to Kennedy some days later on top of NASA 905 to allow for the removal of Spacelab at the Orbiter Processing Facility. Once this job had been done she was flown back to Rockwell International plant at Downey, California, for a complete refurbishment and refit. The first, 'test' Orbiter was to be uprated to the standard of her sister *Challenger*, and the new Orbiter *Discovery*.

41B

The tenth flight in the Space Shuttle programme was the first to carry the new flight designation number — 41B. Numerous last minute changes to flight schedules had led NASA to abandon the old STS numbering system in favour of a new code. In this case *4* was Fiscal Year 1984, *1* for the code for

Challenger's public début at Rockwell's Palmdale facility on 30 June 1982. The boat tail, used on earlier ALT test flights, was retained both to protect the engines during transit and to provide streamlining during the ferry flight across the States to Florida. (NASA)

a Kennedy Space Centre Launch, and *B* for the second planned flight in the fiscal year. The old STS 10 (41A) was to have been flown by *Challenger* with Spacelab; however, when Spacelab was reassigned to STS 9 earlier in the year a secret military payload was assigned to STS 10. Continued problems with that satellite's inertial upper stage booster led to the flight's postponement, and then to its cancellation. STS 11 was then brought forward and designated 41B.

Firsts for flight 41B included the use of the Manned Manoeuvring Units (rocket propelled back-packs), and a landing at Kennedy Space Centre.

The crew were Commander Vance Brand, Pilot Robert Gibson with mission specialists Ronald McNair, Robert Stewart and Bruce McCandless. Together they would deploy two communications satellites, Westar 6 and Palapa-B2.

Of the five men, only Vance Brand had flown in space before, as commander of STS 5 in November 1982 and as command module pilot during the Apollo Soyuz Test Project in 1975. His crew of 'rookies' had put in a considerable amount of simulator hours before the flight which began at 8.00 am EST on 3 February 1984. Lift-off, as was becoming accepted, was faultless, and by its sixth orbit around the Earth, *Challenger* had successfully launched the first of her two satellites, Westar 6. Unfortunately, Westar's own booster rocket failed. Bruce McCandless commented later, 'The deployment was faultless, and we were confident that everything had gone well. It wasn't until several hours later when we got a query from the control centre in Houston that we began to realize that perhaps something had gone awry.

Westar 6, in common with most communications satellites, was supposed to have boosted itself into geosynchronous orbit. Its small booster was to transfer the satelllites from *Challenger's* low orbit. The booster, made by McDonnell Douglas Astronautics and designated 'Pam D', consisted of a solid-fuel rocket motor, and instrumentation. Essentially, it was the most basic and uncomplicated kind of propulsion available. Nevertheless it had failed, leaving Westar 6 functioning normally but in far too low an orbit to be of any use.

The launch of the Indonesian satellite, Palapa-B, scheduled for the second day in space, was postponed. Palapa-B was to use the same kind of booster as Westar 6. Finally, Palapa's sponsors agreed to go ahead with the launch. *Challenger* deployed it perfectly on her fourth day in space, only to hear that it, too, had failed soon after ignition. Bruce McCandless was filming the launch, 'The motor lit exactly 45 minutes after deployment. We found a little white light which was the rocket's exhaust and centred the TV camera on it. Then we got a great big luminous smoke ring that exploded out and we interpreted that as some sort of failure in the nozzle'.

In America, and in Europe, the media pro-

nounced sentence on the Shuttle. Newspapers blamed the satellite's failure on *Challenger*, when in fact she had performed perfectly, deploying each satellite with an accuracy impossible to reproduce with conventional rockets such as Ariane, the European 'expendable' booster. Nevertheless, whilst the media continued their ill-founded condemnation, *Challenger* continued her mission.

To NASA and the crew of *Challenger*, the most important part of the flight was still to come. Loaded in the payload bay were two Manned Manoeuvring Units (MMUs). Bruce McCandless and Robert Stewart would wear these units to move about in space.

The story of the MMUs flown on mission 41B began in the early nineteen-sixties and involved the NASA Gemini spacecraft. At that time USAF proposals were being considered by NASA for an Astronaut Manoeuvring Unit (AMU). The project, designated DoD, experiment D-12, was later accepted by NASA who tentatively scheduled a prototype test flight as part of the Gemini 9 mission in 1966. The USAF wanted to fly another AMU on Gemini 12 in 1967, incorporating the experience gained from Gemini 9.

The AMU was constructed by Ling-Temco-Vought Inc, under the financial auspices of the USAF. Air Force Major and NASA astronaut Edward G. Givens, 34, was assigned to supervise and evaluate the AMU's developmental progress.

The concept of powered astronaut manoeuvring was fundamental to the development of an effective EVA capability which, in turn, was considered to be a routine supporting element in future manned spaceflight. EVA was expected to play a major role in such areas as space rescue, inspection and repair of parent or satellite spacecraft, personnel and cargo transport, and the erection of space structures. The addition of a manoeuvring aid to such EVA tasks was expected to reduce crew fatigue and stress, cut time restraints, offset pressure suit mobility limitations, and facilitate attitude orientation and stabilization.

In February 1966, after 18 months of labour which encompassed design, construction and assembly, the first flight-rated AMU arrived at the Kennedy Space Centre for installation inside the rear adaptor module of Gemini 9. The adaptor module formed both a structural link between Gemini, her retro-rocket module and the Titan II launcher, as well as serving as a container for auxiliary instruments and power fuel cells. The 166 lb AMU was 32 inches high, 22 inches wide and 19 inches in depth. It was fitted snugly inside the adaptor, allowing for easy access by a 'spacewalking' astronaut. In effect, the AMU was a spacecraft in miniature, with its own self-contained

UHF communications, telemetry, manual and automatic stabilization and life support. The AMU's propulsion system utilized 12 small hydrogen peroxide-fuelled attitude thrusters which could be fired via controls on the end of each extendable arm rest, giving the astronaut control over his pitch, roll and yaw motions.

The advantages of having such a device attached to an astronaut on EVA were many. Chiefly, the AMU would permit greater mobility once outside the spacecraft and permit the astronaut to achieve much more productive and ambitious work.

Prior to the flight of Gemini 9, astronaut Eugene Cernan who, together with commander Thomas P. Stafford, would fly the mission, teamed up with fellow astronaut Edward Givens for a number of familiarization tests with the AMU. A modified Air Force transport aircraft was used to fly a parabolic trajectory in which weightlessness could be induced for just under a minute at a time. During these periods, Eugene Cernan practiced 'strapping in' to the AMU, and 'test flying' it around the padded aircraft cabin.

Plans for the Gemini 9 flight of June 1966 called for mission commander Thomas Stafford to remain inside the spacecraft whilst Eugene Cernan opened his hatch and ventured into space attached to the '9' by a 25 ft long umbilical with an emergency life support chest pack. Using handholds deployed at the outset of his EVA, Eugene Cernan would slowly climb back to the open adaptor module, lock his feet into restraints just inside, unfurl the AMU's armrest and strap himself into place by backing into the AMU's form-fitted seat. To protect him from the AMU jet's 'hot' exhaust once free of the '9', Eugene Cernan wore specially reinforced space suit sections of high-temperature resistant material around his rear from the waist down to his feet. Together with the AMU he would conduct a detailed test of the AMU's manoeuvrability having substituted a 100 ft tether for his 25 ft umbilical, attached to the adaptor, and switched life support to the AMU.

On 3 June 1966, Gemini 9 was launched, and on the second day in space Eugene Cernan commenced the EVA as planned. Immediately after leaving the cabin he began a number of tasks which involved him in setting up mirrors and cameras, retrieving experiments, and deploying the handholds to be used in the traverse to the rear of the spacecraft. Half an hour after floating outside he began to climb back to the adaptor module. It was at that point that trouble began. The effort involved in clambering about in the early Gemini air-cooled spacesuit, coupled with difficulty in unstowing an AMU armrest, caused Eugene Cer-

Challenger begins her first journey by road, to Edwards Air Force Base. There she was to join *Columbia*, which had just returned from STS 4 before being ferried to Kennedy Space Centre atop the 905, arriving there on 8 July 1982. (Rockwell International)

nan's suit to overload. He became extremely hot, and was perspiring and fatigued. For a while he waited in the shade of the adaptor until the '9' moved into the Earth's shadow. Strapping into the AMU proved too difficult and Eugene Cernan's visor became fogged to such an extent he was unable to see. The EVA was abandoned and, once his visor had cleared slightly, he returned to the cabin of the '9'.

Shortly before re-entry, the adaptor module, with the untried AMU, was jettisoned into space. The planned AMU excursion on Gemini 12 was subsequently cancelled. It was to be several years before improvements in spacesuit technology and a suitable spacecraft would allow any further flight tests.

In 1968, Martin Marietta began to develop an all-new nitrogen gas-powered AMU (by then renamed the Automatically Stabilized Manoeuvring Unit or ASMU). It was designated the 'M-509' by Martin Marietta for inclusion as part of an experiments package for the orbital workshop Skylab, then in its embryonic stages of development. Scheduled for launch in the early nineteen-seventies, Skylab would carry a basic ASMU inside its 20 ft by 23 ft forward pressurized workshop 'dome'. Principal investigator for the 'M-509' project was Major C.E. Whitsett, Jr of the USAF Space and Missile Systems Organization, Los Angeles, California. He had taken over the project from Major Edward Givens who was killed in a road accident in 1967.

During the second manned flight of Skylab, on 12 August 1973, commander Alan Bean flew the ASMU for 3 hours, 20 minutes, followed by Jack Lousma who made a brief familiarization flight of 10 minutes. Later in the mission the second test of the ASMU had both Alan Bean and Jack Lousma checking out operations in full EVA pressure suits, simulating actual tasks that would one day be carried out in space. Scientist astronaut Owen Garriott, who had not been trained to fly the ASMU, tried it out during an unscheduled run and found it easy to operate and control.

The ASMU was a much more ambitious model of the Gemini AMU. Instead of hydrogen peroxide thrusters, the ASMU was powered by a single rechargeable nitrogen gas bottle and had automatic control maintained by basic rate gyroscopes.

In addition to the ASMU hand-controlled backpack, the Skylab astronauts also experimented with a Foot-Controlled Manoeuvring Unit (FCMU) and a Hand Held Manoeuvring Unit (HHMU). The ASMU's rechargeable high-pressure nitrogen propellant tank powered not only the ASMU, but also the FCMU and HHMU. The electrical systems within the ASMU were powered by a rechargeable battery. The astronaut put on the ASMU over either his pressurized space suit or flight coveralls, using a quick release harness similar to that used on parachutes.

The ASMU was powered in six degrees of freedom (X, Y and Z axis translation; and pitch, yaw and roll), by means of 14 fixed thrusters located in various positions on the backpack. Control of the thrusters was achieved by two hand controllers mounted on arms extending from the backpack. The controllers were identical to those used in the Apollo command module. The HHMU on the other hand was a simple, small, lightweight, completely manual device. It consisted of a hand grip and controls for a pair of tractor (pull) thrusters and an opposing single pusher thruster. The unit was connected to the ASMU propellant tank by a short line. To orientate and propel himself in any direction or attitude the astronaut pointed the HHMU, aligning it so that the thrust vector passed approximately through his centre of gravity and triggered the tractor or pusher thrusters as indicated by his visual cues. Manoeuvring with the ASMU and the HHMU in Skylab was carried out within the Orbital Workshop. Constant checks were kept on the cabin pressure during extended runs to avoid excessive build up of nitrogen. The ASMU was instrumented to record numerous items of engineering and biomedical data during the pressure-suited runs. The data was sensed, collected and telemetred from the free-flying ASMU to a receiver within the OWS. Together with recorded voice commentary, the data was telemetred from the OWS to ground stations. Additional experiment data was provided by inflight TV, postflight still and motion picture data, and logbook entries.

By the end of the Skylab project flights the ASMU had provided engineers with a wide range of valuable information on manoeuvring unit handling qualities, operating techniques, consumable requirements, capabilities and limitations. The way was then clear for construction of a fully-fledged Manual Manoeuvring Unit (MMU) scheduled for the Shuttle in the nineteen-eighties and destined for use in the vacuum of space.

The Shuttle MMU is propelled by 24 cold nitrogen gas thrusters each with a thrust of 1.4 lb. This is enough to propel the astronaut to 300 ft from the Orbiter, conduct work, and return, with an adequate safety margin. Nitrogen was selected as the propulsion in favour of the hydrogen peroxide used on the Gemini AMU, because of the need to protect from contamination sensitive optical and electronic instruments on board a satellite and on the Orbiter itself.

A distance of 300 ft has been calculated precisely according to the dictates of orbital mechanics. At over 300 ft distance from the Orbiter the astronaut and his MMU would fall prey to complex course correction manoeuvres such as those that the Orbiter would encounter when approaching a

Technicians install *Challenger's* tail fin, a job that calls for the utmost care and precision. Manufactured by Fairchild Republic in New York, the tail joined the rest of *Challenger* at Rockwell's Palmdale facility. (Rockwell International)

Challenger's pressurized crew module, hoisted out of its assembly jig, is mated with the forward fuselage structure. The foil is provided as part of the thermal insulation. It consists of a fine coating of gold on a mylar film. (Rockwell International)

Astronaut Bruce McCandless, one of two mission specialists, participating in EVA activities during the 41B mission on 7 February 1984, and seen a few yards away from *Challenger's* cabin. This EVA represented the first use of the MMU. (NASA)

Dale Gardner prepares to dock with the spinning Westar VI satellite and capture it for return to Earth. (NASA)

Joe Allen and Dale Gardner proudly displaying a 'For sale' sign after recovering the Westar and Palapa satellites. Allen is standing on the mobile foot restraint which, in tandem with the RMS arm, served as a 'cherry-picker' during recapture efforts. (NASA)

Right from the early days of the Approach and Landing Trials, crew badges have been produced, each one unique to the mission concerned. (All badges courtesy NASA)

The crew patch worn by all crew-men in the Enterprise *Approach and Landing programme. (NASA)*

The mission badge for STS 1; the first flight of Columbia. *(NASA)*

The mission badge for STS 2; full of patriotic symbolism. (NASA)

The STS 3 mission badge, demon-strating the RMS arm to be used on this flight.

Mission badge for STS 4 depicts the first 'operational' flight of Columbia. *(NASA)*

Mission badge for STS 5 shows the deployment of two satellites; SBS-C and Telsat E. (NASA)

The mission badge for STS 6, the first flight of Challenger *into space. The badge depicts* Challenger *launching the TDRS satellite. (NASA)*

The badge for STS 7, the RMS arm forming the outline of the number seven. The symbols within the sun represent the four male, and for the first time, one female crew. (NASA)

The mission badge of STS 8 depicts the backdrop of space, symbolic of the Shuttle's first night-time launch. (NASA)

The mission badge of STS 9 depicts Columbia in orbit, with the European Spacelab in its cargo bay. (NASA)

Mission badge for Shuttle flight 41B symbolizes two major aspects of the flight, satellite deployment and use of the MMU. (NASA)

The mission badge for 41C dramatically represents the rescue of Solar Max and deployment of the Long Duration Exposure Facility. (NASA)

Mission badge for 41D shows Discovery as the most recent of ships to bear that name, sailing on the ocean of space. (NASA)

Mission badge for 41G depicts both patriotism and the astronaut's symbol of unity; the three vertical paths merging in a star encircled by a ring representing orbital flight. (NASA)

The mission badge of 51A: patriotism, and a dramatic vision of the USA in space. (NASA)

Challenger over a clouded Earth was captured by a 70mm camera on board the temporary free-flying shuttle pallet satellite (SPAS-01) during STS 7's Day Five. Visible in the cargo bay are the protective cradles for the now-vacated Telsat Anik C2 and Plapa-B communications satellites, the RMS arm and the Ku-band antenna. (NASA)

satellite in a different orbit. At 300 ft the astronaut would also be at a distance where return to the Orbiter could be accomplished by 'line of sight'.

Each MMU weighs around 338 lb on Earth (740 lb when combined with astronaut and life support system). NASA's two operational units, making their first flight on mission 41B, cost around $10 million each. Two nitrogen-filled fuel tanks each contain 13 lb of propellant. Two 'arms' extend forward from the MMU, on each of which is a hand controller. Once strapped into the MMU, the astronaut can use the right-hand controller to fire the thrusters and rotate, dip and roll, and the left-hand controller to move forward or reverse. If anything should go wrong, *Challenger* could manoeuvre over to the astronaut and pick him up in the open payload bay.

Stored in the payload bay in a flight station near the forward hinge of the payload bay door, behind the starboard side of the aft cabin bulkhead, the MMUs are securely retained until use. The astronaut backs into the MMU, whereupon two latches clasp his EMU (extra-vehicular mobility unit). He releases the captive latches on the service station and 'flies' away. Each time a thruster fires an audible tone sounds on the astronaut's helmet, similar tones are also employed as warnings for such things as low fuel, malfunction, etc. Automatic gyroscopic stabilization of the MMU allows the astronaut to work using both hands off the controls. After use, the MMU is returned to its flight station for stowage.

For the first time in the history of spaceflight astronauts would be outside their spacecraft with no tethers or umbilicals to keep them safely aboard should either lose their grip. In effect both would, with their own propulsion systems and life support backpacks, be human satellites of the Earth.

The first of two planned EVAs came on 7 February. Bruce McCandless floated out of *Challenger*'s airlock and donned his MMU, with the assistance of Robert Stewart. After a brief series of checks flying within the confines of the payload bay Bruce McCandless headed out into space. Moving at less than one foot per second he tried out the MMU's controls whilst Robert Stewart watched closely. 'Well, that may have been one small step for Neil,' quipped Bruce McCandless, 'but it's a heck of a big leap for me! We sure have a nice flying machine here'. As he drew further away from *Challenger*, a TV camera mounted on his helmet showed live pictures of Robert Stewart in the payload bay far below. 'Just for the record, I don't see too many stars out here,' Bruce McCandless noted. — 'You have a lot of envious people watching you; looks like you're having a lot of fun,' capsule communicator Jerry Ross, monitoring the EVA from Mission Control, Houston, told Bruce McCandless. 'Yeah, it's working very nicely', replied the astronaut, 150 ft away from *Challenger*. 'McCandless and the Manned Manoeuvring Unit constitute a separate spacecraft of

their own now,' said Houston, as Bruce McCandless appeared on TV monitors as a distant white figure far away from home. 'Er, you must get the name as the world's fastest human being there, going along there at around four miles a second!' — 'That record might only stand for the next hour or so!' — 'You've just passed over Florida and Cuba.' Despite the clarity of the TV pictures coming back to Earth and the awesome sights, Mission Control remained calm and professional. 'After all,' said Jim Elliot of NASA's Goddard Space Flight Centre, 'it's not like a guy landing on the Moon for the first time'.

The second EVA of mission 41B came on 9 February. This time Robert Stewart took his turn to fly the MMU. In addition to the tasks carried out during the first EVA, the two astronauts mounted a docking device called a 'Trunnion Pin Attachment Device (T-PAD) on the front of the MMU's armrests. This device would enable the astronauts to practice manoeuvres needed on the next Shuttle flight, planned to rescue an ailing solar observatory satellite called Solar Maximum (known as 'Solar Max' for short).

Armed with this device, both astronauts practised docking with strategically fixed targets within *Challenger*'s open payload bay. Another simulation of Solar Max retrieval had to be abandoned because of a fault in the RMS arm. Originally, mission planners wanted the arm to remove an experiment pallet in the payload bay and hold it aloft whilst at the same time rotating it at one degree a second to reproduce accurately the anticipated rotation of Solar Max. An astronaut, using the MMU, would move in close to the pallet, match its spin rate with the MMU's nitrogen thrusters, and dock. With this test no longer a possibility, there was still one further exercise Bruce McCandless and Robert Stewart could perform. Mounted on the same experiment pallet that would have served as a simulated rotating Solar Max for docking practice, was a reproduction of that satellite's electronic control module. Using a special foot restraint on the end of the RMS arm, Ron McNair, operating it from inside *Challenger*, could move both astronaut and work platform anywhere in the payload bay. Once an astronaut had mounted the framework on the end of the RMS arm and secured his feet in the footholds, Ron McNair could transport him around the Shuttle Orbiter with ease. The small platform also had a faculty for carrying a selection of tools pertaining to the job in hand.

It did not take long to prove to everyone's satisfaction that repair of Solar Max was feasible. Before the final EVA came to a close, Bruce McCandless and Robert Stewart made the first of two planned tests to see if in-orbit refuelling of satellites could be possible. (The second test was scheduled for flight 41G later in the year.) The first satellite to be refuelled in this way would be Landsat 4. Launched several years earlier it was still in working order, but having exhausted its fuel supply, could no longer return useful data on Earth surveying work.

By the time both astronauts had returned to *Challenger*'s airlock they had accumulated over 12 hours outside between them. By that time *Challenger* had achieved most of her flight objectives.

Return to Earth on 11 February began with a de-orbit burn for 169 seconds of *Challenger*'s OMS engines at 6.25 am EST over North West Australia. *Challenger* then, after 127 orbits, began to align herself for re-entry. At 6.50 am EST, north east of Hawaii, travelling at 15,835 mph, *Challenger* entered the atmosphere. Enduring blistering heat, the Orbiter roared over Guaymas, Mexico, at 15,000 mph at 7.00 am EST. Eleven minutes later, at 11,600 mph, *Challenger* crossed the Gulf of Mexico, then the west coast of Florida at 7.14 am EST at seven times the speed of sound. Sixty miles away from touchdown *Challenger*'s speed was down to 1,800 mph. Soon crowds, gathered at Kennedy Space Centre for the landing, heard the thunder of double sonic booms announcing *Challenger*'s arrival. Twenty-six miles from touchdown *Challenger* dropped below the speed of sound. Chase planes closed in on the returning spacecraft as it banked and turned on to final approach. Below, the sea formed a colourful backdrop to the black and white Shuttle as she swooped low over the beaches and mangrove swamps. With a thin vapour trail winding back from each wing tip *Challenger* crossed the threshold of Kennedy's Runway 15 and lowered her landing gear. Touchdown occurred 2,000 ft further down the runway than planned, but well within safety margins. After a roll-out of 10,700 ft, *Challenger* came to a halt from a landing speed of 218 mph. Mission 41B had come to an end after just under 8 days in space.

Shortly after mission 41B landed back at Kennedy Space Centre, NASA cancelled 41E from their schedule. In much the same way as STS 10 (41A) had been deleted, 41E had been a victim of the problematical Inertial Upper Stage booster.

NASA had discovered that the first IUS that launched the TDRS-1 communications satellite from *Challenger* in April 1983 (STS 6) had suffered a failure of its engine nozzle. Designed specifically to transfer satellites from the Shuttle's low Earth orbit to geosynchronous orbit 25,000 miles above the Equator, the IUS was a key part of the Space Transportation System. Whilst engineers attempted to overcome the failure, the launch schedules began to slip.

Originally, 41E was to have flown the secret military satellite (cancelled from STS 10 (41A) for the same reason), but testing of the IUS was taking longer than planned, and the military payload slipped still further down the schedule to 51C, scheduled for launch in early 1985.

Meanwhile, NASA, with an eye to the future, was recruiting its tenth batch of astronauts since the original Mercury 'Seven'. Joining those selected in 1978 the new 'seventeen' were to be selected out of a total of 4,934 applicants whose details had been received by NASA at the close-off date in December 1983. They would begin training in July, before reaching astronaut status in 1985.

41C

The flight of mission 41C was to be the most dramatic, daring and significant of the programme so far. An attempt was to be made to rescue the satellite Solar Max, repair it, and then return it once more to space.

The crew consisted of commander Bob Crippen, pilot Dick Scobee, and mission specialists Terry Hart, George ('Pinky') Nelson and James Van Hoften.

Dick Scobee had transferred to NASA from the USAF in 1980, having distinguished himself both as a fighter pilot in Vietnam and as a test pilot in the X-24-B lifting body programme. Terry Hart had been an employee of Bell Industries in the field of electronic engineering before becoming an astronaut in 1978.

Lift-off of 41C came at just before 9.00 am EST on 6 April 1984. The main engines fired for a few seconds longer than on previous flights to enable *Challenger* to reach a record altitude of 309 miles. Such a height was needed to reach Solar Max. The first day in space was to be a relatively easy one for the crew as it involved very few complex tasks. NASA was also concerned to avoid any space sickness which could jeopardize any planned EVA activity later on. As with all previous Shuttle flights, the first job, once in orbit, was to open the payload doors. This done, astronaut Terry Hart made a preliminary check-out of the RMS arm to make sure that it was functioning correctly.

Mission plans called for rendezvous with Solar Max by *Challenger* on Day Three in space, whereupon George Nelson would make an EVA using the MMU, attended by James Van Hoften. Using the docking device (T-PAD) tried out on 41B, attached to his MMU, George Nelson would fly up to Solar Max, match its rotational spin using the MMU's nitrogen gas thrusters, then close-in and latch firmly into place alongside its spinning axis. He would then once more use the MMU's thrusters to de-spin Solar Max in preparation for Terry Hart, operating the RMS arm from *Challenger*'s flight deck, to grapple the satellite and bring it down into the payload bay for repair. George Nelson would, by then, have undocked and returned

Challenger as seen by Bruce McCandless from a distance of about 180 ft. Robert Stewart can be seen standing beneath the base of the RMS arm. He later donned the same MMU used by Bruce McCandless for his own untethered EVA. This photograph is reminiscent of those taken during STS 7, from the then free-flying SPAS-01. The shuttle pallet satellite is configured mid-cargo bay here as SPAS-01A. Also visible in the cargo bay are the support stations for the two MMU backpacks and the sunshields for the Palapa-B and Westar 6 satellites. (NASA)

his MMU to its parking space in the forward cargo bay.

Solar Max would then be cradled in a special repair platform which, apart from offering a stable base from which the astronauts could carry out operations, would also provide power for the satellite from *Challenger's* own fuel cells until repairs were completed. This was necessary because Solar Max's solar panels would not always be pointing at the sun for power once the satellite was in *Challenger's* payload bay. The platform (known as the FSS or Flight Support Station) would also support Solar Max if repairs could not be undertaken and it had to be returned to Earth.

The first day of 41C came to a close with George Nelson checking out and activating the FSS for the important EVA to come. The only other major activity was two engine 'burns' to trim *Challenger's* orbit for rendezvous. By bed time the crew were relaxed and in good spirits. Bob Crippen talked to Houston Mission Control. 'OK Houston — Challenger, we are getting along here pretty good; how are things going on the ground?' — 'Roger,' responded Houston, 'they look real good Crip.' — 'Up here this is really exciting,' exulted Bob Crippen. — 'Roger, we are looking to several more days of it. We were wondering how it's going up there; you guys having a good time?' George (Pinky) Nelson replied on behalf of the crew (clearly enjoying themselves on TV), 'Stand by, I'll take a poll!'

Next morning the crew, led by Bob Crippen, began preparations for the deployment of 41C's only satellite, a massive 11 ton passive cylindrical structure called the Long Duration Exposure Facility or LDEF. Essentially LDEF would test over 50 experiments that required long-term exposure to the space environment, and would be recovered by a future Shuttle flight in early 1985. Shortly after breakfast Terry Hart, at the aft flight deck console, moved the RMS arm's 'hand' over to the side of the LDEF and switched on the satellite. Then, severing its connection points to *Challenger*, he once more used the RMS arm to pick it out of the payload bay and hold it aloft ready for deployment.

As LDEF had no means of controlling its attitude, great delicacy was required in placing it in space. Several hours were taken up to ensure that once released, the LDEF would remain stable until collected a year or so later by another Shuttle flight. Once set free, George Nelson radioed to Houston, 'Checkout complete, everything went on time, and no anomalies at all.' With deployment successful, *Challenger* moved slowly away and began the hunt for Solar Max.

All through the evening and night of the second day, as the crew slept, *Challenger* gradually closed in on the ailing satellite. By 7.30 am EST she was barely 8 miles away. As *Challenger's* radar and computers made the final closing manoeuvres George Nelson and James Van Hoften were suiting-up with the assistance of Francis Scobee. Both astronauts had to be ready to go outside as soon as *Challenger* drew up next to Solar Max.

Then Terry Hart, using binoculars on the flight deck, reported sighting Solar Max in the distance: a bright speck of light almost indistinguishable from the stars. Shortly afterwards, Bob Crippen brought *Challenger* onto station, keeping position as television viewers in America watched live pictures of Solar Max barely 200 ft away.

In *Challenger's* lower deck airlock George Nelson and James Van Hoften were ready to go. They had completed their pre-breathing time and were switching air and power supply from *Challenger* to their own portable life-support system backpacks. At 9.30 am EST the airlock was depressurized and its outer door opened. George Nelson moved cautiously out into the payload bay towards the MMU. Floodlights illuminated his progress as *Challenger* flew in Earth's shadow. As he strapped himself into position and powered up the unit, James Van Hoften unstowed the T-PAD and attached it to the front of George Nelson's MMU. This done, George Nelson unhooked the MMU from its launch support and began a planned series of tests of the MMU's controls, communications and life-support systems within the confines of the payload bay to make sure that it was working correctly.

As soon as *Challenger* flew into sunrise and the light had increased sufficiently, George Nelson fired the MMU's thrusters to take him out of the payload bay and towards Solar Max. Exactly one hour into the EVA he was alongside the satellite and preparing to dock. Mounted on the side of Solar Max, almost dead centre below its two solar panel wings, was the docking pin. With great care he adjusted his attitude relative to Solar Max and moved in. Nudging against the pin he activated the T-PAD's jaws. They did not latch on. Again he tried, and again met with no success. The jaws of the T-PAD were working, but would not grapple the pin with enough force to remain docked. George Nelson told Houston, 'I hit the thing square on — I bounced out then I went back in again but it didn't snap either time.'

Without a good latch onto Solar Max it would be impossible to use the MMU's thrusters to despin the satellite. Anxious moments passed before Bob Crippen suggested that George Nelson back off and try to stop it spinning by grabbing hold of the outermost edge of one of its two solar wings. As *Challenger* moved once more towards Earth's shadow and darkness, George Nelson was alone struggling with Solar Max. Everything he tried seemed to make matters worse. Holding onto the wing with one hand and firing the thrusters on the

MMU with the other, he became dangerously low on fuel and Solar Max was beginning to tumble. 'OK, come on back in Pinky,' ordered Bob Crippen. He had barely enough fuel to make it.

Undefeated, Bob Crippen flew *Challenger* within a few feet of Solar Max so that Terry Hart could attempt to grapple it with the RMS arm. The plan was too ambitious; Solar Max was moving far too rapidly to be stopped by the arm. Further attempts would probably have damaged both spacecraft. Once more, Bob Crippen moved *Challenger* away from the satellite. Bitterly disappointed, George Nelson and James Van Hoften re-entered the airlock after stowing the MMUs. They had been outside for just over 1 hour 40 minutes.

By the end of their third day in space the crew's spirits were at a low point. The smiles had gone and an air of concern was evident in communications with the ground. Unless Ground Control could come up with something, Solar Max would be a write-off and the Shuttle programme would have suffered a major blow to its prestige.

As Solar Max tumbled, its solar panels spent increasingly longer periods facing away from energy-giving sunlight. Its batteries were running down fast and unless power demands were reduced Solar Max would be finished within seven hours. Then, as is so often the case in spaceflight, just when everything was at its lowest ebb, an amazing stroke of luck occurred. As Solar Max was literally minutes away from closing down permanently, its solar panels caught sunlight for over ten minutes; a short time, but long enough for vital power to come flooding in.

Just before midnight, Ground Control, using electromagnetic torque bars within the satellite, had stabilized it and locked the satellite in such a position that it would have its panels constantly facing the sun. The electromagnetic torque bars, energized by exposure of Solar Max's solar panels were aligned, within the satellite, with the satellite's three axes of rotation. They are designed to work in conjunction with the Earth's own magnetic field to provide Solar Max with a back-up stability control system. With Solar Max now back in action another rescue attempt seemed possible, but there was another, more serious problem — *Challenger* was running low on fuel.

As the crew awoke for their fourth day in space, Mission Control advised them of a change in plan. Instead of the scheduled second attempt to grapple Solar Max with the RMS arm, they decided to postpone any further attempt until Day Five. This would give them a chance to work out the optimum fuel-efficient approach for *Challenger*. By the same constraints, further MMU operations were also out of the question, because if anything were to go wrong with the MMUs (which had already been recharged with nitrogen propellant from *Challenger*'s tanks) then *Challenger* would not have sufficient fuel to rescue the helpless astronaut.

On 1 April, *Challenger* made her last attempt at a Solar Max rescue. Over the past two days the two spacecraft had drifted over 60 miles apart. With only 20 per cent of the original RCS fuel remaining, it took 3 hours to close up once more on Solar Max. Nevertheless, Bob Crippen managed to close up to within feet of the satellite using only jsut over half their reserve.

As the RMS's arm made an attempt to grapple Solar Max, *Challenger* flew into one of the frustrating radio black-outs. No-one on the ground knew what was going on in space until, over Australia, Bob Crippen confirmed capture. Houston called up, watching the TV pictures being transmitted, 'We've got a good picture, looks like you're just about there'. Bob Crippen responded, 'OK, we've got it and we are in the process of putting it in the FSS!' In Mission Control the flight team broke into loud applause; Capcom Jerry Ross exclaimed, 'outstanding!' Later, President Reagan phoned to congratulate the crew and ask them a favour. 'So if you can't fix it up there — would you mind bringing it back. Over?' Bob Crippen, as commander, answered on behalf of his crew, 'Well, we are going to do our best to repair it tomorrow sir, and, if for some reason that is unsuccessful, which we don't think it will be, we will be able to return it.' Terry Hart, using the RMS, stowed Solar Max on the FSS, and by 9.50 am EST had made ready for a second EVA on Day Six.

Once again, at 4 am EST on 11 April, George Nelson and James Van Hoften left *Challenger*'s airlock to begin work on the repair of Solar Max. At the same time, Terry Hart, working from the aft flight deck, had joined onto the end of the RMS arm the work platform that James Van Hoften would use when engaged in repairs. Called the Manipulator Foot Restraint (MFR), this device would support both the astronaut and his tool box. Boarding the MFR, James Van Hoften was transported on the end of the RMS to Solar Max berthed at the far end of the payload bay. Once in position, using an electrically-powered spanner, he began to remove two bolts on the side of the satellite that held its Modular Altitude Control System (MACS) in place. This done he removed the old malfunctioning unit, stowed it, and replaced it with a new system carried aboard *Challenger*.

On 23 November 1980, just eight months after launch, Solar Max was crippled when three fuses blew in its MACS, rendering its main control thrusters inoperative. This cut by 90 per cent the amount of useful data this solar observatory satellite could gather.

Solar Max was the first of an enitrely new series of Earth satellites which was designed specifically to allow in-orbit repairs to be made. All of its major components were modularized for easy replacement in space. Repairs, however, had to be postponed until Solar Max's orbit had wound down to a lower altitude which the Shuttle could reach.

Just one hour into the EVA the new MACS had been installed and was relaying its good health via telemetry to Ground Control. At this point both George Nelson and James Van Hoften busied themselves curing some of the other minor ailments to which Solar Max had succumbed.

The most difficult task was to replace the satellite's coronograph main electronics control box. James Van Hoften, wearing his bulky suit gloves, unscrewed 22 tiny hold-down clips on the box before removing the faulty unit. George Nelson took over to fit the new component, this time secured by plastic non-screwable clips.

Having repaired Solar Max, George Nelson, secured in the MFR on the end of the RMS arm, went on a grand tour of the satellite to take pictures and check its overall condition. High above the Shuttle, on the end of the RMS arm, he exclaimed, 'It's an uncomfortable feeling,' to which Terry Hart replied, 'Feel like you're going to fall?' — 'I feel like I'm going to fall; am I over Africa?' Close-up observations of the satellite's docking pin revealed that a small piece of stray insulation had fouled the pin and caused the docking device on the MMU T-PAD to fail.

Before returning to the airlock, James Van Hoften tried out the MMU that George Nelson had used on the first EVA, keeping within the payload bay at all times. By the time both men were back inside, Terry Hart had restowed the MFR and had removed Solar Max from the payload bay once more. It would, however, remain on the end of the arm until Day Eight in space. Ground Control wanted to make sure that the satellite was 100 per cent before final release.

At 4.26 am EST on 12 April 1984, Solar Max was released to continue its research. NASA was jubilant over the outstanding success of 41C. 'Challenger this is Houston. We'd like the radar movements.' — 'OK, we'll do that.' — 'Thank you; the Solar Max is 'Go' for release.' At this point three flight controllers sang their own ear-piercing rendition of the popular song, *Release me and let me fly again*. A brief pause whilst everyone recovered then, 'Challenger this is Houston. You are 'Go' for release as long as you are within 5 degrees.' TV monitors showed Solar Max drifting away, fluttering slightly. 'That vibration is [*Challenger's*] jets firing, separation burn has been initiated'. — 'Challenger this is Houston. The Solar Max is looking good, you are clear to stop station-keeping any time.'

That evening, the crew put on a special TV broadcast; opening with all five men wearing special tee-shirts bearing the message 'Welcome to the Ace Satellite Repair Company. We pick up, repair, *and* deliver!' The following day, 13 April, *Challenger's* crew prepared for a landing at Kennedy Space Centre. By 5.36 am EST, Bob Crippen was given the go-ahead for the de-orbit burn scheduled for 6.00 am. Weather conditions at Kennedy were deteriorating, however, and by 5.50 am, ten minutes before ignition, Capcom Guy Gardner cancelled the Florida landing in favour of a later landing at Edwards Air Force Base.

At 7.29 am EST, the OMS engines ignited and *Challenger* began the long glide into land. Touch down on Runway 17 came at 8.38 am EST after a flight of just under 7 days.

Solar Maximum Director, Frank Zepollina, announced: 'This mission represents the end of an era of throw-away spacecraft. And what we have been doing here for the first time is spending about $45 million to $55 million to save a $235 million observatory. Well worth the effort!'

If the Shuttle was proving itself a commercial and scientific success, the programme was also beginning to make way for the future defence applications as well. In June, at the Johnson Space Centre in Houston, NASA had announced the names of its seventeen latest astronauts. After giving final interviews to 128 out of the 4,934 original applicants, the Space Agency chose ten mission specialists and seven pilots. They were:

James Adamson,	US Army
Mark Brown,	USAF
Kenneth Cameron,	US Marines
Manley Carter,	US Navy
John Casper,	USAF
Frank Culbertson,	US Navy
Sidney Gutierrez,	USAF
Lloyd Hammond,	USAF
Marshal Ivins,	Civilian
Mark Lee,	USAF
George Low,	Civilian
Michael McCulley,	US Navy
William Shepard,	US Navy
Ellen Shulman,	Civilian
Kathryn Thornton,	Civilian
Charles Veach,	Civilian
James Weatherbee,	US Navy

The bias towards serving military personnel, even though it was an established tradition in NASA, was noted by many observers of the US space programme as an ominous development in the light of President Reagan's commitment to a new Strategic Defence Initiative, and an orbital weapons system for America. The concept that began in the US with Project Bomi in the early nineteen-fifties and continued with the X-20 Dyna-Soar was at last within reach. What Dr Dornberger and Dr Eugen Sanger could never have conceived was the awesome reality their research would eventually lead to in the nineteen-eighties.

8 Discovery

41D

The maiden flight of Orbiter *Discovery* was the most ambitious of the programme thus far. The week-long mission scheduled originally to begin on 25 June 1984, would not only prove *Discovery's* spaceworthiness but also launch a satellite, the military Syncom 4-1, as well as experiment with a new type of extendible solar panel which would power future Shuttle experiments.

The crew of six, which would include America's second spacewoman, was commanded by STS 4 pilot Henry Hartsfield. His pilot on this flight was Michael Coats, making his first trip into space. Michael Coats was a Vietnam veteran who gained his USN wings as late as 1969.

The three mission specialists were Steven Hawley, Richard Mullane and Dr Judith Resnik. Together with payload specialist Charles Walker, they constituted the remainder of the 41D crew, all making their first flight into space.

Steven Hawley, an astronomer, had established a reputation in his field whilst working at most of the major observatories across the USA, before joining NASA. Shortly afterwards he married Sally Ride, the first American woman in space. Judith Resnik, with a Ph.D. in electrical engineering, had worked for a number of commercial companies before joining NASA. Richard Mullane, the Syncom 4-1 specialist, spent four

years in England at Alconbury with the USAF before going to the test pilot school at Edwards Air Force Base, graduating in 1976. He had flown 150 combat missions in Vietnam. Charles Walker was an industry-nominated astronaut, and an employee of McDonnell Douglas. His speciality was the medical experiment called the 'Electrophoresis Operation' which, it was hoped, would eventually be able to produce sophisticated drugs and medicines in space. Certain drugs can be made more purely and more effectively in a zero-g environment. Electrophoresis involves the precise and delicate separation of chemicals in the drug preparation process. The manufacture of new medication is not the only advantage of spaceflight processing. Orbiting space processes can turn out high quality items impossible to manufacture on Earth because of gravity. On Earth, for example, glass tends to be grainy because of convection. Crystal production would be enhanced without gravity, which restricts crystal growth. Perfectly spherical ball bearings could be produced to cut down friction and improve efficiency in rotating machinery.

Also, regional or worldwide inventions could be derived from the Orbiter's payload bay using survey sensor equipment — remote sensing experiments by NASA, the Department of Agriculture, universities and industry have demonstrated the effectiveness of multi-spectral sensing and photo-

Discovery sits poised upon the pad for launch. The complete STS assembly weighs in excess of 2000 tons at launch. (NASA)

graphic techniques for application to agriculture and forest management. Spaceborne high-resolution cameras (with colour and colour infrared, thermal infrared, and multi-spectral scanners) can obtain data on a worldwide basis regarding crop infestations, vigour, total acreage and predicted yields. Careful interpretation of regular space photography can assist in the monitoring of world crop development and land use change.

Discovery represented Space Shuttle 'state-of-the-art'. Most of the thermal tiles covering the upper surfaces of earlier Orbiters had been replaced by new lighter fabric sections. A large part of the total weight saving, which would allow heavier payloads, came about by the extensive use of graphite-epoxy structures in the fuselage instead of heavier aluminium frames.

On 23 June 1984 at 2.00 am EST, the countdown began. Two days later, the crew, after enjoying some last minute flying around the Cape in their T-38s, moved out to *Discovery* and went through the final stages of launch. All went well until one of *Discovery*'s computers became 'distressed'. After anxious minutes, during which engineers struggled to put things right, the decision was made to scrub the first launch attempt, 9 minutes from the planned launch time of 7.43 am EST.

NASA's public affairs commentator explained the problem:

'This is Shuttle launch control. We are at T minus 9 minutes and holding, launch director Bob Sieck has made the decision we will scrub for the day. We do not feel confident in proceeding with the launch this morning, based on the problem that we have had with this back-up flight system. A lot of discussion went on on the network about being able to do some transitions of the computers looking at some data; however, it would appear that it would be a race against the clock whether or not you could find out anything about this computer within our 43 minute [launch] window today.'

Tom Utsman, a NASA spokesman, later commented at an impromptu press conference, 'We ran a quick test, called a built-in test routine, into that computer, and the indication came back that we had a serious hardware failure and that is as much as we really know now.' The crew packed up and left *Discovery*, visibly disappointed but aware that NASA would never risk launching a vehicle not in top condition. As soon as the crew left the launch site technicians began to examine the faulty computer whilst others drained fuel from the giant external tank. The computer was later found to be so badly below par that another unit (taken from *Challenger*) was installed in its place overnight.

The following day the five-man, one-woman, crew went through the pre-launch procedures once more: breakfast, then crossing over to launch complex 39A, which was shrouded in a thick blanket of morning mist that came rolling in across the mangrove swamps. Unlike the previous day, the count-

down proceeded smoothly, the computer behaved, and the mists began to clear leaving an excellent view for the assembled onlookers three miles away across Banana River.

The exchange of conversation between *Discovery* out on the launch pad and launch control two miles away grew rapid and more intense as the final seconds approached. As the count reached the 10 second point, thousands of gallons of water deluged the pad, preparing it for the blast to come. 'We have a go for main engine start,' — a flash and the three Shuttle engines howled into life, swirling smoke and steam gushed out of the flame trench beneath the launch pad and billowed into the sky. Just as everyone expected to see the twin solid rocket boosters ignite, the *Discovery*'s main engines died and her fuel turbopumps ground to a halt. 'We have a cut-off! We have an abort by the on-board computers of the Orbiter *Discovery*.' No sooner had the engines stopped than flames could be seen flashing around beneath the engine chambers. Residual fuel was burning away around the base of *Discovery* as the launch pad fire extinguishers doused the engine chambers with water. High above, the commander and pilot began to 'safe' *Discovery*, fully aware that their actions over the next few seconds would be critical. Not since the aborted launch of Gemini 6 on 12 December 1965 had the launch site at Kennedy Space Centre been so near to disaster, when Tom Stafford and Mercury astronaut Wally Schirra had a similar shut down of their Gemini Titan II rocket just one second after ignition. The correct reactions to such an emergency had their ground rules firmly established then — stay with the ship, remain cool, proficient and professional.

The most important task facing Henry Hartsfield and Michael Coats was to make sure that the solid rocket boosters did not ignite. If that happened (and there was no way of shutting them down once started), *Discovery* would have to lift-off without her main engines, and if their luck held, ditch into the Atlantic Ocean some miles downrange. Below the high explosive stacks of the twin boosters the launch pad fire continued, until doused by the extinguishers. Meanwhile, data received confirmed a fault in one of *Discovery*'s main engines which the on-board computer had recognized, and which then shut down all three engines as programmed in such an event. As Henry Hartsfield and the launch director Bob Sieck considered making an emergency evacuation of *Discovery*, the fire below burst once more into life around the engines and the fire extinguishers again operated and put out the flames.

Henry Hartsfield decided against a rapid evacuation. *Discovery* was settling down again, and there was always the possibility that toxic gases outside could choke his crew in seconds. Forty minutes elapsed before the launch pad access arm was secured in position again. The side hatch of *Discovery* swung open and pad technicians assisted the six crewmen from the Orbiter. Removing their protective white helmets, there was no disguising the strain they had just endured. The Shuttle programme had received its first major setback and, ironically, the event gained more media coverage in a single day than had the nine flights since STS 2 combined!

NASA management and engineers had problems: the Shuttle flight schedules had been thrown completely awry by this failure, and the payload destined for *Discovery*'s next flight, 41F, had to be accommodated in a revised schedule.

The problem in *Discovery*'s engines stemmed from microscopic contamination in one of the main engine's fuel valves. Engine No.3 was checked on the pad over the following days, and consideration was given to replacing the valve with *Discovery* in situ on the pad. Further tests, however, and a mind to safety, led NASA to decide on replacing the engine in its entirety. The work was completed out on the launch pad by 5 July.

Discovery was ready, but NASA had by then decided to change her payload. Moving *Discovery* back to VAB, on 14 July, she was de-stacked from her External Tank and solid rocket boosters. The next step was to transfer *Discovery* to the Orbiter Processing facility behind the VAB. There her cargo was off-loaded and additional supports installed for a new payload, the bulk of which came from the now-cancelled 41F mission.

The Syncom 4-1 satellite was deleted from the inventory of mission 41D, and then, with *Discovery* once more re-stacked and back at launch pad 39A on 9 August, her new cargo was installed. The new 41D was to carry not only a Satellite Business System Communications Satellite (SBS 4) brought forward from the now-cancelled 41F mission, but also Syncom 4-2, and Telstar 3! Syncom 4-1 was postponed, now scheduled for a later flight.

On 27 August 1984, *Discovery*'s second countdown began. Launch was scheduled for 7.35 am EST on 29th. Then came yet another problem. *Discovery*'s Master Events Controller that maintained the correct sequence of major flight functions developed a timing error. In the worst instance this could prevent the solid boosters and External Tank from separating. Scientists at the Johnson Space Centre, Houston, developed a 'software workaround' and the launch was postponed 24 hours to 7.36 am EST on 30 August. Even then, there was a delay for nearly a quarter of

an hour as a Piper Aztec light aircraft, flying along the coast for a view of the launch, strayed into the Kennedy Space Centre's restricted air space. The pilot was ordered out of the area 'for his and his passengers' safety.'

Launch was put back yet again, to 7.51 am EST. The final countdown continued.

'T minus 1 minute and counting. T minus 50 and counting. T minus 45 seconds and counting. T minus 38; repositioning Orbiter vent doors; coming up on a 'Go' from ground computers to start the onboard. T minus 31 seconds; we have a 'Go' for auto-sequence start; *Discovery*'s four computers now having primary control over critical vehicle functions. T minus 20 seconds and counting; T minus 15. T minus 11-10. We have a 'Go' for main engine start; 6. We have main engine start; 3-2-1; we have SRB ignition and ...' we have lift-off. Lift-off of mission 41D, the first flight of the Orbiter *Discovery* and the Shuttle has cleared the tower!'

'Roll Manoeuver,' called Henry Hartsfield. — 'Roger Roll,' responded Houston. NASA's announcer continued his commentary. 'Mission Control confirms roll manoeuvre. Standing by to throttle down to 85 per cent to get through period of maximum aerodynamic pressure. Throttling down in two-step fashion, first to 84 per cent then to 65 per cent. 'Throttling down confirmed, forty five seconds. Altitude 3.5 nautical miles, downrange distance 2 nautical miles; velocity now 2,150 feet per second. Passing through the period of maximum aerodynamic pressure.' *Discovery* flew on, higher into the blue Florida sky; a long streamer-like vapour trail in its wake spanning an arc that marked its progress out across the Atlantic Ocean. — 'Engines running at 65 per cent; velocity now 2,450 ft per second. Engines throttling back up — throttling to 104 per cent.'

'This is Houston; you are go at throttle up!' — 'Discovery; roger, go at throttle up!' Houston's public commentator continued: '*Discovery* given a 'Go' at throttle up 1 minute 30 seconds, velocity 3,400 ft per second; altitude 13 nautical miles, downrange a distance of 8 nautical miles.' '25 seconds away from SRB staging. Three engines running at 104 per cent. Velocity 4,600 ft per second; altitude 20 nautical miles; downrange distance 15 miles. Standing by for SRB separation; crew reports PC less than 50; SRBs separating.' Henry Hartsfield confirmed the manoeuvre, 'Roger staging; yep, SRB sep confirmed, velocity 5,200 ft per second; guidance converging as programmed; altitude 30 nautical miles; downrange distance 30 nautical miles.'

The exchanges continued as *Discovery*, now no more than a distant speck of light, flew out of sight and into orbit.

Once in space, the astronauts' first task was to check out *Discovery*'s systems and open the payload doors. This done, the way was cleared for the next major schedule of 41D, the deployment of

SBS 4. The task was assigned to mission specialists Richard Mullane and Steve Hawley. Soon after leaving the payload bay its solid rocket engine performed 'as advertised' and placed SBS 4 squarely into geosynchronous orbit above Earth's Equator.

The first day in space had gone well, only one problem having arisen. The small TV screen on Mike Coats' right-hand instrument panel was faulty. The screen relayed important flight data to *Discovery*'s pilot during launch and landing, so Houston and the crew decided to swap the screen with another similar unit mounted aft, before the end of the flight.

Discovery seen blasting off from launch pad 39A on a successful first mission, with six crew members and two satellites aboard. *Discovery* returned with the rescued Palapa B2 and Westar 6. (NASA)

Day Two in space for the crew began early. The main task for the next hours would involve, once more, Richard Mullane and Dr Stephen Hawley. They were to deploy the USAF satellite Syncom 4-2. The launch procedure for this particular satellite (built specifically with Shuttle launching in mind) was different from any yet attempted. Instead of being ejected vertically from *Discovery's* cargo bay like SBS 4, Syncom 4-2 would be sent out on its side from the rear of the payload bay. At just after 8.10 EST, Stephen Hawley operated the panel on *Discovery's* flight deck that would release Syncom 4-2's hold down pins. Immediately afterwards Richard Mullane initiated deployment. 'I heard a little bit of a thump when it deployed,' he commented as Syncom 4-2 moved slowly away against the backdrop of Earth.

While both Stephen Hawley and Richard Mullane were busy with launching Syncom 4-2, Charles Walker was getting into difficulties with his CFES medical processing experiment. No sooner had he begun operations down on *Discovery's* lower deck, than the drug processing machine decided to shut down. Rapid changes of pressure inside its mechanical innards rendered further operation impossible. For the rest of the day Charlie Walker made several attempts at repairing it whilst his colleagues at McDonnell Douglas attempted to find a solution to his problems from work at their ground based laboratories. It still did not work, and by the end of the second day Charlie Walker was not the best pleased astronaut aboard *Discovery*.

As the rest of the crew finished breakfast and housekeeping on Day Three, Charlie Walker was engaged in detailed conversations with the McDonnell Douglas CFES director, David Rickman. The McDonnell Douglas team had worked all through the night in an endeavour to find a solution to their spaceborne experiment's pressure problems, but no-one could positively identify the fault. The one ray of hope was that the experiment only seemed to give problems when in its automatic mode. Manual operation (although many times more time-consuming and complex) seemed to be OK. Charlie Walker returned to the mid deck and began to get to grips with his charge.

Meanwhile, on the upper deck, Stephen Hawley and Richrd Mullane were busy at the rearward facing consoles preparing to launch *Discovery's* third satellite of this mission — Telstar 3. Like SBS 4, Telstar 3 would be 'conventionally' launched from the bay. Minutes before launch, scheduled at 8.24 pm EST, the two astronauts started the Telstar spinning up to 50 rpm to set up its stability, then, satisfied all was well, allowed it to spring out clear of the bay and start the second leg

of the journey to its orbital station. At the same time, Henry Hartsfield and Michael Coats, as on two previous occasions, cautiously backed *Discovery* away to avoid any damage as Telstar 3's engine ignited.

Whilst both decks buzzed with activity, Judith Resnik began the first stage of her task of deploying a 150 ft long 13 ft wide extendible solar panel from the payload bay. This unit, a potential source of additional power on later flights, was folded flat in a box 13 ft long and just 7 inches deep! When the aft facing console was cleared by Richard Mullane and Stephen Hawley, Judith Resnik took up station for the first two extension tests of the panel sheduled for the day.

The first test would be to see if the unit would at least come 'out of the box', the second would be a 70 per cent deployment. As *Discovery* flew over the Hawaii tracking station, the panels unfurled, sticking slightly as a result of being close-packed in the box for weeks. When the panel had been 70 per cent deployed, Henry Hartsfield and Michael Coats, in accordance with the flight plan, fired *Discovery's* RCS thrusters in short bursts to see the effect they would have on the panel. As it turned out, the reaction was less than that encountered in deployment. By the time the panel was stowed once more the crew of *Discovery* were tired, and all six crew-members turned in for the night.

The following day was a busy one for Charlie Walker, but his efforts were to be rewarded. Samples were produced from the CFES which were found to be as good, if not better, than the McDonnell Douglas researchers had hoped. For Judith Resnik, too, her solar panel work was proving a success. With the long panel reaching 150 ft from *Discovery,* TV pictures captured the slightest of movements as Henry Hartsfield and Michael Coats attempted to sway it with bursts from *Discovery's* RCS.

Richard Mullane and Stephen Hawley, the bulk of their work completed, were enjoying themselves in front of the TV on the lower deck. Demonstrations for earthbound viewers included a display of acrobatics (somersaults, about turns, handstands etc; a paper aeroplane flight or two; and a quick game of orbital frisbee for good measure). Things were going so well that coverage of the flight in America was becoming limited to brief shots on the news; elsewhere few people knew *Discovery* even existed! By the end of Day Four, however, an event was to occur that brought the Shuttle flight 41D back to the front pages of almost every newsaper in Europe and the US: *Discovery's* toilet had blocked up!

More seriously, the crew discovered that the blockage was caused by a large accumulation of ice particles clogging the water dump outlet port behind and below the access hatch on the port side. To get a better view of the problem the crew used the remote manipulator arm on the end of which was mounted a small TV camera.

Whereas the blockage of *Discovery's* toilet was no more than a nuisance to the crew, who had to resort to plastic bags similar to those used on Apollo, to the flight controllers the ice formation on the hull was a more serious threat. If the ice should break off during re-entry there was always a chance that large chunks would be snapped off before they had been melted completely and, at 17,500 mph, strike any part of *Discovery's* airframe above or on the leading edges of the wings. Severe damage prior to aerodynamic re-entry heating would be a serious threat.

Henry Hartsfield tried to shift the three-foot-long icicle by firing *Discovery's* thrusters in short bursts in the hope that it would jolt the ice free. That did not work, so, during their fourth night in space, the crew manoeuvred the Shuttle so that the sun's rays would fall on to the ice in the hope that it would melt. Before turning in for the night the five-man, one-woman crew had their first encounters with the 'plastic bags'. This indelicate subject was the source of many a terse exchange before the crew retired. All agreed that, to be an Apollo astronaut, you had to be a 'real man'!

On the morning of the fifth day in orbit the ice was still there, albeit a little smaller but still a threat. Mission Control in Houston was becoming seriously worried. Henry Hartsfield tried to shake the ice loose with more powerful, prolonged bursts of the thrusters but to no avail.

Charles Walker was still engaged with his experiment on the lower deck as *Discovery's* other crew members discussed with Houston what to do next. At the Mission Control Centre, Joe Engle had been busy attempting to work out a system on the Shuttle simulator that could be used in orbit to dislodge the ice. The only solutions were the most dangerous. Either the crew of *Discovery* would have to knock the ice off using the RMS or, if that failed, Richard Mullane and Steve Hawley would have to put on their pressure suits and go outside to break it away by hand. To save time, before deciding which method to use, both mission specialists began the lengthy process of pre-breathing oxygen in *Discovery's* airlock, slowly removing all traces of nitrogen from their bloodstreams to avoid the bends when kitted out in full EVA gear for work outside.

Using the RMS would be extremely difficult and so commander Henry Hartsfield would assume the responsibility of control. As Day Five in space drew to a close, Henry Hartsfield decided to try the RMS method first and, if that failed, only then would he send the two men out to perform the task manually. Accordingly, both Richard Mullane and Stephen Hawley were stood down.

The next day started early. For Charles Walker it was time to start packing up his CFES medical experiment. Up above on the flight deck, Henry Hartsfield was beginning to move the RMS out and over *Discovery's* port payload bay door and radiators. On the ground, Joe Engle was

standing by to offer advice if needed, whilst in *Discovery's* left-hand (commander's) seat, Judy Resnik floated next to the side facing window, face pressed against the glass to help guide Henry Hartsfield as best she could. Slowly the RMS moved down along the slab-like side of *Discovery's* fuselage, inches away from the critical yet delicate tiles covering the leading edges of the wing. Closing in on the ice, Henry Hartsfield had to rely entirely on the accuracy of the RMS' TV monitor. Judy Resnik could now no longer see its progress. Gently he tapped the ice with the end of the RMS, and to everyone's relief it snapped away, tumbling harmlessly into space. A small amount remained, effectively still blocking the dump valve, but at least not presenting a hazard for the return trip.

The day ended well, with the ice all but gone, *Discovery's* systems checked out and found to be OK, and equipment stowed for re-entry.

5 September 1984 began with the announcement that one of *Discovery's* oxygen tanks was leaking. The crew were woken early to isolate the problem before re-entry. This being a maiden flight, NASA opted to bring *Discovery* back down to Edwards Dry Lake Runway 17. At 7.35 am EST, Henry Hartsfield and Michael Coats fired *Discovery's* OMS rocket engines against the direction of travel to slow them down and begin the long descent to landing. Below, on the lower deck, Judy Resnik and Charlie Walker sat strapped into their seats. Behind Henry Hartsfield and Michael Coats sat Steve Hawley (who also acted as flight engineer) and Richard Mullane.

Fifty-five minutes after the de-orbit burn, *Discovery* was picked up by chase aircraft streaking across the early morning California sky, small clouds of vapour in its wake evidence of residual RCS fuel burning off. As *Discovery* dropped below Mach 1, Henry Hartsfield switched control to manual and brought America's latest Shuttle into a perfect landing on Rogers Dry Lake.

41G

Challenger's sixth flight into space was to carry the largest single crew ever launched. Commander Robert Crippen and pilot John McBride would fly into orbit for the Shuttle programme's 13th mission: mission specialists Sally Ride, Kathryn Sullivan, and David Leestma together with payload specialists Paul Scully-Power and Marc Garneau.

Objectives for this flight would include Earth observtions — in particular the oceans — and an EVA during which Dr Kathryn Sullivan and David Leestma would try out procedures needed for future in-flight refuelling of satellites.

Neither Marc Garneau nor Paul Scully-Power were NASA astronauts. The former was a representative of the Canadian National Research Council partaking in a joint US/Canadian scientific programme; Scully-Power was an Australian born oceanographer working with the US Navy. His expert observations, combined with data gained from on-board instruments, would greatly enhance the scientific value of 41G.

Flight 41G would deploy just one satellite: NASA's own Earth Radiation Budget Satellite (ERBS). This small satellite would be joined in later flights by two others to measure the amount of solar radiation the Earth receives against that which is reflected back into space (hence the 'budget'). Without a doubt, most of the attention of this flight would focus on the EVA. Future NASA plans called for a visit to Landsat 4 Earth Resources Satellite. Launched in 1982, Landsat 4 performed valuable research work until its fuel ran out. NASA planned to refuel the satellite so that it could continue its work, but before such a mission could be undertaken the procedures had to be thoroughly rehearsed.

After a perfect launch on 5 October 1984 *Challenger* reached orbit, having suffered slight damage to the surface insulation covering each OMS pod. Sally Ride used the camera mounted on the RMS arm to give Mission Control a better view. As things turned out, the damage was minimal and in no way represented a threat to a successful flight.

As soon as the OMS pod inspection had been completed, Sally Ride set about preparing the ERBS for launching. Standing at the rear of *Challenger's* upper flight deck looking out down the payload bay, she activated the little satellite's systems and then used the RMS arm to pick it up gently and hold it high enough away from *Challenger* to enable its solar wings to unfold without hindrance. Mission Control sent the satellite a command to unfold its wings but nothing happened! Again and again they tried, without success. Even Sally Ride tried, shaking the ERBS on the end of the arm in an attempt to free the panels. Stuck solar panels meant that ERBS would be useless. This failure was usually caused by frozen hinges, and with this in mind ERBS was left in direct sunlight to 'hot soak'. It worked, for within minutes its wings had unfurled and at 5.18 pm EST the little ERBS was on its way to its orbit station.

With one problem solved, another developed. *Challenger's* TDRS tracking antenna was not functioning. Without this piece of equipment there would be no communications with Mission Control through the TDRS, and all signals would have to be transmitted through ground stations. Already

the crew were tired after a busy day which had included launch and ERBS deployment. Consequently Mission Control decided to postpone troubleshooting until Day Two.

The proper functioning of *Challenger's* tracking antenna was critical to the operation of 41G's Earth Resources experiment package known as the Shuttle Imaging Radar (SIR-B). This experiment would transmit data through the TDRS at a rate of 46 megabytes a second. TDRS was the only way such a high volume of data could be handled successfully.

Day Two in space was devoted from the outset to attempts at repairing *Challenger's* tracking antenna. Eventually, having tried all conventional methods, the crew, unable to stop the dish antenna from oscillating, locked it into one position and used *Challenger* herself to point it in the right direction! SIR-B would be run at intervals, its data stored on *Challenger's* tape recorder, and then *Challenger* would align with TDRS and transmit the data via TDRS to the ground.

No sooner had this solution been worked out than SIR-B began to malfunction. Its own large radar antenna used to map the Earth was meant to fold up securely when not in use and lock away. Now it would fold but not latch tight. Sally Ride used the RMS arm to gently push the latches home.

Overshadowed by these difficulties other experiments continued as scheduled. Preparations for the EVA began with Kathryn Sullivan and David Leestma checking the fuel transfer plumbing out in the payload bay from the safety of the flight deck. This Orbital Refuelling System (ORS) was carried into space to simulate realistically the kind of difficulties crewmen would encounter at a later date when refuelling Landsat 4. Two fuel tanks, one empty and one filled with hydrazine fuel, were mounted on a pallet in the payload bay. The empty tank was connected to a replica of Landsat's fuel filler panel. During the EVA the two astronauts would install a valve in the Landsat replica panel, then connect the full tank's plumbing to the panel. Once back inside *Challenger,* the crew would then initiate the fuel transfer via the newly installed valve to the empty tank.

The two tanks were linked together before launch by a separate set of pipelines so that, before the astronauts went outside, they could check that fuel would, in fact, flow freely in zero-g.

Day Two had been a disappointment for the crew of *Challenger* and Day Three was to prove no better. SIR-B's antenna still refused to latch when the crew attempted to stow it after the day's operation. As a result Mission Control decided to postpone the EVA of 41G until the final full day of the flight. It made this decision to allow the two spacewalkers to latch the antenna into position manually after its final operation, and at the same time check everything was secure for re-entry and landing. Meanwhile, Marc Garneau was working with the Canadian experiments which included sophisticated investigations into space technology and science. At the same time an advanced 70 mm movie camera was taking a special 360 degree film of *Challenger* in space for public viewing at specially constructed cinemas across the US.

The following day, the mission's fourth, added to 41G's troubles when an error by TDRS Ground Control at White Sands, New Mexico, sent the satellite into a spin, effectively shutting down all communications through the TDRS for the rest of the day. Then *Challenger*'s cabin cooling system broke down and temperatures began to climb towards 100 °F on the crowded flight deck. To cap it all, tropical storm *Josephine* began to threaten *Challenger*'s prime landing site at Kennedy Space Centre.

The crew of *Challenger* spent the evening of the fourth day in a cramped stuffy cabin, before signing-off for an uncomfortable night's sleep. The following day, however, things began to pick up. The TDRS was fixed overnight, and by morning the cabin cooling system was repaired, making life aboard *Challenger* a good deal more pleasant.

Following on from the previous day's intense preparations, the seventh day of *Challenger* flight 41G was to witness the first EVA by an American woman astronaut. At just before 10.45 am EST, David Leestma had opened the outer airlock door and attached his reeled tether to the payload bay side. Slowly he made his way to one of the forward payload bay door hinges where he then began to climb along back to the aft bulkhead to the fuel transfer experiment. Within the space of a few minutes he had been joined by Kathryn Sullivan who had brought with her the necessary tools to perform the transfer plumbing operation. From this point David Leestma began the delicate operation of attaching first the valve, then the fuel feed lines whilst Kathryn Sullivan passed him tools and photographed the operations. The job was completed and preliminary checks were found to be in order.

The major part of their EVA completed, Kathryn Sullivan and David Leestma made their way forward to the SIR-B antenna. If they could not latch the antenna down by hand, they had brought out with them one of *Challenger*'s sleeping bags to tie it into a safe position. Re-entry was not the time during which NASA wanted loose equipment creating havoc in the payload bay. In the event, the sleeping bag was not needed and the antenna was stowed without a hitch. American TV viewers were then given an astounding display of weightless acrobatics by the two astronauts before commander Bob Crippen decided the time had come for them to return. Subsequent fuel flow tests went without fault. The way had been cleared for Landsat reactivation.

Mission 41G's final full day in space was spent, as on all previous flights, preparing for re-entry and landing. On 13 October *Challenger* had entered its ninth day in space when, with hurricane

Josephine now many miles away and no threat to landing, the crew fired the OMS engines to begin re-entry.

Crossing the length of the eastern United States in under seven minutes, *Challenger* had slowed sufficiently to land at Kennedy Space Centre. Crowds applauded as Bob Crippen made a perfect turn in to bring *Challenger* down safely after her sixth journey into space.

51A

The failure of Westar 6 and Palapa-B2 to reach geosynchronous orbits successfully after their deployment from 41B in February 1984, meant a financial loss of $170 million to the insurance underwriters. It was also a particularly frustrating situation for Western Union and Indonesia's Permutel to have two fully-functional satellites in space virtually useless because they were in totally wrong orbits. Only after the triumphant repair and redeployment of Solar Max on 41C did NASA and Lloyds of London (who had suffered the financial loss) start to consider the possibility of retrieving the two satellites on a special salvage mission. By July 1984, the rescue depended on negotiations between Indonesia and its insurance companies rather than technical feasibility. Ex-MOL astronnaut Lt General James Abrahamson, who had recently left NASA to resume duties as head of President Reagan's US Space Defence research project, pronounced that a recovery would be possible.

Although, unlike Solar Max, neither Westar nor Palapa were equipped with a grappling device for the RMS arm to catch hold of, an astronaut would attempt to connect with each satellite using a specially-made docking latch attached to the front of his MMU. The latch would be thrust into each satellite's open rocket nozzle, at which point he would release three spring loaded prongs from the latch probe and grasp the satellite securely by its engine.

By October 1984 the financial haggling had been resolved and NASA announced the objectives of flight 51A, *Discovery*'s second flight into space. In addition to the rescue and return to Earth of Westar 6 and Palapa-B2, 51A would first launch two communication satellites, Telsat H and Syncom 4-1 (Leasat). After launching these two, *Discovery* would manoeuvre up to the disabled Palapa B-2, then, two days later Westar 6 would be retrieved.

By the time of 51A's launch both satellites would, under the power of their own tiny manoeuvring thrusters, have been brought down to circular orbits of 195 miles altitude and only 650 miles apart in order for *Discovery* to reach them. In addition their spin rate would be reduced from 50 rpm down to just 5 rpm to make rescue less dangerous.

The crew for 51A would consist of commander Rick Hauck, whose only other spaceflight had been as pilot to Bob Crippen's STS 7, pilot David Walker, making his first spaceflight, three mission specialists, and one payload specialist. Of these Joseph Allen had flown on STS 5, and Dale Gardner on STS 8. Anna Fisher, the third mission spe-

cialist, was one of the six female astronauts chosen by NASA in 1978 and was making her first spaceflight. Prior to joining NASA she had been a doctor specializing in emergency medicine for the Los Angeles district. Payload specialist was Charles Walker, who would continue work on the McDonnell Douglas pharmaceutical experiment he began on flight 41D in September 1984.

Once in orbit, Joe Allen and Dale Gardner would make the first of two EVAs. In the first Joe Allen, using an MMU, would insert the special docking probe into the Palapa's spent apogee 'kick' motor nozzle and fly back to the *Discovery* using the MMU's nitrogen gas thrusters with the satellite secured. Close to the payload bay Anna

Fisher would use the RMS arm's 'end effector' to grasp a pin on the side of the special docking probe with Joe Allen still attached, and hold Palapa steady whilst Dale Gardner fixed another RMS grappling point on the other (top) end of the satellite. Anna Fisher would then grab this new attachment with the RMS arm and, once Joe Allen had cleared, lower the Palapa engine, nozzle first, into its pallet inside the payload bay for return to Earth.

A similar rescue would occur with Westar. A total of six hours for each EVA was allowed for in the schedule. The second EVA would involve Dale Gardner flying the MMU and Joe Allen attaching the satellite's 'top'-end RMS arm grapple device.

Launch of 51A on 8 November 1984 was flaw-

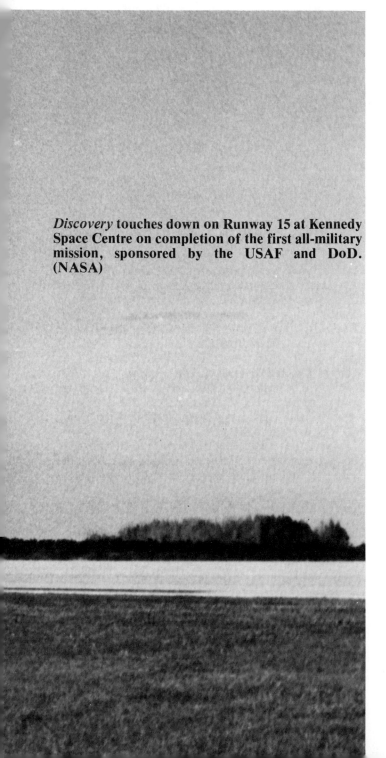

Discovery **touches down on Runway 15 at Kennedy Space Centre on completion of the first all-military mission, sponsored by the USAF and DoD. (NASA)**

less and, shortly after, both Telesat H and Syncom 4-1 had been deployed successfully. That part of the mission completed, *Discovery* started to close up on Palapa-B2.

Once alongside, Joe Allen and Dale Gardner floated out of *Challenger*'s air lock, and Joe Allen powered up his MMU. Flying out to Palapa he managed to dock and latch into position before returning with the 1,250 lb satellite in to the payload bay. Then Dale Gardner and Joe Allen, with the help of Anna Fisher operating the RMS arm, stowed it in the British Aerospace-built and adapted Spacelab pallet. Two days later Westar was similarly saved.

The flight of 51A was a triumph for NASA who, by then, had fulfilled in only 14 flights almost all of the design capabilities of their Shuttle. The two satellites were to be returned and refurbished for relaunch in late 1985.

No sooner had *Challenger* returned from 51A, with both Palapa and Westar safely aboard, than NASA once again announced a postponement and rearrangement of launch schedules.

Mission 51B, the second flight of Spacelab, was postponed until after 51C, possibly as far back as May 1985. Meanwhile 51C was delayed from December 1984 until early 1985.

The reason for this confusion stemmed from what engineers discovered about *Challenger* after her return from space during 41G in October. A critical black tile from the left wing root area, behind and below the crew side access/egress hatch, was missing. Subsequently, removal of almost 100 tiles from the area affected revealed that the adhesive screed used to smooth out surface irregularities in *Challenger*'s aluminium skin had softened. The screed is used in a very similar way on the Orbiter as body filler is used on cars. It dries at room temperature and can be sanded smooth to provide a perfect key for each tile's felt 'strain relief' mounting pad. Used on *Challenger*'s fuselage, body flaps, elevons and sides, engineers and technicians discovered that, fortunately, the problem was confined to only six batches of screed material, and was caused by continual use of a special chemical waterproofing agent.

51C

Mission 51C was the Shuttle flight that brought full circle the programme of USAF space development that began in 1950 with Project Bomi. At last, after almost 35 years, the military had their own winged spaceplane, or at least one on hire from NASA.

The four NASA crewmen, commanded by Tom Mattingly of STS 4, were joined by a Department of Defense military astronaut, Major Gary Payton. They were to lift-off on a secret mission to deploy an electronic intelligence gathering spy satellite.

A few days before the launch the *Washington Post* revealed classified details of the flight which led to outrage by the military, and a suspicion amongst observers that perhaps the 'leak' was intentional. The USAF, by demonstrating a lack of security in using NASA personnel, facilities and equipment, could thus reinforce their case for a fifth Shuttle, of their very own, operating in and out of Vandenburg Air Force Base.

Whatever the motives, for NASA and the American public, who were conditioned to freedom of information during each Shuttle and manned spaceflight since Mercury, it came as a shock to find the USAF demanding a virtual news black-out on the flight. NASA's news centres were shut, and they were instructed to conduct the entire mission from lift-off to touchdown under a blanket of silence. NASA management, traditionally open in their approach to spaceflight, was confronted with a situation never before encountered. Most reacted officially by stating that the USAF was like any other fare paying customer, and if one of their requirements was secrecy, then so be it. Privately many NASA officials, veterans of the early days, objected strongly to the civilian agency being subjected to rigorous security as this was in direct opposition to their 1958 charter which required complete availability and access to information.

Eventually it was to be a compromise. Because *Challenger* would deploy the spy satellite using the first Inertial Upper Stage to fly since the TDRS-1 deployment in 1983, NASA persuaded the USAF to relent slightly on the black-out because of genuine commercial interest in the IUS performance.

As launch date approached, NASA was given leave to reveal that 51C would be launched between 1300 hours and 1600 hours Eastern Daylight Time on 23 January. As was traditionally established, television coverage of the final countdown and launch would be allowed (although not live, but recorded, insisted the USAF). Conversations between the crew and the ground would be made available during countdown and launch up to plus 45 minutes, when all public communications would cease. Every eight hours from then until the end of the flight Houston, unless there was an emergency, would issue brief Orbiter status reports. A full report on the function of the IUS would be made available after the flight. The duration of 51C's mission would not be stated, and only 16 hours before landing at Kennedy Space Centre would the announcement of return be made. After the re-

entry radio black-out, public broadcasts of crew-ground communications would recommence.

The lack of information naturally whetted the media's appetite and, ironically, the flight of 51C attracted more attention in the US than the previous four flights combined. The crew, commander Ken Mattingley and pilot Loren Shriver, together with mission specialists Elison Onizuka, James Buchli and Major Gary Payton, dodged newsmen continually during their final pre-launch training flights and appearances. Finally, after a day's delay caused by unusually cold weather conditions at Kennedy Space Centre, *Discovery* mission 51C lifted off. The satellite was deployed, the IUS worked perfectly and, on 27 January 1985, *Discovery* returned once more to its launch site. For a few weeks the press discussed the precedents that had been set, how 'new' and 'radical' the concept of putting military payloads into space was, and how the Russians would react to being 'second' in the military Shuttle league. Media comments, however, soon dissolved into reports on the general counter-bargaining and recriminations of US/USSR Strategic Arms Limitations Talks on space weapons deployment.

The final irony came with a simple statement by an ex-Apollo astronaut as he watched the recorded launch of 51C on TV.

'To think, we could have been going to Mars today.'

* * * * *

As the Shuttle moves ahead into its first decade of operations, it has already found new commitments in high technology defence applications; in the construction of *Columbus,* the US Space Station scheduled for the nineteen-nineties; and in firm bookings from commercial companies and foreign governments for satellite launchings. NASA still hopes for a fifth spaceflight-rated Orbiter, even though the teams that helped build *Columbia, Enterprise, Challenger, Discovery* and *Atlantis* are now disbanded. Sufficient 'spares' have been set aside to enable assembly of one more Orbiter if and when budgets allow.

NASA's hopes for a two-week turnaround between launches may never be realized, but the mere fact that making regular flights into space has been made routine by Shuttle is a notable achievement in itself.

The Space Shuttle is undoubtedly the most ambitious, technically complex and expensive machine ever built in the entire history of mankind. Like most of our inventions it is a tool, a means to achieve objectives. Whether these objectives lie in the arena of war, or in the scientific understanding of the physical nature of ourselves and the universe, and in the improvement of life for those less fortunate in barren regions of Earth, we have yet to see. The pioneers have given us the key to a whole new future. Which door we choose to unlock with it may decide the survival of our species.

Appendices:

I The X-15 Flight Programme, 1959 to 1968

Flight No.	Date	Pilot		Max speed (mph)	Max altitude (ft)	X-15 Vehicle No.	
1	8. 6.59	Crossfield	(1)	522	37,550	1	(1)
2	17. 9.59	Crossfield	(2)	1,393	52,341	2	(1)
3	17.10.59	Crossfield	(3)	1,419	61,781	2	(2)
4	15.11.59	Crossfield	(4)	660	45,462	2	(3)
5	23. 1.60	Crossfield	(5)	1,669	66,844	1	(2)
6	11. 2.60	Crossfield	(6)	1,466	88,116	2	(4)
7	17. 2.60	Crossfield	(7)	1,036	52,640	2	(5)
8	17. 3.60	Crossfield	(8)	1,419	52,640	2	(6)
9	25. 3.60	Walker	(1)	1,320	48,630	1	(3)
10	29. 3.60	Crossfield	(9)	1,293	49,982	2	(7)
11	31. 3.60	Crossfield	(10)	1,340	51,356	2	(8)
12	13. 4.60	White	(1)	1,254	48,000	1	(4)
13	19. 4.60	Walker	(2)	1,689	59,496	1	(5)
14	6. 5.60	White	(2)	1,452	60,938	1	(6)
15	12. 5.60	Walker	(3)	2,111	77,882	1	(7)
16	19. 5.60	White	(3)	1,590	108,997	1	(8)
17	26. 5.60	Crossfield	(11)	1,452	51,282	2	(9)
18	4. 8.60	Walker	(4)	2,196	78,112	1	(9)
19	12. 8.60	White	(4)	1,772	136,500	1	(10)
20	19. 8.60	Walker	(5)	1,986	75,982	1	(11)
21	10. 9.60	White	(5)	2,182	79,864	1	(12)
22	23. 9.60	Petersen	(1)	1,108	53,043	1	(13)
23	20.10.60	Petersen	(2)	1,280	53,800	1	(14)
24	28.10.60	McKay	(1)	1,333	50,700	1	(15)
25	4.11.60	Rushworth	(1)	1,287	48,900	1	(16)
26	15.11.60	Crossfield	(12)	1,960	81,200	2	(10)
27	17.11.60	Rushworth	(2)	1,254	54,750	1	(17)

Flight No.	Date	Pilot		Max speed (mph)	Max altitude (ft)	X-15 Vehicle No.	
28	22.11.60	Crossfield	(13)	1,656	61,900	2	(11)
29	30.11.60	Armstrong	(1)	1,155	48,840	1	(18)
30	6.12.60	Crossfield	(14)	1,881	53,374	2	(12)
31	9.12.60	Armstrong	(2)	1,188	50,095	1	(19)
32	1. 2.61	McKay	(2)	1,211	49,780	1	(20)
33	7. 2.61	White	(6)	2,275	78,150	1	(21)
34	7. 3.61	White	(7)	2,905	77,450	2	(13)
35	30. 3.61	Walker	(6)	2,760	169,600	2	(14)
36	21. 4.61	White	(8)	3,074	105,000	2	(15)
37	25. 5.61	Walker	(7)	3,307	107,500	2	(16)
38	23. 6.61	White	(9)	3,603	107,700	2	(17)
39	10. 8.61	Petersen	(3)	2,735	78,200	1	(22)
40	12. 9.61	Walker	(8)	3,618	114,300	2	(18)
41	28. 9.61	Petersen	(4)	3,600	101,800	2	(19)
42	4.10.61	Rushworth	(3)	2,830	78,000	1	(23)
43	11.10.61	White	(10)	3,647	217,000	2	(20)
44	17.10.61	Walker	(9)	3,900	108,600	1	(24)
45	9.11.61	White	(11)	4,093	101,600	2	(21)
46	20.12.61	Armstrong	(3)	2,502	81,000	3	(1)
47	10. 1.62	Petersen	(5)	645	44,750	1	(25)
48	17. 1.62	Armstrong	(4)	3,765	133,500	3	(2)
49	5. 4.62	Armstrong	(5)	2,850	180,000	3	(3)
50	19. 4.62	Walker	(10)	3,866	154,000	1	(26)
51	20. 4.62	Armstrong	(6)	3,789	207,500	3	(4)
52	30. 4.62	Walker	(11)	3,489	246,700	1	(27)
53	8. 5.62	Rushworth	(4)	3,524	70,400	2	(22)
54	22. 5.62	Rushworth	(5)	3,450	100,400	1	(28)
55	1. 6.62	White	(12)	3,675	132,600	2	(23)
56	7. 6.62	Walker	(12)	3,672	103,600	1	(29)
57	12. 6.62	White	(13)	3,517	184,600	3	(5)
58	21. 6.62	White	(14)	3,641	246,700	3	(6)
59	27. 6.62	Walker	(13)	4,104	123,700	1	(30)
60	29. 6.62	McKay	(3)	3,280	83,200	2	(24)
61	16. 7.62	Walker	(14)	3,674	107,200	1	(31)
62 *	17. 7.62	White	(15)	3,832	314,750	3	(7)
63	19. 7.62	McKay	(4)	3,474	85,250	2	(25)
64	26. 7.62	Armstrong	(7)	3,989	98,900	1	(32)
65	2. 8.62	Walker	(15)	3,438	144,500	3	(8)
66	8. 8.62	Rushworth	(6)	2,943	90,877	2	(26)
67	14. 8.62	Walker	(16)	3,747	193,600	3	(9)
68	20. 8.62	Rushworth	(7)	3,534	88,900	2	(27)
69	29. 8.62	Rushworth	(8)	3,447	97,200	2	(28)
70	28. 9.62	McKay	(5)	2,765	68,200	2	(29)
71	4.10.62	Rushworth	(9)	3,493	112,200	3	(10)
72	9.10.62	McKay	(6)	3,716	130,200	2	(30)
73	23.10.62	Rushworth	(10)	3,764	134,500	3	(11)
74	9.11.62	McKay	(7)	1,019	53,950	2	(31)
75	14.12.62	White	(16)	3,742	141,400	3	(12)
76	20.12.62	Walker	(17)	3,793	160,400	3	(13)
77 *	17. 1.63	Walker	(18)	3,677	271,700	3	(14)
78	11. 4.63	Rushworth	(11)	2,864	74,400	1	(33)
79	18. 4.63	Walker	(19)	3,770	92,500	3	(15)
80	25. 4.63	McKay	(8)	3,654	105,500	1	(34)
81	2. 5.63	Walker	(20)	3,488	209,400	3	(16)

Flight No.	Date	Pilot		Max speed (mph)	Max altitude (ft)	X-15 Vehicle No.	
82	14. 5.63	Rushworth	(12)	3,600	95,600	3	(17)
83	15. 5.63	McKay	(9)	3,856	124,200	1	(35)
84	29. 5.63	Walker	(21)	3,858	92,000	3	(18)
85	18. 6.63	Rushworth	(13)	3,539	223,700	3	(19)
86	25. 6.63	Walker	(22)	3,911	111,800	1	(36)
87 *	27. 6.63	Rushworth	(14)	3,425	285,000	3	(20)
88	9. 7.63	Walker	(23)	3,631	226,400	1	(37)
89	18. 7.63	Rushworth	(15)	3,925	104,800	1	(38)
90 *	19. 7.63	Walker	(24)	3,710	347,800	3	(21)
91 *	22. 8.63	Walker	(25)	3,794	354,200	3	(22)
92	7.10.63	Engle	(1)	2,834	77,800	1	(39)
93	29.10.63	Thompson	(1)	2,712	74,400	1	(40)
94	7.11.63	Rushworth	(16)	2,925	82,300	3	(23)
95	14.11.63	Engle	(2)	3,286	90,800	1	(41)
96	27.11.63	Thompson	(2)	3,310	89,800	3	(24)
97	5.12.63	Rushworth	(17)	4,018	101,000	1	(42)
98	8. 1.64	Engle	(3)	3,616	139,900	1	(43)
99	16. 1.64	Thompson	(3)	3,242	71,000	3	(25)
100	28. 1.64	Rushworth	(18)	3,618	107,400	1	(44)
101	19. 2.64	Thompson	(4)	3,519	78,600	3	(26)
102	13. 3.64	McKay	(10)	3,392	76,000	3	(27)
103	27. 3.64	Rushworth	(19)	3,827	101,500	1	(45)
104	8. 4.64	Engle	(4)	3,468	175,000	1	(46)
105	29. 4.64	Rushworth	(20)	3,906	101,600	1	(47)
106	12. 5.64	McKay	(11)	3,084	72,800	3	(28)
107	19. 5.64	Engle	(5)	3,494	195,800	1	(48)
108	21. 5.64	Thompson	(5)	1,865	64,200	3	(29)
109	25. 6.64	Rushworth	(21)	3,104	83,300	2	(32)
110	30. 6.64	McKay	(12)	3,334	99,600	1	(49)
111	8. 7.64	Engle	(6)	3,520	170,400	3	(30)
112	29. 7.64	Engle	(7)	3,623	78,000	3	(31)
113	12. 8.64	Thompson	(6)	3,535	81,200	3	(32)
114	14. 8.64	Rushworth	(22)	3,590	103,300	2	(33)
115	26. 8.64	McKay	(13)	3,863	91,000	3	(33)
116	3. 9.64	Thompson	(7)	3,615	78,600	3	(34)
117	28. 9.64	Engle	(8)	3,888	97,000	3	(35)
118	29. 9.64	Rushworth	(23)	3,542	97,800	2	(34)
119	15.10.64	McKay	(14)	3,048	84,900	1	(50)
120	30.10.64	Thompson	(8)	3,113	84,600	3	(36)
121	30.11.64	McKay	(15)	3,089	87,200	2	(35)
122	9.12.64	Thompson	(9)	3,723	92,400	3	(37)
123	10.12.64	Engle	(9)	3,675	113,200	1	(51)
124	22.12.64	Rushworth	(24)	3,593	81,200	3	(38)
125	13. 1.65	Thompson	(10)	3,712	99,400	3	(39)
126	2. 2.65	Engle	(10)	3,886	98,200	3	(40)
127	17. 2.65	Rushworth	(25)	3,511	95,100	2	(36)
128	26. 2.65	McKay	(16)	3,750	153,600	1	(52)
129	26. 3.65	Rushworth	(26)	3,680	101,900	1	(53)
130	23. 4.65	Engle	(11)	3,680	79,700	3	(41)
131	28. 4.65	McKay	(17)	3,273	92,600	2	(37)
132	18. 5.65	McKay	(18)	3,541	102,100	2	(38)
133	25. 5.65	Thompson	(11)	3,418	179,800	1	(54)
134	28. 5.65	Engle	(12)	3,754	209,600	3	(42)
135	16. 6.65	Engle	(13)	3,404	244,700	3	(43)

Flight No.	Date	Pilot		Max speed (mph)	Max altitude (ft)	X-15 Vehicle No.	
136	17. 6.65	Thompson	(12)	3,541	108,500	1	(55)
137	22. 6.65	McKay	(19)	3,938	155,900	2	(39)
138 *	29. 6.65	Engle	(14)	3,432	280,600	3	(44)
139	8. 7.65	McKay	(20)	3,659	212,600	2	(40)
140	20. 7.65	Rushworth	(27)	3,760	105,400	3	(45)
141	3. 8.65	Rushworth	(28)	3,602	208,700	2	(41)
142	6. 8.65	Thompson	(13)	3,534	103,200	1	(56)
143 *	10. 8.65	Engle	(15)	3,550	271,000	3	(46)
144	25. 8.65	Thompson	(14)	3,604	214,100	1	(57)
145	26. 8.65	Rushworth	(29)	3,372	239,600	3	(47)
146	2. 9.65	McKay	(21)	3,570	239,800	2	(42)
147	9. 9.65	Rushworth	(30)	3,534	97,200	1	(58)
148	14. 9.65	McKay	(22)	3,519	239,000	3	(48)
149	22. 9.65	Rushworth	(31)	3,550	100,300	1	(59)
150 *	28. 9.65	McKay	(23)	3,732	295,600	3	(49)
151	30. 9.65	Knight	(1)	2,718	76,600	1	(60)
152	12.10.65	Knight	(2)	3,108	94,400	3	(50)
153 *	14.10.65	Engle	(16)	3,554	266,500	1	(61)
154	27.10.65	McKay	(24)	3,519	236,900	3	(51)
155	3.11.65	Rushworth	(32)	1,500	70,600	2	(43)
156	4.11.65	Dana	(1)	2,765	80,200	1	(62)
157	6. 5.66	McKay	(25)	1,434	68,400	1	(63)
158	18. 5.66	Rushworth	(33)	3,689	99,000	2	(44)
159	1. 7.66	Rushworth	(34)	1,023	45,000	2	(45)
160	12. 7.66	Knight	(3)	3,652	130,000	1	(64)
161	18. 7.66	Dana	(2)	3,217	96,100	3	(52)
162	21. 7.66	Knight	(4)	3,568	192,300	2	(46)
163	28. 7.66	McKay	(26)	3,702	241,800	1	(65)
164	3. 8.66	Knight	(5)	3,440	249,000	2	(47)
165	4. 8.66	Dana	(3)	3,693	132,700	3	(53)
166	11. 8.66	McKay	(27)	3,590	251,000	1	(66)
167	12. 8.66	Knight	(6)	3,472	231,100	2	(48)
168	19. 8.66	Dana	(4)	3,607	178,000	3	(54)
169	25. 8.66	McKay	(28)	3,543	257,500	1	(67)
170	30. 8.66	Knight	(7)	3,543	100,200	2	(49)
171	8. 9.66	McKay	(29)	1,602	73,200	1	(68)
172	14. 9.66	Dana	(5)	3,586	254,200	3	(55)
173	6.10.66	Adams	(1)	2,900	75,400	1	(69)
174 *	1.11.66	Dana	(6)	3,750	306,900	3	(56)
175	18.11.66	Knight	(8)	4,250	98,900	2	(50)
176	29.11.66	Adams	(2)	3,120	92,000	3	(57)
177	22. 3.67	Adams	(3)	3,822	133,100	1	(70)
178	26. 4.67	Dana	(7)	1,163	53,400	3	(58)
179	28. 4.67	Adams	(4)	3,720	167,000	1	(71)
180	8. 5.67	Knight	(9)	3,193	97,600	2	(51)
181	17. 5.67	Dana	(8)	3,177	71,100	3	(59)
182	15. 6.67	Adams	(5)	3,606	229,300	1	(72)
183	22. 6.67	Dana	(9)	3,611	82,200	3	(60)
184	29. 6.67	Knight	(10)	2,870	173,000	1	(73)
185	20. 7.67	Dana	(10)	3,693	84,300	3	(61)
186	21. 8.67	Knight	(11)	3,368	91,000	2	(52)
187	25. 8.67	Adams	(6)	3,115	84,400	3	(62)
188	3.10.67	Knight	(12)	4,520	102,100	2	(53)

Flight No.	Date	Pilot		Max speed (mph)	Max altitude (ft)	X-15 Vehicle No.	
189	4.10.67	Dana	(11)	3,897	251,100	3	(63)
190 *	17.10.67	Knight	(13)	3,856	280,500	3	(64)
191 *	15.11.67	Adams	(7)	3,570	266,000	3	(65)
192	1. 3.68	Dana	(12)	2,878	104,500	1	(74)
193	4. 4.68	Dana	(13)	3,610	187,500	1	(75)
194	26. 4.68	Knight	(14)	3,545	207,000	1	(76)
195	12. 6.68	Dana	(14)	3,545	214,000	1	(77)
196	16. 7.68	Knight	(15)	3,409	218,500	1	(78)
197 *	21. 8.68	Dana	(15)	3,443	264,000	1	(79)
198	13. 9.68	Knight	(16)	3,716	250,000	1	(80)
199	24.10.68	Dana	(16)	3,683	250,000	1	(81)

* Astro-flight
† Number in brackets is cumulative total of pilot's or vehicle's free flights

II The M2F2 Flight Programme, 1966 to 1967

Flight No.	Date	Pilot	Max speed mph (Mach no.)		Max altitude (ft)	Flight time (secs)
1 G*	12. 7.66	Thompson	452	(0.64)	45,000	217
2 G	19. 7.66	Thompson	394	(0.59)	45,000	245
3 G	12. 8.66	Thompson	408	(0.62)	45,000	278
4 G	24. 8.66	Thompson	446	(0.68)	45,000	241
5 G	2. 9.66	Thompson	466	(0.71)	45,000	226
6 G	16. 9.66	Peterson	466	(0.76)	45,000	210
7 G	20. 9.66	Sorlei	421	(0.64)	45,000	211
8 G	22. 9.66	Peterson	436	(0.66)	45,000	233
9 G	28. 9.66	Sorlei	443	(0.67)	45,000	225
10 G	5.10.66	Sorlei	430	(0.62)	45,000	234
11 G	12.10.66	Gentry	436	(0.66)	45,000	227
12 G	26.10.66	Gentry	399	(0.61)	45,000	261
13 G	14.11.66	Gentry	445	(0.68)	45,000	230
14 G	21.11.66	Gentry	457	(0.69)	45,000	235
15 G	2. 5.67	Peterson	411	(0.62)	45,000	231
16 G	10. 5.67	Peterson	403	(0.61)	45,000	223

*G = glide flight

III The HL-10 Flight Programme, 1966 to 1970

Flight No.	Date	Pilot	Max speed mph (Mach no.)		Max altitude (ft)	Flight time (secs)
1 G*	22.12.66	Peterson	457	(0.69)	45,000	187
2 G	15. 3.68	Gentry	425	(0.61)	45,000	243
3 G	3. 4.68	Gentry	455	(0.69)	45,000	242
4 G	25. 4.68	Gentry	459	(0.69)	45,000	258
5 G	3. 5.68	Gentry	455	(0.69)	45,000	245
6 G	16. 5.68	Gentry	447	(0.68)	45,000	265
7 G	28. 5.68	Manke	434	(0.66)	45,000	245
8 G	11. 6.68	Manke	433	(0.64)	45,000	246
9 G	21. 6.68	Gentry	423	(0.64)	45,000	271
10 G	24. 9.68	Gentry	449	(0.68)	45,000	245
11 G	3.10.68	Manke	471	(0.71)	45,000	243
12 P	23.10.68	Gentry	449	(0.67)	39,700	189
13 P	13.11.68	Manke	524	(0.84)	42,650	385
14 P	9.12.68	Gentry	542	(0.87)	47,420	394
15 P	17. 4.69	Manke	605	(0.99)	52,740	400
16 G	25. 4.69	Dana	462	(0.70)	45,000	252
17 PS	9. 5.69	Manke	744	(1.13)	53,300	410
18 P	20. 5.69	Dana	596	(0.90)	49,100	414
19 PS	28. 5.69	Manke	815	(1.24)	62,200	398
20 G	6. 6.69	Hoag	452	(0.67)	45,000	231
21 PS	19. 6.69	Manke	922	(1.40)	64,100	378
22 PS	23. 7.69	Dana	839	(1.27)	63,800	373
23 PS	6. 8.69	Manke	1020	(1.54)	75,800	372
24 PS	3. 9.69	Dana	958	(1.45)	77,960	414
25 PS	18. 9.69	Manke	833	(1.26)	79,190	426
26 P	30. 9.69	Hoag	609	(0.92)	53,700	436
27 PS	27.10.69	Dana	1041	(1.58)	60,300	417

Flight No.	Date	Pilot	Max speed mph (Mach no.)		Max altitude (ft)	Flight time (secs)
28 PS	3.11.69	Hoag	921	(1.40)	63,900	439
29 PS	17.11.69	Dana	1052	(1.59)	64,590	408
30 PS	21.11.69	Hoag	952	(1.43)	79,280	378
31 PS	12.12.69	Dana	871	(1.31)	79,960	428
32 PS	19. 1.70	Hoag	869	(1.31)	86,660	410
33 PS	26. 1.70	Dana	897	(1.35)	87,684	411
34 PS	18. 2.70	Hoag	1228	(1.86)	67,310	380
35 PS	27. 2.70	Dana	870	(1.31)	90,303	416
36 G	11. 6.70	Hoag	503	(0.74)	45,000	202
37 G	17. 7.70	Hoag	499	(0.73)	45,000	252

*G = glide flight
P = powered flight
PS = powered supersonic flight

IV The X-24A Flight Programme, 1969 to 1971

Flight No.	Date	Pilot	Max speed mph (Mach no.)		Max altitude (ft)	Flight time (secs)
1 G*	17. 4.69	Gentry	474	(0.72)	45,000	217
2 G	8. 5.69	Gentry	457	(0.69)	45,000	253
3 G	21. 8.69	Gentry	382	(0.58)	40,000	270
4 G	9. 9.69	Gentry	402	(0.59)	40,000	232
5 G	24. 9.69	Gentry	396	(0.59)	40,000	257
6 G	22.10.69	Manke	387	(0.59)	40,000	238
7 G	13.11.69	Gentry	427	(0.65)	45,000	270
8 G	25.11.69	Gentry	454	(0.69)	45,000	266
9 G	24. 2.70	Gentry	509	(0.77)	47,000	258
10 P	19. 3.70	Gentry	571	(0.87)	44,400	424
11 P	2. 4.70	Manke	571	(0.87)	58,700	435
12 P	22. 4.70	Gentry	610	(0.93)	57,700	408
13 P	14. 5.70	Manke	494	(0.75)	44,600	513
14 P	17. 6.70	Manke	653	(0.99)	61,000	432
15 P	28. 7.70	Gentry	619	(0.94)	58,100	388
16 P	11. 8.70	Manke	651	(0.99)	63,900	413
17 P	26. 8.70	Gentry	458	(0.69)	41,500	479
18 PS	14.10.70	Manke	784	(1.19)	67,900	411
19 PS	27.10.70	Manke	899	(1.36)	71,400	417
20 PS	20.11.70	Gentry	905	(1.37)	67,600	432
21 PS	21. 1.71	Manke	679	(1.03)	57,900	462
22 G	5. 2.71	Powell	435	(0.66)	45,000	235
23 PS	18. 2.71	Manke	998	(1.51)	67,400	447
24 PS	1. 3.71	Powell	661	(1.00)	56,900	437
25 PS	29. 3.71	Manke	1036	(1.60)	70,500	446
26 PS	12. 5.71	Powell	918	(1.39)	70,900	423
27 PS	25. 5.71	Manke	786	(1.19)	65,300	548
28 P	4. 6.71	Manke	539	(0.82)	54,400	517

*G = glide flight   P = powered flight   PS = powered supersonic flight

V The M2F3 Flight Programme, 1970 to 1972

Flight No.	Date	Pilot	Max speed mph (Mach no.)		Max altitude (ft)	Flight time (secs)
1 G*	2. 6.70	Dana	469	(0.69)	45,000	218
2 G	21. 7.70	Dana	440	(0.66)	45,000	228
3 G	2.11.70	Dana	429	(0.63)	45,000	236
4 P	25.11.70	Dana	534	(0.81)	51,900	377
5 G	9. 2.71	Gentry	469	(0.71)	45,000	241
6 G	26. 2.71	Dana	510	(0.77)	45,000	348
7 P	23. 7.71	Dana	614	(0.93)	60,500	353
8 P	9. 8.71	Dana	643	(0.97)	62,000	415
9 PS	25. 8.71	Dana	723	(1.10)	67,300	390
10 G	24. 9.71	Dana	480	(0.73)	42,000	210
11 G	15.11.71	Dana	487	(0.74)	45,000	215
12 PS	1.12.71	Dana	843	(1.27)	70,800	391
13 P	16.12.71	Dana	535	(0.81)	46,800	451
14 P	25. 7.72	Dana	652	(0.99)	60,900	420
15 PS	11. 8.72	Dana	726	(1.10)	67,200	375
16 PS	24. 8.72	Dana	835	(1.27)	66,700	376
17 P	12. 9.72	Dana	581	(0.88)	46,000	387
18 PS	27. 9.72	Dana	885	(1.34)	66,700	366.5
19 PS	5.10.72	Dana	904	(1.37)	66,300	376
20 P	19.10.72	Manke	597	(0.91)	47,100	359
21 PS	1.11.72	Manke	803	(1.21)	71,300	378
22 P	9.11.72	Powell	597	(0.91)	46,800	364
23 PS	21.11.72	Manke	947	(1.44)	66,700	377
24 PS	29.11.72	Powell	890	(1.35)	67,500	357
25 PS	6.12.72	Powell	786	(1.19)	68,300	332
26 PS	13.12.72	Dana	1064.2	(1.62)	66,700	383
27 PS	20.12.72	Manke	856	(1.29)	71,500	390

*G = glide flight   P = powered flight   PS = powered supersonic flight

VI The X-24B Flight Programme, 1973 to 1975

Flight No.	Date	Pilot	Max speed mph (Mach no.)		Max altitude (ft)	Flight time (secs)
1 G*	1. 8.73	Manke	460	(0.65)	40,000	252
2 G	17. 8.73	Manke	449	(0.66)	45,000	267
3 G	31. 8.73	Manke	479	(0.73)	45,000	277
4 G	18. 9.73	Manke	450	(0.69)	45,000	271
5 G	4.10.73	Love	455	(0.69)	45,000	279
6 P	15.11.73	Manke	597	(0.92)	52,800	404
7 P	12.12.73	Manke	645	(0.99)	62,600	434
8 G	15. 2.74	Love	450	(0.68)	45,000	307
9 PS	5. 3.74	Manke	708	(1.09)	60,300	437
10 P	30. 4.74	Love	578	(0.88)	52,000	419
11 PS	24. 5.74	Manke	753	(1.14)	56,000	448
12 PS	14. 6.74	Love	810	(1.23)	65,500	405
13 PS	28. 6.74	Manke	920	(1.39)	68,100	427
14 PS	8. 8.74	Love	1022	(1.54)	73,400	395
15 PS	29. 8.74	Manke	727	(1.10)	72,400	467
16 PS	25.10.74	Love	1164	(1.76)	72,100	417
17 PS	15.11.74	Manke	1070	(1.62)	72,100	481
18 PS	17.12.74	Love	1036	(1.59)	68,800	420
19 PS	14. 1.75	Manke	1157	(1.75)	72,800	477
20 PS	20. 3.75	Love	955	(1.44)	70,400	409
21 PS	18. 4.75	Manke	795	(1.20)	57,900	450
22 PS	6. 5.75	Love	958	(1.44)	73,400	448
23 PS	22. 5.75	Manke	1084	(1.63)	74,100	461
24 PS	6. 6.75	Love	1110	(1.68)	72,100	474
25 PS	25. 6.75	Manke	887	(1.34)	58,000	426
26 PS	15. 7.75	Love	1047	(1.58)	69,500	415
27 PS	5. 8.75	Manke	858	(1.23)	60,000	420
28 PS	20. 8.75	Love	1010	(1.58)	72,000	420

Flight No.	Date	Pilot	Max speed mph (Mach no.)		Max altitude (ft)	Flight time (secs)
29 PS	9. 9.75	Dana	990	(1.50)	71,000	435
30 PS	23. 9.75	Dana	780	(1.20)	58,000	438
31 G	9.10.75	Enevoldson	450	(0.70)	45,000	251
32 G	21.10.75	Scobee	462	(0.70)	45,000	255
33 G	3.11.75	McMurtry	456	(0.70)	45,000	248
34 G	12./11.75	Enevoldson	456	(0.70)	45,000	241
35 G	19.11.75	Scobee	460	(0.70)	45,000	249
36 G	26.11.75	McMurtry	460	(0.70)	45,000	245

*G = glide flight
P = powered flight
PS = powered supersonic flight

VII The Space Shuttle

Flight Programme, 1981 to 1985

	Launch	Landing	Crew	Landing site	Mission objective
STS 1 Columbia	12.4.81	14.4.81	John Young (cdr) Robert Crippen (plt)	Edwards lakebed Runway 23	First test flight of Space Shuttle. Initial check out of Orbiter's orbital systems including function of payload doors.
STS 2 Columbia	12.11.81	14.11.81	Joe Engle (cdr) Richard Truly (plt)	Edwards lakebed Runway 23	Second test flight to further evaluate Orbiter systems, test remote manipulator arm and expose OSTA 1 Earth resources experiment package
STS 3 Columbia	22.3.82	30.3.82	Jack Lousma (cdr) Charles Fullerton (plt)	White Sands lakebed Runway 17	Third test flight — full use of remote manipulator arm. Also tests of prolonged Orbiter space exposure.
STS 4 Columbia	27.6.82	4.7.82	Ken Mattingly (cdr) Henry Hartsfield (plt)	Edwards concrete Runway 22	Final extended Orbiter engineering test flight. Loss of two solid rocket boosters due to parachute failure.

	Launch	Landing	Crew	Landing site	Mission objective
					First test of autoland system. First military payload (classified DoD 82-1 package).
STS 5 Columbia	11.11.82	16.11.82	Vance Brand (cdr) Robert Overmyer (plt) Joseph P.Allen (ms) William Lenoir (ms)	Edwards concrete Runway 22	First fully operational Shuttle flight. First to carry two mission specialists. Launched two commercial satellites successfully (Satellite Business Systems 3 and Anik-C). Also carried first 'Getaway Special' experiment package in cargo bay.
STS 6 Challenger	4.4.83	9.4.83	Paul Weitz (cdr) Karol Bobko (plt) Donald Peterson (ms) Story Musgrave (ms)	Edwards concrete Runway 22	First flight of *Challenger* fully operational flight with two mission specialists. Launched TDRS-A successfully. Second 'Getaway Special' carried. First Shuttle EVA within payload bay by Story Musgrave and Donald Peterson.
STS 7 Challenger	18.6.83	24.6.83	Robert Crippen (cdr) Frederick H.Hauck (plt) Sally Ride (ms) John Fabian (ms) Norman Thagard (ms)	Edwards lakebed Runway 15	Second flight of *Challenger*. Three mission specialists including first US woman astronaut. Successful launch of the two satellites, Anik-C and the Indonesian Palapa-B. Evaluation of SPAS-1 prototype free-flying platform. Exposure of OSTA 2 Earth resources package.
STS 8 Challenger	30.8.83	5.9.83	Richard Truly (cdr) Daniel Brandenstein (plt) Guion Bluford (ms) Dale Gardner (ms) William Thornton (ms)	Edwards concrete Runway 22	Third flight by *Challenger*. Successfully launched Insat-B (Indian satellite). Remote manipulator arm test with 7,460 lb 'dumb bell' payload; first shuttle to take off and land at night.

	Launch	Landing	Crew	Landing site	Mission objective
STS 9 Columbia	28.11.83	8.12.83	John Young (cdr) Brewster Shaw (plt) Robert Parker (ms) Owen Garriott (ms) Byron Lichtenburg (ms) Ulf Merbold (ms)	Edward lakebed Runway 17	First flight of European space lab. First six man crew. First launch of US spacecraft with non-US national aboard (Dr Ulf Merbold — West Germany).
41B Challenger	3.2.84	11.2.84	Vance Brand (cdr) Robert Gibson (plt) Bruce McCandless (ms) Robert Stewart (ms) Ronald McNair (ms)	Kennedy Space Centre Runway 15	Successful deployment of Westar 6 and Palapa B-2 satellites. Successful evaluation of manned manoeuvring units developed by Martin Marietta, during two EVAs by Bruce McCandless and Robert Stewart. Check out of EVA procedures needed for Solar Max repair on 41C. Failure of two satellites to reach proper altitude due to problems with their McDonnell Douglas Pam-D second stage motors. First to land back at Kennedy Space Centre.
41C Challenger	6.4.84	13.4.84	Robert Crippen (cdr) Francis Scobee (plt) Terry Hart (ms) James van Hoften (ms) George Nelson (ms)	Edwards lakebed Runway 17	Capture and repair of Solar Max satellite using combination of MMUs and remote manipulator arm. Successful redeployment of Solar Max and launch of 'long duration exposure facility' satellite. Two EVAs, by George Nelson and James van Hoften.
41D Discovery	30.8.84	5.9.84	Henry Hartsfield (cdr) Michael Coats (plt) Judith Resnik (ms) Steven Hawley (ms) Richard Mullane (ms) Charles Walker (ps)	Edwards lakebed Runway 17	First flight of *Discovery*. Initial launch attempt on 25.6.84 aborted due to engine failure. Subsequent successful flight launched SBS4 satellite, Syncom IV-2, and Telstar 3C.

	Launch	Landing	Crew	Landing site	Mission objective
					Test of extendible solar panel from cargo bay.
41G Challenger	5.10.84	13.10.84	Bob Crippen (cdr) John McBride (plt) Sally Ride (ms) David Leestma (ms) Kathryn Sullivan (ms) Marc Garneau (ps) Paul Scully Power (ps)	Kennedy Space Centre Runway 15	First EVA by US female astronaut. Simulated satellite refuelling operation within cargo bay. Deployment of Earth Radiation Budget Satellite (ERBS). Use of Shuttle Imaging Radar (SIR-B) for Earth terrain photographs.
51A Discovery	8.11.84	16.11.84	Frederick Hauck (plt) David Walker (plt) Joe Allen (ms) Anna Fisher (ms) Dale Gardner (ms) Charles Walker (ms)	Kennedy Space Centre Runway 15	Successfully launched two satellites, Anik D2 and Syncom IV-3. Successfully recovered Palapa B2 and Westar 6 (after failing to achieve proper orbits after successful deployment from 41B). Palapa recovered on 12 November and Westar on 14 November. Two EVAs, by Joseph Allen and Dale Gardner using MMUs.
51C Discovery	24.1.85	27.1.85	Ken Mattingly (cdr) Loren Shriver (plt) Elison Onizuka (ms) James Buchli (ms) Maj Gary Payton (USAF)	Kennedy Space Centre Runway 15	USAF/DoD Classified. First flight totally devoted to military.

Index